VOLUME
ONE

A RADICAL THOUGHT

A DAILY **THROUGH-THE-BIBLE** DEVOTIONAL

RICK LANCASTER

W
RADICALWORD

A RADICAL THOUGHT: VOLUME ONE
By Rick Lancaster

Hard Cover: ISBN-13# 978-1-60039-125-5
Paperback: ISBN-13# 978-1-60039-124-8

www.radicalword.com

RADICALWORD

IN COLLABORATION WITH:

LAMP POST
publishers
lamppostpublishers.com

God's Word promises that all who seek the LORD will find Him.

This book is dedicated to those who hunger and thirst for more of God.

It is my prayer that these devotionals will be used by the Holy Spirit

to plant seeds of truth in the hearts of God's people.

It is my further prayer that these humble offerings will spark

a love for God's Word that will draw you ever closer to Him.

JANUARY

JANUARY 1

Read: Genesis 1:1 – 2:25, Matthew 1:1 – 2:12, Psalm 1:1-6, Proverbs 1:1-6

PSALM 1:1

Oh, the joys of those who do not follow the advice of the wicked, or stand around with sinners, or join in with scoffers.

Psalm 1 is one of the undated and anonymous psalms. There is no definitive information as to when it was written or by whom. It opens the book of Psalms with a contrast between the godly and the ungodly. Psalm 1 begins with a warning regarding our relationships. In the very first verse of the book of Psalms we are told to be very careful about the people that we allow to be close to us.

As Christians we have got to be very careful about who we are taking advice from and who we are joined together with. This is especially true of those that have been called by God to be involved in a ministry or church. As Christians and Christian leaders we must stay away from the advice of those whose worldview is different than ours. No matter how wise a person might be by the standards of the world, if they are looking at the world differently than God does than their advice is going to be different than God's desires.

Our text also tells us not to "stand with sinners." This means that we are not to have strong ties to unbelievers. It doesn't mean that we have to be separated from them. You would have to leave the earth to accomplish that. This is referring to deep rooted relationships that we invest into. We should be investing into our relationship with Jesus and with other believers. Our relationships with nonbelievers should be deep enough that they can see Jesus in us but not so deep that they can influence us with their beliefs and lifestyles.

Last we are told not to join in with scoffers. A scoffer is someone that mocks God and His church. God wants us to separate ourselves from these people and have nothing to do with them. Unless you have been specifically called to minister to a group that openly mocks God, then you should avoid them as they will be a continuous source of pain and discouragement to you.

God created you to be filled with His joy. Then He gives you the choice whether or not to enjoy that joy. Our text opens up by saying that there is joy in doing what God says. If God tells you to stay away from a certain group or type of people it is because He has a different plan for them that does not include you. Your choice then is to obey God and stay away from those people and experience His joy or disobey Him and experience God's rebuke and maybe punishment. The choice is always ours to make. Personally, I prefer to experience the joy of the Lord. Jesus, help us to love and pray for those that you have told us to stay away from.

JANUARY 2
Read: Genesis 3:1 – 4:26, Matthew 2:13 – 3:6, Psalm 2:1-12, Proverbs 1:7-9

MATTHEW 2:14

That night Joseph left for Egypt with the child and Mary, his mother...

Jesus' birth in Bethlehem had been prophesied by the prophet Micah about 700 years before His birth. The "wise men" from the east come to see if this prophesy had come true. They have been following a star that leads them directly to where Jesus is. Herod, the governor of Judea finds out and is very concerned that the Messiah, the Jew's deliverer has been born during his time as governor.

God warns Joseph that he needs to flee from Bethlehem and go to Egypt. He does that very night. There is no indication from the text as to how long it was before Herod ordered the murder of every male child two years old and under. Herod's plan was to do evil to Jesus and God had a plan that prevented it. The thing that struck me about this verse is that Joseph seems to have responded immediately. It is not normal to travel at night; especially with a young child.

Joseph sensed the urgency in God's warning and responded immediately and packed up his family and took them to Egypt. What a beautiful lesson there is for all of us. When God says go, it is time to go. When God says stop, it is time to stop. Joseph didn't wait for morning. He didn't wait for confirmation. He simply responded to what God told him to do.

The world is always at work to find ways to defeat us and the work that God is trying to do in us and through us. The enemy is always at work developing plans on how he can thwart the works of God. God is so much greater than that. He simply gives us directions that if we will follow them we will avoid the harm that might come to us. But sometimes that means packing up everything and moving to a new place for a while. Everything that Joseph and Mary knew was in Bethlehem; it was their home. Bethlehem was where Joseph made a living.

God might call you to give something or someone up that is very important to you. That doesn't mean that He is trying to punish you or test you. He might be trying to protect you from an upcoming attack of the enemy. The sooner that we realize this the sooner that we will avoid experiencing some of the consequences of our slow responses. God wants us to move when He says move. He wants us to do when He says do. He wants us to speak when He says speak. He is the Master and we are His servants. Our response should always be immediate. God is looking for men and women with a heart like Joseph's; ready to obey right now. Jesus, help us to be looking for your direction and teach us to respond immediately.

JANUARY 3

Read: Genesis 5:1 – 7:24, Matthew 3:7 – 4:11, Psalm 3:1-8, Proverbs 1:10-19

MATTHEW 4:4

But Jesus told him, "No! The Scriptures say, 'People need more than bread for their life; they must feed on every word of God.'"

After Jesus is baptized the Holy Spirit leads Him or compels Him to go out into the wilderness. For forty days Jesus has no food. The Bible records that he was hungry. I imagine He was. He was probably also very weak from lack of food. It was at this time of apparent weakness that Satan comes to tempt Him. That is Satan's style; attacking when we are weak and vulnerable.

It is Jesus' response that we should see and understand. Satan challenged Jesus to turn a stone into bread so that he could eat. Jesus could have done that. In our reading for today, Jesus turned water into wine.

Later in the gospels Jesus will multiply a few fishes and loaves to feed thousands of people. It would have been an easy task for Jesus to turn a stone into bread so that He could stop being hungry.

The problem is that God the Father had sent Jesus out into the wilderness to fast and to pray. God was preparing Him for the ministry that lay ahead of Jesus; specifically the cross of Calvary. For Jesus to have responded the way that Satan tempted Him to would mean that Jesus would have to stop trusting God and trust in Himself or Satan instead. Turning a stone into bread would have made Jesus' life easier but that wasn't the plan that God had for His life.

There will be times in all of our lives and ministries where we are tempted to make life easier. There will be times when we are tempted to compromise so that we can shortcut the process. Jesus knew the truth about compromise and shortcuts with God; it always leads to less than what God wanted to give you.

Jesus responded to Satan by saying that we need more than bread. The things that we know and see are not enough to sustain our lives. If we settle for "bread," those things that we know and see, than we have settled for something that may keep us alive but won't allow us to flourish. To truly flourish we need to feed upon every word of God.

Your Bible is a banquet! It is filled with some of the most incredible dishes that when eaten will fill your life to overflowing with the amazing character of God. In this banquet there is nothing that is bad for you and there is nothing that you can eat too much of. Nothing will make you sick and I find that each time that I read a section of scripture again it has a new taste from the last time that I ate of it. God's word is alive and it is the thing that feeds your soul and spirit. It also defends you from the temptations and attacks of the enemy. Thank you Father for giving us the Bible that we might so freely and easily partake of Your life-giving Word. Jesus, teach us to eat a well-balanced diet of every word of God.

Then God said to Noah, "Leave the boat, all of you."

Noah and his family and all the animals have been in the boat for over a year. Five of those months they have floated around in the midst of the flood. For the last seven months they have been waiting on the top of Mount Ararat as the earth has been drying. Several times during this wait, Noah sent out birds to test and see if the land was ready for them or not. The last dove that Noah sent did not come back. For the last two months they just waited.

In our verse for the day, God instructs Noah to leave the boat. This is a great picture of waiting patiently for the Lord. We can learn a lot from the way that Noah waited for the Lord to direct him with his next move. Noah waited until the Lord had told him before leaving the boat.

Noah had sent out the birds to check and see how things were going but his intent was to do what the Lord directed him to do. Noah and his family didn't need to leave the boat. They had everything they needed there to live. I can imagine that they wanted to leave; it couldn't have been a fun place to live for a year. For a year they have been feeding and cleaning up after who knows how many animals. The sounds and smells must have been overwhelming at times. There was probably a great desire to leave.

In our own lives there are decisions that we are faced with just like Noah was here. Noah could have been out of the boat two months earlier than he was; when the dove did not return. But what would that have meant for him, his family, and for the animals. If the earth had not been dry enough, it may have been very dangerous and harmful for them to leave early.

We have decisions that we are thinking about making and have been waiting on the Lord to direct us. We need to be just like Noah. He couldn't see what lie beyond what he could see from the deck of the boat. There are things outside of your vision that only God can see. God was busy drying up the land for Noah and his family and the animals while they waiting safely in the boat.

Don't get out of the boat until God tells you to. You can't know what God is still working on to make things ready for you. If you leave before everything is ready you may be putting yourself in danger or at least depriving yourself of the blessing that God is preparing for you. God blessed Noah for his patience and obedience. The Bible teaches that those that wait on the Lord will not be disappointed. Be patient; let God finish preparing the way for you so that you can experience all the blessing that He desires to pour out into your life. Jesus, help us to wait.

JANUARY 5

Read: Genesis 11:1 – 13:4, Matthew 5:1-26, Psalm 5:1-12, Proverbs 1:24-28

PSALM 5:3

Listen to my voice in the morning, LORD. Each morning I bring my requests to you and wait expectantly.

David begins this psalm with a commentary on prayer. As we study the life of David we can see that there were times when David had a strong connection to God through prayer. Sadly, there are also times when David was disconnected from God and he wasn't listening for God's voice. Those times seem to be fewer than more and David seemed to have had a fairly healthy prayer life. I believe that is why God blessed him as he did and referred to David as "a man after God's own heart."

Prayer is the air of our spiritual life. Without prayer our spiritual life will suffocate and die. Breathing is a natural process that we don't need to be taught; we just do it without thought. I have learned that there are times when we need to be taught to breathe differently than how we would naturally.

During exercise for example, it is important to breathe in the appropriate way to get the greatest benefit from your exercise and to prevent injury. During times of stress we can minimize the stress by regulating our breathing. Women are taught techniques for breathing during childbirth. Breathing in the right way can make an enormous difference in your life. The same is true of prayer.

Our spiritual life is not natural; it is supernatural. And to live a spiritual life, we must learn to breathe properly. King David started his mornings in prayer. We also need to start our days in prayer. Our spiritual day should begin before our feet hit the floor. Just like you wouldn't get out of bed without breathing, don't get out of bed without praying. Give your day to God before the world comes to take it away from you.

After David gave his day to God he waited for God to do something. This is one of the great truths about a successful prayer life; believe that God can and will do something about the things that you pray for. David believed that God was going to act on his behalf and he waited expectantly for him to do it. He waited for God to act just as a father waits for their child to be born; they know it is going to happen, just not when.

When I breathe I know that the air is going to supply me with what I need to live and function. Our prayer life should be very similar; we should know that our prayers are heard and that God will answer them. He may not answer them the way that we think He should but He always answers them the way that is best for us. We need to wait expectantly for the Almighty Creator of the Universe to respond to our prayers because He has promised to and He ALWAYS keeps His promises. Jesus, let every breath that we take be a reminder to take spiritual breaths of prayer.

JANUARY 6
Read: Genesis 13:5 – 15:21, Matthew 5:27-48, Psalm 6:1-10, Proverbs 1:29-33

GENESIS 15:6

And Abram believed the LORD, and the LORD declared him righteous because of his faith.

God told Abram that He was going to do something, to make Abram the father of a great nation. Abram's only responsibility at that time was to believe God. And because Abram believed God, it was counted to him as righteousness. There are times when all that God is asking us to do is believe Him. There are going to be times in all of our lives when the only thing that we can do is believe God. And that action will result in God counting us as righteous.

What an incredible thought, sometimes all we have to do to please God and be righteous in His sight is believe Him. And there also comes with believing God something for us as well. When we believe God, we experience peace, joy, hope, and love. We have a confidence in our situation and circumstances that the world looks at and is astounded.

Noah believed God and it gave him the confidence and strength to work for 100 years building an ark. Even in the midst of what must have incredible criticism and ridicule and persecution. Just by believing God we can cross through any wilderness or valley that may enter our lives.

Abraham believed God and it gave him the patience that he needed to wait for that promise to be fulfilled. And because Abram believed God, God used him in a supernatural way. Both he and Sarai were well past the age where they could have children. But because Abram believed God, they conceived and had a son.

God is the same today as He was then. He is still looking for people that will believe Him. And when He finds people that will believe Him, He will give them everything that they need for the day and will use them to do radical, supernatural things in the future.

Your church or ministry will only be as successful or effective as your ability to believe God. Do you want to be blessed in your life, in your ministry, and in your church? Then believe God! When God says that He is going to send a flood, believe Him! Noah waited 100 years to see what God said come to pass. When God says that He is going to make you a father of a great nation, believe Him. Abram waited 15 years! What has God told you? How long have you been waiting to see it come to pass? Do you believe God?

If you do, God counts it as righteousness and is standing ready to provide you with everything that you need and He is preparing a miraculous, supernatural thing for you to be a part of. Lord, help us to believe you.

JANUARY 7

Read: *Genesis 16:1 – 18:15, Matthew 6:1-24, Psalm 7:1-17, Proverbs 2:1-5*

MATTHEW 6:5

And now about prayer. When you pray, don't be like the hypocrites who love to pray publicly on street corners and in the synagogues where everyone can see them. I assure you, that is all the reward they will ever get.

Jesus was a man of prayer. He knew the power of prayer and rewards of prayer. Jesus modeled an active and effective prayer life. The gospels report that He often got up before everyone else so that He could get away to pray. There were at least a couple of occasions when He prayed all night long. We also have recorded Jesus teaching His disciples about prayer.

Here in our text for the day, we have an example of Jesus teaching His disciples and us how not to pray. Sometimes it is useful to teach what not to do as well as what to do. In our verse we are told not to do as the hypocrites do. These men would make a big show out of their prayers. They would make sure that they were on public street corners when prayer time came and then would stop right there and make a big thing out of how religious they were in the middle of everything.

These hypocrites would also go to the synagogue and compete with others to make their prayers longer and louder than anyone else's. They would practice to make their prayers as religious as they could. It was all meant to impress men. Jesus tells His disciples that the recognition that they receive from men, if any, is all the reward that they will get. The implication is that God will ignore prayers like that.

It might not be obvious just how hypocritical that really is. These men were praying to God under the pretense of wanting God to answer their prayers and do something in the world that they couldn't do for themselves. But because of the way that they were praying they were blocking their prayers from getting to God at all. Their prayers were sinful and therefore there was no chance that God was going to answer them.

Prayer is a very personal thing, even public prayer. When you pray, you, and you alone are talking to God. If you are praying publicly, you are inviting others to agree with you in prayer but the fact remains that it is to be a very personal thing. Jesus goes on to tell His disciples that if they want to receive a reward for their prayers, that they should humble themselves and go off by themselves to pray.

The reward that we all seek is God's grace and mercy in our lives. We might think that we want God to answer our prayers but I have found that sometimes I am much better off when God has done what he wanted to do rather than what I was asking Him to do. God's plan is infinitely better than what I think. Jesus, help me to get alone with You.

JANUARY 8
Read: Genesis 18:16 – 19:38, Matthew 6:25 – 7:14, Psalm 8:1-9, Proverbs 2:6-15

PROVERBS 2:7

He grants a treasure of good sense to the godly. He is their shield, protecting those who walk with integrity.

A study of the book of Proverbs is a study of wisdom; not as the world sees it but as the Lord sees it. These proverbs were written mostly by King Solomon who had received a special gift of wisdom from the Lord. These proverbs teach us what wisdom is and is not. In our verse for today we also see that there are also promises and conditions attached to the acquisition of wisdom.

Our verse for today begins with a promise. The godly are given a treasure; good sense, which is another way of saying wisdom. Wisdom is a treasure that can only be experienced by people that are living lives in accordance with God's plan and under His direction. An interesting thing about this treasure is that the only way that it is valuable is when it is being used. Wisdom that is held and not used is not wisdom at all; it is just knowledge. Our verse also reminds where that good sense comes from; the Lord. We can, through our own efforts acquire knowledge, but it is the Lord that grants good sense or wisdom. This should work to keep us humble. There is a real temptation for those that have received good sense from the Lord to become proud and arrogant, thinking that they are the source of the wisdom rather than the Lord.

Today's verse goes on to say that the Lord is the shield to those godly people that He has given good sense to. What a wonderful promise to grab hold of. God has promised to protect those that are living lives according to His plans and direction. This is a conditional promise as are most of God's promises. To experience this protection we must walk with integrity.

There are a couple of definitions of integrity that apply to this statement found in our verse. First, integrity is the moral character of a person. God protects those that are of the moral character that he desires. Integrity has been defined as the person that you are when no one else is watching. This really speaks to the condition of the heart.

The second definition of integrity is to be undivided or whole. This could also be an appropriate definition of godly. God desires that we would be wholly devoted to Him and wholly committed to doing things His way. It is when we divide our affection between God and the things of the world that problems begin to develop in our relationship with God. God wants to give us the treasure of wisdom and good sense and He wants to protect us, but He will only do it if we are walking with integrity and in godliness. We need to be wholly committed to and surrendered to the will and direction of the Lord. Jesus, teach us to be men and women of integrity.

JANUARY 9

Read: Genesis 20:1 – 22:24, Matthew 7:15-29, Psalm 9:1-12, Proverbs 2:16-22

GENESIS 22:8

"God will provide a lamb, my son," Abraham answered. And they both went on together.

Isaac, the child that God promised to Abraham would be the one from whom the uncountable ancestors of Abraham would come is being led up this mountain to be sacrificed to God. Isaac observes that they have the wood and the fire but where is the lamb for the sacrifice. And in Abraham's response we see his faith. Abraham knows that the promises of God are faithful and true. He is confident that whatever God has said, will come to pass.

In his heart I am sure that he doesn't understand what is going on. Why would God give him this son and promise that he will be the one through whom the countless ancestors would come and then ask him to kill him on this mountain? How is God going to fulfill His promise if Isaac is dead? Will God bring Isaac back to life after he has been sacrificed? All of these questions must have been going through his mind as they made this long journey to the mountain.

Abraham's response to Isaac is one of a great confidence in the power and ability of God. Abraham was convinced that God had a plan that he couldn't understand or know. And Abraham trusted God so completely that he was willing to walk up this mountain and sacrifice his promised son to Him.

God calls us to have this same confidence in Him. As we build this church or ministry, God is going to ask you to sacrifice something that is very special to you. He isn't going to ask you to take your son onto a mountain to sacrifice Him. But He might ask you to lay down a dream that you have held on His altar. He might ask you to give up something that He has given you as a special possession.

Is there anything in your life that is so dear to you that you would not lay it on the altar as a sacrifice to God if He asked for it? If there is, then it will prevent you from fully experiencing the power of God flowing through your life. Nothing can take a higher place in your life than God.

Daily look through your life to see what you have not laid on God's altar in your life. If you find something ask God to help you to sacrifice it. If you do that you will unleash God's power more fully in your life. There may come a time when God will ask you to give that thing up. Will you have prepared yourself to be willing, like Abraham, to give up that precious thing that you have to God in obedience, submission, and love of God? Will you trust that God is able to provide a substitute for that sacrifice? Lord, help us to trust and believe.

JANUARY 10

Read: Genesis 23:1 – 24:51, Matthew 8:1-17, Psalm 9:13-20, Proverbs 3:1-6

I know, because I am under the authority of my superior officers and I have authority over my soldiers. I only need to say, "Go," and they go, or "Come," and they come. And if I say to my slaves, "Do this or that," they do it.

This is a scripture that I have often marveled at. This Gentile Roman officer comes to Jesus because one of his servants is seriously sick. There is much about this text that is fascinating and interesting. The Romans of this time are often pictured as being uncaring, cruel masters of those nations that they had conquered. This officer cares enough about his servant to humble himself and ask Jesus, a citizen of the nation that the Romans had conquered, to heal him.

Servants and slaves in this time were more considered property than people. There was a very active slave market. The Romans had a ready supply of people from the nations that they had conquered. This Roman could have easily replaced this sick servant with another. But what is most striking about this Roman officer is his faith. He has an understanding and grasp of faith that is remarkable. So striking is it that Jesus commends him as having more faith than anyone else in Israel. This Roman officer believed that Jesus could, should He desire to do so, heal his servant. Belief is the foundation stone of faith. There is no faith where there is not belief. The Roman soldier believed and so he had the faith to ask.

Faith alone is not enough! Our faith must also be based on truth. No matter how strongly I might believe that I can fly, if I step off of a building, I will not fly. The Roman officer knew who Jesus was and believed what was being said about Him. This Roman officer believed that Jesus' power came from God. And it was this knowledge that allowed him to believe that Jesus could save his servant.

This is the truly amazing part of this account. The Roman told Jesus that He didn't need to come to his house to heal the servant. He needed just to give the command and it would be done. The Roman officer understood that God's power was far beyond the reach of any person. This Roman officer understood that Jesus was under the authority of the Father.

He understood that Jesus' presence in his home was unnecessary if God wanted to heal the servant.

Sometimes we lack the faith of this Roman officer. Sometimes we think that we need to go or to be in some place or with some person so that we can experience the power of God working in our lives. The only thing that limits the power of God is our faith. If we will just believe that God wants to do a thing; then it can happen. The Roman officer did not know that Jesus would heal his servant, but he believed that He could. Do you believe? What doubts prevent you from getting all from God that He wants to give you or do for you? Jesus, teach to understand who you are and what you want to do in our lives.

JANUARY 11
Read: Genesis 24:52 – 26:16, Matthew 8:18-34, Psalm 10:1-15, Proverbs 3:7-8

GENESIS 25:32

"Look, I'm dying of starvation!" said Esau. "What good is my birthright to me now?"

Esau has just come in from a long day of hunting and is hungry. His brother Jacob has made stew and Esau asks for some. Jacob as we will see is his habit uses this as an opportunity to advance himself within the family. Jacob as the younger son (by a couple of minutes) is not entitled to much within the family. Because Esau is the oldest son he will be entitled to a larger share of his father's estate and he will assume the role of the leader of the family once his father dies. This is called the "birthright." Jacob tells Esau that he will give him a bowl of stew if Esau will give him the birthright. Esau agrees and trades his birthright for a bowl of stew. This is a fulfillment of the prophecy that was given to their mother Rebekah while she was pregnant with them. Rebekah was told by the Lord that her older son would serve her younger son.

What has always struck me about this account is the foolishness of Esau. Esau traded his future for a simple bowl of stew. Was he really that foolish or did he not believe that he was actually trading away his birthright. Later in the reading we see that Esau acknowledged that he had lost his birthright to Jacob. For the momentary satisfaction of a bowl of stew Esau gave his whole future away.

How many of us have done something very similar to what Esau did? How many of us have traded a future that was rich and full of promise for something as temporary and meaningless as a bowl of stew? Esau's flesh drove him to make a very poor decision that affected the rest of his life. In all of our lives there will come times where we are faced with these same types of choices; choices that will affect the rest of our lives. And some of them will be like this one that Esau made; affecting the rest of your life.

Esau responded in his flesh when he should have thought about what he was doing. He wasn't really starving but he put his immediate desires over his future dreams. We have got to be so careful not to do the same thing. Satan will tempt us to accept some small thing that brings happiness to us now in exchange for a future dream. This is especially true when it comes to things of God. The Devil would gladly trade you today some small physical pleasure for a future that is rich and full and blessed by God.

Jesus told us to deny ourselves so that we could inherit the kingdom of God. We have been promised so much by God; we shouldn't trade it all away for something that makes us happy today. Jesus also told us to seek first His kingdom. If we do that He promises to add all that other stuff to our lives. Oh, you may miss a bowl of stew or two but you won't starve; God won't allow it. Just keep your eyes on the prize that has been set before you and keep moving up toward God. Jesus, help us to keep our minds off of our flesh and on heaven.

JANUARY 12

Read: Genesis 26:17 – 27:46, Matthew 9:1-17, Psalm 10:16-18, Proverbs 3:9-10

GENESIS 26:22

Abandoning that one, he dug another well, and the local people finally left him alone. So Isaac called it "Room Enough," for he said, "At last the LORD has made room for us, and we will be able to thrive."

This is the third time that Isaac's men dig a well so that they can get water for their families and flocks. The two previous times, the local Philistines would come and claim the well and drive Isaac's men away from it. This third time, they did not. This time they allowed the men of Isaac to keep this well.

Fresh water is an absolute necessity. In Genesis 26, there is a famine in the land. That means water is especially scarce. These wells are of great value because they are providing life to the people and animals that so desperately need it.

If you are involved in planting a church or starting a ministry, there are a couple of great lessons in this text for you. First, as we begin a ministry or church, we are digging a well. There is a famine in the land and all around us people are dying. People are starving from a lack of God in their lives and they are dying without God. The well that we are digging will supply something that they need so desperately.

Twice Isaac was blocked after his men had done the work. And yet he persisted. He did because the need was so great. Just because our work is hindered or blocked by the Philistines around us, we shouldn't allow it to deter us from the work that God has given us. If you have to, move to a new location and start again. On the third attempt to provide water, Isaac was successful. Be persistent!

Twice the Philistines came in and took the fruit of what Isaac had done. It wasn't fair! It shouldn't have happened! And yet it did. Isaac didn't sit around moaning and complaining. He got to work to complete the work that was before Him. If you are successful at starting a church or ministry that provides life-giving water there will be people that will try to take it away from you.

And if they do, what should you do? Sue them? Fight them? No, you start digging. You move to a new location and you start digging. God blessed Isaac not because he had dug these wells, but because he had provided for the needs of the people. And while we can see no justice in this, we need to keep in mind that three wells ended being dug instead of one. Not only was Isaac and his family provided for but so were the families of many of the Philistines. What might not seem fair or just to us may be a part of God's plan to bring life to more than just you and yours. No matter what happens you keep digging! Jesus, help us to persevere.

JANUARY 13

Read: Genesis 28:1 – 29:35, Matthew 9:18-38, Psalm 11:1-7, Proverbs 3:11-12

MATTHEW 9:28

They went right into the house where he was staying, and Jesus asked them, "Do you believe I can make you see?" "Yes, Lord," they told him, "we do."

Jesus healed untold thousands of people during His three years of public ministry. Not all of those miracles are detailed in scripture and so every time one is, it is an opportunity to learn about Jesus and the way that he desires to work within our lives. We have just such an example in our verse for the day. These two blind men hear that Jesus is passing by and begin yelling out for Him to stop and heal them. It appears from the text that He did not stop but instead went into the home where He was staying.

That is where this account becomes fascinating; they follow Him right into the place where He is staying. These guys were serious about getting their sight back. And this is something that we look for in ministry; people that want to be helped. I have come to realize that there are people that say they want help but then will do nothing to cause that help to take place. I now understand that you can only help the ones that want to be helped. This makes it so hard when someone comes to me and says that someone they love needs help. I have to tell them that their loved one can't be helped until they want to be helped.

It is not enough to know that you need help to deal with some trial or tribulation in your life. It is not enough to know that your marriage is bad or that your relationship with your children is not good. It is not enough to know that your finances are a wreck. The only way that you will be able to find victory is to decide to do whatever it takes to obtain victory. These two blinds guys were determined to gain back their sight.

We see another important truth in gaining victory in our lives, marriages, families, every other area of our lives in the question Jesus asked them. He asked them if they believed that He could heal them and they said yes. In addition to making the decision that you will do what it takes to gain victory you must also believe that Jesus can do for you what you need to have victory. These two guys were determined to regain their sight and they believed that Jesus could help them.

Faith and action combined is what will result in the great victories in our lives. We must believe that God can do anything and everything that we desire and then we must act like we believe that and do the things that are necessary to gain victory. If these two guys had stayed outside of the house, they would not have gotten their sight back. What is missing in your life, marriage, family, ministry, or church because you are still standing outside complaining about how cold it is. Believe God and act like you believe God. Jesus, help us to come in out of the cold.

JANUARY 14

Read: Genesis 30:1 – 31:16, Matthew 10:1-23, Psalm 12:1-8, Proverbs 3:13-15

GENESIS 30:27

"Please don't leave me," Laban replied, "for I have learned by divination that the Lord has blessed me because you are here."

What a great testimony of God working through Jacob. Laban is telling Jacob to stay with him because he knows that his blessings are coming from God because of Jacob. Laban has made the connection between the material wealth that God has blessed him with and Jacob's work. Laban is an unbeliever that can't deny the existence of God because of how God is working on behalf of Jacob. As Christians, we are called to be a light to this dark world. We should be a living testimony of God to the rest of the world. Jacob's life made it an undeniable fact to Laban that God existed.

Few church-planters or ministry workers are employed by their ministry. Many are employed or self-employed, often in the secular world. Would your employer or clients say as Laban did: "God has blessed me because of you"? If you were to leave to accept a full-time position in ministry would they be disappointed and saddened that you are leaving? Would they sense, somehow, that they will not be as blessed as before? Or will they be glad that you are gone?

As a church planter or ministry worker, you have a holy occupation. You have a responsibility to work at your job in such a way that it brings glory and honor to God. You need to be praying for God's blessing to be upon your employer. After all, God might bless an unbeliever so that you might be blessed. And God might use that blessing as a way to show that unbelieving employer or client that He exists.

As a church planter or ministry worker, the church or ministry can become more important and more fulfilling than your employment. Jacob worked for twenty years to earn the price of his brides and to provide for his family. What is God's plan for your employment? You don't know, only God does. Your goal should be to create a testimony in your employer or clients about the power, grace, mercy, and blessings of God.

Even if, like Laban, your good character doesn't change their attitude toward God, you keep working to be a blessing. God wants us to keep working to earn that bride-price, as long as it might take. He wants us to work with integrity and strong character. He wants us to be a blessing and to bring a blessing to all that we come in contact with.

Lord, let us never forget that whether we are employed in the secular world or by a ministry or church, that you are our employer. Lord, help us to be a blessing to them and to you.

JANUARY 15
Read: Genesis 31:17 – 32:12, Matthew 10:24 – 11:6, Psalm 13:1-6, Proverbs 3:16-18

PSALM 13:1
O Lord, how long will you forget me? Forever? How long will you look the other way?

David expresses great anguish in this psalm. You can sense that he feels very alone; as though God has totally and completely abandoned him. David does a great job with imagery here to help us to sense what he was feeling as he was inspired to write this psalm. In his heart, David feels as though God has forgotten him. To feel forgotten is a desperate and fearful thing. The picture that I have is of someone on a island in the middle of the ocean with no one to rescue them. Before very long, that person is going to start to feel as though everyone has forgotten them and stopped looking for them. That is how David is feeling as he writes this psalm.

We can all get to that place of feeling that way sometimes; as though God has forgotten us. It might feel as though He has turned His back on us and stopped looking for us. As we mature in the Lord and learn to walk closer and closer to Him, the more profound is this feeling when it is missing. And even though we should not live by our feelings, they are real and are signs of what might be going on inside of our hearts.

It is usually during times of great distress that we feel the way that David describes here. Something has happened in our life that causes us to look for God in a deeper way than we currently are. We are probably looking for God to rescue us from some situation that appeared in our lives. It is at times like this that we are more likely to recognize that we don't sense God's presence in our lives. It is on those deserted islands of the circumstances of our lives that we can find ourselves as feeling alone and separated from God.

David's response at the end of this psalm is the key to how we should respond when we do not feel God's presence. In verses five and six of this psalm David did three things to rekindle the fire in his heart toward God. First, he chose to trust God. In the midst of our circumstances, we must choose to trust God to be our protector and provider. Trusting God begins by believing God and believing comes through the power of His Word.

David then says that he will rejoice because God has rescued him. It is real easy to miss what David is saying here. David feels alone as he writes this psalm. To combat that feeling David is going to rejoice because God has rescued him before. God has been faithful to every one of us and done tremendous things for us. Remember those things and rejoice. The third thing that David did was sing to the Lord because God has been so good to him. There is great power in praising God, especially when we feel distant from Him. The next time you feel like God is far from you, do as David did and you will soon find you are right back in the presence of God. Jesus, teach us to seek You when we don't feel You.

JANUARY 16

Read: Genesis 32:13 – 34:31, Matthew 11:7-30, Psalm 14:1-7, Proverbs 3:19-20

GENESIS 32:10

I am not worthy of all the faithfulness and unfailing love you have shown to me, your servant. When I left home, I owned nothing except a walking stick, and now my household fills two camps!

Jacob is on his way home after twenty years at his uncle Laban's home. God has blessed Jacob tremendously in these twenty years. He has four wives and eleven children. He has flocks of sheep and goats and herds of cattle and camels. God has made him wealthy. As he is returning home he sends messengers to his brother Esau to let him know that he is on his way. The messengers return saying that Esau is coming with four hundred of his men. God has also blessed Esau in the last twenty years. The news of Esau's coming with such a force sends Jacob to his knees to pray to God for his help.

Jacob's prayer is a great picture of how we can pray as well. He doesn't waste a lot of words getting to what he wants and reminds God of the promises that He had made to him. Jacob started this very simply by acknowledging who God was. Jacob was also reminding God that he was doing what God had told him to do; return to his father's home. Jacob knew God and knew that he could speak to Him boldly about the things that God had said to him.

It is the verse for today that caught my attention in this prayer. Jacob told God that he didn't deserve all that God had given to him. He knew that it was all from God and that without God he would still have nothing but a walking stick. Jacob was a wealthy man but he had not allowed his wealth to replace God in his life. All of us have stuff that God has given us. Even if all that we have is a walking stick we need to understand that it came from God. Everything we have was a gift from God. Jacob told God that he was not worthy of all that God had given him. It is because of God's grace that we have all that we have. There is a real risk when we have been blessed by God to forget that it came from God. Jacob didn't do that.

Jacob maintained a clear focus of who God was and what He had done for him. I think that is the message that this prayer has for us. By keeping our eyes on the Lord all the time we will not lose sight of Him no matter what happens in our lives. Whether we are in abundance or despair, keeping our eyes on the Lord assures a right approach to God and His blessings and protection.

In your family, ministry, or church there will be times of both plenty and little. If you will keep your eyes firmly focused on Jesus during all of those times you also will be able to walk boldly into the throne room of God and entreat Him for His help because it will be a natural thing for you to do. Jesus, help us to focus upon you rather than our circumstances or stuff.

JANUARY 17

Read: Genesis 35:1 – 36:43, Matthew 12:1-21, Psalm 15:1-5, Proverbs 3:21-26

GENESIS 36:7

There was not enough land to support them both because of all their cattle and livestock.

Jacob has returned to the land of his father Isaac. In the twenty years that Jacob has been gone God has prospered his brother Esau. They are both very prosperous and their herds and flocks combined are too much for the land they are living in to support. And so Esau moves away from his brother Jacob. In the text there is no sense of animosity in this move on Esau's part. It appears that it was just the logical thing for him to do.

The fact that it was Esau that moved may be based on his understanding that it was through Jacob that God was going to fulfill His promise to their father, Isaac. It could also be that Esau was being honorable. Even though, at least at one point, he felt that Jacob had stolen his birthright. The birthright entitled Esau to stay but because Jacob had his birthright, it was Esau that moved away.

How easy it would have been for Esau to demand his rights and challenge his brother. This issue of the birthright was between him and his brother. He could have easily claimed that it had never happened. He could have easily have claimed that he had been cheated and therefore deserved his birthright back. But Esau didn't do that. Instead he moved his family and his rather sizable household away from Jacob. And the result for Esau was that God continued to prosper him and bless him.

There are times in ministry when we have the opportunity to make a decision like Esau made. The decision might make life more difficult and awkward. It might not even be fair in your eyes. It might even be because of someone else's sin. But ultimately God blesses the honorable decisions, especially those that are made sacrificially. And just like God blessed Esau for his honorable decision, He is likely to bless you in some way. We understand, of course, that blessing might not be in some material way but we can rest in the knowledge that His blessings will follow our obedience.

If there is conflict or stress in your life and one of your options is to make a decision that is awkward or uncomfortable or you, it might be because He desires to move you to place where He has more room to bless you. Too often we look at our current situation like it can't be better, or that if we move it will be worse. When we do this we are limiting a God that has no limits. Be looking for those times when God is looking to do radical things in your life by leading you into the greener pastures that He has been preparing for you. Lord, help me to see you in the tough choices that I need to make in my life.

JANUARY 18

Read: Genesis 37:1 – 38:30, Matthew 12:22-45, Psalm 16:1-11, Proverbs 3:27-32

GENESIS 37:4

But his brothers hated Joseph because of their father's partiality. They couldn't say a kind word to him.

Joseph was Jacob's eleventh son. He was born to him by his favorite wife Rachel. It was obvious to everyone that Jacob loved Joseph more than his other sons. This created incredible tension with at least ten of his brothers. From our verse for the day we are told that they couldn't say anything nice to him at all. There was a severe hatred that had developed by the brothers toward Joseph.

We all know the story; the brothers plotted to kill Joseph but instead sold him into slavery to some Ishmaelite traders going to Egypt. We also know that God works that out to the good of Joseph and to his family; including the brothers that wanted to kill him.

Every time we read this story we are appalled at the behavior of the brothers and feel that they should be punished. It seems that the only thing that they ultimately experienced was a bit of a guilty conscience. Those kinds of stories tend to bother us. We want to see justice and believe they should experience some penalty for what they did.

Have you ever thought how you might have behaved if you were in the same place as the brothers of Joseph? Do you think you would have handled it differently than they did? Those are great questions but we can't put ourselves in that situation so it is difficult to respond. However, we probably do find ourselves in similar situations on a fairly regular basis. There are usually people all around us that appear to be God's favorites. They are blessed beyond what seems reasonable and nothing ever goes wrong in their lives. That can very easily lead to feelings of jealousy and envy. The Bible teaches that God has no favorites but it is obvious that some people are experiencing greater blessings than others. Be careful, you can very quickly find yourself in the same place as Joseph's brothers.

Ministries and churches experience the same thing. As you look around and see other ministries and churches that are experiencing great success and growth while yours may not, it can lead to very wrong thinking and actions. Or if it is your ministry or church that is being blessed you might expect to experience some negative responses from those around you. Why God chooses to bless one and not another is God's sovereign will at work. We may not understand it but we have a choice in how we respond to it.

The best way to defeat hatred is to love. The way to defeat jealousy is to rejoice with those that are successful. Go to that person that God is blessing and give glory to God for what they are doing. Praise God for that ministry or church and what He is doing there; even if you don't agree with the way that it is done or the style it is done through.

You have to choose to fight against the natural tendency toward jealousy, envy, and hatred. Jesus, help us to rejoice with those that you have blessed more than us.

JANUARY 19

Read: Genesis 39:1 – 41:16, Matthew 12:46 – 13:23, Psalm 17:1-15, Proverbs 3:33-35

MATTHEW 13:11

Then he explained to them, "You have been permitted to understand the secrets of the Kingdom of Heaven, but others have not."

Jesus' disciples came and asked Him why He spoke in stories and parables. These stories were intended to teach people about the kingdom of God using real-life illustrations. The listeners would have immediately understood the context of the story and if able would be able to make the spiritual interpretation. But when the disciples ask the question, Jesus makes this interesting statement in our verse for the day.

He tells them that they have been permitted to understand but there are some that have not been permitted to understand what He is saying. On first glance at this verse you might think this is unfair but you would be reading it out of context with the following verses. The Father knows absolutely everything and He knows who will listen to the message that Jesus is proclaiming. To those that are listening, the Father gives them understanding so that they can correctly interpret the things that Jesus is saying.

To those that will not accept the truth of the things that Jesus is saying, He does not give understanding. God knows that some people will not accept the truth no matter what you say and so he will not let them understand the truth; it just won't make any sense to them. I remember from my own life that this was true. The things that my wife would tell me about God made no sense to me and no matter how hard she tried to explain I just couldn't get it. God knew I wasn't going to accept it anyway.

Then a time came when God changed my heart and I was willing to accept those things and the very same things that I couldn't understand before began to make sense. Don't be concerned when those around you just don't get it. They can't because they are not ready. Only after God has thoroughly prepared their hearts are they going to be ready to start understanding.

In the meantime you need to do just what Jesus did; keep telling them the truth. It doesn't matter if they are going to receive it or not; you just keep telling them the truth. What you need to do is stop expecting them to understand. What that will do for you is eliminate the frustration that you feel because they are not responding. They can't respond until God has finished doing the work in their heart. Your responsibility is to keep planting seeds of love and truth so that when the time comes you are there to help them to understand. Just keep loving them even thought they don't really understand it. Just keep showing them God's grace and mercy even though they don't understand it. Just keep living like Christ, even though they don't understand it. Someday they might and you will have played a part in getting them there. Jesus, teach us to be patient.

JANUARY 20

Read: Genesis 41:17 – 42:17, Matthew 13:24-46, Psalm 18:1-15, Proverbs 4:1-6

GENESIS 42:5

So Jacob's sons arrived in Egypt along with others to buy food, for the famine had reached Canaan as well.

Jacob sends ten of his sons to Egypt to buy food because a famine is in the land of Canaan. Little does Jacob know but he is sending his ten sons to meet with his other son that they had sold into slavery that he thinks is dead. This is the second year of the famine that will last for another five years.

One of the questions that can get your mind all twisted up is: Did God cause the famine to happen so that Joseph's brothers would have to come to Egypt? Or did God know that the famine was going to happen and so He caused events to happen in Joseph's life so that he would be reunited with his family as a result of the famine? Scripture doesn't answer that question and so that means that we don't need to know the answer.

What we do need to take from that though is that God could do either one. It is kind of fascinating to think of questions like that because it gives you a picture of some of the things that God could do to carry out His will and plans in this world. There is nothing that is beyond the ability of God. If God wanted to change the weather patterns to cause a famine, that is no great feat for Him. If God wanted to arrange that Joseph was able to interpret dreams, that is nothing to Him.

However it happened, God was using circumstances to bring His plan to pass. He was reuniting the sons of Jacob and setting them up to grow into a great nation. While they are living in Egypt they grow to be well over one million people; all descendants of Jacob and his twelve sons. As we go through life there are going to be famines. They will be of all kinds and causes. They can be material, physical, emotional, relational, or spiritual. Some of them we bring on ourselves. Others are imposed upon us by others. And some might even be brought on by God. Regardless how it happens God is still in control and has a plan that He is working out in your life and in the lives of everyone around you.

"Can God make a rock that is too big for Him to lift?" is a stupid question. "Can God rearrange the world and nature to cause His plan for my life to happen?" is a great question. These types of questions should remind us of the grace, mercy, and power of God. They should bring us back to His incredible love for us. And ultimately they should bring us back to the cross.

Any time we come to a question about God that His word doesn't answer then we need to go back to His character and nature; they will answer the question for us. Jesus, teach to let our questions draw us closer to You.

JANUARY 21

Read: Genesis 42:18 – 43:34, Matthew 13:47 – 14:12, Psalm 18:16-36, Proverbs 4:7-10

GENESIS 43:18

They were badly frightened when they saw where they were being taken. "It's because of the money returned to us in our sacks," they said. "He plans to pretend that we stole it. Then he will seize us as slaves and take our donkeys."

Joseph has been in Egypt for some time now. His brothers don't recognize him but he knows each one of them. It probably appears that they hadn't changed much at all. That is, except for Benjamin. When Joseph was sold into slavery Benjamin was but a boy. Now he would be an adult just a few years younger than Joseph.

It is hard to guess what all the brothers were feeling but we get a sense from the text that they were pretty worried about this trip to Egypt. They were expecting the worst and when Joseph told his manager to take them into his house for lunch they assumed that they were in deep trouble. There is a great sense of fear in this whole story of the famine.

The problem lies in their consciences. They carry a sense of guilt about what they did to Joseph. They know that they sold him into slavery and they believe that he is most likely still a slave somewhere or possibly dead. This guilty conscience has kept them in a state of fear since they sold Joseph into slavery.

They thought selling Joseph into slavery would make their lives better because it eliminated their problem. Joseph was never their problem. Their problem resided in the deepest parts of their hearts; they didn't really love or trust God. It seems that the closest the brothers get to God in this account is to believe that He is punishing them for what they did to their half-brother Joseph. Instead of making their lives better, it made their lives miserable.

Making a problem go away seldom solves the problem. This is true because the problem is usually not outside of you but in your heart. If you want to solve your problems, stop looking at the circumstances around and trying to devise ways of selling them into slavery. Instead, open your heart to the Lord and allow Him to change the part of your heart that is causing you to feel the way that you are.

It was always God's plan to send Joseph to Egypt because that was how He intended to save them and countless thousands of others during the seven-year famine that was devastating the land. God used Joseph's brother's sin to get him to Egypt. But I believe that God wanted them repent of that sin and submit their hearts to Him. Instead they lived in fear and guilt and misery. Don't let guilt ruin your life. Lay it down at the foot of the cross and allow Christ's perfect blood to cleanse you. Allow His perfect love to cast out all fear from your heart so that you can live the life that He intended you to live. Jesus, help us to empty our hearts of everything but You.

GENESIS 45:16

The news soon reached Pharaoh: "Joseph's brothers have come!" Pharaoh was very happy to hear this and so were his officials.

Pharaoh hears that Joseph's brothers have come to Egypt. Joseph is so well-respected and appreciated that this is good news to everyone. Pharaoh tells Joseph to send his brothers back to Canaan and to bring back their families and Joseph's father Jacob (or Israel) to Egypt to live. Egypt and Canaan were in the midst of a severe famine. God had told Pharaoh through Joseph that this famine would last for seven years. There were still several years left and chances are that the rest of Joseph's family would have suffered greatly as a result of this famine.

But God had promised to make them as numerous as the sands of the seashore or as the stars of the sky. To do that, they would need to not just survive the famine but prosper through it. And to do that they would need the favor of Pharaoh. They had that favor because of Joseph.

Joseph held a position of great power and authority in the nation of Egypt. He was second only to Pharaoh himself. It is easily understood why Pharaoh was pleased with him. The plan that Joseph had recommended was working perfectly. In the midst of a severe famine, they had food to eat. But it was not just Pharaoh that was pleased but also his servants.

This means that Joseph had developed a reputation and a relationship with these servants that led them to be happy for him when something good happened to him. To do that Joseph had to have caused them to believe that he cared for them. People are fickle and funny, especially where great power and authority are concerned. Pharaoh's servants, including high ranking officials who might have envied his position and power, cared for Joseph.

As we build a church or a ministry, we must care for people. That seems like such an obvious thing to say. But I am not just speaking of those that our church or ministry is trying to touch. We must care for all people. First we do that because that is what Jesus would have us to do. But from a practical standpoint, God might want to use someone in your life, an unbeliever perhaps, to bless your church or ministry.

Our minds cannot comprehend the complexity of God's plan. Our eyes cannot see His hand moving the game pieces around the board to accomplish His grand plan. Our role in that plan is to try to eliminate obstacles that God has to work around. One of the ways that we do that is by truly caring for everyone around us. And yes, that includes the ones that you don't like. God loves them and so should you. Lord, help us to care for everyone!

JANUARY 23

Read: Genesis 46:1 – 47:31, Matthew 15:1-28, Psalm 19:1-14, Proverbs 4:14-19

GENESIS 46:2

During the night God spoke to him in a vision. "Jacob! Jacob!" he called. "Here I am," Jacob replied.

Jacob's sons have returned from Egypt to get food and told him that they met Joseph there. He is stunned by the news and then his sons tell him that they have been invited to move to Egypt to escape the famine that is going to last for the next five years. So they pack up everything they own and start off to Egypt.

During the night, the Lord speaks to Jacob in a vision. At first you might wonder why the Lord would speak to Jacob as he is making this journey. But as you look at what the Lord says to him it starts to make sense. The Lord had promised the land of Canaan to Abraham and his descendants. Jacob may very well have been unsure about leaving Canaan to go to Egypt. He may have been questioning whether he was showing a lack of faith. He might have been concerned that something would happen in Egypt. There may have all sorts of questions in his mind as he was making his way out of the Promised Land.

God knew what was going through Jacob's mind and so He gives him a vision to reassure Jacob that this is all a part of God's great plan for the nation of Israel. God goes on to tell Jacob that He is going to make them into a great nation while they are in Egypt and that He will bring them back. We know from the Exodus that there was an estimated 1 to 2 million people in the nation of Israel when they left Egypt. God kept His promise to Abraham, Isaac, and Jacob.

It was Jacob's reply in the verse above that I loved. When the Lord called to Jacob in the vision, he replied "Here I am." Part of the reason why God was able to do the things that He did in people's lives like Jacob is because they were waiting for Him to call them. I believe this was why men like Jacob heard the voice of God the way that they did; they were listening for it. Jacob was expecting to hear from God and he was waiting to hear from God.

God still speaks to His people. He especially wants to speak to those that have been called to shepherd His people. As leaders of families, ministries, and churches we need to be expecting God to speak to us; we need to be waiting for Him to call out to us. This involves preparation. We must prepare ourselves spiritually so that the lines of communication are clear. We start by opening a channel of communication through prayer. Next we continue to familiarize ourselves with God through His Word. We also need to be looking for things in our lives that will hinder our ability to hear from God; namely distractions and sins. Then we must believe that He is going to call. If we will do things like these, when the Lord does speak to us, we will answer immediately like Jacob did, "Here I am Lord." Jesus, teach to answer the phone from You on the first ring.

JANUARY 24

Read: Genesis 48:1 – 49:33, Matthew 15:29 – 16:12, Psalm 20:1-9, Proverbs 4:20-27

MATTHEW 16:1

One day the Pharisees and Sadducees came to test Jesus' claims by asking him to show them a miraculous sign from heaven.

The Pharisees and the Sadducees were seldom in agreement about anything. They had two different ways of looking at the worship of God. They coexisted but they didn't hang out together. But when it came to Jesus they were united in their attempts to get rid of Him. They combined for the purpose of proving that He was not who everyone was saying He was; the Messiah. Jesus didn't fit the profile that they had created for the Savior of the Jewish people. They expected a king to come riding in on a white horse to cast down the oppression of the Roman occupation. A carpenter from Nazareth was not what they were looking for.

The Pharisees and Sadducees came to Jesus and asked for a miraculous sign so that they would be convinced. Jesus knew their hearts and knew that they were trying to prove Him false and that He was not the Messiah. Jesus had already performed signs without number. People have been healed. People have been delivered from demons. He has fed the multitudes. Jesus had already provided all the proof that they needed that He was real, only their hard hearts prevented them from believing.

It is still the same today. Jesus has provided all the proof that we need to believe. And for those of us that do believe, we have seen that proof. But to those that don't believe, many won't because their hearts are hard and wouldn't believe even if Jesus appeared in front of them and handed them a loaf of bread. Sometimes in the ministry that can be very discouraging. People will come to challenge what you are doing. They are challenging you to prove that what you are doing is real. They don't care to know if you are real or not; they are more interested in proving that you are false.

If God blesses your family, ministry, or church you can be pretty sure that there are some Pharisees and Sadducees right around the corner to test you. When they come, rejoice! If they are coming it is because the Lord is at work in your midst. Jesus' response to them was tell them to look around and watch for the fruit. The fruit of your family, ministry, or church is all the testimony you need of the power of God working in your midst.

The Pharisees and the Sadducees didn't want to see the proof and there will be people that come to test you that don't want to see the proof either. That is not your concern. If Jesus didn't make a point to prove to them that He was real, then we don't need to either. Only those with eyes to see will see. Only those with ears to hear will hear. Only those with hearts that are open to receive will receive. Just like Jesus, focus on the ministry that God called you to and leave the Pharisees and Sadducees to God. Jesus, teach us to keep our eyes on the task at hand.

JANUARY 25

Read: Genesis 50:1 – Exodus 2:10, Matthew 16:13 – 17:9, Psalm 21:1-13, Proverbs 5:1-6

But because the midwives feared God, they refused to obey the king and allowed the boys to live, too.

It has been about 350 years since Jacob and the rest of his family have come to Egypt. They have multiplied from about seventy people to well over one million. A new pharaoh takes the throne in Egypt and this pharaoh does not remember the things that Joseph did for Egypt. He doesn't remember that this Hebrew saved the nation of Egypt and made the previous Pharaoh wealthier through his efforts. All this pharaoh could see was that there were a lot of these Hebrews and they could be a threat to his rule.

So the pharaoh began to oppress the children of Israel. His plan was to make life very hard on them so that they would not multiply and grow stronger. This plan backfired on him and the Hebrews continued to prosper.

During this period Egypt was very prosperous and powerful. Egypt represented all the good things that the world had to offer. The Hebrews considered Egypt to be their home. And for the Christian, Egypt is a type or picture of the world around us. We look around and see all the good things that there are and that they are beautiful and appealing. We look at this world and see it as our home.

Egypt was not home to the Hebrews. But they were comfortable in this place. And once you become comfortable in a place, it is difficult to separate yourself from it. And once you become comfortable, that place will begin to influence you. And at some point, you will be asked to compromise. Pharaoh told the Hebrew midwives to kill all the boys born to Hebrew women. He told these women to murder these babies.

Most of us will never be faced with anything remotely as obvious as that. We will not be told to compromise what we believe to that awful degree. But all of us that are living and ministering in this world will be told to compromise our faith to some degree. And if you give in to that compromise, eventually you will be killing babies. I don't mean literally, but I do know that one compromise leads to another. And with each new compromise, we are told to compromise more.

The midwives feared God more than they feared the pharaoh. As Christians, do we fear God more than we fear the world? Which of the two do you hold in higher reverence and authority? Which one will you obey, even if it costs you something? This world is not your home. Heaven is your home and God is your King! Resist this world and refuse to compromise even a little bit! Jesus, help us to see heaven as home and your word as law.

JANUARY 26
Read: Exodus 2:11 – 3:22, Matthew 17:10-27, Psalm 22:1-18, Proverbs 5:7-14

PROVERBS 5:8

Run from her! Don't go near the door of her house!

Solomon takes three chapters in the book of Proverbs to warn us against immorality in our relationships. And within these three chapters you find some of the strongest language on the subject in the entire Bible. Here in chapter five we are told that an immoral relationship will result in utter ruin. We are warned that an immoral relationship will cost us everything; our reputation, our wealth and possessions, and even our health and life are at risk.

And as we look around this world we can see that things are true. Most of us know someone that has been in an immoral relationship and we have seen the pain and suffering that they caused and that they endured as a result of it. And even though we have seen the carnage left behind because of an immoral relationship, we are still tempted and sometimes even flirt with the idea. Why do we do that?

Our problem is that we think that we are somehow different than those other people. We can make ourselves believe that we could do it without getting caught. Somehow we believe that we can hide it from everyone. And in some bizarre chain of logic we might even convince ourselves that God doesn't mind. How foolish!

God does mind and He gives us some very clear instructions on what to do so that we don't get involved in an immoral relationship. RUN! If you are tempted, RUN! If you have been flirting with the idea, RUN! If you are in an immoral relationship, RUN FAST! The sooner you remove yourself from the source of the problem the better, RUN!

God will not allow our sins to hide forever. If we don't deal with them ourselves, He will do something to cause our sins to be revealed to the world. He is faithful and patient. He will try to get you to do it on your own. And if we do, the pain and suffering are reduced. But if God has to reveal it, the pain, suffering, and loss are always great.

It seems that the number one reason for Christian leaders to fall is because of immoral relationships. Whole churches have suffered because of the fall of a Christian leader. They are human just like anyone else and vulnerable to the same temptations as anyone else. But the burden of responsibility is much greater. As a leader in your family, ministry, or church your sin affects not only you but all those that look to you for leadership.

A good defense is a strong offense. We must defend ourselves against this sin by attacking the source of it. Do everything that you can to prevent and eliminate the temptation. Put in safeguards to protect you. Develop accountability relationships to provide you with a way to verify how you are doing. Don't relent and don't relax; our enemy is waiting for an opportunity to devour us. Jesus, help us to RUN!

JANUARY 27

Read: Exodus 4:1 – 5:21, Matthew 18:1-20, Psalm 22:19-31, Proverbs 5:15-21

EXODUS 4:18

Then Moses went back home and talked it over with Jethro, his father-in-law. "With your permission," Moses said, "I would like to go back to Egypt to visit my family. I don't even know whether they are still alive." "Go with my blessing," Jethro replied.

Moses has just met with God and been told by God from the burning bush to go back to Egypt to lead the people of Israel out of Egypt and into the land that God promised them. Moses then goes and talks it over with Jethro, his father-in-law. I found that interesting. Why would Moses talk it over with Jethro and seek his permission to leave? Was it a lack of faith on Moses' part? I don't think so. I believe it was respect for Jethro that prompted Moses to do this.

Just because God had told Moses to go didn't mean that he could just walk away from everything else to go. Don't get me wrong, nothing should interfere with our obedience to God. However, God is not a god of chaos but of order. When He tells us to do something He wants us to do it well. When that something includes a change from one thing to another, God wants us to do it in such a way that He is glorified and honored. If Moses had just walked away from everything it would have been very disruptive to Jethro's household and would have had a negative effect on his relationship with his wife's family.

If Moses had done this poorly it may have closed the door to his relationship with Jethro. Because Moses didn't close that door, Jethro is there to help Moses as he is trying to lead the Israelites through the wilderness. The help that Jethro gives to Moses does more than just save him from leadership burnout but it also establishes the leadership system that they will need once they enter into the Promised Land.

Moses did not need Jethro's permission to do what God had told him to do. But by showing Jethro the respect that he did, God was glorified and God used that relationship to bless Moses and the Israelites later. We don't need anyone's permission to obey God. However, there are going to be circumstances that require us to go to someone else and seek their blessing or permission to do what God is directing us to.

There are going to be times when the only way that we can obey God is by getting someone's blessing or permission. This is not a "necessary evil" as some might perceive it; it is a part of the process that God wants you to go through as He positions all the pieces to help you to accomplish the things that He is directing you to do. If we do it well God is glorified and His will is accomplished. If we resist it and fight this process, God must rearrange things to cause His will to be done and it will be much harder on us. God's instructions do not depend upon man's blessing but they often are found together. Jesus, help us to be humble enough to ask for a blessing on what God wants from us.

JANUARY 28

Read: Exodus 5:22 – 7:25, Matthew 18:21 – 19:12, Psalm 23:1-6, Proverbs 5:22-23

EXODUS 6:2

And God continued, "I am the Lord."

God is setting the stage to perform this incredible work of delivering the nation of Israel out of the bondage of Egypt. But as God is preparing for this great miracle, things are getting a little tough for the Hebrews. Pharaoh has put unreasonable demands upon them. And the people are blaming Moses and calling him a troublemaker.

Moses goes back to God and asks Him why this is happening the way that it is. Moses is confused because he thought God was going to make things easier for the Hebrews. Moses didn't expect things to get worse.

We behave just like Moses did. When God gets our attention and tells us that He has a plan for our lives that is more than just sitting in the pews, we believe that it is going to be easy. But it isn't easy and God never promised that it would be.

Egypt is a type or picture of this world that we live in and pharaoh is a type or picture of our enemy, Satan. And just like Moses, if you have been called to serve in a ministry or church (which everyone has), your role is to lead people out of Egypt and away from pharaoh. But pharaoh doesn't want to let them go. While they may be a threat to his rule, as long as he can hold on to them, he can use them for his purposes.

God reassures Moses by telling him that He is the Lord. He tells Moses: I am God! God then continues on and tells Moses about what He is going to do. It was God's intention and plan to free the nation of Israel from the bondage of Egypt. That is still the plan of God. He is still about that same plan; freeing people from the bondage of this world and sin. And just like God used Moses, He wants to use you.

Moses was no different than any other man. There were no great features about Moses that led God to choose him. In fact Moses resisted God and didn't want to do what God wanted him to do. God can and will use anyone that He chooses to do His will. And if we will just rest in the fact that He is God, then we will be used to do incredibly miraculous things for His kingdom.

The Hebrews didn't believe Moses because their circumstances were so difficult. And in ministry and church, there will be times that you might feel as Moses felt. You know that God has given you a task, but no one sees that but you. It is during those times that you need to hold on the fact that God is God. He is working even when you can't see it and don't understanding it. His plan will be carried out and you have the honor and privilege of being a part of it. Jesus, help us to do our part and to let you be the Lord.

JANUARY 29
Read: Exodus 8:1 – 9:35, Matthew 19:13-30, Psalm 24:1-10, Proverbs 6:1-5

EXODUS 9:16

But I have let you live for this reason – that you might see my power and that my fame might spread throughout the earth.

God keeps sending Moses to Pharaoh to get him to let the people of Israel go. God intends to deliver them from their bondage but wants to send a message to the whole world as a result of what He is doing here in Egypt. The first thing that you notice about this message that God is sending to Pharaoh through Moses is that God is in control. Egypt is one of the most powerful nations in the world at this time. And the Egyptians considered their Pharaoh to be god on earth. This message from God to Pharaoh is to tell Pharaoh that there is only one God and Pharaoh is not it.

God tells Pharaoh not only that He is in control but that Pharaoh remains only because He has allowed it to be. God is telling Pharaoh that his very life is in God's hands and control. He then goes on to tell Pharaoh that He has allowed him to remain for a purpose. That purpose is so that God's power can be seen by the whole earth and so that His name can be proclaimed to the ends of the earth.

We live in a world that is filled with people that think they are gods, or at the very least kings. They might not use those words to describe themselves, but that is how they behave. They believe that they are in control of everything around them and that they are where they are because they deserve to be there or because they have earned the right to be there. And God allows them to stay there so that He can show His power and so that His name can be spread to the furthest parts of the earth. We also live in a world that is filled with things that hold people in bondage just as the Hebrews were in bondage in Egypt. Drugs, alcohol, pornography, sex, gambling, power, position, hatred, fear, and bitterness are just a few of the things that hold people.

God used Pharaoh to demonstrate His power and to proclaim His name. And God is still using the Pharaohs and "gods" and "kings" of this world to demonstrate His power and to proclaim His name. The reason your ministry or church exists is to be used by God to deliver His chosen people from the bondage of whatever their Egypt is. The reason that you are still on this earth and not in heaven with God is so that He can use you to demonstrate His power and proclaim His name through you.

Moses didn't volunteer to be the vessel that God used to deliver the Hebrews from Egypt; God picked him. You didn't volunteer either; God picked you. And just like Moses, if you will let Him, God will use you to deliver His people from bondage. And you will see incredible things being done in and through your life, ministry, and church. Jesus, help us to be clean vessels for your power and help us to proclaim Your name clearly to the world.

JANUARY 30
Read: Exodus 10:1 – 12:13, Matthew 20:1-28, Psalm 25:1-15, Proverbs 6:6-11

MATTHEW 20:15

Is it against the law for me to do what I want with my money? Should you be angry because I am kind?

Today we read the parable of the vineyard workers. In this parable the vineyard owner hired workers to work in his field. He went out several times throughout the day and hired groups of men. As was the custom of the day, each man was paid at the end of the work day. The vineyard owner paid each man a full days wage even though some of them only worked for an hour.

The guys that had been there all day long objected to the fact that some of the men had worked far less and received the same as them. They considered this to be unfair. They labored long and these others received the same thing as them. This parable is meant to teach us about God's incredible grace. Because God's grace is unmerited, nothing that we do determines the reward that we get. While this particular parable speaks primarily of salvation, the principle applies to all areas of our life with God.

This is especially true of those that serve the Lord. Our human nature will sometimes convince us that because we have been faithful in service to God that we have earned something for our service. God's grace does not depend upon our service but upon God's good pleasure. It is a dangerous thing to think that you deserve something from God. According to the Bible the thing that we deserve is death. In God's incredible mercy He does not give us what we deserve. Instead He pours out His amazing grace and gives us what we have not earned or deserve.

This is such an important truth for servants and leaders to embrace. It can determine the effectiveness of everything that we do in our marriages, families, ministries, and churches. When we believe that we deserve something for our efforts we begin to remove ourselves from the flow of God's blessings. His grace is still dispensed but His blessings can dry up and turn to curses.

We serve God because He is worthy of our total devotion and commitment to Him and because of what Jesus did for us. We cannot look to others to determine if our rewards are fair; only God can determine that. Our attitude should be that we are thankful for everything that we have regardless of what someone else has received. We should celebrate when God chooses, in His grace, to bless someone abundantly. Pride will convince us that we deserve more. We need to daily remind ourselves that we deserve nothing and that the very breath in our lungs is a gift from God. The only reward that we should desire from God is growing fellowship with Him. If you keep that attitude, you will be able to serve as long as the Lord has need of you and you will be blessed every time He rewards you. Jesus, help us to have humble and thankful hearts.

Take special care of these lambs until the evening of the fourteenth day of this first month. Then each family in the community must slaughter its lamb.

God is about to keep His promise to the nation of Israel and deliver them from their bondage and bring them to a land of their own. To do that He is going to send one last plague to the nation of Egypt; He is going to send the Destroyer to kill the firstborn son of everyone in the land of Egypt. Here we see the institution of the Passover for the Israelites. The Passover lamb was slaughtered and its blood was smeared on the doorposts of the houses as a sign to God to pass over those houses. Some might say that God instituted the Passover to protect the Israelites from the angel of death. God didn't need the sign to tell Him who was an Israelite; He is God, He knows everything. The blood on the doorposts was to tell God who would follow Him. If an Israelite family did not smear the blood of the lamb on their doorposts they were no safer than the Egyptians.

The thing that struck me about this verse is that each family was to take special care of the lamb for four days. Tradition says that each family would bring this lamb into the house and it would be treated like one of the children. It would be bathed and fed and would probably play with the children. For four days this lamb would be a part of the family. It is not hard to imagine that even after such a short time that some amount of attachment would develop. This would be especially true if there were small children in the house.

As someone who has spent most of my life in the city it is very hard for me to imagine what it would be like to slaughter an animal. For that culture it would have been a fairly regular occurrence but I wonder what it would have been like to slaughter this animal that had been part of the family. It would almost seem to be like slaughtering a pet.

The Passover lamb is a picture of what Jesus would later do for all mankind with His sacrifice on the cross. The sacrificial lamb was Jesus. By having the Israelites take special care of this lamb before it is sacrificed they get a taste of what the Father would be feeling when He allowed Jesus to be sacrificed. It is just a taste; we could never really know the depth of the pain of the separation even for the brief time that God and Jesus were separated.

We do not have to annually take a lamb into our home and care for it because Jesus was the Lamb that saves us from spiritual death. But instead of bringing the lamb into our home we are to bring Jesus into our hearts. And there we are to care for Him; not just for four days but for our whole lives. Jesus, help us to bring you into our hearts and treat you with the love and respect that you deserve.

FEBRUARY

FEBRUARY 1

Read: Exodus 13:17 – 15:18, Matthew 21:23-46, Psalm 26:1-12, Proverbs 6:16-19

MATTHEW 21:31

Which of the two was obeying his father? "They replied, "The first, of course. "Then Jesus explained his meaning: "I assure you, corrupt tax collectors and prostitutes will get into the Kingdom of God before you do.

Jesus on a regular basis had to respond to the interrogations of the religious leaders of the Jews. They were trying to trap Jesus into saying something that they could use to have Him arrested. He was always aware of what they were doing. The time is rapidly approaching in our reading that Jesus will be arrested and be taken to "stand trial" before these religious leaders. They are turning up the heat and are relentless in their desire to destroy Jesus. Jesus has just driven the merchants and money-changers from the temple and the religious leaders want to know what authority that He had to do it. After refusing to allow them to manipulate Him, Jesus gives them this parable about the two sons.

Jesus tells these religious leaders very plainly that they are the disobedient son. They have told God that they worship Him and will obey Him but their actions are completely opposed to their words. They put on a show of worship and obedience but their hearts are far from God. Jesus tells them that those people, the tax collectors and prostitutes, whose outward lives appear to disqualify them from the Kingdom are more likely to get there than the religious leaders are.

Religious pride is absolutely devastating. Too often people believe that going to the right church is all they need to get into heaven. Or they might believe that being the citizen of the right country will get you there. Maybe it has to do with their heritage; their parents were Christians, "so I am too." Jesus is telling these religious leaders and us that church affiliation, nationality, or heritage is meaningless when it comes to the Kingdom of God.

God looks at one thing; your heart. He is looking for only one thing in your heart and that is His Son, Jesus Christ. We have to be very careful that we don't fall into the same trap that the religious leaders did by assuming their place in heaven based on their place in life. Our only way to heaven is by accepting The Way, Jesus Christ, as our Lord and Savior.

Not only that but we need to be actively making sure that everyone that we know has that same knowledge. If God has placed you in a position of leadership anywhere in life; which He has with most people, then you are expected to help God communicate this truth to all of those that you influence. The people in your family, workplace, ministry, or church need to know that the only way to heaven is through a personal relationship with Jesus Christ.

Religious pride is very prevalent in this world. People will gravitate toward a group or church and adopt a title that they think will give them a ticket to heaven. Jesus came to shine a light on the darkness of this belief. He wants us to keep that light shining. Jesus, help us to keep that light burning brightly until you return.

FEBRUARY 2

Read: Exodus 15:19 – 17:7, Matthew 22:1-33, Psalm 27:1-6, Proverbs 6:20-26

EXODUS 18:17

"This is not good!" his father-in-law exclaimed.

Moses' father-in-law Jethro brings Moses' wife and sons out into the wilderness to join him. Jethro witnesses Moses' ministry to the people of Israel and is disturbed by what he sees. Moses is sitting before the people and helping them resolve all of the disputes that they have with one another. The people line up in the morning and stay in line all day long to present their cases to Moses. Jethro takes one look at this and tells Moses that what he is doing is not a good thing.

At first glance, you look at this and wonder what Jethro is talking about. Moses is representing God to the people. They are having disagreements and Moses is trying to minister to them by helping them to resolve these arguments. And on the surface that is a great thing that he is doing. The trap that Moses has fallen into is the same one that many in ministry fall into. Moses thinks he has to do it all!

Too many great Christian servants think the same way that Moses was thinking here. They think that they need to do everything. They might think that they are the only ones that can do it. They might believe that if they don't do it, it won't get done.

If that is the way that you think in your ministry or church, than I would say to you as Jethro said to Moses; this thing that you do is not good. Either you are going to burn out or your people are going to burn out. You must realize that you don't have to do everything. And you must learn to accept the fact that some things might not get done.

But a truth that many good people in ministry fail to apprehend is that there are people around you that God has been equipping to help you to minister. For Moses, there were literally hundreds of men all around him that were perfectly capable of helping him to minister to the flock around him. Around you also, while it may not be thousands, are people that are capable of helping you to minister. Many of them are just waiting to be invited. Some will need to be encouraged to help. Some of them might need some training or discipleship. A small investment in the people around you will reap incredible fruit for the Kingdom of God.

Don't be so arrogant as to think that you are the only one that can do it. And don't be so faithless as to believe that someone might do it better and see that as a threat to your "position." Your ministry or your church is not yours. It is God's! And He loves you and your flock more than you ever will. The best way to grow your ministry or church is to give it away. The more of it you give to capable men and women, the more God will bless you and your ministry or church. Jesus, help us to let go of the things that we can't do and give them to the ministers that you are preparing to do them.

FEBRUARY 3

Read: Exodus 17:8 – 19:15, Matthew 22:34 – 23:12, Psalm 27:7-14, Proverbs 6:27-35

PSALM 27:1

The Lord is my light and my salvation – so why should I be afraid? The Lord protects me from danger – so why should I tremble?

This psalm asks a couple of questions that teach us a lot about our relationship to God and our behavior in this world. We are reminded that the Lord is our light and salvation. Light is the opposite of darkness. Instinctively people have a fear of the darkness. We know that danger and enemies lurk in the darkness. We also know that it is much easier to get lost in the dark than it is when it is light. The Lord is our light. He provides us the light that we need to see our enemies and to find our way.

The Lord is our salvation. There is incredible power in that statement. I love the fact that it doesn't say that I need to do something for the Lord to be my salvation. I don't need to go anywhere and I don't need to become something to receive salvation; the Lord IS my salvation. I just need to accept that and I am saved.

If the Lord is my light and salvation, what should I be afraid of? The answer is simple; nothing! If we would just embrace this truth we would live such radically different lives. If we could simply accept and believe the fact that Jesus is our light and salvation, we would fear absolutely nothing. That's the life that I want to live; a life of fearlessness.

The verse goes on to say that the Lord protects me from danger. I know in my heart that if I will just believe God and follow him as my Lord that no danger will befall me. This allows me to respond to His calling in my life without hesitation or compromise. I know that I can walk boldly where He leads because He is not going to allow me to wander into danger.

Our problem is that we sometimes forget that Jesus is more than just our Salvation; He is our Lord. That means that He has the right and obligation to direct our lives. We wander into fearful and dangerous situations because we have stopped letting Jesus be Lord of our lives. If you want to make sure you are kept free from danger, you need to keep Jesus as Lord of your life.

There is a plaque on my desk that says, "The will of God will never lead you where the grace of God cannot keep you." We would be more effective in our Christian lives and ministries if we would truly apprehend this truth. We need more fearless Christians; men and women that will boldly go and do what the Lord directs them to do.

God wants to do spectacular, supernatural things in this world and He is looking for fearless men and women that will rest in the power of His hands as they go where He leads them. Do not fear or tremble; stand up and go; He is right there with you. Jesus, help us to trust in the power of your love.

FEBRUARY 4

Read: Exodus 19:16 – 21:21, Matthew 23:13-39, Psalm 28:1-9, Proverbs 7:1-5

EXODUS 20:24

The altars you make for me must be simple altars of earth. Offer on such altars your sacrifices to me – your burnt offerings and peace offerings, your sheep and goats and your cattle. Build altars in the places where I remind you who I am, and I will come and bless you there.

Exodus 20 is best known as the place in scripture where the Ten Commandments are first given. In addition to the Ten Commandments God also gives to Moses to give to the people some instructions that will help them to live with, relate to, and worship God. And in the chapters that follow God gives them instructions on how to live with and relate to one another. As you study these commandments and instructions it will give you a clearer idea of the nature and heart of God.

Here in verse 24 God tells the Israelites that when they sacrifice offerings of animals to God it is to be on an earthen altar. The concept of sacrificing animals to God is not new. It has been happening since the Garden when God killed animals to cover Adam and Eve's nakedness. The thing that I would like you to think about is the style of altar that God asked them to make the sacrifices on. God told them to build simple earthen altars. It goes on to say that if you use stones, those stones are to be natural, uncut stones. God didn't want the Israelites building enormous, elaborate altars. He wanted them to be simple, humble things.

As Christians, animal sacrifice is not a part of our worship of God. He no longer desires the sacrifice of animals. He asks for something much greater. In Romans 12 God calls us to be "living sacrifices." And we can take from the above text that the altar that we are a living sacrifice upon should be a simple, humble thing.

As Christians, one of the ways that we can most fully obey the command to be a living sacrifice is to serve others rather than ourselves. Some people believe that to serve God you must have some kind of training or theology degree. God doesn't need any of that stuff to use you.

The same is true in our ministries and churches. God doesn't need large impressive structures or elaborate sophisticated systems to reach people for

Christ. What He needs are simple, humble people that desire to be a living sacrifice to Him by serving others. Don't get me wrong, God also uses the mega-churches to do this work. But even there He is still looking for humble, simple hearts.

This instruction to build these simple earthen altars comes with a promise. If we will worship God in this way, He will come to us and bless us. God will bless the person, ministry, or church that is being a living sacrifice, regardless of any of the outward things that the world might look for. Jesus, help us to live each day for others sacrificially.

FEBRUARY 5
Read: Exodus 21:22 – 23:13, Matthew 24:1-28, Psalm 29:1-11, Proverbs 7:6-23

EXODUS 22:29
Do not hold anything back when you give me the tithe of your crops and your wine. You must make the necessary payment for redemption of your firstborn sons.

God commanded the Israelites to bring a portion of their crops and the things that they produced from their crops to God as an offering. It was to remind them that what they had came from God. The firstborn sons were dedicated to and redeemed from God to remind the Israelites of the mighty miracle that God did to deliver them from Egypt.

Any time we talk about offerings and tithes pastors and people start to get squeamish. It is as though we are talking about something that we shouldn't be. Some are more comfortable talking about sex than this topic. Some are even afraid that if we talk about giving to God that it might scare some people away. We should be more afraid of not talking about it. God commands in the Old Testament and Jesus confirmed in the New Testament the practice of tithing and offerings to God. To not do it is to be in disobedience to God (also called sin) and it sets you up to lose the blessings of God.

The book of Malachi teaches clearly that there is a direct correlation between our giving to God and the blessings that He pours out into our lives. God's blessings come in all forms, so don't get caught up in the false teaching of prosperity theology. But it is a fact that God blesses His children that obey Him. The first part of this verse teaches that we are not to delay in giving from our harvest (income) and our vintage (investments). It has been said that you should only give to God from the part of what God gave you that you want Him to bless. If you give reluctantly and sparingly, expect similar blessings from God. If you give joyfully and generously, expect the same from God. It has also been said that you can't out-give God.

In your ministry and church, this principle and command is the same. Some portion of what you do must be an offering to God. This must be different than what you are normally doing in service to and for God. It must be sacrificial in nature, meaning you reap no benefit from it. And for every ministry or church it is going to be different and very specific to that ministry or church. It could be some form of outreach that is outside your normal area. Or it could be an offering to another ministry.

And let us not forget that when we speak of offerings to God, we are not just speaking of money. God can also use our time and things. In our verse for today, God claims the firstborn sons as His. This was to remind the Israelites that He saved them from bondage and death. These firstborn sons were to be redeemed with a sacrifice. Every one of us also has been saved from the bondage and death of sin. We redeem our lives by giving of ourselves and our stuff to God for His use. Everything you have, including your life, was given to you by God. God expects us to give to Him what He asks for. Jesus, help us to give freely of all that you have given us.

FEBRUARY 6

Read: Exodus 23:14 – 25:40, Matthew 24:29-51, Psalm 30:1-12, Proverbs 7:24-27

EXODUS 25:8

I want the people of Israel to build me a sacred residence where I can live among them.

God told Moses to have the people gather materials and build the Tabernacle. It was to be a sanctuary, a sacred or holy place where the nation of Israel was to focus their worship of the Almighty God. And then

God said that He would dwell among them. This literally means that God would live with them. In verse two of this chapter God told the Israelites that they could make an offering to Him. But it was conditional; they had to want to give it. It wasn't required and it wasn't expected. God wanted them to give willingly from their hearts. The Tabernacle and everything in it was built from the willing giving of the people. We will see later in the reading that the people had to be told to stop giving because there was more than enough materials.

The Israelites were to build this tabernacle so that God would live among them. What an awesome thing; the Almighty Creator of the universe living in their midst. And this meant for the Israelites that God was right in their presence when they needed Him for leading, guiding, provision, protection, and strength.

The Tabernacle was to be a place where the people would come to hear from and learn about God through the priests. It was at the Tabernacle that they would receive cleansing of their sins. It was at the Tabernacle that the people would focus their attention on God; it was the center of their worship of God.

God still wants to build Tabernacles. God still desires to dwell with us. But instead of there being only one Tabernacle, God wants there to be millions of them. After Jesus was raised from the dead and ascended into heaven, He sent the Holy Spirit. As children of God, the Holy Spirit lives within us and we are the Tabernacle that He dwells in. And as a Tabernacle of the living God, we should be a place of worship.

God also wants to build Tabernacles within ministries and churches. Our ministries and churches must be places where God is dwelling and people are worshipping Him. And we will know that is happening when the power of God is seen in the lives of the people. Are people being changed to be more like Christ? Are people being cleansed from their sins and unrighteousness? Are people being drawn to Jesus? Are people learning how to worship God?

The people gave to the building of the Tabernacle because of God's presence and promise. Too many people believe that if they build a ministry or church that people will come. Invite God to come and build your ministry or church and then God will bring the people. Jesus, help us to invite you into the Tabernacle before we start building it.

FEBRUARY 7

Read: Exodus 26:1 – 27:21, Matthew 25:1-30, Psalm 31:1-8, Proverbs 8:1-11

EXODUS 26:30

Set up this Tabernacle according to the design you were shown on the mountain.

For several chapters here in the book of Exodus God has been describing to Moses how He would like the Israelites to build the Tabernacle. In some aspects there is great detail given but in some cases the instructions are relatively vague about just what it is to look like. It seems to me that while God had a specific design in mind, He left some of the details to the people that would use the creative abilities that He had given them. That is an important lesson for any leader; give your people the plan but let them use their God-given talents to work out some of the details.

In our verse for the day God tells Moses to set up the Tabernacle just as he had seen it while he was on the mountain. Moses spent forty days (without food or drink) with the LORD on Mount Sinai. He did this not once but twice. During that time in intimate fellowship with God, the Lord taught Moses the Law of God and showed Moses many things. One of those things was the Tabernacle. Elsewhere in Scripture we are told that the Tabernacle on the earth was to be like the one in Heaven. God allowed Moses to see into heaven to see the Tabernacle.

Moses was given this incredible privilege for a reason. After seeing the heavenly Tabernacle, Moses would be better able to build the earthly Tabernacle. As I read through God's description I often wish that I could see what is being described. I marvel at people that can hear a description like this in Exodus and then go make it. I need to see what I am building before I can build it. In leadership we refer to this as vision.

One of the things that sets a true leader apart from others is an ethereal thing called vision. Vision is a leader's ability to see the task that they are working on already completed. They can see in their minds that the task can be completed and they can see what it will look like when it is done. If you are following a true leader that can create a real challenge for you because he can see it but you might not be able to. We might be working on one small piece of the project and have no idea what the whole thing looks like.

For the Tabernacle to be complete all the pieces had to be completed. All of the pieces were important. As we serve, especially in a large organization, we may not understand the vision. We might understand what the whole thing is going to look like when it is completed. That's Okay, you don't need to understand. You just be faithful to complete your small piece and then trust God to use it to build for Himself a grand and beautiful Tabernacle. Jesus, teach us to work diligently on our small piece of Your Tabernacle.

FEBRUARY 8

Read: Exodus 28:1-43, Matthew 25:31 – 26:13, Psalm 31:9-18, Proverbs 8:12-13

MATTHEW 26:2

"As you know, the Passover celebration begins in two days, and I, the Son of Man, will be betrayed and crucified."

We have reached the point in our reading where we are on the eve of Jesus' crucifixion. Jesus knows that this is His last meal with the disciples and that very soon events that have been foretold for over a thousand years will begin to unfold. Jesus is about to complete the work that he was sent to the earth to accomplish.

The text does give us a glimpse into Jesus' thoughts and emotions but it is impossible to know entirely what was going on in Jesus' mind during this meal. One thing we can tell from His words and actions is that He wasn't thinking about Himself. In our reading Jesus gave us the example of washing the feet of our brothers and sisters. While this was not meant as a literal act, it was meant to teach us to serve others rather than ourselves.

How many of us could be so selfless at a time like this? All of us have those high-stress moments where the big events of our lives are laid out before us. It began in school with the tests, especially final exams. Later it was job interviews and performance reviews. In the ministry it is board meetings and confronting sin in the church or church body. For some it is waiting for the test results from the doctor.

How can any of that compare to what Jesus was going through at that time? It can't; not by a long shot! None of us will ever experience anything that will even be the minutest fraction of what Jesus was experiencing at that moment. The reason is that He knew exactly what was going to happen to Him. The Father had showed Him precisely what was going to take place. It is as though the Father showed Jesus the movie *The Passion of the Christ* in advance of the event. Jesus knew what was coming.

We don't have that opportunity to see the events in advance of them occurring. We are stressed out over the fear of what might happen. Our attention focuses intensely upon what might happen. What we need to understand is that means that we have taken our focus off of God. Jesus knew the suffering and abuse that He was about to experience and yet He still kept His eyes on the Father and completed the task that was before Him. Never for a moment did He not have others in His mind.

Too often our stress is a result of our eyes being on ourselves or our circumstances. Only by taking our eyes off of ourselves and putting them on God can we have the peace that Jesus possessed at this very stressful time in His life. The greatest antidote for stress in your life is to imitate Jesus; keep your eyes on God and think of others rather than yourself. Jesus, thank you that You are our strong tower and our source of power.

FEBRUARY 9

Read: Exodus 29:1 – 30:10, Matthew 26:14-46, Psalm 31:19-24, Proverbs 8:14-26

MATTHEW 26:41

Keep alert and pray! Otherwise temptation will overpower you. For though the spirit is willing enough, the body is weak!

Jesus is in the Garden of Gethsemane preparing Himself and His disciples for the most important day in the history of the world; the day that God pays the redemption price for mankind through the sacrificial death of Jesus. As Jesus prepares Himself, He gives His disciples two commands; keep alert and pray. He also explains what will happen if they don't and why it will happen.

His first instruction is to keep alert. At first glance you might think Jesus is telling them to stand guard because Judas is coming back with a gang to arrest Him. Jesus knows that but that is not the context from which he is speaking. Jesus' focus in on them not on what is going to happen to Him. Jesus is calling them to stay alert to themselves and what is going on in their own lives and hearts.

We can't just sleep through this life and expect to be successful, growing followers of Christ. In order to truly experience the fullness of the life that Jesus intends us to have we need to continually be examining our heart and the circumstances around us. Jesus is telling them to be on guard, not for Him but for their own hearts.

Jesus then tells them to pray. The only offensive weapon we have in the fight to live an abundant, victorious life is prayer. Jesus didn't tell them to build a church; He said He would do that. He didn't tell them to start a program; He told them to let the Holy Spirit lead them. He didn't tell them to raise an army; He said He already had one at His disposal. The only thing He told them to do was pray.

We would be so much more effective in our lives and ministries if we would spend more time in prayer. It is in prayer that we get the instructions that we need to go forward to live the life that Jesus came to give us. We need to be in the habit of praying more before doing more. Jesus then explains why.

Our text says that we if we don't stay alert and pray that we will be overcome by temptation, suggesting that it will pursue us and overpower us. In the original language the idea is not that we would be overcome but that we will enter into temptation. If we are not alert and praying we will wander into temptation.

It used to be a saying of mine, "I can resist anything except temptation!" The reason why is because our body, or flesh is weak. I now know that all temptations can be resisted but it takes vigilance and prayer. If we keep our eyes on Jesus and stay in communication with Him we will resist all the temptations that the enemy lays before us. Jesus, help us to keep our eyes open and the phone lines clear.

FEBRUARY 10

Read: Exodus 30:11 – 31:18, Matthew 26:47-68, Psalm 32:1-11, Proverbs 8:27-32

EXODUS 30:19

Aaron and his sons will wash their hands and feet there...

God speaks to Moses and tells him to make a washbasin for Aaron and his sons. This basin is to be used to wash their hands and feet before they minister before the Lord. God puts an exclamation on the requirement to be cleansed by saying that if they don't wash before they minister they will be killed.

This washbasin was outside of the Tabernacle. Before Aaron and his sons entered into the tabernacle they were to wash themselves at this washbasin. The previous chapter of Exodus described the process that Moses was to institute to sanctify the priests that would minister before the Lord. That process made them holy and set apart for that service. And even though they had been set apart as holy, they still needed to wash before entering the Lord's presence.

Aaron and his sons were to cleanse their hands and feet. Just because they had been made holy, they still lived in a world that was not holy and so they needed to be cleansed of the unholiness that they come into contact with. They would wash their feet as a way of cleansing them from the places they may have been. They would wash their hands to cleanse them of the things they touched.

Jesus made a similar statement as He washed the feet of His disciples. As born-again believers of Jesus Christ we are washed by His blood and cleansed of our sins and unrighteousness. But we live in a world that is not clean. And we need to be cleansed of the dirt of this world on a regular basis. It would be great if once we accepted the cleansing of Jesus' blood that we would no longer be affected by the dirt of this world. But that is not the case. No matter how long you have walked with the Lord, your feet are still going to get dirty and need to be washed. And no matter how much your heart is turned to God, your hands are still going to get dirty and need to be cleansed of the things that you chose to touch. As long as we live, we will always need to be cleansed of the dirt that we pick up along the way.

This is especially true if we are ministering before the Lord. If you are involved in ministry or in a church, then you are ministering before the Lord. No matter how small your role might seem to you, when you do it you are entering into the Tabernacle and ministering before the Lord. And before we do it, we need to wash in the washbasin of God's grace and mercy and be cleansed. We need to ask God for His cleansing often. We need to ask the Lord to wash us clean of any sin or unrighteousness that we have picked along our path. We need to confess our sins and receive the cleansing of the blood of Jesus. Jesus, help us to come before you to be cleansed before we go before you to minister.

FEBRUARY 11

Read: Exodus 32:1 – 33:23, Matthew 26:69 – 27:14, Psalm 33:1-11, Proverbs 8:33-36

EXODUS 32:1

When Moses failed to come back down the mountain right away, the people went to Aaron. "Look," they said, "make us some gods who can lead us. This man Moses, who brought us here from Egypt, has disappeared. We don't know what has happened to him."

Moses has been on the mountain with God for almost 40 days. All the people can see is that the mountain is covered by clouds so they have no idea what is going on up there. They have been forbidden from going too near the mountain or they will be killed. When Moses went up on the mountain to receive the Ten Commandments, he left Aaron and Hur in charge. The people get tired of waiting and so they go to Aaron and ask him to make them gods so that they can follow them back to Egypt. And Aaron responds by telling them to bring their jewelry so that he can make an idol for them to worship. Aaron failed to do one thing here, lead the people like Moses would have in this situation.

As the man selected to be "in charge" in Moses' absence, Aaron should have responded the way that Moses would have responded. His thoughts should have been, "What would Moses do in a situation like this." Aaron's failure was in that he did not do what his leader had instructed him to do.

Aaron was to keep things under control until Moses got back. He didn't do a very good job of that.

Aaron should have pointed them back to God. He should have reminded them that it wasn't Moses that led them out of Egypt but it was God. He should have reminded them that it was God that had performed all of the mighty miracles. And he should have told them to wait for God to tell them what to do next.

As a servant within a ministry or church you have a responsibility to the leader of that ministry to keep things going the way that they have told you. If you are in submission to that leader as you should be then you have the belief that the Holy Spirit is leading him or her. If the Holy Spirit is leading them then any directions they give are to be obeyed as if they came from God (unless they contradict scripture of course). To not do so is to be in rebellion against God.

The leaders absence is not a time to change things to be the way you want them but an opportunity to prove to that leader that you trust God. Any ministry or church that you have even a tiny responsibility in or for deserves your faithful trust of those that God has placed in the leadership position. Ask yourself how your leader would make the next decision that you make. Jesus, help us to follow you by teaching us to follow the leaders that you placed over us.

FEBRUARY 12

Read: Exodus 34:1 – 35:9, Matthew 27:15-31, Psalm 33:12-22, Proverbs 9:1-6

EXODUS 34:29

When Moses came down the mountain carrying the stone tablets inscribed with the terms of the covenant, he wasn't aware that his face glowed because he had spoken to the LORD face to face.

Moses is just returning from having spent forty days on Mount Sinai alone with the LORD. This is the second time he has done this. He is carrying the second set of stone tablets that replaced the ones that he smashed after finding the nation of Israel dancing around the gold calf

A Radical Thought · 59

that Aaron made for the people to worship. This time his face is glowing. Something different happened on this trip that caused his face to glow.

In the previous chapter of Exodus we read that the thing that was different was that the LORD passed before Moses and He allowed Moses to get a glimpse of His glory. It was this glimpse of the glory of God that caused Moses' face to glow. However, I would suggest that was not all that was different about this event.

Moses was speaking to the LORD before God revealed His glory to him. Moses was begging the Lord to accompany them into the land that the LORD had given them. This was not a lack of faith in Moses; it was a revelation of his increased faith. Moses had previously spent forty days in the presence of God. None of us can truly appreciate what that might have been like; daily in the presence of Almighty God for almost six weeks.

Then, immediately after that huge spiritual experience Moses comes down the mountain to find God's Chosen people practicing the worst kinds of sins out in the open. It stirred within Moses a very natural human response; anger. In an instant Moses' mountaintop experience is shattered just like the stone tablets he smashed on the rocks at the base of Mount Sinai. Moses went up that mountain differently than he had the first time. He realized how desperately they needed the presence of God with them as they entered the Promised Land. He realized that but for the presence of God; they were no different than the people that they were going to displace in the land. He also realized that he was no different than the rest of the people.

Much is made about getting into the presence of God. Books are written about how we climb the spiritual mountain to get into the presence of God. It is my belief that the trip is not upward but down. Moses was humbled before the LORD because he realized just how desperately they needed Him. Moses didn't know that his face glowed until others responded to him. He was not seeking the effects of being in the presence of God; he was simply seeking God with a desperate heart. God loves to reveal Himself to people that seek Him in this way. And after He does reveal His glory to you, others will know it and will either be afraid of it or be drawn to it. Don't seek the glow, seek to see His glory. Jesus, help us to have hearts that desperately seek You.

FEBRUARY 13

Read: Exodus 35:10 – 36:38, Matthew 27:32:66, Psalm 34:1-10, Proverbs 9:7-8

EXODUS 35:26

All the women who were willing used their skills to spin and weave the goat hair into cloth.

Moses over the last several chapters has described the Tabernacle and all of its furnishings. The Tabernacle is to be the place that God uses to focus the attention of the Israelites upon Him. Moses then told the people to make a contribution to the cause of building the Tabernacle. He gave them a list of the materials that were needed for the construction. Moses did not require them to donate to the construction. He did not institute a tax to provide for the construction of the Tabernacle. He asked for a donation from those that were willing.

The people responded by bringing everything that was needed. In fact, Moses had to tell the people to stop bringing materials because they had more than enough to complete the Tabernacle.

Moses also put out a call to all the craftsmen to come and assist with the construction of the Tabernacle. God had gifted a few with exceptional skill, but some He had given ordinary skills. The craftsmen also responded and worked to construct the Tabernacle.

In our text, women were also involved in the Tabernacle construction. God had also given them talents that were very useful to the project. But the thing that makes these women special is not their skills but their hearts. They had willing hearts! Their hearts had been stirred to help in this project to build a place where God would dwell.

God has given every person some sort of gift, skill, or ability. And those skills would be useful in building, not the Tabernacle but something much grander, much greater, the Church. Every person, whether man or woman, has a place of service in building Jesus' church. Every person, whether highly skilled or with ordinary abilities, is necessary to build the Church in which the Savior of the world dwells.

But God doesn't want your skills, gifts, and abilities by themselves. First, He wants your heart. He wants you to bring the gifts, skills, and abilities that He gave to you with a willing heart. God is looking for people that want to help in the construction project of His Church because their hearts have been stirred to do so.

No one has to serve God; it is our choice. God can take a heart that is serving out of obedience and stir within it the desire to serve God. God is not glorified by a heart that serves because of selfish motives or out of compulsion. If you are serving God in any way, but especially in a leadership position, are you doing it because the Holy Spirit has stirred your heart? Are you helping to build the church of Jesus Christ because of your love for Him? If not, ask the Lord to change your heart. Jesus, stir our hearts to serve You out of a deep and abiding love for You.

FEBRUARY 14

Read: Exodus 37:1 – 38:31, Matthew 28:1-20, Psalm 34:11-22, Proverbs 9:9-10

EXODUS 38:8

The bronze washbasin and its bronze pedestal were cast from bronze mirrors donated by the women who served at the entrance of the Tabernacle.

The Tabernacle is being constructed as it has been directed by the Lord to Moses. All of the materials have been donated by the people for the construction process. So much has been donated that the construction team had to tell Moses to tell the people to stop bringing stuff. One of the things that they made was a bronze washbasin. The purpose of the washbasin was that Aaron and his sons could wash themselves before they go in to the Tabernacle to serve before the Lord. The instruction to them was that every time they passed this washbasin they were to wash themselves of any dirt they may have picked up along the way.

The thing that I found interesting was what this bronze washbasin was made from. Apparently there was a group of women serving at the entrance to the Tabernacle. There is no indication what they were doing or how many there were; just that they were there. These women donated their bronze mirrors to the construction of the temple. The purpose of mirrors has not changed in the last 3,500 years. It is fascinating to me that

God would use something that would be used to reveal beauty to create something that would be used to remove filth.

The fact that the washbasin was made from women's mirrors is a great picture for all of us and especially those that have been called to lead families, ministries and churches. God desires that we would be cleansed as we go about the daily tasks that have been assigned to us by God. Whatever you do today, at least that which is not sin, was assigned to you by God to do today. God wants you also to wash in the washbasin before you minister before Him to your family, ministry, or church, or anywhere else that you may find yourself today.

To do that you must look into the mirror of God's word, the Bible. The Bible was given to us so that we would be able to see what in our lives is filthy and not pleasing to God. But to look into that mirror and see clearly what we need to be cleansed of is not possible apart from the work of the Holy Spirit within us. As we look into the mirror of God's word we need to ask the Holy Spirit to help us to see clearly what He sees. Otherwise we will only see what we want to see. Once we have seen that we need to be cleansed we must go to the washbasin and wash. Aaron and his sons had to wash every time they passed the washbasin. We also need to be washed that often. The difference for us is that the washbasin is with us always in the person of Jesus Christ. His work on the cross made a way for us to be cleansed of all the filth that we pick up during the day. We are washed by His blood through repentance and forgiveness. The picture that God is painting here for us is that we ought to be regularly being washed by that forgiveness through our repentance. Jesus, help us to get clean.

FEBRUARY 15
Read: Exodus 39:1 – 40:38, Mark 1:1-28, Psalm 35:1-16, Proverbs 9:11-12

MARK 1:1

Here begins the Good News about Jesus the Messiah, the Son of God.

In our daily reading we finally get to the New Testament. The Old Testament is so rich and full that it is a joy to read and study. It points to the coming of the Savior, Jesus Christ, and gives us hope about our future. The Old Testament is filled with examples of God's grace, mercy, patience, blessings, and kindness. It also reminds us that He deals with disobedience and unfaithfulness very harshly. It teaches us that God will not tolerate our turning from Him because it separates us from Him.

Today we turn a new page and begin to read the New Testament. We see the direct revelation of Jesus Christ. And for the next several weeks we will watch as the life and ministry of Jesus Christ is laid out for us. Mark begins his gospel very simply by saying this is the beginning. The word gospel means "good news." Jesus is the Messiah; sent by God to save the world. The Word "messiah" is also translated as "Christ." The gospels are the good news about Jesus Christ, the Son of God

As we begin reading the gospels it should always be with the view that we are looking at a picture of God. The gospels paint the closest thing to an image of God for us to see. Jesus said if you have seen Me, you have seen the Father in heaven. As we read through the gospels, let it create in your mind the picture of God. No other part of scripture can do that like the books of Matthew, Mark, Luke, and John.

This picture is so critical because it forms the basis on which we build our faith. Without the right foundation of who Jesus is and what he has done for us, the rest of the Bible can't impact us the way that it is supposed to. By seeing Jesus the way that He really is, the rest of the Bible makes more sense and can reach further into your life to change you into the person that God wants you to be.

Every word of the Bible was inspired, breathed by God, and will help you to live a life that is full and rich and filled with all the blessings that God wants to pour out into your life. Over the next several weeks as we go through the gospels together, pray and ask God to show you Jesus in a new and fresh way. Ask the Holy Spirit to open your spiritual eyes to some new facet of Jesus that you have missed before.

Take a little extra time in your reading as we go through the gospels. Don't rush through this part. Take your time and allow the Spirit to minister to you about the amazing God that we worship. Allow this time to be a sanctuary from your life. Here begins the good news about your Savior, your Messiah, your God. Jesus, help us to see you.

FEBRUARY 16

Read: Leviticus 1:1 – 3:17, Mark 1:29 – 2:12, Psalm 35:17-28, Proverbs 9:13-18

Give the following instructions to the Israelites: Whenever you present offerings to the LORD, you must bring animals from your flocks and herds.

Some people have great difficulty reading or understanding the book of Leviticus. It seems to be filled with repetition and mundane instructions. It comes after all the action and adventure of Genesis and Exodus making it even more tedious. The book of Leviticus was written by Moses, probably at the foot of Mount Sinai or shortly after they left there. It was written for the tribe of Levi to instruct them on how to conduct worship within the Tabernacle and to teach the Hebrew people how to be set apart as holy to the LORD. It is within that context that this "mundane" book has incredibly important lessons to teach us all about our relationship with God.

In today's verse we have the LORD instructing Moses to tell the Israelites in the correct way to make a sacrifice to him. The Israelites have just been delivered from bondage in Egypt for the last four hundred years. Generations of Israelites had been born and raised in the culture and ways of the Egyptians. All they knew about worshipping God was what they had learned from the culture that they had lived among. God didn't want His people to worship Him the way the Egyptian people worshipped their gods.

In this very first instruction, the LORD tells them to bring animals from their flocks and herds. The Lord is telling them that their sacrifice must cost them something. They were not to go out and catch a wild animal and bring it as an offering to the LORD. Their sacrifice had to come from the flocks and herds that they had been building up and investing into. For it to be an acceptable offering it had to be a sacrifice; it had to be of value to them personally.

Today, we don't go to the flocks and herds to bring an offering to the LORD. Our offerings come out of our day-planners and checkbooks. Instead of lambs, goats, and bulls the LORD wants our time, talents, and treasures as offerings to Him. But just like the Israelites grew up in a culture that did not know how to worship God, we have all grown up in a culture that worships different gods.

God created us to worship Him and Him alone, and to be in an intimate relationship with Him. Our first step to fulfilling that great purpose of our lives is to acknowledge that we don't know how to do it and that we need to be taught how. The book of Leviticus might still be difficult to read, but it and the rest of the Bible is there to teach you how to be what God created you to be; a child of Almighty God. Jesus, help us to see the beauty contained in every book, chapter, and word of the Bible.

FEBRUARY 17

Read: Leviticus 4:1 – 5:19, Mark 2:13 – 3:6, Psalm 36:1-12, Proverbs 10:1-2

LEVITICUS 4:2

Give the Israelites the following instructions for dealing with those who sin unintentionally by doing anything forbidden by the LORD'S commands.

At first glance the verse for today is a little confusing. God is instructing the Israelites to make an offering for sin that was committed unintentionally. The question that might be raised with this instruction is; if it was unintentional did they know they committed the sin. As you read further in the text for today you find that God expects this sacrifice after they become aware of their sin. This is comforting to me because it means that I don't have to worry if I have done anything contrary to God's laws until He reveals it to me.

People have come to me with that very concern. They are worried that they have done something against God and they don't know what it is. They are afraid that God is going to judge them because they have sinned in some way that they don't know about. I will usually encourage them to pray much like Job did for his children; asking God for forgiveness of sins that may have been committed.

This viewpoint that God is going to judge us for sins that we are not aware of is contrary to the grace of God. God in His incredible love for us wants us to be in a right relationship with Him. He wants us to know where we have strayed away from His will and sinned against Him so that we can return to that right relationship. One of the primary responsibilities of the Holy Spirit is to convict us of our sin; that is make us aware that we have sinned against God.

If we have a desire to please God and obey His word as best as we are able, then we will know those areas that God wants us to repent of and get right in. He is not going to keep it a secret and pound us the first chance He gets. The fact that we are concerned that we might have sinned against God is an indication that our heart is turned toward God. What God desires is that when we discover that we have sinned either intentionally or unintentionally that we repent immediately and do whatever it is that His Holy Spirit directs us to. Fortunately, we are not required to bring a goat or a bull to be slaughtered because of our sin but there may be another type of sacrifice or consequence that we need to bring to God as a result.

Unintentional sins are those that are committed by accident or in ignorance. To avoid these kinds of sins we need to make it a priority in our lives to get to know what God wants from us and learn what the things are that God wants us to avoid. We do that by making the Word of God a part of our everyday lives. We also do it by learning to hear the voice of God as He speaks to us in our daily activities. This will not completely eliminate unintentional sins but it will gradually reduce them until they are a rare occurrence. Jesus, help us to keep our hearts tender before God and our ears sensitive to His voice.

FEBRUARY 18

Read: Leviticus 6:1 – 7:27, Mark 3:7-30, Psalm 37:1-11, Proverbs 10:3-4

MARK 3:14

Then he selected twelve of them to be his regular companions, calling them apostles. He sent them out to preach...

Jesus is surrounded by people that have decided that He is someone that they need to follow. This is relatively early in His public ministry. One day Jesus goes up on top of a mountain and stays there the whole night praying. Upon coming down He selects the twelve men that will be His constant companions. He calls these twelve men apostles.

Our reading for the day gives us a list of the names of the men that He selected. It is fascinating to look at the men that Jesus selected to be His regular companions. I don't think that any of us would have made the same selections if we were in Jesus' place. A couple of these men we know very little about; Thaddeus and Simon, the zealot for example. Others we know quite a bit about and might wonder what Jesus was thinking.

Why would Jesus pick Judas Iscariot? Jesus knew that Judas was going to betray Him right from the very moment that He first met Judas. It seems a little odd that Jesus would deliberately select Judas to be one of His closest companions. But then as we read the Old Testament; this very thing was predicted. It had to happen that way.

The thing that caught my attention in this verse was the very last part; "He sent them out to preach…" The very first thing that Jesus does with these twelve guys was send them out to tell people about the kingdom of God. This is probably the exact opposite of what we would have done. We would have put these twelve guys into the local seminary or at least into some kind of internship before we sent them out.

What we need to learn from this is that we don't always have to prepare everyone for what God might want to do through them. I believe that sometimes the best school of ministry is to do ministry. By getting out and doing the work that Jesus wanted them to do, they learned much about God and His plan for the world. In many cases I think we would be much better off to let God teach people about ministry through the work of the ministry than through some sort of "training process."

Many of the people that God has called us to lead have all the training and experience they need to be used by God to do very cool things for the Kingdom of God. All we need to do is to send them out into the field to get to work. People are often waiting for someone to tell them to go. They might not think that they are ready but we should never stop someone from trying to do something great for God. This is where faith is built and strengthened. This is where God is glorified; through His power working through the weaknesses of men. As leaders it is our responsibility to send them out into whatever field we see that is ripe. Jesus, help me to see them and send them.

FEBRUARY 19

Read: Leviticus 7:28 – 9:6, Mark 3:31 – 4:25, Psalm 37:12-29, Proverbs 10:5

LEVITICUS 8:30

Next Moses took some of the anointing oil and some of the blood that was on the altar, and he sprinkled them on Aaron and his clothing and on his sons and their clothing. In this way, he made Aaron and his sons and their clothing holy.

God is teaching the people how to worship Him. The Tabernacle has been constructed and all the furnishings and holy objects placed inside. God is now establishing an intermediary between Himself and the people. The people could not approach God themselves. It was the role of the priests to come before God on behalf of the people. Aaron and his sons were given special clothes to identify them as priests. These clothes were of the finest materials and were finely made. They were then sprinkled with the anointing oil and blood of the sacrifice making both themselves and their clothes holy before the Lord. We will see in tomorrow's reading that sprinkling did not make them "holy" or perfect, as two of Aaron's sons will prove. This sprinkling sets them aside for a special use by God.

It was the responsibility of the priests to teach the people the statutes of God and to assist them in their worship of God through the sacrificial system. The sacrifices served two purposes. The primary purpose was to cause the people to see their sins and to give them a way to get right in God's eyes. The sacrifices also provided for the needs of the priests. Only a few of the sacrifices were completely burned up. Parts of the sacrifices were given to the priests as "their portions."

The sacrificial system continued for about fifteen hundred years until 70AD when the Temple was destroyed for the last time. When the Temple is rebuilt in the Tribulation period, the sacrificial system will be revived for a short time. The need for this system of the people paying for their sins with animal sacrifices ended with the perfect sacrifice of Jesus Christ on the cross at Calvary. There is still a need for someone to teach the people the statutes of God and to teach them how to worship. And interestingly enough, there is still a need for a sacrificial system, not to pay for sin but to provide for the needs of the "priests." The priestly order is no longer in

A Radical Thought · 69

effect but those that are called to minister to the people need to be provided for. And God calls the people to support those that serve in this role.

Aaron and his sons were sprinkled with the anointing oil and the blood of the sacrifice. Every born-again believer has also been sprinkled with the sacrificial blood of Jesus. And as the guarantee of His salvation we have been anointed with the Holy Spirit. Our role in ministry is to teach the people what that means. They no longer need anyone to approach God because they have been sprinkled with the oil and the blood. Jesus, thank You for Your blood shed on the cross for us and thank You for the Holy Spirit You sent to live within us. Lord, help us to support those that serve as Your "priests" to the people.

FEBRUARY 20
Read: Leviticus 9:7 – 10:20, Mark 4:26 – 5:20, Psalm 37:30-40, Proverbs 10:6-7

MARK 5:7

He gave a terrible scream, shrieking, "Why are you bothering me, Jesus, Son of the Most High God? For God's sake, don't torture me!"

Here the tremendous power that Jesus has over demons is displayed. Jesus comes to the area of the Gerasenes where a man is possessed by demons and lives among the tombs. As soon as the man sees Jesus he comes and falls at Jesus' feet. In our verse for the day we are told that he shrieks; He is terrified about what Jesus can do to him. He begs Jesus not to torture him.

This demon recognized Jesus the moment he saw him and its first response was to fall at his feet in worship. It recognized Jesus' absolute power and authority over it and the whole world. It also recognized and acknowledged that Jesus was the Son of God. This demon knew exactly who Jesus was and what He could do. I wish I had that same level of knowledge that this demon did; I am certain that my worship would be more real and powerful. It is my prayer that my knowledge of Jesus grows to that level some day.

Today's reading goes on to reveal that it is not just one demon in this man but many. The demon identifies himself to Jesus as "Legion" because there are many of them. A Roman legion consisted of six thousand men. We also know that these thousands of demons were cast into a herd of two thousand pigs, driving them mad and causing them to run into the sea.

The idea that there are demons and evil forces in the world is often something that we try to ignore or downplay. But any serious student of the Bible has but to look at the world around us to know that these forces are still at work all around us. Today's verse encourages me and helps me not to fear these evil spirits.

One of the basic truths about my relationship with Jesus is that He lives within me. There is great power in that truth that I believe we too often neglect to draw upon. And because we don't access this power we are terrified by the very thought of demons. The fact that Jesus lives within me means that the power that drove these thousands of demons to terror lives within me also. We don't need to be afraid of demons; we can stand in the power of Jesus against them.

To do that means that we need to have Jesus showing forth from our lives. That means allowing the Holy Spirit to do His work in our lives to shape us and mold us into the image of Jesus. As more and more of Jesus shines forth from our lives we are more able to stand against the attacks of an enemy that desires to destroy our souls. Even thousands of demons are no match for a believer that has Jesus firmly rooted in his heart and life. Jesus, help me to let your light shine forth from my life into the darkness that surrounds me.

FEBRUARY 21

Read: Leviticus 11:1 – 12:8, Mark 5:21-43, Psalm 38:1-22, Proverbs 10:8-9

PROVERBS 10:9

People with integrity have firm footing, but those ho follow crooked paths will slip and fall.

Integrity is something that our culture has diminished in clarity severely. Most people today couldn't even tell you what the word means. That is sad because our verse of the day tells us that there is a significant blessing for those that walk in integrity. Integrity is defined as: adherence to moral and ethical principles; soundness of moral character; honesty. A person of integrity is, first and foremost, honest.

A person of integrity has a moral compass that guides them along a path that keeps them from slipping and falling. Having spent a great amount of time on board ships I know how important it was to keep a close watch on the compass. When you are far out to sea and there is nothing but ocean all around you the compass is the only thing tells you whether or not you are going in the right direction. The consequences of not watching the compass could be very serious.

Our moral compass is God's word. When we use it to direct our paths we can be assured that we will not slip and fall. It is when we take our eyes off the truths found in the pages of Scripture that we start to run into reefs. It is impossible to steer your life, marriage, family, ministry, or church where God would have it to go if you don't follow the compass.

Integrity is especially important if you are called to lead in any area of your life or ministry. The sad truth about people that do not have integrity is that when they fall, they are not the only ones that are harmed. All those that follow are also harmed. It is not a matter of if a person without integrity is going to slip and fall but when. Those leaders will someday stand before God and give an account for why they did not follow the compass that God gave them to ensure safe passage for themselves and those that follow them.

The first person that we need to have integrity with is God. If we are not honest with God, who already knows everything about us anyway, then we won't be honest with anyone else either. Being honest with God is very freeing and cleansing. Once we are honest with God we need to start being honest with everyone else also. This doesn't mean that we are to be mean and cruel but we don't deliberately mislead them.

There are many reasons why people are dishonest but virtually all of them stem from a lack of trust or faith in God. Abraham lied about his wife Sara and said that she was his sister because he was afraid of the foreigners. Abraham didn't trust God to protect him while he was where God had told him to go. Believe God for everything and keep your eyes on the compass of His word. Jesus, teach us to follow the course that You have laid out for us.

FEBRUARY 22

Read: Leviticus 13:1-59, Mark 6:1-29, Psalm 39:1-13, Proverbs 10:10

And Herod respected John, knowing that he was a good and holy man, so he kept him under his protection. Herod was disturbed whenever he talked with John, but even so, he liked to listen to him.

What a powerful verse we have in today's reading. There is a great contrast seen between these two men; Herod and John the Baptist. The thing that spoke to me is the way that Herod behaved around John. It is an amazing testimony of the witness of a man of God. It is a lesson that we can all learn a great deal.

John was a simple and austere man. He lived very humbly and did not seek fame or luxury. Herod on the other hand was consumed with power and position and the pursuit of personal pleasure. He denied himself nothing that he desired. John is a great example of a man that lived to please God while Herod is a nearly perfect example of a man that lived to please only himself.

Herod had arrested John and placed him in prison but even there our verse tells us that Herod protected him; probably from the guards, other prisoners, and Herod's wife Herodias, who wanted John dead. Herod was the picture of a man that was consumed by wickedness and evil. As he looked at John he recognized something radically different about him; Herod could tell that John was a good and holy man. Something about this fascinated Herod.

Our verse tells us that Herod liked to listen to John speak. It also says that whenever he did it disturbed him. John's style of speaking, teaching, and preaching was very bold and in some cases confrontational. A man like Herod could have John killed for speaking in a confrontational way. Why did he hesitate? Executing people was a relatively common occurrence in the court of Herod but for some reason he hesitated to execute this man of God. Herod knew that John's words were the truth. He wasn't going to accept them as such but his spirit recognized it.

As we go through this life we will have opportunities to speak forth the truth. We should be more like John. John was not afraid of what Herod

A Radical Thought · 73

or anyone else could do to him. Ultimately it cost John his head upon a platter. It is very unlikely that you will ever face that kind of a consequence to speaking the truth with boldness. So why do we hesitate? We hesitate because we are afraid of consequences of far less significance than death. We need to begin to trust God with every part of our lives and speak out against the evil that exists in this world. Jesus, take away our fear and loosen our tongues.

FEBRUARY 23
Read: Leviticus 14:1-57, Mark 6:30-56, Psalm 40:1-10, Proverbs 10:11-12

LEVITICUS 14:34
When you arrive in Canaan, the land that I am giving you as an inheritance, I may contaminate some of your houses with an infectious mildew.

The Lord is giving instructions to Moses and Aaron to give to the people so that they know how to deal with different things once they enter the land of Canaan. This one deals with what to do if they find a certain kind of mildew in their homes. God is teaching them how to protect themselves from diseases.

What struck me about this verse was that it says "I may contaminate." Since it is the Lord speaking, He is saying that the Lord may contaminate some of their houses. Why in the world would He do something like that? Isn't that mean? Isn't that unfair? Be careful, asking those kinds of questions can quickly lead to blasphemy. It is against God's character to be mean or unjust.

The Hebrew word that is translated as "mildew" is actually more accurately translated as "leprosy." In Scripture leprosy is often associated with judgment or punishment. You might remember the account of when Aaron and Miriam challenged Moses' leadership of the nation of Israel. God struck Miriam with leprosy as a punishment. Moses prayed for her and she was healed but not until after she had been driven from the camp for a period of time.

Contracting this disease would have been a terrible inconvenience for Miriam. A family living in a house with infectious mildew would also be greatly inconvenienced. The text of our verse doesn't say clearly whether God will do this as a form of punishment or for some other purpose. But for a period of time, their lives will be interrupted by this thing. Even in our modern times we need to be watching out for infectious mildew but I believe there is a different lesson in this verse than that.

Life is filled with interruptions, inconveniences, and disruptions. These are things that are not a part of our plan for life. Some of them might be small like a flat tire and some of them may be large like a serious illness. Usually we examine them in relation to how they affect our lives. What we usually forget to do is to use it to draw us to the Lord.

The Israelites were to go to the priests and report this problem and then a priest would come out and examine it to determine what they should do. And whatever the priest told them to do, they did. As Christians, we don't have priests that we can go to. You might be thinking that is what the pastor is for. He is no more a priest than you are. In fact, as Christians we are called into a holy priesthood. Jesus would have us to minister to one another. Surround yourself with people that are spiritually more mature than you are and then invite them into your life to examine the mildew that you find there. But if you do that, be prepared to do what they tell you. Jesus, help us to examine our lives.

FEBRUARY 24
Read: Leviticus 15:1 – 16:28, Mark 7:1-23, Psalm 40:11-17, Proverbs 10:13-14

LEVITICUS 15:31
In this way, you will keep the people of Israel separate from things that will defile them, so they will not die as a result of defiling my Tabernacle that is right there among them.

God has just given to Moses to give to the people of Israel the laws of cleanliness. These laws deal with all sorts of things that will make the people unclean in the Lord's sight and also gives them the instructions of what they need to do to become clean in God's sight. The issue of "clean" and "unclean" served two purposes. The first was very practical. There were more than two million people living in close proximity to one another. Many of these laws are very practical for keeping contagious diseases from spreading through the camp. If these controls weren't in place, a contagious disease could easily have wiped out the population of the children of Israel.

The second and more important reason for these laws of cleanliness is given here in our text. These laws were to protect the Hebrews from the separation of uncleanness. God was living in their midst and He is perfectly clean. If they were to enter His tabernacle while they were unclean, His cleanness would have no choice but to separate Himself from it permanently.

The tabernacle was the place that God chose to live among them. It was a holy place. It was ceremonially clean. To enter into the presence of God, you also had to be ceremonially clean. To come into the tabernacle while being "unclean" would defile the tabernacle making it "unclean" and this was punishable by death. There is great symbolism in the laws of cleanliness and the tabernacle. Each of these laws spoke of a physical truth that also showed a spiritual truth. Jesus was speaking of that when He said that it is not what goes inside of us that defiles but what comes out. He said that the things that we say and do come from our heart and that are what defile us.

We are now the tabernacles of God. How much more important is it for us to be clean since God chooses to live in us rather than in our midst? While the dietary laws and cleanliness laws do not apply to us as New Testament Christians, we still need to separate ourselves from the things that make us unclean. Uncleanness will separate us from the blessings, provision, and protection of God.

And we need to teach others how to be "clean" in the presence of the Lord. We do that through our testimony and the witness of our lives. Some of us are also have the responsibility of teaching these truths to others. It is a very high calling to be a priest in the Tabernacle of God. If you are in a ministry or starting a church then that is exactly what you have been called to. Even if you aren't involved in ministry, you are still called to keep your tabernacle clean. Jesus, help us to separate ourselves from anything that would defile us.

FEBRUARY 25

Read: Leviticus 16:29 – 18:30, Mark 7:24 – 8:10, Psalm 41:1-13, Proverbs 10:15-16

LEVITICUS 18:3

So do not act like the people of Egypt, where you used to live, or like the people of Canaan, where I am taking you. You must not imitate their way of life.

God gives Moses to give to the children of Israel some basic guidelines on how they should live. And as we read through the list of sexual behaviors that are forbidden most of us would say: Of course you shouldn't do that. The problem is that these were regular practices of the land of Egypt and of the land of Canaan. Everywhere the people of Israel looked these improper sexual relations were taking place.

For more than four hundred years the Hebrews have been in Egypt living among the people of Egypt. It is very possible and likely that the people had adopted many of the ways and customs of the Egyptian people, including the immoral sexual behaviors. The land of Canaan was as bad, or possibly worse, than Egypt in that regard.

Those behaviors were evil and wicked and God wanted the nation of Israel to be holy. There is no way that the nation of Israel could have figured this out without God's help. If God hadn't told them that it was not OK to have sex with their mothers, they probably would have because that it is what both of the nations around them were doing.

The culture that we live in determines in the minds of the people what is right to do and what is wrong to do. The things that people do without punishment are the right things to do. And the things that people will be punished for doing are the wrong things to do. It is a simplistic way of looking at it, but that is the way that a great many people think.

Without God clearly defining the boundaries between right and wrong, our behavior would most likely mimic the behavior of everyone else in our culture. If we did not have God telling us that those things are wrong, it is very likely that we would be doing those very same things.

God called the Israelites to be different than the peoples of the land they were leaving and different from the people of the land where they were going. God also calls us to be different than the people of the land that we are in. We are not to imitate their ways. The regulations that God laid out for the Israelites were designed to set them apart from the rest of the world. God wanted them to be perceived by the rest of the world as different. He wanted people to notice that these people were different. And in so doing, the world would want to know why they were different. And then God's name would be proclaimed.

It is no different today. God is calling you, your ministry, and your church to be different from the world. And in so doing the name of Jesus will be proclaimed. Are you different from the world? Jesus, help us to be holy, just as You are holy.

FEBRUARY 26

Read: Leviticus 19:1 – 20:21, Mark 8:11-38, Psalm 42:1-11, Proverbs 10:17

MARK 8:23

Jesus took the blind man by the hand and led him out of the village. Then, spitting on the man's eyes, he laid his hands on him and asked, "Can you see anything now?"

Everywhere that Jesus goes, people come to Him looking to be healed, fed, and delivered. And because of Jesus' compassion He would heal, feed, and deliver them. Everywhere that Jesus went there were people that needed Him to touch them and make them well. There are several accounts of Jesus healing the blind. The thing that fascinates me is that each time that He healed someone He did it a different way.

This one in particular was especially different. Not only did Jesus use a different technique to heal the man's blindness but the results were different as well. This is the only account that suggests that Jesus had to touch a person twice to heal them. Scripture doesn't explain why it took two touches to heal this man's blindness so it is not appropriate to presume to know why. It just did!

The way Jesus met the needs of all the people He came into contact with varied based on the person and the situation. There was no method or model that He followed. There was no ritual that He implemented to minister to the people. The Holy Spirit led Him to minister to each person in a special and unique way. There is an important lesson there for us.

In ministry there will never be an end to the people that need to be ministered to. Each one of those people is different and unique. God wants us to see them in that way. There is no model, or process, or program that can minister to every single person that we come into contact with. Too often as ministry or church leaders we get caught up in the mindset that one-ministry-fits-all. That wasn't true when Jesus was ministering and it isn't true today. Ministries and programs and procedures and policies are tools that we use to love God by loving others. It is inappropriate to try to modify the person to fit the tool. We should modify the tools to fit the person that needs to be ministered to.

Jesus met the needs of those that God put in front of Him using techniques that the Holy Spirit led to Him to use. God doesn't need our programs and policies to minister to His people; He just needs us. Programs and policies have their place but only as a framework through which we can minister to whomever the Holy Spirit leads us. If that framework makes it difficult or awkward to minister to God's people then it is time for it to be modified or dismantled. We should never let something that man has created interfere with God's plan to heal, feed, or deliver His people. Jesus, help us to see past our models and methods to see the people that You are bringing to us to receive an outpouring of Your love.

FEBRUARY 27
Read: Leviticus 20:22 – 22:16, Mark 9:1-29, Psalm 43:1-5, Proverbs 10:18

MARK 9:24
The father instantly replied, "I do believe, but help me not to doubt!"

Jesus is coming down from the mount where He was transfigured. Peter, James, & John have just seen Jesus with Moses and Elijah. The very first thing that He is faced with after this mountaintop experience is this need to minister. That is often the way that it goes; you have a tremendous encounter with God and you are immediately faced with a great need in the body for ministry.

This father's need was great. His son has been plagued by a demon since he was a small child. This demon must have made life for the child and for the family very difficult. The father asks Jesus to heal the child "if He can." The disciples had already tried and failed to deliver the boy from this demon. We learn later in the reading that there was something unique about this demon because it required prayer and fasting to be cast out. We are not told what makes it unique; just that it was.

Jesus then responds to the father's statement by saying that anything is possible if you believe. Jesus is referring to faith. Also in our reading today, Jesus referring to this incident said that a small amount of faith could move a mountain. Jesus was calling the father of the child and His disciples to a deeper level of faith. It is the father's response that I found interesting. This father did believe but he also readily admitted that there was doubt. He did believe that his son could be delivered by Jesus; that was why he was there with his son. But in the back of his mind he was uncertain; either that Jesus would be willing to do it or that He could do it.

Believing God is the first and most important step that we take as Christians. But it doesn't end when we accept Jesus as our Savior. We then spend the rest of our lives believing God for every area of our lives. The problem is that this world, and our enemy, and our own experiences conspire to create doubts in our minds. One of the greatest tactics of Satan is to create doubt; to try to get us to question the things of God.

As long as we are wrapped up in this flesh we will have doubts. Only once we have our glorified bodies and we have complete knowledge will all doubt be forever removed from our minds. Until then we need to be working on eliminating one area of doubt after another in our minds. By doing that we will draw nearer to God and we will see His miraculous hand at work more often.

The only way that doubt can be removed is by a complete and total surrender to the truth. We must know and accept what God says and develop in our minds a clear picture that there is no question that it is the truth and that nothing can change that. It is a choice that we must decide to make if we want to move the mountains in our life. Jesus, I do believe; help me not to doubt!

FEBRUARY 28

Read: Leviticus 22:17 – 23:44, Mark 9:30 – 10:12, Psalm 44:1-8, Proverbs 10:19

LEVITICUS 23:3

You may work six days each week, but on the seventh day all work must come to a complete stop. It is the Lord's Sabbath day of complete rest, a holy day to assemble for worship. It must be observed wherever you live.

In Leviticus 23 God describes the festivals that the people of Israel were to celebrate. Each of these festivals or celebrations was created to remind the people of what God has done for them in the past. By celebrating these festivals at their appointed times, God intended for the people to not forget that what they had and where they were because of their special relationship with God.

The very first thing mentioned is the Sabbath. It is actually not a festival or celebration. The Sabbath was a day of rest. The purpose was to give the people and their servants a day off each week. During this day, the Israelites were to be turning their minds to God. God modeled this behavior in the creation of the world. For six days He worked to create the world. And on the seventh day He rested. This was a holy day. The Sabbath is holy because God said it was holy.

God knew that if He didn't give the Israelites the Sabbath day, that they would likely work seven days a week. They would also make their servants work seven days a week. The problem with that is that it is difficult to think about God while you are working. And the less you think about God, the further you get away from Him. God also knows that without rest, people are more prone to illness and sin. God gave the Israelites the Sabbath so they would be protected from both.

There is also a tendency with those in ministry and especially those starting churches to forget the principle of the Sabbath day of rest. There is always so much that needs to be done. The work of the ministry never ends. You could easily work seven days a week and 365 days a year and not be finished with the work of the ministry. While we are not under the Law and not required to rest on the Sabbath, the principle remains sound. You need to take time to rest. If you don't then you are eventually going to run out of strength or you are going to get sick. Or worse, if you don't take the time to reconnect with God on a regular basis, you will fall into sin.

Give yourself permission and be faithful to take time for you to meditate on the things that God wants to tell you. That demands that you slow down long enough for your mind to become clear. You can't do that while you are busy working. If you are too busy to spend time with God, you are too busy. As a leader of people, you need to lead by example and then make sure that your people are getting the rest that they need so that they are connecting with God. The Lord will bless you for being obedient to His Word and taking time to be alone with Him. Jesus, help us to make our time with you more important than our time working for you.

FEBRUARY 29
Read: Read from your favorite Scripture

LEVITICUS 23:22

When you harvest the crops of your land, do not harvest the grain along the edges of your fields, and do not pick up what the harvesters drop. Leave it for the poor and the foreigners living among you. I, the LORD, am your God.

As you are reading scripture and this devotional I pray that you are learning to catch some of the cool things that many people miss as they read the most incredible book ever written; the Bible. Today is another example of something cool that God would like us to glean from this reading. That was a play on words because what God is telling the Israelites is that they should not glean their grain or other crops. To glean is to come after the harvesters and gather what they missed.

God wants the Israelites to have giving attitudes about the things that God is going to give them in the Promised Land. Remember, right now they are living in the desert and living off of manna. Before that they were living as slaves in Egypt. It is likely that the people would have a tendency to hoard everything they got from God because they had gone so long without anything. That was not how God wanted them to be.

God had promised them abundance and His desire was that they would share that abundance with others that had a need. By leaving the edges of the fields and what the harvesters dropped, the poor and foreigners would have something to eat. This precept is played out beautifully in the book of Ruth.

God has also promised us abundance and His desire is that we would share what we have with those that are in need. One of the truths that many people miss in their lives is that God gives us what He does so that we will share it with others. God wants us to take care of the poor and the foreigners. The problem is that most of us don't have fields that we are harvesting and even if we did we live in a culture that doesn't operate this way.

What God wants us to glean from this text is that our abundance serves a purpose. God will give to you all that you can safely enjoy without being drawn away from Him and all that you will give away. If you will not give away some of your abundance to those that need it, He will not give it to you. If you cannot have abundance without it drawing you away from God, He will not give it to you.

Here is the hard part for some people; God wants you to have a giving heart before He gives you abundance. If you are not willing to help those that have need with what you have right now; God may not give you any more. God will only give us what we can bear. That also means that He will only give us what we can carry. If you cannot carry abundance; He will not give it to you. God wants you to live today just as if you have abundance right now. Jesus, help us to give away what You have given us.

MARCH

MARCH 1

Read: Leviticus 24:1 – 25:46, Mark 10:13:31, Psalm 44:9-26, Proverbs 10:20-21

LEVITICUS 24:2

Command the people of Israel to provide you with pure olive oil for the lampstand, so it can be kept burning continually.

There is tremendous symbolism in all of the furnishings of the tabernacle. In each item, its placement, and its use we are shown some aspect of Christ and God's plan of redemption for the world. The lampstand alone is rich in symbolism with its seven stems, the light, the flame, and the oil. Many of these things God commanded Moses to tell the people pointed to something they would not see or understand in their lifetimes. The fulfillment of the symbols was not to take place for over a thousand years.

What caught my attention in today's verse was the word "continually." The Israelites were to provide oil for the lampstand so that it would burn without ceasing. The priests were also tasked to tend to the lampstand through the night so that it didn't go out. The oil is a picture of the Holy Spirit. The light is a picture of Jesus Christ. The lampstand points to believers. The New Testament tells us that Jesus is the light of the world. Jesus instructed His followers to let their light shine for the whole world to see. The light is the declaration or witness of the gospel of Jesus Christ. And in the book of Acts, Jesus told His disciples that they would receive power from the Holy Spirit so that they could be witnesses.

What we sometimes forget is that God's instruction to keep the lamp burning continuously still applies to us today. The priests were instructed to tend the lampstand all through the night. All through the dark night they were to make sure that the light did not go out as they waited for the dawning of the day. We also wait for the dawning of the day, the day when Christ returns. While we wait we need to be tending the lamps of our life to keep the flame burning brightly.

This means keeping the oil of the Holy Spirit flowing in our lives. We must daily commit to being open to the moving of the Holy Spirit in all areas of our lives. This also means removing from our lives anything that might hinder the work of the Holy Spirit; which means eliminating sin, disobedience, and rebellion from our lives.

We also need to make sure that our lamps are placed where others can see the light. Sharing the gospel with others is the reason why we weren't taken to heaven the instant we accepted Jesus. There are as many ways to share Christ as there are believers in the world. Some will do it through sharing the gospel. Others will do it through good deeds. Some will do it by living the abundant blessed life that Jesus promised.

We can't make the light or the oil. Our only part is to tend the lamp. If we will do that, the light will shine out from us in the way that Jesus wants it to. This is not something we can do once a week or even once a day. Tending to the lamp of our faith is a continual thing. Jesus, help us to not let the light dim for even a second.

MARCH 2

Read: Leviticus 25:47 – 27:13, Mark 10:32-52, Psalm 45:1-17, Proverbs 10:22

LEVITICUS 26:3

"If you keep my laws and are careful to obey my commands..."

Here in Leviticus chapter 26, God gives the people of Israel a very clear description of what will happen if they are obedient to His Law and commands. He also contrasts this description of His blessings with the curses that the people will experience if they are disobedient to His Law and commands. We see a similar accounting in Deuteronomy 28. And you will notice in both places that the curses take twice as long to describe as the blessings.

God expects the people to be obedient. And in these two chapters He describes all the good things that will happen to them if they will obey His Laws and commands. The curses are given to create a sense of fear. God doesn't give the curses to make the people afraid of Him but to give them a fear of the consequences of not obeying God. The curses listed in Leviticus 26 turn out to be prophetic. The people will turn away from God's Law and His commands and He does inflict the curses upon them. And ultimately the people are sent into exile and the land is given rest as is required in the Law. God never fails to do what he says He is going to do.

As you look at the curses listed there you will notice that they come in waves. And before describing each wave God says: "If you fail to obey" and "If you fail to listen." Each curse is intended to get the attention of the people and cause them to start obeying God's Law and commands. It is God's desire that His people would stay in the place where He can bless them. But most of the blessings of God depend on our obedience.

If we choose to be disobedient, God will send a warning to us, maybe several warnings. And if we refuse to listen to the warnings and continue to be disobedient, God will begin to withdraw His hand of blessing from our lives. And if that still doesn't get our attention He will start allowing curses to come into our lives. And then if after experiencing the curse that he allows we still don't turn to Him and be obedient to Him, He will punish us Himself.

This applies not just to people but to ministries and churches as well. God has a plan for your life, your ministry, and your church. To fulfill that plan He has established laws, the Bible, that he expects you to follow. He will then through the Holy Spirit give you direction to cause you to fulfill the specific plan that he has for your ministry or church.

If you refuse to obey His Laws as they are described in the Bible and fail to listen to the Holy Spirit as He leads you, you should not expect to receive God's blessing on your ministry or in the church that you are starting. In fact, you should expect to experience the curses. God will bless your obedience and will curse your disobedience. As with most things with God, it is your choice. Jesus, help us to choose obedience and blessings.

MARCH 3
Read: Leviticus 27:14 – Numbers 1:54, Mark 11:1-26, Psalm 46:1-11, Proverbs 10:23

LEVITICUS 27:30
A tenth of the produce of the land, whether grain or fruit, belongs to the Lord and must be set apart to him as holy.

Here in the last book of Leviticus, God gives to Moses instructions about how the people are to devote things to the Lord. It was a practice of that time to dedicate to the Lord for His use and purpose. This could be done with things, animals, and even people. God concludes this chapter describing those things that the people can't dedicate to the Lord. The reason they can't be dedicated to the Lord is because they already belong to Him. Certain things like the firstborn male of the people and the animals are holy and set apart for the Lord. They are His and they cannot be redeemed.

And in the verse above we are told that the first of the harvest is also the Lord's. That means that a portion of the things that the people produced also belonged to the Lord. This included not only the crops but the animals that were born to the people. God was to be given a portion, a tithe, of them as well.

The word tithe means a tenth. God told the people of Israel that of all that He gave them they were to give back to Him a tenth. The act of tithing is first seen being done by Abraham after rescuing Lot. Abraham gave a tenth of the spoils to the King of Salem.

About a thousand years after God spoke the above verse to Moses, God spoke to the prophet Malachi. God was upset because the people had neglected to give Him what was due to Him. Within the rebuke he made to the nation of Israel, He made a promise. God told the people that if they would bring the tithe in that He would bless them beyond their imagination. It was been about 2,400 years since the Lord spoke to Malachi and people need to be reminded all over again. There are some that say that we shouldn't talk about tithing. There are two reasons why we should. First, the first tenth of all we have belongs to God. It is holy; it has been set aside for His use. The only correct thing to do with God's portion is give it to God. Doing anything else would be treating holy things as common.

The second and much less important reason why we should encourage people to obey God and tithe is that they will receive a blessing as a result. God has never made a promise that He hasn't kept. If He says that He will "open up the windows and pour out a blessing so great that you cannot contain it," then you can count on it coming true.

The New Testament teaches that God loves a cheerful giver. That doesn't mean that until you are happy about tithing that you shouldn't tithe. Tithe out of obedience and then let God work on your emotions. Teach your people that tithing is a natural and important part of their relationship with God. Jesus, teach us to give back to you a part of what you gave to us, not because we have to but because we love you.

MARCH 4

Read: Numbers 2:1 – 3:51, Mark 11:27 – 12:17, Psalm 47:1-9, Proverbs 10:24-25

NUMBERS 3:7

They will serve Aaron and the whole community, performing their sacred duties in and around the Tabernacle.

The Levites had a very special place in the nation of Israel. God chose them from among all the other tribes as His chosen servants among the Chosen People. They were identified as God's; as a substitute for all the first-born sons of Israel which God claimed as His own. And they served a special purpose for God and for the nation of Israel. Theirs was a sacred calling to serve God by serving the High Priest and the community as a whole.

God is still calling people to this same role; He is still calling people to serve the High Priest and the community. The Levites were called to serve Aaron and his descendants as they fulfilled the role of High Priest. Today, we serve the perfect High Priest, Jesus Christ. And we are called to serve the community.

You should notice that the Levites were not called to serve the Tabernacle. They performed their duties in and around the Tabernacle. As Christians, we are not to serve the church but we perform our duties in and around the church. The church is where we perform our duties; it is not the reason why we perform our duties. The church is never to take the place of God; it is a conduit that we use to connect people to God.

The duties of the Levites are also described as "sacred." When we think of sacred duties we will often think of things like preaching or praying or visiting the sick. The Levites were responsible for everything that happened in and around the Tabernacle and God described all of their duties as sacred. Anything and everything that we do for the Lord at church is a sacred duty. Whether it is picking up trash in the parking lot or changing a dirty diaper in the nursery or greeting people at the door as they come in; all is sacred in the Lord's eyes.

The Levites were a very special people to God and everything that they did was considered sacred to Him. Those people that serve God today are very special to the Lord and He considers all that they do as sacred and special. If you are involved in serving at your local church, know that God smiles down upon you and looks upon you in a special way. And no matter how mundane or menial the task is that you perform, it is a holy thing to the Lord. If you are not serving in your local church, God invites you to join the ranks of those special people doing a sacred thing. Jesus, help us to serve you in the smallest ways with a deep respect for the work that we are doing.

MARCH 5

Read: Numbers 4:1 – 5:31, Mark 12:18-37, Psalm 48:1-14, Proverbs 10:26

MARK 12:34

Realizing this man's understanding, Jesus said to him, "You are not far from the Kingdom of God." And after that, no one dared to ask him any more questions.

Jesus regularly had run-ins with the Pharisees and religious leaders and teachers of His day. Most of those events were strained at least and some were very confrontational. Later on in the text that we read today Jesus blasts the religious leaders and teachers for leading the people astray and preventing them from seeing the Kingdom of God.

In our verse for the day, Jesus has just had a conversation with one of these teachers of religious law. He had asked Jesus about which of the laws of God was the most important. Jesus told him that there is only one God and to love Him and to love others is the most important thing that anyone can do. This teacher of religious law understood what Jesus was saying. Jesus could see that this man understood what He was saying and so told him that he was not far from the Kingdom of God. He was not far from the Kingdom of God but he wasn't there yet. He was only missing one thing. All that this religious teacher needed to do was believe that Jesus was who He said that He was; the Son of God, the Messiah.

This teacher of religious law knew all about God. He knew what the Law of Moses and the prophets had taught. He knew what God had said about Himself and about the Messiah that He would send to save the people of Israel. Knowledge by itself will not help us to see the Kingdom of God. To see the Kingdom of God we must believe in the King of the Kingdom of God; Jesus Christ.

As we go through this life we are going to meet a lot of people that know about God. We are going to meet people that have been in church for their entire lives. We are going to meet people that know the Bible better than we do. If these people do not know Jesus Christ, all of their knowledge and experience is meaningless. They are no better off than the Pharisees and teachers of religious law. Only a personal knowledge of Jesus Christ will allow them to see the Kingdom of God.

It is not enough just to know about God. To see the Kingdom of God we must be in a relationship with Jesus. As leaders of families, ministries, and churches we need to also help others to do the same. As leaders, one of our primary roles is helping others to understand that not only do they need to get to know Jesus, but they need to help others to get to know Jesus also. We need to teach them how to do that through their lives, actions, and words. The role of a religious leader is to lead people to Christ and then to teach them to lead others to Christ. You don't have to be an evangelist to do that; you just need to know Jesus. Tell people what you know and show it to them in your life. Jesus, help us to be living testimonies of the Kingdom of God.

MARCH 6
Read: Numbers 6:1 – 7:89, Mark 12:38 – 13:13, Psalm 49:1-20, Proverbs 10:27-28

PSALM 49:16

So don't be dismayed when the wicked grow rich, and their homes become ever more splendid.

There are some things in life that just don't seem to be fair. Today's verse is one of those things. It doesn't seem fair that the wicked prosper and grow rich and have great things. To us, it would be fairer if the wicked were all punished with poverty and had to live on the streets. To us it would be fair if the godly people were blessed with the great riches and fabulous houses.

Life isn't fair but not for the reasons that you think. God has a plan for the wicked just as He does for the godly. When we think something like this is unfair we are criticizing God. You are not in a position to criticize God. In a recent message that I taught, God helped me to see this more clearly. To criticize God, you must understand what He is doing and you must be able to think like He does. That is not possible; if it were, He would not be God. He is God and you are not.

We have no idea what awaits the wicked; either in this life or in eternal life. If we could get a glimpse of what their eternity is going to be like I believe that we would be much less likely to be bothered by the fact that they are given good things in this life. If we could even imagine the pain and suffering they will endure for all time, we probably would be thankful that they have at least this short life to enjoy.

Also, if we were able to imagine what our own eternity is going to be like in heaven, the things that the wicked have now would pale in comparison. The wealth and riches of this world are garbage compared to the things of heaven. The greatest home on the earth probably wouldn't be suitable for a pig in heaven. If we truly understood those things we would have a totally different outlook on the things that the wicked enjoy in this life.

When we look at the wicked and are dismayed by the things that they get to enjoy in this life we are also revealing the condition of our hearts. It shows that our hearts have an unhealthy desire for the things of the world. As we surrender more and more of our lives to God, the things of the world should begin to fade in importance in our lives. And it is not that we have or have not those things, it is just their importance that fades. As that happens, the things of others also don't impress us.

We have to be careful that we don't allow a desire for the things of the world to replace our desire for a relationship with God. Sadly, God will allow us to trade our relationship with Him for a pursuit of the things of the world. But by sacrificing our relationship with God, we also sacrifice the blessings of the relationship. Don't be dismayed by the apparent blessings that the wicked are receiving; instead pray that God would be able to reach their souls before it is too late. Jesus, help us to be satisfied with You.

MARCH 7

Read: Numbers 8:1 – 9:23, Mark 13:14-37, Psalm 50:1-23, Proverbs 10:29-30

MARK 13:22

For false messiahs and false prophets will rise up and perform miraculous signs and wonders so as to deceive, if possible, even God's chosen ones.

Jesus has just told the disciples about the things that are going to happen during the time between His ascension to heaven and His return to get His Church at the rapture. He very plainly describes the kinds of events that will precede His return. Anyone that is paying attention to the world around them can tell that we are seeing these very things happen. Jesus tells the disciples not to be afraid or to worry. Instead He tells them to stand up straight and look toward the heavens; for that is where their salvation will come from.

Jesus also gives them a warning. He tells them that people will come and say that they know where the Messiah is or even worse, they will say that they are the Messiah. And some of these false messiahs and prophets will be able to do some of the miracles that Jesus did. They have only one purpose; to draw as many people away from God as they possibly can. If possible they will even deceive the children of God.

The warning is clear; these people are false, they are coming, and they will be able to deceive even the children of God. Warnings like this are given to us so that we will be prepared and equipped to deal with whatever we are being warned about. Jesus wants us to know what to expect and be prepared to deal with it without being deceived. To keep from being deceived we have got to keep our relationship with Jesus fresh and strong. We do that by knowing what God's word says and by spending time with Jesus allowing the Holy Spirit to speak to us and minister to us. We do that by staying connected to the body of Christ and by using the gifts and abilities that God gave us for the body.

Most people have some level of influence in their families, ministries, or churches. This influence was given to you so that you could use it to help others get prepared for what is coming. We must be helping to equip the saints so that they know a false prophet or messiah when they see one. Jesus never hesitated to confront false teaching when it was revealed to Him; neither should we. Daily we need to put on the armor of God and go out into this strange and dangerous world. We are to take the light of Jesus Christ into the darkness that surrounds us so that the lost can find their way to eternal life. The enemy wants to deceive everyone that he can and we can see in this world that he is doing a very good job. Each of us has a responsibility to try to do what we can to bring the truth that reveals the deception.

Jesus told us that His return would be preceded by the very things that we are seeing. He also told us that His return would be sudden and unexpected. People all around us are being deceived into believing that they have nothing to worry about. Each of us has a role to play in revealing the truth and promise of Jesus Christ. Jesus, help us to be an oasis of truth in this false world.

MARCH 8

Read: Numbers 10:1 – 11:23, Mark 14:1-21, Psalm 51:1-19, Proverbs 10:31-32

MARK 14:7

You will always have the poor among you, and you can help them whenever you want to. But I will not be here with you much longer.

Jesus is having dinner at the home of a man with leprosy. It is very unlikely that this man actually had leprosy at this time but had once had leprosy and very possibly had been healed by Jesus. In his gratitude he invited Jesus to dine with him. During this time a woman, who is believed by some to be Mary Magdalene, comes in and pours a vial of expensive perfume on Jesus. Many commentators suggest that this perfume was worth upwards of a year's wages. There is much debate over how she would have obtained such a valuable thing. Some suggest it would have been as a result of her occupation which is believed to have been prostitution.

Upon anointing Jesus with this perfume she receives a rebuking from the disciples. It is suggested that she shouldn't have "wasted" it on anointing Jesus and instead she should have sold it and given the money to the poor. Jesus' response to His disciples was to tell them to leave her alone. He goes on to commend her and tells the disciples that this act of devotion and love will be spoken about wherever the Good News is preached.

This text is rich with things to share about Jesus and the Kingdom of God and our lives but space is limited and so dig into it and find out what the Holy Spirit would say to you. The Holy Spirit prompted this woman to an extravagant act of adoration. Imagine for a moment taking something that is worth as much as one year's salary and giving it to Jesus. This woman had that opportunity and took it and for the rest of time people will speak about her love and adoration of Christ.

We don't have the opportunity to walk up to Jesus and thank Him personally for what He has done for us. But if we could would we be like this woman or would we be like the disciples? This woman recognized the value of what Jesus had done for her and counted it more valuable than anything that she owned. God calls us to this same level of adoration and worship of Jesus. Hold nothing back in your worship; lay at His feet everything that you have as an act of extravagant worship.

Jesus said that the poor would always be with us. It is true that throughout all of time there have been people that are in great want. That is not going to change in the future. Every once in a while God will give us an opportunity to lavish Jesus with something extravagant. The disciples didn't understand the significance of this woman's act of adoration. We need also to be very careful that we don't fall into this same trap as disciples of Jesus Christ. If we see someone lavishing Jesus with this kind of love, we must not object and question them, but we must rejoice with them. Jesus, help us to lavish all of our stuff and lives on you as a sacrifice of extravagant love and adoration.

MARCH 9

Read: Numbers 11:24 – 13:33, Mark 14:22-52, Psalm 52:1-9, Proverbs 11:1-3

MARK 14:36

"Abba, Father," he said, "everything is possible for you. Please take this cup of suffering away from me. Yet I want your will, not mine."

Jesus is in the Garden of Gethsemane on the eve of the most important day of His earthly ministry. He has spent the last evening with His disciples trying to prepare them for what is going to happen on this day.

He enjoyed one last and special meal with them. Now He is spending some time by Himself preparing Himself for what is coming next.

Jesus knew exactly what was coming. He knew the suffering that was ahead of Him. He knew precisely how the events of the next day were going to unfold. The pain and suffering that He was about to experience is beyond our comprehension or description. And yet that is unlikely to be what Jesus is referring to here.

Jesus was a man and as a man the idea of what He was going to experience is likely to have been highly undesirable. The Bible teaches that Jesus was tempted just as we are tempted so that He could relate to and understand us. There is no question that the idea of the beatings and crucifixion would create a sense of dread in Him.

Jesus was also God and had an incredible communion with the Father in heaven. As God He is eternal; He has existed since before there was time. The events of the next day would be virtually instantaneous in His life. A day in God's perspective is an incredibly short period of time. It is possible that Jesus' anguish in the Garden was as a result of the suffering that He was about to experience. It is much more likely that it has to do with something much greater than that.

Jesus was about to go to the cross and take the sins of the whole world upon Himself. "He that knew no sin became sin..." There is no way that our human minds can truly fathom what that meant to Jesus. I know that my sins separate me from God. I know that Jesus took my sins to the cross on my behalf. What I don't understand is how my sins separated Jesus from God the Father. I know it to be truth but there is no way that I can comprehend totally the significance of that truth. Jesus' anguish in the Garden was great. The knowledge that He was to be separated from the Father for even a short time was what He dreaded most.

That dread and that anguish did not overshadow His mission. This was the very reason why He had come to the earth. Jesus would gladly have chosen another way but He was resolutely determined to do what the Father willed. Most of us will not be asked by God to suffer the way that Jesus did in a physical way or in a spiritual way. How can our response to God's call be any different than Jesus'? God understands our dread and anguish; and still expects our surrender to His will. Jesus, help us to submit our will to Yours in all things and in all ways.

MARCH 10

Read: Numbers 14:1 – 15:16, Mark 14:53-72, Psalm 53:1-6, Proverbs 11:4

MARK 14:61

Jesus made no reply. Then the high priest asked him, "Are you the Messiah, the Son of the blessed God?"

Jesus has been arrested by the Jewish religious leaders. He is now standing trial before them. Even though they find several people that will testify against Jesus, none of them can get their lies to line up. Even the two that they find that have similar testimonies are not close enough to condemn Jesus. The Law was very clear that a person could not be condemned to death without the testimonies of two witnesses. The religious leaders were very strict about this. They are determined to follow the letter of the Law as they murdered Jesus. These Jewish leaders knew they were murdering Jesus. We know that because they would not receive back the money they paid Judas. Instead they used the money to buy a field that was used to bury foreigners.

It wasn't until the high priest asked Jesus directly if He was the Messiah that they had something they could use. The significance of this event is usually overshadowed by the events that follow and for good reason but this is a tragic thing. The Jews, especially the religious leaders have lived their lives waiting for one thing; the Messiah. A savior and deliverer was promised to them for a thousand years. Prophecy after prophecy had been fulfilled through Jesus. Standing in front of them was what they had lived their entire lives for. Their only thought was what they needed to do to destroy this threat to their position and authority.

These religious leaders had lost sight of the reason for their existence; to prepare the people for the coming Messiah. Like the religious leaders many of us have a similar responsibility. God has called us and placed us into places of leadership and authority. He did that for one reason; to help the people prepare for the coming of our Savior, Jesus.

The religious leaders of Jesus' day were more interested in where they fit in the scheme of the arrival of the Messiah than they were in His arrival. Anything that might upset their personal kingdom was to be fought and destroyed. Could we be accused of the same thing? Are we building a kingdom that might be resisting the return of Jesus? If Jesus were standing in front of us and we asked Him the same question that the high priest did, would we fall down on our face before Him in worship? Or would we be angry that His arrival has upset our little plans?

Nothing prevents Jesus from returning at this very moment. We need to live our lives as though we believe that. We need to be looking for Jesus and helping others to prepare their lives for His imminent return. If He came now would you be rejoicing or angry? Jesus, help us to live our lives as though you could arrive at any moment.

MARCH 11

Read: Numbers 15:17 – 16:40, Mark 15:1-47, Psalm 54:1-7, Proverbs 11:5-6

MARK 15:2

Pilate asked Jesus, "Are you the King of the Jews?" Jesus replied, "Yes, it is as you say."

Jesus has been delivered to Pilate for judgment. The Jewish leaders are accusing Him of all sorts of things. Pilate asks Jesus a simple question; "Are you the king of the Jews?" Jesus' response is to say that He is. This results in the Jewish religious leaders unloading barrage of accusations. Jesus' response to them and their accusations was silence. He refused to acknowledge or respond to the things that they said.

Jesus' response to the accusations made against Him is a lesson for us all in life and especially as we are called to lead ministries and churches. As Christ-followers, watching Christ on the day of His crucifixion can teach us about the way that we should and can walk in this life. If we will just follow Christ and His example and teachings we can know Him better and be better equipped to minister to the flock He has entrusted to us.

Most of us will never even come close to experiencing what Jesus experienced on that Friday morning. Few people will ever experience the pain and suffering that Jesus did at the hands of the Romans. It is very unlikely that anyone we know will endure a death as terrible as crucifixion. But it is very likely that all of us will be exposed to accusations. Anyone that has obeyed God's voice and accepted their role as leader in a family, ministry, or church will have to face some amount of accusations. When we do, we should strive to respond as Jesus did.

The Jewish leaders accused Jesus of inciting riots and of attempting to overthrow the Roman government. They accused Him of teaching people not to pay their taxes to Caesar. Jesus' response was a profound silence. He chose not to say a word in response to the lies that were being told about Him.

We live in a world that teaches and expects people to defend themselves. This society promotes the exposure of people's lives. People seem to feed off the failures of others. The better or godlier that someone is, the more the world seeks to discredit them. Even if that means that they need to make something up to do it.

Jesus chose not to respond to the false accusations brought against Him. We don't need to defend ourselves. Jesus is our advocate. We sometimes expend way too much energy defending ourselves against lies. We need to learn to respond with the same silence that Jesus did. If your heart is pure before God, let the accusations fall to the earth and die as they should. Respond only to those things that bring glory to God. Trust Jesus to be your defender. Jesus, help us not to waste our time trying to defend ourselves and help us to focus on our King.

MARCH 12
Read: Numbers 16:41 – 18:32, Mark 16:1-20, Psalm 55:1-23, Proverbs 11:7

MARK 16:20
And the disciples went everywhere and preached, and the Lord worked with them, confirming what they said by many miraculous signs.

Jesus' work on the earth is now complete and we move into the age of the church. The age of the church began at the Pentecost and will continue until Jesus comes to take His beloved bride, the church up into heaven to be with Him forever. One of the last things that Jesus told His disciples was to take the message of Jesus with them everywhere that they went. Here in our verse for the day we see they immediately do just that.

It is the God-given responsibility of every Christ-believer to tell those around them about Jesus. Some people are gifted greatly in this area and they can't help but share the Lord with others. Some people are very timid and the idea of speaking to anyone about anything is a little frightening; let alone sharing Jesus with them. It was what Jesus did for the disciples that encourages me to share more openly the good news of Jesus; the Lord worked with them.

Sometimes I think we may overlook this fact in our lives and especially as we go to share Christ with others. Jesus assigned them the task of "making disciples of all the nations" and to help them accomplish this task he was planning to work right alongside of them. How much bolder do you think you could be if Jesus were standing right beside you as you shared what you know about Jesus? I know that it would greatly embolden me.

The fact is that He is standing right beside you always. We should never even hesitate to respond to the leading of the Holy Spirit to share God's truth with someone. If God has led us to that person because He has something that He wants us to say to them, then He will also go with us to work with us to see that work is completed. As a proof of His sending us He will perform amazing signs in and through our lives to give people something substantial in which to believe.

We must not be tempted to take this to mean that we can do anything that we desire to and assume that Jesus is going to work with us. Jesus will only work with us as we go out to do the will of the Father in heaven. Don't be fooled into believing that just because it is a noble thing that God wants you to do it. Many people have been harmed because they decided to do something great for God that He didn't ask them to do. They get shipwrecked spiritually because they expect God to approve of their plan and they expect Jesus to work with them. That is the wrong view of God and it is very dangerous for you and harmful to the cause of Christ. We need only be humble and follow the directions of our King as He guides to those things that He desires done. Then we can expect great and mighty things to be done. Jesus, help us not get ahead of You.

MARCH 13

Read: Numbers 19:1 – 20:29, Luke 1:1-25, Psalm 56:1-13, Proverbs 11:8

NUMBERS 20:12

But the LORD said to Moses and Aaron, "Because you did not trust me enough to demonstrate my holiness to the people of Israel, you will not lead them into the land I am giving them!"

Our verse for today comes out of a text that many of us are familiar with. As leaders this is a text that we should study and become very familiar with. This is the account of when Moses responded to the people's request for water. Two million or so people and all of their animals are in the middle of the desert and they have no water. It seems like a reasonable request that they would want water. Scripture does record that they were grumbling and complaining and blaming God and Moses for this situation. Moses goes to God and is told to speak to the rock to bring forth water for the people. Instead Moses rebukes the people drawing attention to himself and then strikes the rock with his staff.

God does bring forth water from the rock but then tells Moses and Aaron that they will not be allowed to enter into the Promised Land. For nearly forty years Moses and Aaron will lead the nation of Israel around in the desert. It could not have been a pleasant life. The hope of the land filled with milk and honey had to be one of the things that drove them on. That hope was now gone. Moses would get to look upon the land but he was not allowed to enter into it.

Moses was accused by God of not trusting Him enough to demonstrate His holiness to the people. Because of his lack of trust in God, Moses lost the greatest physical blessing that he might have received. God did the miracle that He had planned to do through Moses and He continued to work through Moses after this event. It was a future blessing that Moses had sacrificed for this one moment of poor judgment. Moses allowed his flesh to get the best of him and it cost him dearly.

As God uses us to lead the families, ministries, or churches that He has entrusted to us He is going to give us opportunities to demonstrate His holiness to those around us. Moses should have simply gone out and told the people that their God had heard them and then spoken to the rock to produce the miracle. That would have focused the people on God and they would have honored and glorified His name. We will be given those same kinds of opportunities as we minister to the people that God has given us. Moses disobeyed God and paid a steep price for his disobedience. We need to take this for the warning that it is to us. God will use us as long as we let Him to lead and guide His people. He will bless us in ways that are beyond our ability to comprehend. But He demands our trust and obedience. If we fail to give them to Him as He deserves then we sacrifice our future blessings. How strongly do you think Moses wished he could take back those few seconds of time? Don't let a few seconds of the flesh ruin what God wants to give you. Jesus, help us to trust and obey.

MARCH 14

Read: Numbers 21:1 – 22:20, Luke 1:26-56, Psalm 57:1-11, Proverbs 11:9-11

NUMBERS 21:8

Then the LORD told him, "Make a replica of a poisonous snake and attach it to the top of a pole. Those who are bitten will live if they simply look at it!"

This is a section of scripture that has always fascinated me. The people are grumbling and complaining which seems to be their normal pattern. The problem is that the people do not trust God. Because they are faithless, God is punishing them. God has been traveling with them providing for them every step of the way and yet they still don't trust Him to do what he says He is going to do. God will only tolerate that from His people for so long before He starts to discipline them. God gets angry and sends poisonous snakes to punish them. They cry out to Moses and ask him to pray for them. God tells Moses to make this replica of a snake and put it on a pole.

There is a greater message in this text which we see explained in John chapter three as Jesus speaks with Nicodemus. Jesus refers to this incident in Numbers and says to Nicodemus that He must be raised up just as the bronze serpent was raised up so that anyone that looks upon Him will live.

One of the realities of our relationship with God is that He gives us the ability to choose. God does not make us love Him or trust Him. God will not make us believe in Jesus. God will not make us look upon Him upon the cross so that we can live. He gives us the ability to choose to look upon the bronze serpent.

While this is not in the text, it is not hard to imagine that there were some that chose not to look upon the bronze serpent. I can easily imagine people lying in their tents dying from the bite of the serpent and someone coming in to say that if they want to be healed they just need to come outside and look up at this serpent upon the pole. How many of those people refused to come outside because they didn't believe it was possible to be healed that way? It is not hard for me to imagine that because we see that on a regular basis as we share the truth of the gospel with others and they refuse to look up at Jesus on the cross so that they might have life.

We can't make them put their trust in Jesus; they have to choose. All we can do is be the ones that carry the pole around to as many people as we can and invite them to look up to the bronze serpent that brings healing from the poisonous snake of sin. We can't make them do it; they have to choose just like you did. Sadly, there will be many that will choose death rather than life. When that happens we need to be very clear that it was their choice not God's. God's desire was that they would choose life; eternal life with Him.

The Israelites chose not to trust God and it cost them dearly. God still expects His people to trust Him. Don't wait until the snakes are slithering around your ankles to believe and trust God. Jesus, teach us to trust You.

MARCH 15

Read: Numbers 22:21 – 23:30, Luke 1:57:80, Psalm 58:1-11, Proverbs 11:12-13

LUKE 1:64

Instantly Zechariah could speak again, and he began praising God.

Zechariah had the incredible privilege of getting a visit from Gabriel the archangel. Gabriel told Zechariah that he was going to have a son and that he was to name him John. This child would grow up to be John the Baptist and be chosen to proclaim the arrival of Jesus. Zechariah did not believe the angel and so Gabriel made him mute; unable to speak until the child's birth. After the baby is born, Elizabeth, his mother, names him John much to the surprise and questioning of the friends and family that are there to celebrate his birth. Zechariah confirms that the child's name is to be John and instantly he is able to speak again.

God punished Zechariah for unbelief. The punishment lasted for nine months. We must never forget that God is not pleased when we do not believe Him or His word and He has every right to punish us in any way that He chooses. Try to imagine what it must have been like to try to describe to everyone that he met after he met Gabriel about the experience. It must have been very frustrating and humiliating.

The Bible teaches that it is impossible to please God if we don't have faith. Faith is simply the act of believing God. For nine months Zechariah couldn't praise God or share with others the incredible event that had taken place in his life. We must also be so careful to walk in faith; believing God wherever and whenever we are faced with the opportunity. Too often we sacrifice or delay the blessings of God because we neglect to believe Him first.

It was Zechariah's response to the end of his punishment that caught my attention. His first action was to praise God. He did not vent the nine months worth of things that he wanted to say but couldn't; he praised God for His faithfulness. God was just and right to punish Zechariah. He is also just and right when He punishes us. We need to be ready to respond as Zechariah did and praise Him at the end of it. What the Bible doesn't tell us is what Zechariah was doing during his punishment. I believe that the way we prepare ourselves to praise God at the end of our punishment is to praise Him during our punishment. Zechariah knew that God had been fair with him and while he might have been unable to say that he was probably thinking it.

In the midst of all the hard things that might be going on in your life, never cease to praise God. Then when the end of those trials, tribulation, and punishments come, you will naturally and without hesitation praise God. God blessed Zechariah for the way that he responded by giving him a word of prophecy. Only God knows how else he was blessed. God is even right at this moment preparing something special for you; get ready for it by praising Him in the midst of the storm. Jesus, give us hearts that never cease to praise You.

MARCH 16

Read: Numbers 24:1 – 25:18, Luke 2:1-35, Psalm 59:1-17, Proverbs 11:14

NUMBERS 25:3

Before long Israel was joining in the worship of Baal of Peor, causing the LORD'S anger to blaze against his people.

God had led the nation of Israel through the wilderness for almost forty years. They will soon be entering into the Promised Land. God is traveling with them and providing for them every day and every step of the way. And yet, here they are in this text worshipping the false god of Baal. It started with the men seeing the women of Moab and being attracted to them. They then began to have sex with these women. Before long they are going to these women's festivals and religious ceremonies. And then ultimately they have turned away from the one true God to worship a god that allowed them to satisfy their sinful desires.

Baal was the supposed god of fertility and both male and female shrine prostitutes were available to assist in the worship of this pagan deity. As the men of Israel were prostituting themselves to this pagan false god, they were also acting as the prostitute to the one real God. God made it very clear to the descendants of Abraham that they were to have only one God. God is a jealous God and will not share our affections with anyone.

It is very unlikely that any of these men that were ultimately killed because of their sin believed that their first lustful look at the women of Moab would lead to Baal worship and then death. They simply saw something they wanted that would temporarily make them happy. God had warned them of this very thing. He had told them to separate themselves from the rest of the world because the world would draw them away from Him. As always, what God said would happen if they didn't listen to Him, is exactly what happened.

We live in a world today where there are so many more idols that can be worshipped than there were in the time of the Israelites. With television, movies, sports, and the internet there are literally thousands of idols that people can and do worship. And then there are the ones that have always been around; money, power, influence, and sex.

God gave the Israelites the Tabernacle and the sacrificial system and the Law to separate them and to protect them. We, as Christians, have something even more powerful than that, the Holy Spirit. The Holy Spirit was sent to us so that we could resist the temptation of the idols of this world. But we have to allow Him to work in our lives. We have to surrender control to Him so that he can teach us how to recognize and refuse the false gods of this world.

And we are called to reveal the futility and wickedness to others that are practicing in these things. It is our role to let God use us to save them from the penalty of worshipping any god other than the Almighty God. Jesus, help us to see the unclean things as they are and help us to worship only You.

MARCH 17

Read: Numbers 26:1-51, Luke 2:36-52, Psalm 60:1-12, Proverbs 11:15

NUMBERS 26:51

So the total number of Israelite men counted in the census numbered 601,730.

The Israelites have almost finished their forty year wilderness hike. They are camped out on the edge of the Promised Land and they will soon enter into it and begin to possess what God had promised their ancestors. Before they go in, God has them do a census to count all the men that are twenty years and older. Forty years earlier God did the same thing when He was preparing to take them in the first time. What caught my attention was that the totals were very close to the same. In the first chapter of Numbers the Israelites took a census and the total counted was 603,550; just a couple of thousand higher than the second count.

The interesting thing about the two counts was that none of the 603,550 that were counted in the first count was counted in the second count. That means that the 601,730 consisted of two groups of people. The first group was all the boys that were less than twenty years old when the first census was taken. The second group was all the boys that were born in the wilderness during the first twenty years of the wilderness journey.

This speaks to me of God's faithfulness. God had made a promise. That promise was that He was going to lead the people into the Promised

Land. His plan was to take over 600,000 men and their families into the land. God's plan didn't change just because the people were unfaithful and rebelled against Him. Their unfaithfulness and rebellion just delayed God's plan for forty years. God was faithful and kept His promise and stuck to His plan to take more than 600,000 men and their families into the Promised Land.

This applies to us as well. God has a plan and He has made promises that apply to all of our lives, families, ministries, and churches. Our faithfulness and obedience will have an impact on how and when God fulfills those promises and plans. Nothing we do will stop them from happening but we do have a choice about our role and involvement in those things happening.

If the first 600,000 Israelites had trusted and believed God and acted upon their trust and belief, they would have entered into the land and seen God's promises fulfilled. Because of their disbelief and rebellion they didn't and another 600,000 were allowed to get what God had offered to them first. The first 600,000 had to live with the consequences of their bad decisions. We also have to live with the consequences of the way that we believe and act in relation to God. Many people are wandering around in the wilderness of their disbelief and rebellion against God, while someone else is reaping the fulfillment of God's promises. We owe it to our families, ministries, and churches to believe God and obey Him so that He can be glorified and they can experience the fulfillment of God's promises. Jesus, teach us to trust, believe, and obey.

MARCH 18

Read: Numbers 26:52 – 28:15, Luke 3:1-22, Psalm 61:1-8, Proverbs 11:16-17

NUMBERS 27:17

Give them someone who will lead them into battle, so the people of the LORD will not be like sheep without a shepherd."

God has just told Moses that it is time for Moses to die. Moses was not going to be allowed into the Promised Land because He had rebelled against God when the people complained about water. God wanted Moses to reveal to the people His holiness. But Moses revealed his own humanity instead. This cost Moses his trip into the Promised Land. It was time for Moses to go the way of his ancestors. But before he died Moses asked God to replace him as leader of the community. Moses wanted God to pick someone to lead the people of Israel after he was gone. Moses' was concerned that once he was gone that the people would be like sheep without a shepherd.

Sheep will do whatever comes into their minds. They will wander off whenever they feel like wandering. Moses' concern is that the people would scatter and be destroyed by the inhabitants of the land. Moses is a shepherd to the people and he wants them to have a shepherd even if it is not him.

People are often referred to as sheep in the Bible. That is because in many respects that is exactly how we behave. And if we don't have a shepherd, we are very likely to wander off into some kind of trouble. God doesn't want that to happen to His people and so He assigns shepherds to tend the flock of God. After Moses' request God selected Joshua to take Moses' place as shepherd-leader of the nation of Israel.

Jesus is the Good Shepherd. Through the influence of the Holy Spirit He leads, guides, protects, and feeds us. Some of us have the responsibility of under-shepherd to a portion of Jesus' flock. We have been assigned by God to lead in our family, in a Bible study, in a ministry, or in a church. That is a holy thing to be called to be used by God this way.

The under-shepherds responsibility is to tend the flock that has been entrusted to him or her. To tend the flock is to take care of all of its needs. Just as the shepherd has to do almost everything for the sheep in his flock, you as an under-shepherd will need to make sure that the sheep in your care are healthy, well-fed, and safe. And sometimes you need to deal with unruly and rebellious sheep.

As under-shepherds, we carry a greater weight of responsibility. But that weight shouldn't be heavy because we have the Good Shepherd assisting us the whole way. There is nothing that we can't do while Christ leads and guides us, even tend to an unruly or rebellious flock. We need to tend our flocks well because our Good Shepherd, Jesus, has entrusted them to us to bring them, all of them, to Him safely. Jesus, teach us to tend to the flock, however great or small, that you have entrusted to us just as you would tend to it.

MARCH 19

Read: Numbers 28:16 – 29:40, Luke 3:23-38, Psalm 62:1-12, Proverbs 11:18-19

PSALM 62:1

I wait quietly before God, for my salvation comes from him.

David's life often had trials and tribulations. It was a regular occurrence that enemies were attacking him. His king attacked him, his son attacked him, his friends attacked him, and the enemy attacked him. David was no stranger to the attacks of people around him. David was also no stranger to the help of the Lord. On many occasions God had interceded on his behalf. David understood clearly where his help came from. He knew that salvation came from God and from Him alone.

The interesting thing about this psalm is the use of the word "quietly." Twice it is used in this psalm; or song. Other translations render this word as "silently" or "wait in silence." This describes a different form of waiting that many people are not accustomed to. Too often people's waiting is anything but quiet; it is filled with crying, complaining, or griping.

Recently I was with my wife at a resort in Palm Springs and many of the people that served us expected some form of compensation. But none of them expressed that to us; they stood by quietly and waited for us to tip them. These "servants" were being paid by the resort and so tipping was not required for them to make their living. They were anticipating some measure of grace from the person that they had served.

As Christians, we have received our "compensation" in the form of the free gift of salvation. God is under no obligation to save us from our trials and tribulations. But just like the resort workers anticipated tips from their service we can anticipate God's grace to be given to us through salvation from our attackers. We can't expect it because God is not required to give it but we can anticipate it because of God's love for us.

And just like those resort workers stood by quietly, we also need to stand quietly waiting for God to act on our behalf. Those resort workers do not always receive a tip for the services that they provide. And God doesn't always act in the way that we want Him to. Sometimes He responds instantly and sometimes He takes a very long time.

Our role is to wait and to do it quietly; knowing that God is capable and inclined to help us because we are His children. Often people are so busy telling God and others that they need to be rescued that they can't hear God telling them what they need to do before He will rescue them. Only by waiting quietly can we hear the small, still voice of the Holy Spirit guiding us to our part in our being saved from our attackers. Jesus, help us to be patient and to wait quietly for You to do what You are going to do.

MARCH 20

Read: Numbers 30:1 – 31:54, Luke 4:1-30, Psalm 63:1-11, Proverbs 11:20-21

NUMBERS 30:2

A man who makes a vow to the LORD or makes a pledge under oath must never break it. He must do exactly what he said he would do.

Moses gives to the leaders of the people some laws regarding how to conduct themselves in the use of vows. These vows were commitments or promises made to God. And Moses instructed the people that if they make a vow to God, that they have to keep it.

Moses also gave them some exceptions to this law. Fathers could annul the vow of an unmarried daughter and husbands could annul the vows of their wives. This was done because the man was responsible for the decisions of his daughter and wife. If he felt that the vow was made foolishly or was harmful to the person or family he had the authority to over-ride. And this would leave his daughter or wife innocent before the Lord.

The man does not have this exception to the making and keeping of vows. If a man makes a vow, he is expected to keep; to never break it. This law of vows was meant to prevent people from making foolish or rash vows before the Lord. God didn't want them making promises that they couldn't keep.

Elsewhere in scripture it tells us that it is better not to make vows. The reason for that is that you cannot foretell the future. You don't know what twists and turns the Lord has planned for your life. It is risky to make a vow to the Lord because chances are you don't know what He has in the future for you. It is better to make no vows at all than to make a vow and not keep it.

Ultimately, the issue of vows is a matter of integrity. God was teaching the Israelites to be people of integrity. In this text He is using the matter of vows as the example for that lesson but elsewhere He uses other things. The Law of Vows refers specifically to vows made to God but it is also inferred to be between people. God also expects us to keep our vows, commitments, and promises whether they are made to Him or to other people.

Few things will harm a relationship like a lack of integrity. If you are someone that cannot be trusted to do what you say you are going to do it will seriously harm any relationships that you are in. If you are involved in service or leading a ministry or starting a church integrity is a must. It is one thing if you show a lack of integrity in your personal relationships, it is quite another if your lack of integrity involves people that God has entrusted into your care.

It is absolutely critical that we are very careful regarding the commitments and promises that we make. It would be better to make no commitment or promise than to make one and not keep it. Sometimes saying "no" or "I can't" is the right thing to do. Jesus, help us all to be people of integrity doing what we say we are going to do.

MARCH 21
Read: Numbers 32:1 – 33:39, Luke 4:31 – 5:11, Psalm 64:1-10, Proverbs 11:22

"Master," Simon replied, "we worked hard all last night and didn't catch a thing. But if you say so, we'll try again."

Jesus has just finished preaching to the crowds as He is standing in Simon's boat. He tells Simon to cast off and to let down the nets. Jesus tells him that they will catch many fish. Simon, being a fisherman, lets Jesus, who is a carpenter, know that they have already tried. Fishing is what Simon did; it was his strength. He had been working in his strength all night and it resulted in nothing.

How many of us can relate to Simon. There are some things that we are good at; either from experience or gifting. And even though we are good at it, there will be times when that is not enough. Even though we are good at it, we still come up with nothing. Simon's response to Jesus may have been because he was frustrated with himself for not producing any results. Or it may have been because he was frustrated with Jesus for thinking that He knew something about fishing that Simon didn't.

Whatever Simon was thinking he did the right thing; he did what Jesus told him to do. But you can tell from Simon's response to the large catch that he did not believe that it was going to do any good. Simon was obedient but he didn't believe; that is until the nets were full to the breaking point.

There will be times when our best efforts result in nothing. Even though we have experience and gifts, there will be times when nothing is working. It is at times like those that we need to look and determine who is doing what. Is it you that is doing the work or the ministry or is it the Holy Spirit doing it through you. It is within our strengths that we experience the greatest temptation to take control away from God. Even when doing those things that you are good at, you should be dependent upon God for everything.

Also, if Simon had not been obedient he would have missed the blessing of the catch. In those times that things are not going the way they should we need to be very sensitive to the leading of the Holy Spirit because He might be telling us to cast off and try again. And it might not make sense to you but if you will obey you will experience a blessing.

Our strengths can be our greatest weaknesses. God wants to use us to do incredible, miraculous, supernatural things in this world. To be used in that way we must surrender our strengths to God. We must allow Him to use them and direct them as He desires. If you will stay humble in your strengths, God can use them to do amazing things in this world. Jesus, help us to lay our strengths, abilities, and experiences at Your feet.

MARCH 22

Read: Numbers 33:40 – 35:34, Luke 5:12-28, Psalm 65:1-13, Proverbs 11:23

NUMBERS 33:55

But if you fail to drive out the people who live in the land, those who remain will be like splinters in your eyes and thorns in your sides. They will harass you in the land where you live.

The Israelites will soon be making the trip that their fathers had failed to make forty years ago, entering into the Promised Land of Canaan. And before they go into the land Moses gives the people some instructions from God. These instructions are meant to make them successful once they get into the land. One of the most important instructions that Moses gave them was to drive out the people of Canaan from the land. God had earlier told the Israelites that part of His plan for bringing the Israelites into the land was to cleanse of the filth of the Canaanite's sin and wickedness from the land.

Moses tells them to make sure to do and then gives them the reason why he is telling them to do this. If the Israelites do not drive the Canaanites from the land they will harass them. The Canaanites that remain will be a constant irritant like a splinter in the eye or a thorn in the flesh.

The Canaanites are a type or picture of the enemies in our life. All of us have enemies and strongholds that we have allowed into our life or were introduced into our life. God expects us to drive out those enemies just like He expected the Israelites to drive out the Canaanites. And if we leave any remnant of those enemies in our lives they will be a constant irritant.

God had told the Israelites that He would be the one to drive the enemies out. All the Israelites had to do was to face these enemies one at a time. God would then tear down the stronghold that protected the enemy. But then it was up to the Israelites to eradicate that enemy. History has proven this warning from God through Moses to be true. The Canaanites that they allowed to remain in the land harassed them continually and ultimately drew them away from true worship of God.

Our role as leaders in God's ministries and churches is to teach, exhort, and encourage people to come against each of the strongholds in their life and then celebrate with them as God brings about the victory in their lives. Our personal goal should be personal holiness through a systematic destruction of all of the enemies that currently are taking up residence in our lives. At the same time, we need to be helping those in our ministries and churches to do the same thing.

We must strive to eliminate even the slightest trace of that enemy or it will come back to torment and irritate us and those in our ministries and churches. We must be ruthless with the enemies in our lives. We must aggressively seek to destroy every vestige of sin our lives so that it doesn't interfere with our relationship with God. Jesus, help us to hate sin enough to allow you to destroy it within our lives.

MARCH 23
Read: Numbers 36:1 – Deuteronomy 1:46, Luke 5:29 – 6:11, Psalm 66:1-20, Proverbs 11:24-26

DEUTERONOMY 1:17
When you make decisions, never favor those who are rich; be fair to lowly and great alike. Don't be afraid of how they will react, for you are judging in the place of God. Bring me any cases that are too difficult for you, and I will handle them.

The book of Deuteronomy is a record of the last words of Moses before he dies. These are his final instructions to the people that he has led for the last forty years. He is about to die and they are about to enter the Promised Land and so he tells them everything that he wants them to know before he goes. Much of the book is a recap of things that happened during the last forty years as well as some further instructions.

Here as the book opens Moses reminds them about the time when he set up the leadership structure of the nation of Israel. His father-in-law Jethro is the one that recommended it to Moses. The problem was that there were too many people for Moses to deal with all of their problems all by himself. He was killing himself trying and all of the people's needs weren't being met. Jethro suggested that Moses assign other capable men the task of doing what Moses was doing. And that is exactly what Moses did. There is a great leadership truth in this for us as well.

As leaders of ministries and churches we cannot do everything that needs to get done ourselves. If you try to you will find yourself in the same place that Moses did; killing yourself and the needs of the people not being met. The big difference is that the people that were following Moses didn't really have anywhere else to go. Those that God has given into your care do have other options. Or worse yet, they can wander away from the flock.

It is not part of God's plan that you work so hard to minister to everyone around you that you burn out. God's plan includes you finding capable people around you that can come along side of you to help you. If God has called you to lead and has brought people to you that are following, then He has also brought people that can help you. It is your responsibility to look for them and to invite them to join you. And while they may not be able to do it as well as you; they can do things that you can't get to do.

Select and equip people to do much of the work that you do. You'll be surprised how this will cause your ministry to grow and to flourish. Be there to help with the hardest of situations but release your people to do everything else and you will see them all grow in their relationship with God as well. Jesus, teach us to give the ministry away so that it can grow and be all that You desire it to be.

MARCH 24
Read: Deuteronomy 2:1 – 3:29, Luke 6:12-38, Psalm 67:1-7, Proverbs 11:27

DEUTERONOMY 3:22
Do not be afraid of the nations there, for the LORD your God will fight for you.

Moses is getting the people ready to enter into the Promised Land. God brought them out of Egypt and lead them to the edge of the land. God told them that He was going to drive out nations that were greater than they were so that they could possess the land. The spies that had gone into the land also reported that there were strong nations in the land. Moses tells them not to worry about those other nations because God is going to fight for them.

This is a beautiful picture of the Christian life, especially to someone that has fully surrendered their life to God and committed to serve Him. God has not promised us a land like He did the Israelites. What He promised us is a life that is rich, power-filled, and full of all the goodness of God. To get this life we need to go in and possess it just like the Israelites had to do with the Promised Land. And just like the Israelites had to dispossess enemies from the Promised Land, we need to dispossess enemies from the life that Jesus gave to us.

In our lives those enemies are sin. To experience all of the life that God wants us to, we must drive sin from our lives. We do that by surrendering our lives fully and completely to the work of the Holy Spirit and strive to obey every word of the Bible. Then we will find that God will drive those enemies from our lives.

As we surrender more of our lives and give ourselves to serve God and His people we will also find enemies in that area as well. The reason for that is that by committing to serve you are actually stepping further into the Promised Life. The enemies there are greater and fiercer. That is because now you are not just working on your life with God but you are also impacting the lives of others and their relationship with God.

Moses told the Israelites not to be afraid of those enemies that they would face in the land because God was going to fight for them. God has not changed and He is still fighting the battles of those that are actively seeking to possess the life that He promised them and those that they serve. We have absolutely nothing to fear; God is bigger and badder than any enemy that could possibly come into our lives.

God wants us to fearlessly pursue the life that Jesus came to give us. He wants us to face those enemies just as David faced Goliath; with a bold confidence, not in his own ability but in the power of the living God. The people of God should be fearless as they face the things that the world throws at them. The people that have been called to serve Him (that is everyone) should be even more fearless. We are on God's side and no one or nothing can beat God. Jesus, help us to face our enemies with fearless confidence in You.

MARCH 25

Read: Deuteronomy 4:1-49, Luke 6:39 – 7:10, Psalm 68:1-18, Proverbs 11:28

DEUTERONOMY 4:12

Do not add to or subtract from these commands I am giving you from the LORD your God. Just obey them.

Moses is giving his last speech before he dies. In this speech he will remind the nation of Israel of all the great things that God has done for them and he will remind them of God's laws. Much of the book of Deuteronomy is a restatement of the laws of God. And here in our verse for the day we see Moses making a very important statement. In a very simple statement Moses describes what our response to the laws of God should be.

First we are told not to add to or subtract from these laws. God's laws, commandments, and statutes are complete. They need nothing added to them. There is nothing that man can say that can add anything to what God has said. All man can do is to attempt to explain to others what God said. And even in that man has to be very careful that his explanation lines up with the Word of God.

There is no part of God's word that is not necessary. If you subtract anything from God's Word, you are making it incomplete. Every word is there for a reason. Only by examining all of God's Word do you get a complete picture of God. If you leave things out of what God said you have a lesser view of God's holiness. God is jealous of His holiness and anything that diminishes it will be met with His anger and judgment.

God's word is absolutely perfect and complete. It needs nothing and it has nothing extra. It contains everything that we need and nothing in it is unimportant. The only way the Bible can be viewed is completely. Anything less than that will cause you to view God in a way that cannot help you the way that you need to be helped.

Moses concludes this exhortation with a very simple instruction of what to do with the laws of God; "just obey them." How simple is that! We tend to spend too much time trying to understand the theology and prophetic aspects of scripture when the most important thing that God wants us to do is obey scripture. We need to understand scripture well enough that we can obey it.

Don't complicate scripture! Don't diminish scripture! Just do what it says! If we would spend more time obeying scripture and teaching others to obey scripture, there would be less conflict in the church and in ministry. Jesus, help us to see the Bible as a work of absolute perfection to be held in awe and reverence and to be obeyed absolutely.

MARCH 26

Read: Deuteronomy 5:1 – 6:25, Luke 7:11-35, Psalm 68:19-35, Proverbs 11:29-31

DEUTERONOMY 6:6

And you must commit yourselves wholeheartedly to these commands I am giving you today.

M oses is continuing his last speech to the people of Israel before he dies and Joshua takes them into the Promised Land. Moses is reminding them of everything that the Lord has told them. He is also reminding them of the mistakes that they and their fathers have made and exhorting them not to make the same mistakes again.

In our text for today Moses tells the Israelites to follow these commands wholeheartedly. The NKJV says that these commands "shall be in your heart." God is very concerned about the condition of the hearts of His people. God knows that it is in the heart that obedience begins. In the verse prior to this, Moses told the children of Israel to "love the Lord your God with all your heart, with all your soul, and with all your strength." Our obedience should be born out of our love for God.

The way that we show God that we love Him is by obeying Him. And the way that we obey God is by living a life that imitates the life of Christ. Christ lived a life that was sacrificed to others in service. The way that we show God that we love Him is by obeying Him in a life that is lived wholeheartedly for others.

That's where it sometimes can become difficult for some people. They love the Lord Jesus and they want to serve Him wholeheartedly but they are not in the ministry or church that they feel called to be in. Because of the needs of the ministry or church that they are in, they find themselves doing something that is not "their ministry" or "using their gifts." And unfortunately they are not serving wholeheartedly. They are doing it out of sense of duty or "because the pastor told me to."

Let us not forget that Jesus also served in a ministry that was not His primary calling. Jesus is God! But for a time the needs of His ministry to the world called Him to serve in a very humble way; as a man in Galilee. If Jesus could do that, is it too much to ask us to set up chairs, or to be an usher or greeter, or even to serve in the Children's Ministry. We should not think so highly of ourselves as to think that any service to God is below us.

God has you where you are in your ministry or church for a reason and a season. He is trying to teach you to be more like His Son and He is preparing you for the next step of the journey that he has you on. The length of the season may depend on whether or not you serve God whole-heartedly even in a ministry or place of service that you don't enjoy. Jesus, help us to love you so much that we will pour our heart completely into whatever act of service that YOU have placed before us.

MARCH 27
Read: Deuteronomy 7:1 – 8:20, Luke 7:36 – 8:3, Psalm 69:1-18, Proverbs 12:1

PSALM 69:6

Don't let those who trust in you stumble because of me, O Sovereign LORD Almighty. Don't let me cause them to be humiliated, O God of Israel.

David was a king of great power and ability. He had done amazing things while king of Israel. But he was also a humble king. He recognized his weaknesses and wasn't afraid to confront his sins and unrighteousness. It was this that earned him the title of: A man after God's own heart. And here in our verse for the day we see another example that heart that seeks to be like God's heart.

David's prayer here is that he not be the cause of any that follow him from falling away from the Lord. David is concerned that his own foolishness and sins might be the cause of someone else stumbling and falling. And he has good cause to be concerned about that. After David's son

Solomon dies we will see a whole series of kings that does what is evil in the sight of the Lord and they lead the people of Israel to follow them into sin.

As a leader, you have the ability to influence people toward God or away from God. And it doesn't matter what you are leading; your family, in your neighborhood, at your workplace, a ministry, or a church. As a leader at any level or place you will be influencing people, that's what leaders do. And your heart should burn like David's did to lead well.

Knowing that your actions, attitudes, behaviors, sins, or foolishness could be the stumbling block that prevents someone from coming to Jesus should cause pain to your heart. It should create within you a passion to control your members so that the only thing that anyone around you sees in you is Jesus.

Knowing that you are leading others which means that they are following you to where you are going should give you a burden to always be checking your compass to make sure that you are headed toward Jesus. If God has called you to lead He expects you to lead people to His Son.

All of us have the responsibility to lead people to Jesus. Our lives should be living signposts directing people to the Savior of our souls. And with that responsibility should come the awareness that our lives can also lead people away from Christ.

To be a leader is to bear a burden that is impossible to carry. But if we are doing it in the power of the Holy Spirit and leading people toward Jesus, then it is also one of the greatest joys that you will experience on this earth. Jesus, help me to look back and see who is following me and help me to look forward and make sure that I am leading them to You.

MARCH 28

Read: Deuteronomy 9:1 – 10:22, Luke 8:4-21, Psalm 69:19-36, Proverbs 12:2-3

PROVERBS 12:1

To learn, you must love discipline; it is stupid to hate correction.

As we study God's word we sometimes find ourselves trying to under-stand what He is trying to teach us. At other times it is so simple that a small child can understand it. Today's verse is one that seems very simple to understand and yet we often struggle to live it out. And for some reason it is leaders that seem to have the greatest difficulty with this.

To be a good leader you must have a desire to learn. To be a great leader you must be a great student. For reasons of pride mostly, a lot of leaders fail to understand this because they think since they are the leader that they must know all that they need. The problem with that is that we live in a world that never stops changing. To stop learning is to allow the world to move past you and the longer that you allow that, the less effective you are as a leader.

Two words are used in our verse today to describe the tools of learning; discipline and correction. Both words have similar meanings and often instill within the minds of the hearers negative emotions and connotations. Both words carry with them the sense that the person receiving them is not where they are supposed to be and are in need of adjustment. To admit that is to be humbled and that is often a difficult thing for a leader to do.

Our verse tells us that we should love discipline. Elsewhere in scripture it tells us that God disciplines those that he loves. We should love discipline because it proves that we are loved by our Father in heaven. When we are disciplined by the Father it is so that we can become better at whatever it is that we are being disciplined for. As leaders of our families, ministries, and churches we ought to desire to be the absolute best there is at whatever God has called us to do. To accomplish that we need to learn what we don't do perfectly and then be humble enough to change.

This verse goes on to say that if we don't love correction that we are stupid. Most people are offended if someone were to call them stupid. That is exactly what God is calling you if you reject and despise His attempts to make you into the person that he wants you to be. His will for our lives is perfect and His plans for our lives are good. To see His plans come to pass in our lives we must be changed into the person that He desires us to be. That is accomplished through discipline and correction. To hate that process is an attitude of stupidity.

Learning is a life-long process that draws us nearer and nearer to being the men and women of God that we were created to be. Learn to love the process of being changed; don't fight the work that God is doing in you. He is doing it for your own good and for the good of those that He called you to lead. Jesus, help me to be a straight "A" student.

MARCH 29

Read: Deuteronomy 11:1 – 12:32, Luke 8:22-39, Psalm 70:1-5, Proverbs 12:4

DEUTERONOMY 11:2

Listen! I am not talking now to your children, who have never experienced the discipline of the LORD your God or seen his greatness and awesome power.

M oses is laying out what the Israelites need to do when they cross over the Jordan River into the Promised Land. He is giving them instructions and letting them know what God is going to do on their behalf. Moses is telling them of all the great things that God is going to do. Then Moses makes this interesting statement in our verse for the day. His point is clear; they should know that everything that he is saying about God is true because they have seen the same things before. Besides Caleb, Joshua, and Moses the oldest people in the camp are sixty years old. Everyone that is from forty to sixty years old was alive when God brought the Israelites out of Egypt. Everyone less than forty years old was born during the wilderness wanderings.

These people that are between forty and sixty years of age are most likely the leaders of the community. Moses is reminding them that they have seen God do to the Egyptians what Moses is telling them that He is going to do the nations in the Promised Land. If God did something once and He says He is going to do it again we can absolutely trust Him that He will.

Anyone that has spiritual eyes to see what God is doing will see Him work powerfully in their lives or in the lives of those around them. Moses was telling the leaders of the community to remember these wonderful works of God and to tell their children so that they can believe as well. God is calling anyone that has seen God work in their life or someone else's to use that knowledge to encourage and exhort the others around them to believe God.

That belief is the source of the faith that is needed to see God work all around us. If we don't believe that God can work in our lives, we may not be able to see it when it happens. It is critical that we share what God is doing and has done in our lives so that others can have the same faith that we do that God is going to act and work in their lives. If we don't, then those people may not get to experience the amazing, power-filled life that God desires for them.

That can be a burden to think that someone else's life depends upon your actions, but it is not a burden, it is a privilege. God has chosen to use us to be His special vessel to share with others so that they can receive something very special from God. Instead of being a burden that we bear, this truth should give us tremendous boldness. We get to be a part of helping people experience God in a powerful and radical way. God has worked in your life; share that with others and watch how it affects their life. Jesus, give us good memories about the radical things that You have done in our lives and then give us the boldness to tell others.

MARCH 30

Read: Deuteronomy 13:1 – 15:23, Luke 8:40 – 9:6, Psalm 71:1-24, Proverbs 12:5-7

DEUTERONOMY 13:4

Serve only the LORD your God and fear him alone. Obey his commands, listen to his voice, and cling to him.

Moses in his farewell speech tells the Israelites not to get caught up in the worship of false gods. God knows that we can easily be distracted by the things of this world. And even the innocent things that are harmless, if not kept in their proper place, can draw us away from worshipping God the way that He wants for us.

Moses instructed the people that if anyone in the community of Israel was found to be actively drawing others away from God and to the false gods that they were to have no mercy upon them. They were to destroy them to make sure that their influence would not spread.

In our text for today we are given five things that will help us to keep our focus where it needs to be. First, we need to serve God alone. Jesus also taught about this. We cannot serve two masters. We have to choose to serve God.

Second, to keep our focus on God we must fear Him alone. Only God deserves our greatest respect and admiration. No other person or group should be held in the awe and respect in which we hold God.

Third, if you are not obeying God then you are at very high risk of being drawn away from Him. It is through obedience that all of the power, blessings, mercies, and grace are poured out from God into your life.

Fourth, God is speaking to us all the time through His Word, through prayer, through others, and even through nature itself. For us to keep our focus on God, we must learn to listen for when He is warning us and directing us away from trouble spots.

Fifth, God is our loving Father and He wants us to run to Him every time we need Him. The more that we cling to the Lord; the less likely we are to fall away from Him. Just like a small child staying close to their parents finds comfort and strength; we need to stay close to the source of our comfort and strength.

In our roles within ministries and churches, we are the models of these types of behaviors for those that have not experienced them. We need to show the people around us how to live like this. And then we need to teach them how to live that way. And then we need to teach them how to teach others how to live that way. Jesus taught twelve men and those twelve men taught others. Those twelve men changed the world through what Jesus taught them. That should be our model for ministry; learn to live it, learn to teach it, and then teach others to do the same. Jesus, help us to follow the model that you established for growing your church by first learning to live what you taught.

MARCH 31

Read: Deuteronomy 16:1 – 17:20, Luke 9:7-27, Psalm 72:1-20, Proverbs 12:8-9

DEUTERONOMY 17:1

Never sacrifice a sick or defective ox or sheep to the LORD your God, for he detests such gifts.

The Israelites had a very elaborate sacrificial system. The sacrifices to be made were rigidly inspected for quality; meaning they couldn't be anything other than excellent. Moses says this the other way in our verse for the day. Moses says that if the animals they sacrificed were sick or defective that God would view them as detestable. That is pretty strong language. It is not that God won't like it; he will be upset and reject it.

People in our culture really can't relate to things like this. The whole idea of a sacrificial system is a bit repulsive to us. The idea that we would need to kill an animal to atone for our sins and to please God is far from our Western sensibilities. The fact that Jesus came to make the final atonement for us makes the need for animal sacrifice unnecessary.

As always, that fact does not make this verse unimportant to us. There are no verses in the Bible that do not have a place in our lives. Paul told Timothy that ALL scripture is useful. The thing that is sometimes difficult is trying to understand how to relate a verse like today's to our lives.

The key in this verse is the word "gifts." God still calls us to give Him gifts. Many of the sacrifices that the Israelites made had nothing to do with sin. They had to do with celebrating and recognizing what God had done for them. God asked them to give a portion of what He gave them back to Him by giving it to the Levites. The people were also encouraged to give freewill offerings and offerings related to vows that they had made. The Israelites were also exhorted to take care of the widows and orphans with gifts. Jesus said that when we do that we are actually doing it to Him.

Since we are called to give gifts to God, the above verse does apply to our lives. God doesn't want us to give our junk as gifts to Him. It is disrespectful of God and it is detestable to Him. God expects our very best. God also doesn't want our leftovers; He wants and deserves our first-fruits. The Israelites were to bring the first of their crops and the first animals that were born to their flocks as gifts to God.

There is an obvious connection to tithing but that is not what this is talking about. Tithing is what you owe to God; gifts are what you want to give to God. There is a difference but the above verse applies to both. Too many Christians treat tithing like some sort of curse that is associated with their faith. They tithe when they have extra or if things are going well. God has promised that if you will give Him the "first" tenth that He will provide so that you can live on the remaining 90%. Gifts do not take the place of tithing. Gifts are given because you are thankful for what God has done in your life or they are a way for you to join God in some work that he is doing. God wants your best; not your least. Jesus, help us to give You the best of our time, talents, and treasures.

APRIL

APRIL 1

Read: Deuteronomy 18:1 – 20:20, Luke 9:28-50, Psalm 73:1-28, Proverbs 12:10

PSALM 73:3

For I envied the proud when I saw them prosper despite their wickedness.

The psalmist describes a very natural tendency for those that are seeking the Lord and trying to follow Jesus. It is natural to look around at the proud people around us, those that have no desire for God, and envy their success. It can be very frustrating to see them prosper even though they are arrogantly rebelling against God. We will comment in our spirits that it is not fair and we can become envious of their success.

There are a couple of reasons why we shouldn't do this. The first one is that we shouldn't be spending that much time admiring the things of the proud. If we are envying the success and prosperity of the proud, then we do not have our eyes on Jesus and we are likely to find ourselves in a dangerous place. You can't drive your car without keeping your eyes on the road. You can't live this Christian life without keeping your eyes on Jesus.

Second, we need to keep in mind that the things that the proud have in this life is all that they are going to get. None of it will follow them into eternity. They may enjoy the success and prosperity in this life but as Christians we will enjoy Christ for all of eternity. Nothing on this earth can compare to that.

Our problem as finite humans is that we don't really grasp that concept very well. Eternity is vague and uncertain in our little minds. What we can see, touch, and feel is more real to us and so it draws our attention very easily. We can't really understand the joy and satisfaction that we will experience in the presence of Christ. If we could we would never consider envying the things of proud people; those things would more likely disgust us.

Families, ministries, and churches are not immune to this ailment. We can regularly look around at other groups that are having great success and envy the work that they are doing and the success they are having. Some of those groups are doing what they do for all the wrong reasons. They are proud and arrogant and are far from God and His plan for the world. Don't envy them; pray for them.

God called you to do a certain thing. He is not going to compare you to that "successful" ministry down the street; He is going to compare you to the mission that He gave you to accomplish. Your success will be measured by God and your faithfulness to follow Christ will be the ruler that measures your success. Don't envy someone just because they have the outward appearance of success; it takes your eyes off Jesus and off the goal that He set before you. Jesus, help us to fix our eyes on You and the things that You have set before us.

APRIL 2

Read: Deuteronomy 21:1 – 22:30, Luke 9:51 – 10:12, Psalm 74:1-23, Proverbs 12:11

DEUTERONOMY 22:4

"If you see your neighbor's ox or donkey lying on the road, do not look the other way. Go and help your neighbor get it to its feet!

In our reading today, Moses lays out various laws that the Israelites are to follow as they live in the Promised Land. These laws cover all aspects of their lives and were meant to teach them about who God is and how they were to relate to Him and each other. Unfortunately, the Israelites in many cases took these laws and made them into something they were not intended to be. They began to develop systems for following the letter of the Law while ignoring the heart of God found within the Law.

In our verse for today, we find a very simple instruction. If an Israelite was walking along the road and saw an ox or a donkey, he was to help get the animal back on its feet. This is a very practical instruction. It can be a two person job getting one of these animals up on its feet and it is usually bad for one of these animals to be down for too long. Basically, God wanted the Israelites to help each other. This would be another way that they would be different from the nations around them. Some Israelites then started to debate what it meant to be a neighbor. They did that to determine who they would or would not help. This allowed them to justify walking past someone that needed help without helping and without feeling they had violated the Law. Jesus condemned this practice and rebuked those that felt justified by living that way.

God doesn't want us to be legalistic, unloving, uncaring, and unhelpful people. God doesn't want us to find ways to get around His commands. God wants us to find ways to fulfill His commands. God wants us to find ways to love and help people; not look for ways to avoid loving and helping people.

Being in ministry or starting a church, we usually understand. It is our desire to reach out to help and love people. That is why we exist; to help people. First and foremost, we want to help them begin and grow in their relationship with Jesus Christ. And secondarily, we want to meet their physical, emotional, and spiritual needs.

It is my belief that God would call us to be neighbors to other ministries and churches. Too often we view these ministries and churches as the competition and avoid contact and withhold help from them. This, I believe, is contrary to scripture. There are some religious organizations that we should avoid because they are in fact enemies of God. Moses, in his instructions to the Israelites, told them what nations to avoid and why.

But if our only reason for not helping another ministry or church is because we are afraid that it will cost us something, then we are in disobedience to God's Word and we don't trust God enough. The Apostle Paul described the Church as a body with many members "working together." Too many have forgotten the "working together" part and the body is suffering as a result. Jesus, help us to see other ministries and churches as neighbors and not as enemies, and give us Your heart to reach out and help them.

APRIL 3
Read: Deuteronomy 23:1 – 25:19, Luke 10:13-37, Psalm 75:1-10, Proverbs 12:12-14

DEUTERONOMY 24:5
A newly married man must not be drafted into the army or given any other special responsibilities. He must be free to be at home for one year, bring happiness to the wife he has married.

The book of Deuteronomy is a review of the instructions that God gave to Moses to give to the nation of Israel. These instructions covered all areas of life, including their relationships. Many of those instructions were only relevant to a culture that existed 3,000 years ago, but some are just as relevant today as they were then. Such is the case for our verse today.

It is often amazing to discover how much of our language and culture has been impacted by the Bible without our realizing it. Here in a text written 3,400 years ago we see the concept of "newlyweds." A newlywed is a person that has been married for less than a year. Most people that use that term have no idea it came from the Bible.

Moses instructs the Israelites not to draft any newlywed men into the army and to refrain from giving them any special responsibilities. Instead the newlywed men are to focus their attention on "bringing happiness" to their wife.

There is a saying that I adopted some years ago, "Happy wife, happy life!" I have found in my own life, that when my wife is happy, I am happy. There is direct connection between her happiness and my own. I have also discovered that bringing happiness to my wife is not a natural thing. We have been married since 1981 and I am still learning what it means to bring happiness to her.

God's wisdom in this instruction is beyond question. In my own experience, if a man doesn't take the time to do this at the beginning of his marriage, it becomes increasingly difficult as the years pass. Life has a way of filling up our time and making it virtually impossible to invest this kind of time to learning how to bring happiness to a wife.

Whether you are leading a family, ministry, or church, take note of this concept. Give the newlyweds a great gift by not filling their lives with "special responsibilities." Give them time to better understand the meaning of "one flesh." Those other responsibilities will be taken care of by others or can wait. Trust God's wisdom in this and give the newlyweds the time they need to become happy in each other.

Our verse also says that they shouldn't be drafted into the army. It is not stated implicitly but I believe this speaks of God's promise to protect the nation or organization that follows this instruction. Sometimes we think we need every able-bodied man in the battle if we are going to win. Thinking like that assumes that you are the one that will determine the outcome of the battle. You aren't, God is. Leave the battle in His hands and follow His instructions. Jesus, help us to be bringers of happiness.

APRIL 4

Read: Deuteronomy 26:1 – 27:26, Luke 10:38 – 11:13, Psalm 76:1-12, Proverbs 12:15-17

DEUTERONOMY 26:19

And if you do, he will make you greater than any other nation. Then you will receive praise, honor, and renown. You will be a nation that is holy to the LORD your God, just as he promised."

In these next few chapters of Deuteronomy Moses explains to the nation of Israel that God expects them to obey His commands. This is not a new concept that Moses is describing. But starting here Moses explains that there are benefits and consequences to the response of the Israelites. Within these chapters God explains to the people that there are great blessings to be experienced through obedience and that there are terrible curses resulting from disobedience. That is very graphically described in Deuteronomy chapter 28.

For some reason people have a hard time believing that God would curse them. Their view of God is that He will only bless and would never curse someone. There is no basis for that viewpoint in Scripture. God's blessings are a result of our obedience and God's curses are a result of our disobedience. This can become complicated because we can also experience the blessings or curses of someone else's obedience or disobedience. A great example of this is the people that Moses is talking to in this text. These are the children of the people that refused to obey God and enter the Promised Land at Kadesh-Barnea. As a result of that disobedience their children were forced to wander around in the wilderness for forty years until all of their parents had died.

But even though the children were experiencing the curse that was brought on by their parents, God used this time to teach them to obey His commands more readily. During this time God caused them to become a great nation that was feared and respected by every other nation around them.

Our role as leaders of families, ministries, or churches is to guide people through their wilderness times. Everyone, including those in leadership will experience those times; either self-inflicted as a result of sin and disobedience or as a result of someone else's disobedience. We need to show them the path that God has laid out for them through the wilderness time. We need to help them to see their sin and disobedience so that their wilderness time can be as short as possible. And we need to help them to see the lesson or lessons that God is trying to teach them through this time.

And if we will be faithful to do those things God will bring praise, honor, and renown to us. This is not the reason why we do these things; it is one of the fruits that you look for so that you know that you are doing it the way that God wants you to. God's promises are faithful; we can trust them no matter what. If our lives are marked by blessings than we can feel confident that we are being obedient. If our lives are marked by curses; than we need to examine our lives for disobedience in our lives or the lives of those around us. Jesus, help us to obey your commands not just for the blessings but because we love You.

APRIL 5

Read: Deuteronomy 28:1-68, Luke 11:14-36, Psalm 77:1-20, Proverbs 12:18

LUKE 11:15

But some said, "No wonder he can cast out demons. He gets his power from Satan, the prince of demons!"

Jesus has just cast out a demon that was preventing this man from speaking. Some people in the crowd attributed this miracle to Satan's power. They suggested that Jesus was able to do this amazing miracle because the prince of demons had given Jesus this power. We can infer by the reading a little later that it was the religious leaders that had made this accusation against the source of Jesus' miraculous power.

It sometimes amazes me the things that the religious leaders did to discredit and minimize the amazing works that Jesus was performing by the power of God. As we read through the New Testament we might think that we might have done things differently but I am not so sure that is true. If it were to have come during our time rather than two thousand years ago I am certain that people would have been saying the same kinds of things.

And it would have been the spiritual leadership leading the way to discredit His mighty works.

Why did they do that? Why would it happen again today? It's pretty simple; pride! The religious leaders believed that they were the spiritual reservoir of all human holiness and that great works of God would come through them. This Galilean carpenter did not fit into their view of the Messiah. Their pride would not let them see the truth.

The world is not that different than it was two thousand years ago, people still think that they are the spiritual banks of their time. They for some reason believe that they are the vessel that God will use to do great things and that anyone else that is doing anything great for God must actually be doing it in their flesh or as a result of the work of Satan.

As leaders of God's people we need to understand that we are just simply clay pots that He uses to contain and distribute His power. We have no control or responsibility for that power. Too often we think that just because God has used us for something that we are suddenly something that we are not; our pride begins to swell.

Just because God uses us in some small way or even in some great way to work a miracle or do some great work doesn't change our relative importance to God. In fact it ought to humble us every time that He uses us because the Bible teaches that God uses the foolish things of the world. If God is using you, it must mean that you are one of those foolish things. I know that every time I think of that it reminds me just how small and insignificant I truly am. But then it also makes me very thankful because the Almighty God used someone as foolish as me to do something amazing for Him. The fact that God would use me at all is a miracle. Never forget that you are no more than a clay pot being used by God. Don't let pride cause cracks in your pot that will prevent you from being a useful pot. Jesus, help us to be useful to You.

DEUTERONOMY 30:8

Then you will again obey the LORD and keep all the commands I am giving you today.

In the reading for today, Moses prophesies that the people of Israel are going to be unfaithful to God and that He is going to drive them from the land of Canaan that He is just about to give them. Moses has just gotten through explaining to the people all the blessings that they will receive if they are obedient to God and the curses they will receive if they are disobedient. God told them very plainly what was going to happen in the future and then allowed them to choose the option that they wanted; His blessings or His curses.

God has not changed! He still allows us to choose whether or not we will receive His blessings or curses. People don't like to look at God that way; that He would send a curse to you. Their view of God is that He should always bless and never curse. What they fail to understand is that His love for us is so great that He must curse us when we are being disobedient. He does that because when we are disobedient or in sin (which is disobedience) it separates us from Him. We were created to be in intimate personal fellowship with Him. God will do anything to eliminate anything that separates us from Him; including sending curses.

In our verse for the day God tells the reason why He will allow all the bad to happen to Israel that he ultimately does. It is because they will turn away from Him and He wants them to turn back. By turning back to Him and obeying His voice and His commandments, they will again be in that place where God can be in fellowship with them and bless them.

God does not want to curse you or anyone else. To be cursed by God, you must make a decision to be cursed by God. The Bible teaches that God waits to bless us, not curse us. His desire is that we would be in a place where He can pour out blessings so great that we can't contain them. All we have to do is obey His voice and His commands. Our problem is that our sinful flesh would much rather do things our own way even if it means taking ourselves out of the blessings of God and placing us in the curses of God.

God cares so much for you that He will do anything to cause you to be in a place where you can receive all that He desires to give you. He will even allow great pain and suffering in your life if that is what it is going to take to get you to turn back to Him and obey His voice and His commands. The choice is yours! It is an absolutely incredible fact that God lets us choose whether or not He will bless us. I know for myself and for my family and for my church that I am going to choose to obey God as well as I am able. I am going to be looking for signs that I am out of God's blessing and then run back to Him as quickly as I can. What life will you choose? Jesus, help us to choose well.

APRIL 7

Read: Deuteronomy 31:1 – 32:27, Luke 12:8-34, Psalm 78:32-55, Proverbs 12:21-23

DEUTERONOMY 32:15

But Israel soon became fat and unruly; the people grew heavy, plump, and stuffed! Then they abandoned the God who had made them; they made light of the Rock of their salvation.

When we think of Moses, most us of do not think of him as a song-writer. Here in our reading for today we have a song that he wrote under the inspiration of the Holy Spirit. Music has a tremendous impact on people; either for the good or for the bad. Songs can be used to draw people from God and they can be used to curse God and draw people into sin.

Songs and music can be used in all sorts of ways. We use songs often to teach things to people; especially children. We use music and songs to teach children their alphabet and in Sunday School we teach them about Jesus through song. We also use songs and hymns to remember the amazing things that God has done for us. This song written by Moses was intended to remind and warn the children of Israel. God wanted the people to remember some things and one of the tools that he gave them to do that was this song.

This song was intended to remind the Hebrews about their Rock of salvation and to warn them not to turn away from Him. It also speaks to the future and tells the Israelites about what is going to happen to them in the future. Moses knows that the children of Israel are going to fall away from worshipping the One and Only True God and turn to worthless idols. Moses even describes how it is going to happen. The Israelites are going to be blessed by God because that is what He wants to do with all of His people. That blessing is going to cause them to get very comfortable in their lives. God will protect them from their enemies and they will rest from conflict. The more God blesses them the more comfortable they get. Eventually they will begin to get fat and grow lazy. And then they will begin to forget the things that God has done for them and they will begin to turn away from God.

It is amazing that while things are tough how close we stay to God. But almost as soon as things start going well that we tend to lose focus on who He is and what He has done for us. Prosperity can be a great challenge; possibly the greatest challenge that we face as Christians. The more prosperous and successful that we become; the more likely we are to forget that it is God that has provided all that we have.

Music and songs can be a great way for us to keep our focus on God where it belongs. Keep a song in your heart; especially a song that reminds you about all that the Lord has done for you. Sing about the beauty, glory, grace, mercy, and blessings of God. Let them remind you of all that He has done for you. Look in the spiritual mirror. Are you getting fat from the blessings of God? Keep your eyes on the Lord and let Him help you to stay spiritually fit and strong. Jesus, teach us to do our spiritual exercises.

APRIL 8

Read: Deuteronomy 32:28-52, Luke 12:35-59, Psalm 78:56-64, Proverbs 12:24

LUKE 12:38

He may come in the middle of the night or just before dawn. But whenever he comes, there will be special favor for his servants who are ready!

Jesus is speaking to His disciples about what is to be expected of them after He is gone. And here in out text for today Jesus brings out the idea of being ready; being prepared for His return. He has already told them that He is leaving. He has told them that He is going to die and that He will be raised from the dead on the third day. He has even said that He is going to return to His Father in heaven who sent Him. It is obvious through much of our reading of the gospels that His disciples didn't really understand what He was telling them much of the time. They all figured it out as the things that Jesus said came to pass just as He said.

The idea of us getting ready for Jesus' return is one that man has wrestled with since He left. The disciples stood watching the sky immediately after Jesus left. Two angels came and asked them what they were doing. The inference is that being prepared for Jesus' return is not about getting your bags packed and standing at the train station to heaven. That is why Jesus used the example of the faithful servant. We are to serve faithfully tending to the Master's household while we are watching for His return.

This was one of the reasons that Jesus was so harsh with the Pharisees and religious leaders. It was their responsibility to tend the Master's house and make sure that everybody was ready and watching for His return. Not only were they not doing that but they would not open the door when the Master of the house, Jesus, came and knocked.

As leaders in families, ministries, or churches we have the responsibility of making sure that the Master's house is being properly attended to and that all those that we are responsible for are doing what is expected of them and help them to prepare for the Master's return. This means that we do not get too attached to the things of this world. Our minds and thoughts ought to be on heavenly things while we tend to the physical things for which God has made us responsible.

There is a warning in our reading against not being prepared. We can't allow ourselves, or anyone that we are responsible for, to believe that the Lord is not going to be here for a long time. His arrival will be completely unexpected. Having the Lord arrive while we are unprepared will result in great punishment. You have a responsibility to the Lord and to those that have been entrusted to you to keep them ready for His imminent return. That means that we are helping them to live their lives as though Jesus could return before you finish reading this devotional. It also means that we live our lives with the understanding that people have been waiting for two thousand years for the imminent return of Jesus Christ. He might not return in our lifetimes. But if He does, will

He find you and those that you care for prepared? Jesus, help us to keep our eyes on the heavens and our hands on the plow as we wait for your imminent return.

APRIL 9

Read: Deuteronomy 33:1-29, Luke 13:1-21, Psalm 78:65-72, Proverbs 12:25

DEUTERONOMY 33:11

Bless the Levites, O LORD, and accept all their work. Crush the loins of their enemies; strike down their foes so they never rise again.

Moses is praying a blessing over the people of Israel right before he dies. He gives a blessing to each of the tribes. It is fascinating to study the many times that the patriarchs blessed people. Often the blessings were prophetic; telling what was going to happen in the future of the person or tribe that was being blessed. In our verse for the day, Moses is blessing the Levites. It might be interesting to spend a little time thinking about Moses' request concerning the enemies of Levi but it was the reference to work that caught my attention.

The Levites were a special people among the Chosen people. They had the responsibility to assist Aaron and his sons in the work of the priesthood. They alone were to do the work in and around the tabernacle and ultimately in the temple that Solomon would build. No one else was allowed to do this work.

How does this relate to the modern church? The closest comparison we might have to Levites in the modern church is the volunteers that serve in our churches and ministries. The volunteers serve God by assisting the pastors and ministry leaders in the completion of their religious responsibilities.

There is a lesson in this verse for the ministry leaders and pastors; pray for God to bless your volunteers. We should also be praying for God to crush their enemies so that they cannot rise again to hinder the work of God in which they are involved. I believe that if more pastors were praying for their volunteers, they would have more volunteers.

The main thing that caught my attention was that Moses asked God to accept their work. We might think that because we are working for God that He has to accept our work but that is not the case. When we think of giving to God we usually think of money but that is not the only thing that we have that we can and should give to Him. In addition to our treasures, we also have our time and our talents. When we are working for God we are often using both time and talents. These then become an offering to the LORD.

In many places in the Bible we are taught that there is more to giving to God than simply the giving part. God cares about the condition of the heart of the giver. Gifts and offerings that are given out of the wrong heart are not acceptable to God. Work done for the LORD for the wrong reasons is not acceptable to Him. If we are doing things for the LORD because we think we have to or because we believe that we are going to get something out of it is not acceptable to God. The Lord wants us to do work for Him because we love Him and because we know that it will please Him. He desires that we do the things that we do because it proves our love for our God. That kind of work, however small it might seem, is very pleasing to the LORD. Jesus, teach to be pleasing to You in all the works that we do for You.

APRIL 10

Read: Deuteronomy 34:1 – Joshua 2:24, Luke 13:22 – 14:6, Psalm 79:1-13, Proverbs 12:26

PSALM 79:13

Then we your people, the sheep of your pasture, will thank you forever and ever, praising your greatness from generation to generation.

In this psalm Asaph is calling out to God and asking him to save them from the enemies that are coming against the nation of Israel. He is crying out and asking God to rescue them. This psalm ends with our verse for the day telling us what should be the natural response after God has rescued us from our enemies; thankfulness and praise.

Our verse begins by likening God's people to sheep. We see this picture being painted throughout the Bible; God's people are like sheep and God is the owner of the flock. Jesus described himself as the Good Shepherd and we see many references throughout the Bible that the leaders of God's people as shepherds of the flock of God.

Asaph suggests that if God rescues His people that they will thank Him forever and praise His name throughout the generations. Sadly, most people are like sheep in that they do not have very good memories. We might thank God for the times that He rescues us and we might even praise His name for a while but it doesn't take long before we have forgotten the amazing things that He has done.

A few years ago I started keeping a journal. I am trying to make it a habit of going back in that journal and reading it. It amazes me the things that I have not thought about that God has done in my life. It concerns that if it weren't for that journal that I might completely forget some tremendous thing that God has done in my life.

As you read through the Bible you will often come across an accounting of some of the amazing things that God has done for the nation of Israel. It was a way of reminding themselves and others about the wonderful things that God did for them. God would have us do something very similar to that; He wants us to remember what He has done for us so that we can remember to thank Him and to praise His holy name.

We also need to find ways to remind ourselves and others of the amazing things that God has done in our lives. This is part of the way that other people are going to come to know Jesus. As you share with others through thanksgiving and praise they come to know the Jesus that has performed these mighty works in your life. We don't need to preach at people for them to be saved; we need to show them Jesus. That happens as they watch our lives change and they see the things that He is doing. The only way that they will see these things is if we show them. Celebrate the incredible things that God is doing. They might not be excited about it as you are but that doesn't matter; God wants us to thank Him and praise Him. As we do that, the world will see how they also can experience God's grace and mercy in their own lives. Jesus, remind us to remember what You have done in our lives so that we might thank You and praise Your name.

LUKE 14:28

"But don't begin until you count the cost. For who would begin construction of a building without first getting estimates and then checking to see if there is enough money to pay the bills?"

Great multitudes of people are following Jesus. They are there for count-less reasons. Some are there because He feeds them. Some are there because He has healed them of sickness, disease, or infirmities. Some may be there because He cast out demons from them. I am certain many are there because they want to see what Jesus was going to do next. Jesus, knowing that, turns and challenges them to think about what they are doing.

It might seem kind of odd that Jesus would challenge these people that were following Him in this way. But in doing so Jesus teaches us a valu-able lesson in regards to our relationship with Him. There are two kinds of Christians; believers and disciples. If you believe and accept Jesus and what he did for you, you are a believer, but that doesn't make you a disciple. Every disciple is a believer but not every believer is a disciple.

Jesus described the criteria for a disciple in the previous verse; love Jesus more than yourself or others, and carry your own cross. This speaks of a total surrender of your life to the kingship of Jesus. Most believers never achieve this level of surrender; they are satisfied with just being saved, just being believers. It is my belief that the abundant life that Jesus promised in John 10:10 can only be experienced by a disciple. All believers must at some point decide if they will live out their lives as believers or if they will give up their lives to become disciples.

That is precisely what Jesus is telling the multitudes to do in today's reading. He is telling them to think about what they are doing and then decide if that is really what they want to do with their lives. This is one of the amazing things about God; He gave us our lives and then He lets us decide how we are going to live them. It has been said: "Life is a gift from God, what you do with it is your gift back to Him."

It is a big decision to give your life fully to Jesus and He wants you to think about it fully before you make that decision; He wants you to "count the cost." He goes on to use a construction analogy to help us to understand what He is saying. Before you build a house you need to determine how much it is going to cost and then make sure that you have enough money. Before you start building, you should know you can afford to finish. The same is true with being a disciple. Before you make this decision, you need to make certain that you are willing to pay the price. The price is your whole life. If you are not willing to give every part of your life to Jesus then you are not ready to be His disciple. You don't need to fully understand every aspect of surrendering your life to Christ to be a disciple; you just need to be decided to do it. Jesus, help me to give up what I can't hold without you; my life.

APRIL 12

Read: Joshua 5:1 – 7:15, Luke 15:1-32, Psalm 81:1-16, Proverbs 13:1

PSALM 81:12

So I let them follow their blind and stubborn way, living according to their own desires.

God is an awesome God. He has done exceedingly beyond all that we could hope or think. God has delivered us from the bondage of sin through His Son Jesus and made a way for us to enter into heaven. Every breath that we take and every beat of our heart is a gift from our Heavenly Father. Everything that we have and are comes down from Him. Even our skills and abilities were given to us by the God Almighty. He also guards and protects us from our enemies. If it weren't for God's mighty hand in our lives many of us would have been destroyed long ago. When we sense the presence of the enemy we just need to run to our strong tower Jesus for protection and strength.

All God asks in return for everything that He has done for us is that we worship and obey. And His desire is that we worship and obey out of a sense of thanksgiving and love rather than duty and obligation. And the odd thing is that God does not make us worship and obey which He could do. Instead, He invites us to fellowship with Him through our worship and obedience. But we have the choice to enter into that fellowship or not.

And if we choose not to worship and obey, God will respect that decision. But He also wants us to understand the consequences of choosing our own way. In our verse today we see one of the many verses that talks about God allowing us to follow our own path. And we see here how our way differs from God's way.

Our way is blind! Only God can see the future. We are blind to it. At best the future is a vague guess about what might happen. By walking our own way, we have decided that we would rather wander around like a blind man without a guide than allow God, who can see all time just like a photograph to direct our paths. Our way is stubborn! To be stubborn means that you will not turn from your path even when you know it is wrong. Stubbornness is rooted in pride and will cause people to make the most foolish decisions rather than changing their path. Our way is driven by our desires! When we live our way, it is our desires that are driving and motivating our actions. And often we will allow desires that are harmful to us to be the driving force of our lives. God's pathway is never harmful to us. God has a plan for our lives that is good and will prosper us and brings with it a future and a hope.

God's way is the right way! Through worship and obedience, we are brought into a sweet fellowship with God that brings protection, provision, and guiding. Because of our relationship with Jesus, we have a strong tower for refuge and the hand of Almighty God to provide for us. Jesus, remind us to run to you and to come to you in worship and obedience out of a heart filled with thanksgiving and love.

APRIL 13
Read: Joshua 7:16 – 9:2, Luke 16:1-18, Psalm 82:1-8, Proverbs 13:2-3

JOSHUA 8:2
You will destroy them as you destroyed Jericho and its king. But this time you may keep the captured goods and the cattle for yourselves. Set an ambush behind the city.

The background for this verse is fascinating and important. Joshua and the nation of Israel have been in the Promised Land for about two weeks. They defeated the fortress city of Jericho in a spectacular way. The Lord had instructed them to utterly destroy the city and everyone and everything in it. Only the precious metals were to be spared and those were to be put into the Lord's treasury. For you Bible students this was a form of the first fruits of the Promised Land.

Israel's victory at Jericho went to their heads and they turned their gaze upon the much smaller city of Ai and attacked it. Israel was soundly defeated by a much weaker force. Upon seeking the Lord about the defeat they discovered that Achan had disobeyed God and had kept some of the spoils from Jericho for himself. Once that was dealt with, God told the Israelites to go back to Ai and destroy it.

God changed the rules when He sent them to Ai; He told them they could keep all the captured goods for themselves this time. This then became the pattern for most of the rest of the conquest of the Promised Land. The second time they attacked Ai, they were victorious and kept the captured goods for themselves. God had a plan to bless them abundantly, but they had to follow God's plan to receive God's blessings and abundance.

Many are like Achan, they see the riches of the world and don't want to wait for God's blessings. Because he wouldn't wait for God, Achan lost everything, including his life. For us to experience the fullness of God's blessings we must do what He tells us to do. Patient obedience always leads to blessing and disobedience always leads to destruction.

There are times when it doesn't make sense from a worldly perspective to give God that which He is asking. From a human perspective it would make more sense to take care of ourselves. Our problem is that we can't see clearly how God's plan is going to bless us. That's where faith comes in; we simply need to trust God and His Word to us.

Achan's lack of faith and impatience destroyed him and his family. Many Christians are also suffering from the same spiritual disease that Achan had. By grasping at a blessing today, they are sacrificing even greater blessings in the future and potentially heading toward destruction.

Give God what He is asking for and wait for His blessings in your life. Trust God at His word even when it makes no sense to you. God is not a liar; He promised to bless us if we would just obey His Word without hesitation or question. Keep your eyes on the Lord and not on what you want or what you don't have. Jesus, teach us to trust You.

APRIL 14

Read: Joshua 9:3 – 10:43, Luke 16:19 – 17:10, Psalm 83:1-18, Proverbs 13:4

PSALM 83:16

Utterly disgrace them until they submit to your name, O Lord.

As you read this psalm it sounds pretty harsh. Asaph wants God to judge and destroy the nations that are enemies of God and Israel. All of the nations and leaders that are named in this psalm are all ones that were destroyed by the nation of Israel at some time. And Asaph wants all the rest taken care of. At least that is what it looks like until you get down to the last few verses.

It is in the last few verses that we find that what Asaph is wanting God to do is to push these enemies into a place where all they can see is who God is. Asaph wants these nations to know the God that they are fighting against. That may not change their heart but at least they will know the truth.

All around us are enemies that seek to destroy us and take away the things that God gave to us. And this can make us angry and bitter toward the world. And it might cause us to pray as Asaph did that our enemies would be destroyed. This is what the people of the Old Testament thought was the right way to deal with the enemies of God. But then Jesus came and taught a new way to deal with our enemies. Jesus taught that we are to love our enemies. And through our love for them they will see the love of God toward them. The problem is that the gospel of love fights against our nature. Our nature wants to lash out at anyone or anything that we view as an enemy. What we need to keep in mind is that the only enemy that God wants us to destroy is sin. But we have to love the sinner while fighting against the sin.

As leaders in families, ministries, and churches this is one of our great challenges. As long as there are people in our families, ministries, and churches there will also be sin. It is our responsibility to battle against that sin while at the same time building up the sinner in love. This battle will continue until the Lord comes back for His church.

But we need to start in our own hearts. We shouldn't be telling others to love their enemies if we do not love our enemies. It will be difficult for us to teach others the gospel of love if we are not practicing this gospel in our own lives. It is a difficult thing to do to battle sin and love the sinner. But by the grace of God and through the power of His Holy Spirit we can do it.

As long as we are in this world we will live with enemies all around us. God can make it so that you can live at peace with those enemies that surround you. But for that to happen we must first deal with the enemies within us; the enemies of sin. As we surrender more of our lives to God, He will keep our enemies at bay. Jesus, help us to love the sinner while hating the sin.

APRIL 15

Read: Joshua 11:1 – 12:24, Luke 17:11-37, Psalm 84:1-12, Proverbs 13:5-6

JOSHUA 11:15

As the LORD commanded Moses his servant, so did Moses command Joshua, and so did Joshua; he left nothing undone of all that the LORD commanded Moses.

Joshua was one of the most successful leaders that Israel ever had. And in this verse we see the reason why. Joshua did what he was told! He had spent a large chunk of forty years under the tutoring of Moses. Joshua was there as many of the commands that he was to obey were given to Moses by God.

Joshua was a great leader. Few leaders have accomplished similar things in their lives. And his success can be directly linked to his obedience. Whatever he was commanded to do, he did. Even when he didn't understand the instructions, he did it anyway. Joshua's obedience was linked to his faith. Joshua believed God and so he obeyed God. So strong was his faith that he could ask God to make the sun stand still so he could destroy God's enemies and God did it. Joshua was a man of faithful obedience. And that faithful obedience allowed God to win great victories through Joshua.

God is always looking for someone that He can show Himself strong through. He is looking for men and women that have the faithful obedience of Joshua so that He can win great victories through them. He is looking for ministries and churches that will faithfully obey His calling and commands. And when He finds those faithful ones that will obey, there is no limit to the things that he will accomplish through them.

This world is in desperate need of people like Joshua. This world needs people that, in faith, will ask God for the impossible so that they can fulfill His will. No one had ever heard of God stopping the sun from setting. And yet Joshua asked for it because it was the only way he was going to be able to complete the task that God had given him. We need to have that same faith to ask God to do something that has never been done before so that we can accomplish His works.

This world needs leaders like Joshua that obey God and His commands without hesitation and without question. We need to be leaders that don't ask God for an explanation or even a confirmation. Just simply obey! If we will just believe and obey there is no limit to the things that God can accomplish through us. Joshua believed because he was there as God gave all the commands to Moses. God is no further away from us than He was from Joshua. Every time you read God's Word know, believe, and act as though every word is true; because it is true. And then, ask God for the impossible to complete the work He has given you.

God uses ordinary people, ministries, and churches to do extraordinary things. In fact, the more ordinary you are, the more God wants to use you because he will receive more glory when extraordinary things are done. Jesus, help us ordinary people be used by an extraordinary God by building in each us Joshua-sized faith and obedience.

APRIL 16
Read: Joshua 13:1 – 14:15, Luke 18:1-17, Psalm 85:1-13, Proverbs 7-8

LUKE 18:11

The proud Pharisee stood by himself and prayed this prayer: "I thank you, God, that I am not a sinner like everyone else, especially like that tax collector over there! For I never cheat, I don't sin, I don't commit adultery..."

Jesus told this story. It was directed at people that were self-confident in their own righteousness. Jesus challenges them with this story to take a closer look at their hearts and attitudes. In this story, the Pharisee has been doing everything he could to follow the Law of Moses. He has obeyed the commandments and tithed and fasted. In his heart this convinced him that he was no longer a sinner. This Pharisee is very similar to Nicodemus whom Jesus discussed this very same matter with in John 3.

This Pharisee had allowed his "righteous" deeds to create within him a sense of pride regarding his place in the Kingdom of God. The problem is that his righteousness was in fact the source of his greatest sin; pride. He didn't really need God.

The tax collector knew that he was a sinner and that his sins separated him from God. This created in his heart a great sense of his need for God's mercy in his life. He knew that if it weren't for God's mercy that he would be lost and eternally separated from God. Unlike the Pharisee, this tax collector knew in the deepest parts of his heart that he needed God and that he was lost without Him.

Jesus said that it was the despised tax collector that went away from that time being justified by God. Which do you think God would compare you to; the tax collector or the Pharisee? As men and women that seek to be pleasing to God, we can fall into the same trap that the Pharisee did, thinking that we are somehow better or more righteous than those that are around us.

God wants all of His people to behave like the tax collector. He wants us to be broken and contrite over the sin in our lives. He doesn't want us to be proud about the righteousness of our lives. Paul says that our righteousness is like filthy rags to the perfectly righteous and holy God. No matter how "righteous" we become we will still have sin in our lives. It is God's desire that these sins cause us deep pain and drive us to seek God's help to eliminate it. The moment we start looking at our righteousness as anything other than the work of God in our lives we are on a slippery path that may lead to God having to take us to the woodshed.

The Pharisee was doing the things that he thought made him righteous but didn't see the sin in his life that was separating him from God. The tax collector saw his sin and it broke his heart causing him to cry out to a loving God that wants to help him change. Let us not get so caught up in the things that we are doing for God that we forget to allow the Holy Spirit the chance to show us the sin in our lives and the condition of our hearts. Jesus, help us to feel the pain that our sin causes you.

APRIL 17

Read: Joshua 16:1 – 18:28, Luke 18:18-43, Psalm 86:1-17, Proverbs 13:9-10

JOSHUA 15:63

But the tribe of Judah could not drive out the Jebusites, who lived in the city of Jerusalem, so the Jebusites live there among the people of Judah to this day.

This is a recurrent theme with the nation of Israel. God promised the land of Canaan to Abram and his descendants. God then told Joshua that He would drive out all the inhabitants of the land from before them. Even with those promises we see the nation of Israel failing to drive out the inhabitants and failing to take the whole land.

There was nothing special about the Jebusites that prevented the tribe of Judah from driving them out of Jerusalem. They were not some great nation that was too powerful for the tribe of Judah to defeat. So why is it that the tribe of Judah could not drive out the Jebusites? Every other time that they had faced an enemy they had been greatly victorious. What has changed?

Each of the tribes is receiving its inheritance and going and taking possession of the land that was given to them. The greatest change that has taken place is leadership. Up until this point, Joshua has led the nation of Israel. Each tribe also has a leader that took Joshua's orders and carried them out through their tribe. Now each tribe is leading itself.

Any time there is a change in leadership there is usually some amount of chaos that comes with it. The preparation by the previous leader will determine how great that chaos might be. That doesn't really explain what is going on here; most of these leaders have been with Joshua for most of their adult lives. They have watched him very closely for the seven years of the conquest; they really have no good excuse.

The problem is not in the change of leadership but in who the leader is depending upon. Joshua has led the nation of Israel from one victory to the next. Joshua was a great example of a leader that depended upon the Lord to determine his steps. Every time the Israelites did what the Lord told them to do they were successful. Joshua had an intimate fellowship with God that allowed him to be victorious everywhere that he went.

The leaders of Judah have not developed this same level of intimacy with God. They were not able to hear from God the way that Joshua was and so they were not successful like Joshua was. Caleb is another leader that had this close fellowship with God and was successful at driving out the people that were living in the land that was allotted to him.

Success and victory can only come through a finely developed relationship with Jesus Christ. There are likely Jebusites that God has called you to drive out of the land of your life. You will not be able to do it completely until you have surrendered your whole life to God and allow Him to direct your path. Jesus, lead us to victory.

APRIL 18

Read: Joshua 16:1 – 18:28, Luke 19:1-27, Psalm 87:1-7, Proverbs 13:11

JOSHUA 18:3

Then Joshua asked them, "How long are you going to wait before taking possession of the remaining land the LORD, the God of your ancestors, has given to you?"

Seven of the tribes still have not taken possession of the land that had been promised to them. Joshua challenges them in our verse and asks them why they are still waiting around and not taking the gift that was given to them. God had promised them the entire land of Canaan and had promised to drive out all of the nations from before them. For the last seven years they have been marching through the land and defeating one enemy after another.

They have defeated all of the major enemies in the land and all that remains is that they go and take possession of the land that has been allotted to each individual tribe. It is difficult to say why they didn't do that. They had been fighting for seven years and so they might have been tired. It is hard to imagine a great leader like Joshua challenging them like that if that was the case.

It is more likely that they were just being lazy. They had conquered large chunks of the land of Canaan and they may have been satisfied living in the land of someone else's inheritance rather than going out and taking their own. The problem with that was that wasn't God's plan. God wanted them to spread out and fill the land and to drive out all the other nations so that He could make them a completely separated nation. God had a special blessing for each tribe that they could only receive from within their inheritance. And so Joshua tells them to stop sitting around and go out and take what God has given them.

We also can fall into this same problem in our lives, ministries, and churches. Sometimes it is much easier to just sit in the comfort of someone else's inheritance than it is to go and take possession of the one that was promised to you. The problem with that is that you will not experience all that God has for you nor will you be in the center of His will for your life if you do that.

God's promises are not just so that we can be blessed; they are also so that we can be positioned where God wants us so that He can fulfill the plan that He has for our lives. If we fail to take possession of the promises that He has made to us then we are not where He wants us to be. And because we are not where we are supposed to be we will miss out on the future blessings that God has for us there and we are not where He can use us most effectively.

Joshua told the seven tribes to stop free-loading off of the other tribes and to go and take what was theirs. Would God tell you the same thing? If you are not where you are supposed to be; stop sitting around and go there! Jesus, lead us to where we need to be.

APRIL 19

Read: Joshua 19:1 – 20:9, Luke 19:28-48. Psalm 88:1-18, Proverbs 13:12-14

JOSHUA 20:3

Anyone who kills another person unintentionally can run to one of these cities and be protected from the relatives of the one who was killed, for the relative may seek to avenge the killing.

After the Promised Land has been divided God reminds Joshua of an instruction that He had given Moses regarding setting aside cities to serve as places of refuge. These cities had a very special purpose, to provide a place of sanctuary to anyone that unintentionally killed another person.

The slayer could flee to one of these cities and would be safe there from anyone that might seek vengeance.

God considers the taking of any life a serious matter. In fact, He tells us that it is His responsibility; not man's. In God's economy there are serious consequences associated with the taking of a human life. Even if someone were to take a life unintentionally, the consequences were significant. They had to flee, ahead of the family avenger, and stay in a city of refuge until the ruling High Priest died. That could mean years of separation from their previous life.

On the other hand, someone that committed murder had no such hope. A murderer had no place to run. If they ran to a city of refuge, the leaders of the city were to determine his guilt and then turn him over to the family avenger who would execute him immediately.

In the Law that God gave to Moses to give to the people of Israel there were numerous capital offences. If someone were to break one of those laws, the punishment was death. God explained that this was so that the impurity could be cleansed from the land. God was trying to send a clear message that the only behavior that was acceptable to Him was one that conformed with His commands. He wanted people to think carefully before they decided to commit one of the capital offences listed in the Law.

God is absolutely just. This means that we can be absolutely certain that we will experience the consequences of our behaviors. If we violate one of the laws or commandments of God, we will experience some kind of consequence. We live in a society that gives hope to people that there will be no consequences for bad behavior. The legal system as it exists gives people hope that they can get away with breaking the law or at least not experience the full consequences that should come with breaking the law.

By giving people the hope of evading the consequences, they more freely challenge the laws and rules. We see this in all areas of our society, including in our homes. Society then begins to change our view of God; if we can get away with it in the world, maybe we can get away with things with God. God is gracious and merciful, but if you test Him you will find yourself on the wrong end of His rod of correction. Jesus, teach us to take Your commands seriously.

APRIL 20

Read: Joshua 21:1 – 22:20, Luke 20:1-26, Psalm 89:1-13, Proverbs 13:15-16

JOSHUA 21:44

And the LORD gave them rest on every side, just as he had solemnly promised their ancestors. None of their enemies could stand against them, for the LORD helped them conquer all their enemies.

The nation of Israel has successfully conquered all of the land that they have attempted to occupy. There was much of it that they still needed to occupy but God fought for them every time they went out to occupy the land that God had promised them.

For many years, the Israelites have been fighting to take the land that God had promised to their ancestors. God had promised that if they would go in and fight that He would drive their enemies out before them. And as always, God has been faithful to His promises. And now He is giving them rest. That doesn't mean that they don't have any more battles to fight. It just means that God is going to keep their enemies at bay for a while. Their enemies will not come after them for a while so that they can have a chance to rest.

We often forget this truth about God. He is in control of everything, including what our enemies can and cannot do. If God didn't want the enemies of Israel to attack them, then He would prevent them from being able to attack them. But the other side of that truth is that God can allow them to attack when it suits His purposes and plans.

As we go through this life, especially as we are involved in ministry, it seems like we are always in some battle or another. These battles and attacks come in all forms and effects. Some of them seem to wear us down and others seem to strengthen our resolve.

What we need to keep in mind is that we are in enemy territory. God may have promised us victory but there are still many enemies in the land that need to be defeated. And God intends to use our enemies to teach us and to discipline us. The battles and attacks that we face with our enemies teach us to depend upon God and His strength and not our own. And when we forget that, God will use our enemies to remind us to depend upon Him alone.

God will also provide for us times of rest. These times are for us to regain our strength and to focus our attention on Him and His grace and mercy in our lives. Unfortunately, we often take these times of rest and focus our attention on ourselves. And if we do that God will use an enemy to get our attention back where it belongs.

When the battles are raging, it seems like they will never end. But God has a plan and that plan includes us having victory over our enemies and having times of rest. This verse should bring great hope to those that are in the midst of great battles. The Lord has planned a time of rest for you. Keep at it until that time comes! Jesus, help us to keep marching forward until we reach Your place and time of rest.

APRIL 21

Read: Joshua 22:21 – 23:16, Luke 20:27-47, Psalm 89:14-37, Proverbs 13:17-19

JOSHUA 23:14

Soon I will die, going the way of all the earth. Deep in your hearts you know that every promise of the Lord your God has come true. Not a single one has failed!

Joshua knows that his life is nearing its end. He brings all the leaders together and gives them his last instructions and warnings. Here in this text he warns them against turning away from the one true God to worship the idols of the nations that the Lord has driven out of the land. Joshua was concerned that after he was gone they would start to corrupt themselves by getting involved with the people of the land of Canaan which would ultimately corrupt their worship of God.

Joshua had good cause to be concerned because the people had already shown a tendency toward this behavior. Sadly, the people did not heed the warnings of Joshua and did get involved with the peoples of Canaan and did end up corrupting their worship of God. In his warning Joshua told them that God would not tolerate such behavior and that He would punish them if they did turn away from the Lord.

Joshua tells them to look deep within their hearts. He tells them what they will see there; that God has been faithful to keep every promise he has ever made. Their experience with God proves that God is faithful and that His word is absolute. His point was that if God has always kept His Word, He will do so again in regards to their association with the idols of the land of Canaan.

They did not listen and God did keep His word to punish them. Every time that they persisted in turning from Him to the false gods of the land, God sent a punisher into the land in the form of an enemy nation. Ultimately, He kicked them out of the land that He had promised to their ancestors because they would not remain faithful to Him.

God's word is just as absolute today as it was when Joshua uttered these words. If we persist in rejecting God's grace and chasing after things of this world rather than Him, we should expect to be punished. Some would tell you that a loving God would never punish His children. The fact is that if He is a loving God, He must punish us. It is one of the ways that He proves that He loves us.

We were created to be in intimate fellowship with God. Sin and rebellion breaks that fellowship and God will be faithful to do His part to restore that fellowship. God warned us not to rebel or sin and He promised us that He would punish us if we did. He could not be God if He did not follow through with those promises.

God's punishment of His children is for correction of behavior, not judgment. Thankfully, all of our sins and rebellion were judged on the cross of Christ. God's punishment is meant to bring us back to the cross and remind us what He did for us and so that He can continue to pour out His love, grace, and mercy. Jesus, don't spare the rod.

JOSHUA 24:15

But if you are unwilling to serve the LORD, then choose today whom you will serve. Would you prefer the gods your ancestors served beyond the Euphrates? Or will it be the gods of the Amorites in whose land you now live? But as for me and my family, we will serve the LORD."

Joshua is nearing the end of his life and he is giving the Israelites some last minute instructions before he leaves them. They have been in the Promised Land for about twenty-five years and have still not conquered the whole land. Joshua is concerned that after he dies that the Israelites are going to turn away from God and turn to either the gods of their ancestors or the gods of the people of Canaan.

Joshua challenges them by telling them to choose whom they will serve. He has just finished reminding them of all the great things that God has done for them and reminded them of the mistakes of their fathers that resulted in the anger of the Lord. Joshua finishes his challenge by telling the people what choice he is making.

The people respond by telling Joshua and then making a covenant with God to follow Joshua's example. They commit to follow the Lord and turn away from any of the worthless idols that they have been worshipping. Joshua reminds them of the punishment that awaits those that turn away from the Lord and they seem to respond in the right way.

The people do follow the Lord as long as Joshua lives. The text tells us that the people obeyed until all the elders that had witnessed the mighty works of God had died. We will see as we get into the book of Judges that it wasn't long after that the Israelites did what Joshua was warning them not to do.

We can learn from this text three things that every leader must do. First, we must teach people the truth. They need to understand what God expects of them and warn them of the danger of disobeying and rebelling against God. Second, God's leaders must be examples of the things that they are teaching to the people. We should be living examples of the things that we are teaching to God's people. Our lives must model faith and obedience to God. Third, as leaders in God's ministries and churches we must be raising up leaders to take our place that will continue in the first two steps.

We must find and train leaders to teach and model God's truth. Any leader that is not recruiting and training leaders is not fulfilling his or her greatest responsibility. Who will lead the flock if something happens to you? A healthy ministry or church has shepherds ready to assume any responsibilities needed to protect and grow the flock no matter what happens to the leader. Jesus, help us to follow Your example of teaching the truth, living a life that models those truths, and teaching other leaders to do the same.

APRIL 23

Read: Judges 1:1 – 2:9, Luke 21:29 – 22:13, Psalm 90:1 – 91:16, Proverbs 13:24-25

JUDGES 2:2

For your part, you were not to make any covenants with the people living in this land; instead, you were to destroy their altars. Why, then, have you disobeyed my command?

God had told the nation of Israel not to make any covenants with the nations in the land of Canaan; the Promised Land. And He also promised them that He would drive out all of the people in the land. God had promised to give the land of Canaan to Abraham and his descendants forever. And the one thing that God wanted them to do was avoid making agreements with the nations that were in the land.

God had wanted them to do only one thing with those nations and that was to drive them out of the land. God had promised to drive those nations out before the nation of Israel. The nations that were living in the land were practicing all sorts of wickedness and evil and God knew that if those nations remained in the land that it was just a matter of time before His people turned away from Him and turned to the worthless idols of the people of Canaan. And that is exactly what happened.

The people of Israel did not drive out the nations that were living in the land and instead they started to get comfortable and began making agreements and covenants with the people of Canaan. And before very long they were intermarrying the people of Canaan and worshipping their gods.

The people of Canaan are a type or picture of the sin in our lives. They represent the evil and wickedness that lives within all of us. And God would also tell us not to make any agreements with those sins. Our only objective should be to conquer our lives for Jesus Christ and with the power of His Holy Spirit drive out all the sin in our lives. God has also promised that He will drive out those enemies to our life as we engage them in battle.

We must never get comfortable with the sin in our lives and we must never allow sin to exist peacefully within our lives. Because if we do, we will soon be bowing down to the altar that those sins will erect in our lives and we will hear God saying to us that we have not kept our part of the agreement with Him. The only way to live the life that God has promised us is to wage a never-ending war against the enemies to our soul; the sin that threatens to separate us from the God that gives us everything that we need and desire.

And when we engage in those battles, God is right there before us to defeat those enemies but it is up to us to march up to that enemy and attack. Jesus, help us to hate the sin in our lives as much as You do.

APRIL 24

Read: Judges 2:10 – 3:31, Luke 22:14-34, Psalm 92:1 – 93:5, Proverbs 14:1-2

PSALM 92:1

It is good to give thanks to the LORD, to sing praises to the Most High.

The very first words of this psalm struck me as I read them this morning. It is good to give thanks to the Lord. As I thought about this verse it struck me that I hadn't been doing that. Not that I hadn't been thankful but that I hadn't been giving thanks to God for everything in my life.

For the last seven months my family and I have been dealing with a trial at our home. By itself this trial is not that big of a deal when I compare it to what other people have been going through. But lately I have sensed in myself that it is wearing me down. Everything we do to attempt to resolve the issue seems to be ineffective or serves to reveal more of the problem.

This morning the Lord revealed to me that I had allowed this circumstance in my life to distract me from being thankful to the Lord. He reminded me that I should be thankful to have a home so that I could have a trial like this going on. He reminded me that He is bigger than this circumstance and that He is going to overcome it; not me.

What struck me about all of that is that as a pastor, I know all these things. On nearly a daily basis I am telling people that is how they should respond to their circumstances. And what I have discovered is that I had somehow separated what I believed from what I did. I didn't do it consciously but I can see that it happened.

As leaders in families, ministries, and churches we are going to experience more than our fair share of trials. As a leader standing up for what God wants and leading people to Jesus, the devil is going to resist you. The more effective we are; the more resistance we are going to experience. I allowed my shield of faith to slip and some of the darts got through to wound me.

It is good to give thanks to the Lord. When? Always! It is good to give thanks to the Lord. For what? For everything; including the trials! It is good to give thanks to the Lord. Why? Because absolutely everything in your life was sent by God or was allowed by God. Nothing comes into your life that didn't first pass before God and receive His permission to be sent.

It can be very easy to forget this when you are in the midst of a trial. And just because you are the one that is telling people how to deal with their circumstances doesn't mean that you won't make the same mistakes they do. The remedy is the same for everyone; give thanks to the Lord. Blessed be the name of the Lord! Jesus, thank you for everything in my life; the things that I would describe as good and the things that I see as bad.

APRIL 25

Read: Judges 4:1 – 5:31, Luke 22:35-53, Psalm 94:1-23, Proverbs 14:3-4

"Very well," she replied, "I will go with you. But since you have made this choice, you will receive no honor. For the LORD'S victory over Sisera will be at the hands of a woman." So Deborah went with Barak to Kedesh.

The book of Judges reveals a very consistent pattern in the nation of Israel. While a prophet or judge is alive, they will follow the Lord. Shortly after the death of the prophet or judge, they turn away from the Lord and begin worshipping worthless idols. God then sends an enemy to remind them of their relationship with the Almighty God. Here in our account today we have the same scenario being played out. The Israelites have done what is evil in the Lord's sight and God has sent the Canaanite king Jabin to bring the Israelites back to God.

God selects Barak to be the one that He will use to defeat King Jabin and his commander Sisera. This is a great honor to be selected like this to do a great work for God. But Barak lacked the faith to go by himself and wanted Deborah to come with him. Because of his lack of faith some of the glory and honor that God had determined to give him was going to be given to a woman.

This would be a slap in the face to Barak. The person that defeated the enemy commander was the one that would be given great honor and respect. As the commander of the army of Israel, Barak would expect that to be him or at the very least, one of his soldiers. It was not uncommon for the soldiers to capture the enemy commander and bring him to their commander so that he would receive the honor of killing the enemy commander. Barak would be humiliated to have a woman do what he should have done.

As leaders of God's ministries and churches, God has given us the opportunity to do great things for Him. If we will have faith, He will win great victories and He will give us some measure of honor and glory. But if we lack the faith, He will still have the victory but He will use someone else and give them the honor and glory that He wanted to give you. And the person He picks will be someone that normally you would say is not capable to be used in that way.

The Bible teaches that God is searching the whole world to find people with the faith to do great things for Him and then He shows His might and power through those people. Those people do not have great power or might, but they believe that God does. When we believe that God has great power and might, we then become conduits for the use of that power and might.

God used a donkey to speak to Balaam in Numbers 22. He could use anyone or anything to do the things that He has asked me to do. Jesus, help me to have the faith to respond to your will immediately and completely, so that I might receive the honor and glory that you have determined to give me, so that I in turn can give it back to you.

APRIL 26

Read: Judges 6:1-40, Luke 22:54 – 23:12, Psalm 95:1 – 96:13, Proverbs 14:5-6

JUDGES 6:14

Then the LORD turned to him and said, "Go with the strength you have and rescue Israel from the Midianites. I am sending you!"

Gideon receives a visit from a very special person; the angel of the LORD. Some say that this person is a special messenger from heaven, possibly the archangel Gabriel. However, verses like the one above that in the Hebrew use the proper name of God, Yahweh, would lead us to see this as a Christophany, the physical appearance of the second person of the Trinity, Jesus Christ.

God had told the Israelites that if they rebelled against Him and turned to worship the false gods of the land they were occupying, that he would hand them over to enemies that would oppress them. That is exactly what has happened at the point in history to which this account relates. The Midianites regularly come in and steal their crops and cause havoc in Israel. Finally, they cry out to God for help and He responds by appearing to Gideon. The LORD addresses Gideon as "Mighty hero." The LORD saw him as He was going to be, not as he was.

Gideon didn't consider himself a hero. In our verse, the LORD tells Gideon to go and defeat the Midianites. He then assures Gideon by telling him that He was going with Gideon. At first Gideon is not sure that God is really going to do what He said and asks for proof, which to my surprise the Lord provides to Gideon.

The LORD tells Gideon to go with the strength that he had. That is one of the fascinating parts of this verse. What strength did Gideon have? If he had had any real strength he might already be doing something to resist the Midianites rather than hiding in the bottom of a winepress threshing grain. To Gideon, this task was far beyond any puny strength he might have.

We all know the rest of the story. God uses Gideon and a small band of Israelites to route the Midianite army. All the work was done by God, Gideon and his little army were just allowed to be in the front row to watch what God was doing.

How much strength do you have? How much strength do you need to have to do the thing that God has told you to do? According to this verse you have enough strength to do what God is telling you to do. The question then is, "Will you obey?"

Gideon did and was allowed to participate in a great victory for the LORD. As small as your strength is, it is all you need when it is coupled with the LORD's strength and His command to "Go." Your little bit of strength and obedience combined with the LORD's infinite strength is a recipe for victory every time. Jesus, teach us to trust and obey.

APRIL 27

Read: Judges 7:1 – 8:17, Luke 23:13-43, Psalm 97:1 – 98:9, Proverbs 14:7-8

PROVERBS 14:8

The wise look ahead to see what is coming, but fools deceive themselves.

The book of Proverbs spends much of its time contrasting things. Good is contrasted to evil; wisdom is contrasted to foolishness, and many other contrasts. This allows us to see each of these topics in a much clearer light and allows us to examine our own hearts and determine where we stand in that contrast.

Someone once encouraged me to read one chapter of Proverbs every day. There are thirty one chapters and so in a month you can read the entire book. They encouraged me to do this every month. The amazing thing to me was that after two years of doing that I still found that something in the chapter I read every day spoke to me about something that was going on in my life at that time. Try it! It is a powerful thing.

In our text for today, we have another contrast of wisdom to foolishness. The wise person looks ahead to see what is coming. This is contrasted with a foolish person who does not and deceives themselves into believing that everything is OK.

The wise person understands that there is a balance that must be walked. We must walk in the present but we must be mindful of the future. The wise person trusts God for the future but also understands that he has a role to play in that future. Only by looking to the future can he develop plans that will take him where the Lord would want him to go.

The foolish person leaves all that to chance. The foolish person does not consider how God might be working and try to determine what their role is. They are waiting for someone to tell them what to do.

God tells us plainly in scripture that He expects us to do our part in our relationship with Jesus. One aspect of our part is looking to see how God might be working and attempting to develop plans so that we can be prepared for what He wants to do. God will honor that even if His plans are different than what we thought they were going to be. God will do what He is going to do even if it conflicts with our plans. The wise person sees that and then alters the plan to fit how and where God is working.

Our role as people leading families, ministries, and churches is to lead. And one of the characteristics of a leader is that they have an idea of where they are going. The only way to do that is to look ahead of where you are and set out to reach that point. It is foolish to entrust your family, or God's ministry, or church to chance. Jesus help us to be wise enough to see where you are working and help us to develop plans that bring us alongside You to join You in the work.

APRIL 28

Read: Judges 8:18 – 9:21, Luke 23:44 – 24:12, Psalm 99:1-9, Proverbs 14:9-10

JUDGES 8:27

Gideon made a sacred ephod from the gold and put it in Ophrah, his hometown. But soon all the Israelites prostituted themselves by worshipping it, and it became a trap for Gideon and his family.

God has just won a tremendous victory through Gideon and the nation of Israel by defeating the wicked Midianites. God had used the Midianites to punish Israel for turning away from Him to worship other gods. The Bible teaches that God is a jealous God; He will not share our affection with anything else.

Unfortunately, we humans have this bad habit of creating our own gods and objects of worship. If we would honestly evaluate our lives, all of us would probably find several objects of worship in our lives that God disapproves of. Many of them could have started out as good things. Gideon creates a golden ephod from the earrings of the fallen Midianites. The scriptures don't tell us why he does this. It is possible that it was done to serve as a memorial to God's victory.

Before long the Israelites are worshipping this object. God's description of that response is to call it prostitution. Prostitutes are not held in high regard in most cultures. In fact, they are shunned by most people because their lifestyle/profession is demeaning and offensive. By referring to their worship of the ephod as prostitution, the Lord is trying to help them to be repulsed by their own behavior. The golden ephod became a trap for Gideon and his family. It is not hard to imagine that the attention that God's victory and the worship of this ephod had an intoxicating effect upon Gideon and his family. That was the bait that lured them into the trap. The trap was sprung when they didn't recognize what was going on and turn away from it.

Another feature of the human race is that we will often continue in behaviors long after they are productive or understood. We do what we do because that is the way we have always done it. We also refer to this trait as habits. We form habits that in some cases turn into tradition. If a tradition exists long enough, its source can be lost and therein lies the danger. For some reason we resist the urge to question tradition.

Gideon allowed his family to develop a tradition that drew them away from God and ultimately played a role in Israel's fall back into idolatry. There is nothing wrong with traditions, as long as they draw us to God and not away from Him. Traditions can be very useful and uplifting. It is up to us as leaders to challenge those traditions with God's Word and the guiding of the Holy Spirit to make sure that we are not allowing those we lead to spiritually prostitute themselves.

Traditions should draw us together and lead us to the Lord. If they don't, we are at risk of experiencing what the Israelites went through; the punishment of God. Because they allowed their tradition associated with Gideon's golden ephod to lead them away from the Lord, He used one of Gideon's own sons to bring trouble into his family. Jesus, help us to stay away from the traps.

APRIL 29

Read: Judges 9:22 – 10:18, Luke 24:13-53, Psalm 100:1-5, Proverbs 14:11-12

LUKE 24:31

Suddenly, their eyes were opened, and they recognized him. At that moment he disappeared!

Jesus meets two guys that are walking to the village of Emmaus. As the two men are walking they are discussing the events that they have just witnessed in Jerusalem. Jesus asks them what they are talking about and they tell Him everything that happened to Jesus. Jesus rebukes them for not believing the scriptures that spoke of all the things that the Messiah must suffer. They were then approaching Emmaus and the two men convince Jesus to come to their home. As He breaks the bread and asks God's blessing the two men's eyes are opened and they recognize Him as Jesus.

To me this is a fascinating account that is filled with mystery. Why did Jesus hide His appearance from them? Why did He reveal Himself as He broke the bread? Why did He disappear after He had they recognized Him? We may never have the full answers to these questions but they are marvelous to meditate upon.

It was the matter of recognizing Jesus that really spoke to me about this verse. These two men knew Jesus and were familiar with His appearance. They has probably traveled with Him and witnessed His miracles and teachings. They may have even witnessed the crucifixion. But they didn't recognize Him as He walked with them on the road or even as they sat at the table to eat.

We also struggle with the same thing that the two men experienced; walking with the Lord and not realizing it. When we accept Jesus He begins a journey with us. That journey is the trip that we all take through the remainder of our lives. Jesus walks every step of that journey with us but sometimes we don't recognize Him there. These two men were consumed with their own concerns and fears and so they didn't recognize their Savior and Lord.

Life has this way of getting us to take our eyes off Jesus. Sometimes we can get so distracted that even when we look back we fail to recognize Him walking there beside us. We just need to do as these two men did and keep walking and letting Him speak to our hearts through the scriptures. If we will let Him, His words will warm our hearts and make them tender toward Him again.

It would be better to not take our eyes off Jesus as we walk through this life but there will be times when we do. When we realize that we don't recognize Jesus we just need to focus our eyes on His word and turn our heart toward Him in prayer. At some point He will open our eyes again. Jesus, help us to watch where we are walking.

APRIL 30

Read: Judges 11:1 – 12:15, John 1:1-18, Psalm 101:1-8, Proverbs 14:13-14

JUDGES 11:31

I will give to the LORD the first thing coming out of my house to greet me when I return in triumph. I will sacrifice it as a burnt offering.

There are some accounts in Scripture that are difficult to understand and in some cases are a little disturbing. This is one such account. The armies of Ammon are preparing to attack Israel and the Israelites cry out to God to rescue them. The LORD accuses them of turning away from Him to worship false gods, again. They agree to change and so God raises Jephthah as leader of the Israelites.

The Spirit of the LORD comes upon Jephthah and he gathers together an army to fight against the Ammonites. Before going into the battle, Jephthah makes a vow to give the LORD the first thing that comes out of his house if the LORD gives him the victory. The disturbing part is that he promises to burn it as a sacrifice.

After the victory Jephthah returns home to be greeted by his daughter. The text says that his heart was broken because she was his only child. There is much controversy over what happened next in this account. Human sacrifice was forbidden by God for the Israelites but was practiced by the people of the surrounding nations. It is hard to imagine that God would allow Jephthah to sacrifice his daughter as a burnt offering.

The account ends in such a way to believe that rather than sacrificing her, she was never allowed to marry and ultimately died as a virgin, presumably of natural causes. So the outcome of this account is a little unclear. The outcome is not the main point of the account and it is easy to miss that. The main point of this account is that God had already determined to save the Israelites; Jephtath's vow was unnecessary and irrelevant.

God does not need our vows or promises, but He requires our obedience. Jephthah had already been given the victory; he only needed to obediently go out with his army and fight. He thought he was being spiritual by making a vow, and it is my guess this was not a private vow but very public. His vow was foolish and it cost him more than he ever imagined it would, regardless of the actual outcome.

If the LORD wants you to do something, you don't need to make a vow so that God will help you. If He wants you to do it He has already decided to help you. All you then need to do is just do it. Jesus, help us not to make foolish vows and simply obey.

MAY

MAY 1

Read: Judges 13:1 – 14:20, John 1:29-51, Psalm 102:1-28, Proverbs 14:15-16

JUDGES 13:8

Then Manoah prayed to the LORD. He said, "Lord, please let the man of God come back to us again and give us more instructions about this son who is to be born."

An angel of the Lord has appeared to the wife of Manoah and told her that she was going to have a son even though she was barren. Not only was she going to have a son, but this son was going to deliver the Israelites from the oppression of the Philistines. She tells her husband and he prays and asks that God would send back this messenger so that they can get additional instruction regarding this miracle.

What a great example of faith! Manoah did not question God about the miracle and he did not ask for proof. He asked God to provide them with more information so that he could complete the task that God was giving them. God answered Manoah's prayer and sent the messenger again. This is further proof of the heart of this man and his wife. God had selected them to do this great work because they had the faith to do it.

When the messenger returns he doesn't give them any more information than he did the first time. And his second visit serves no real purpose beyond blessing and encouraging Manoah and his wife. It was as though God was saying to them that He was pleased with their response to the first visit of the angel of the Lord.

When God speaks to us, He wants us to listen. He will send us messages in many different ways. He will speak to us through His Word, the Bible. He will speak to us in prayer. He will often give us a message while we are listening to someone teaching through the Word. He will also send people to deliver a message to you. When He does, He wants our response to be like that of Manoah and his wife.

They believed God and were ready to do whatever was asked of them. It wasn't a question of will God do this thing; it was a matter of what is our part in this thing that God is doing through us. And it is OK to ask God for more information but know that God might not give you any more information. That doesn't change the fact that He wants you to do what you can with the information you have. God will often only give us just enough information so that we can obey Him but not enough that we can do it without trusting Him to provide more in the future.

Men and women of faith receive messages from God. And when they do, they respond in faith to accomplish whatever it is that God is asking them to do. What has God asked you to do lately? What was your response? If you want God to do radical, supernatural, miraculous things in your life, you must believe that He can and will. And then when He tells you that He is going to do it, He will tell you what your part is. It is then up to you to do your part, trusting that God will do His. Jesus, help us to be men and women of faith that are used to do incredible things in Your name and for Your glory.

MAY 2
Read: Judges 15:1 – 16:31, John 2:1-25, Psalm 103:1-22, Proverbs 14:17-19

PSALM 103:1

Praise the Lord, I tell myself; with my whole heart, I will praise his holy name.

This psalm is a beautiful description of all that God has done for us. We could spend many days and many pages discussing each verse of this amazing psalm of praise from David's heart. I would encourage you to do that and discover for yourself the treasures that are laid out for us here in our text for today.

In today's verse I was impressed by the words, "I tell myself." That really struck me and so we are going to spend a little time in that. David, whom God describes as "a man after My own heart" says in this verse that he tells himself to praise the Lord. David is talking to himself about how he should respond to all that God has done for him. It occurred to me as I was reading how very important it is for us to do that.

As humans we have this terrible tendency to forget the good things that have happened in our lives. Or if we don't forget them we will take them for granted. We can look in virtually every part of our lives and see places where something amazing has happened and yet we treat it as something very common and ordinary.

Our salvation is a perfect example of that. When we were first saved, our salvation was the most amazing thing in the universe. It was cause for rejoicing and celebration and praise to the God that loved us enough to save us from our own sinful desires. As time goes on, those emotions and feelings fade and we don't rejoice and praise God for the miracle of our salvation like we used to. Our salvation is just as much a miracle today as it was on the day it happened.

David is telling himself to remember to praise God with his whole heart. He knows that his natural tendency is to forget or minimize the great things that God has done in his life. He knows that the only way that is going to change is if he regularly reminds himself to do it. David was so serious about it that he wrote it down in this psalm.

God is amazing and wondrous; He has done and will do marvelous and miraculous things in your life. Tell yourself, just as David did, that you will praise God with your whole heart. You will be stunned by the way that changes your outlook on your day and on your life. Praising God is good medicine for your soul. It can also be a great encouragement in times when things are not going all that well.

It is often at times when things are hard that we need to remind ourselves to praise God. Remembering the great things He has done can help us to believe that He will do great things in our current situation. It all begins by making a decision to praise God with your whole heart. Try it and see what God does. Jesus, help us to choose to praise You.

MAY 3

Read: Judges 17:1 – 18:31, John 3:1-21, Psalm 104:1-23, Proverbs 14:20-21

JOHN 3:4

"What do you mean?" exclaimed Nicodemus. "How can an old man go back into his mother's womb and be born again?"

Nicodemus comes to Jesus under the cover of darkness to ask Him questions. Nicodemus sees something different in Jesus and recognizes that it is the power of God working in Him. Jesus responds to

Nicodemus' first statement with a statement of His own and the statement amazes Nicodemus. Jesus tells him that he needs to be born again.

Nicodemus doesn't understand; he doesn't get it. It doesn't make sense that an old man has to be born again. It is not logical that an old man can go back into his mother's womb to be born again. Of course Jesus isn't talking about a physical birth but about a spiritual birth. We all understand that we need to be reborn by the Spirit of God. That's what Jesus was telling Nicodemus. We understand that but Nicodemus didn't. Why is that? It is simple; we have been reborn or born again already. It is a spiritual truth that can only be understood by someone that has the Holy Spirit within them.

As we minister in our families, ministries, and churches we sometimes forget this truth. People that do not have the Spirit of God are not going to understand spiritual truths. Before we can expect them to get it they need to get Him; the Holy Spirit. Before we can expect them to understand what it means to be born again they need to receive the gift of salvation and the Holy Spirit

The longer that we are walking with the Lord; the more likely we are to forget this truth. It seems that we forget that it takes the Spirit of God for people to behave like Christians. And even with the Spirit people can behave very badly and do some very un-Christian things. The longer that we allow the Spirit to shape us and mold us, the harder it is for us to remember what it was like before. We must not expect people to act like us. We need to encourage them to imitate us as we imitate Christ but to expect them to behave a certain way just creates frustration and disappointment.

Our responsibility is to follow Christ! That is your first and foremost responsibility. As you are following Christ, God is going to have some people follow you so that they can learn how to do it on their own. Don't be surprised when they don't get it. Don't be too disappointed when they don't do it "right" every time. You just keep following Christ and you just keep inviting others to join you. Every time they stumble and fall, you reach down and help them up and show them how they can do it better the next time. That is exactly how Christ did it with you. Jesus, teach us to follow closely after you and help us to teach others to follow.

MAY 4

Read: Judges 19:1 – 20:48, John 3:22 – 4:3, Psalm 104:24-35, Proverbs 14:22-24

JUDGES 19:1

Now in those days Israel had no king. There was a man from the tribe of Levi living in a remote area of the hill country of Ephraim. One day he brought home a woman from Bethlehem in Judah to be his concubine.

Here we have the peculiar account of a Levite and his concubine from Bethlehem. This Levite is traveling home after finding this woman that he wants to bring to his home. She runs back to her home and then the Levite comes back to get her after four months. After several days of the father stalling, the Levite heads for home again.

They travel until dusk and stop in a town to rest. They bypass the city of Jerusalem because the Levite does not want to stay with foreigners. While in this town, they are invited into the home of an old man. While there, the men of the town, later identified as leaders of the town, come and tell the old man to send the visitors out so that they can have sex with them. Then the Levite does the unthinkable, he pushes his concubine out the door and locks it behind her.

The men of the town rape her all night and then she finally crawls back to the doorstep and dies. The Levite takes her body to his home and then dismembers it and sends the pieces to the twelve tribes of Israel. This creates great outrage within the nation and justice is demanded. The tribe of Benjamin is asked to hand over the wicked men that have done this evil thing. But instead they mobilize their army and a civil war breaks out that virtually wipes out the tribe of Benjamin.

Most of us cannot imagine many of these events taking place but to have them all take place in a single account is bizarre. We are reminded of the account of Sodom and Gomorrah being destroyed by God because of its great wickedness. And here the children of God are doing the same thing. The last verse in the book of judges sums up what was going on. It reminds us that Israel did not have a king and so they did what they thought was right to do.

In the three thousand years since this event took place very little has changed. Most people still have no king and so they do what they think is right and best, usually for them. It is our responsibility as leaders in God's ministries and churches to bring them to the King of kings, Jesus Christ. Without a leader, people will do whatever feels right to them. We need to bring them back to the light of truth in the Bible and teach them to listen to the leading of the Holy Spirit.

Sadly, many of our churches also do what seems right in their own eyes and have forgotten their first love. Let us be the ones that relight that torch that provides light to lead God's people back to His throne so that they might find grace and mercy. Left to themselves people will do horrific things and think nothing of it. Jesus, teach us to chase after holiness and to lead others toward it as well.

MAY 5

Read: Judges 21:1-Ruth 1:22, John 4:4-42, Psalm 105:1-5, Proverbs 14:25

PSALM 105:4

Search for the LORD and for his strength, and keep on searching.

One of the attributes or characteristics of God is His strength. There is no way to measure or describe God's strength because it is infinite, just as He is infinite. Our finite minds will never fully grasp that concept. Humans, by nature, seem to have an insatiable desire to measure the world around them. We seem to never tire of exploring and finding those things that have not yet been found. Today's verse tells us that this characteristic was placed in us by God.

In our verse for the day we are exhorted to search for God and for His strength. We need to be careful not to miss the implication that this carries for all of us. This means that our relationship with God must be an active one. We can't be passive and find God or His strength; just as you can't be passive and discover some thing that has never been discovered before.

One of the obvious places to do this is in God's Word. God reveals Himself through His word and His strength is acquired as we take hold of His promises. As we learn about God in His word, more and more of His strength is revealed to us. Another area where God is found and His strength appropriated is in prayer. As we pray, God reveals Himself to us and the Holy Spirit strengthens us.

To find God and His strength also means that we need to go places that we have not been before if we want to discover the unknown things. That can be a very scary thing for some people; especially in times of trial or tribulation but it is exactly in those places where God and His strength are most profoundly manifested. Too often we will run away or avoid the very things that we need in order to discover the secret things of God and His strength.

The thing that struck me about this verse are the last words: "and keep on searching." This search is not a one-time thing; it is not even a seasonal thing, it is a life-long journey. The Bible teaches that all wisdom and knowledge are hidden in Christ Jesus. Our lives should be marked by a growing passion to know Jesus and to discover all the hidden things that we can find in Him. As we do this we will find ourselves growing in strength.

Jesus was the ultimate example of the strength of God being revealed in a living person. As we search for God and His strength we will find ourselves growing daily to be more like Jesus and we will experience His strength flowing through us into the lives of others. It requires faithfulness and diligence to daily search for God and His strength. Even that cannot be found outside of God and the work of the Holy Spirit in your life. Daily, ask God to give you the passion to continue searching for all that He has for you. Jesus, create within us a burning desire to discover all there is to know about You.

MAY 6
Read: Ruth 2:1 – 4:22, John 4:43-54, Psalm 105:16-36, Proverbs 14:26-27

RUTH 4:16

Naomi took care of the baby and cared for him as if he were her own.

While the main character in the book of Ruth is Ruth, the role of Naomi is fascinating and gives us much to learn from. Here as the book of Ruth comes to a close we see the happy ending. Ruth marries

Boaz and they have a son that they name Obed. Naomi then cares for that son as though he was hers. By Jewish law this son would grow up to inherit all the land of Naomi's dead husband and sons. But he wasn't really related to her.

Ruth was a Moabite and Boaz was at best a distant relative of Naomi. And yet she cares for this child as if it were her own son. It almost makes you wonder if she had some sense of how precious this infant was. It is not likely that she was alive when this baby's grandson was born and even less likely that she was alive when he became the king of Israel. Obed's grandson was David, the son of Jesse.

As far as scripture tells us, she or no one else had been told of the incredible things that God was going to do through David. It wasn't until Samuel anointed David as the next king of Israel that we even know who he is. This has often caused me to wonder about the people around me. Are there children and people around me that are going to be used by God like He used David or Moses or Joshua?

As the leaders in God's ministries and churches, we need to be like Naomi. We need to care for God's children as though they were our own. Not just because they may grow up to be used by God in some mighty way but because they are God's children. And this doesn't mean just the children. Some people used by God were called before their birth and others were called late in their life.

We need to take care of the people of God just as though they were our children. No matter how rebellious or stubborn they might be, we must care for them. No matter how wild and uncontrollable they are, we must take care of them as our own. We can never write them off and stop caring for them, because God never will.

There is no way for us to know what the future holds for ourselves, let alone anyone else in our ministry and so we must always try to look at the people in our ministries and churches with the eyes of Christ. Just like Naomi cared for the child Obed, we are to care for everyone that God places in our care. It is a huge responsibility and it carries with it eternal consequences and rewards. Jesus, help us to care for and love the people and children that you bring to us just like you would. Help us to see them through your eyes and to see that there are great things that you can do through them.

MAY 7

Read: 1 Samuel 1:1 – 2:21, John 5:1-23, Psalm 105:37-45, Proverbs 14:28-29

JOHN 5:6

When Jesus saw him and knew how long he had been ill, he asked him, "Would you like to get well?"

Jesus comes to the pool at Bethesda in Jerusalem. Around this pool are crowds of people that are suffering from all sorts of illnesses, diseases, and frailties. One of the men there had been sick for thirty-eight years. It is hard for most of us to imagine what it must have been like to be sick for that long. He was at the pool because it was believed that angels would come down to stir up the waters of the pool. If you got into the water quickly enough you would be healed.

For who knows how long, this man has been coming to the pool with the hopes of getting healed. He was not able to be healed because He had no one to help him get into the pool in time. Jesus comes along and looks at him and knows how long he has been sick. He knew this because the Father had told Him; The Father wanted to heal this man.

There are several things that fascinate me about this account, such as the fact that it is only recorded that this man was healed even though there were "crowds of people" there. It also fascinates me that God would have this kind of a thing going on; an angel stirring up the water occasionally to heal a few people at a time. Each of those is worthy of greater focus and meditation but one thing really grabbed me; it was the question that Jesus asked the sick man.

Jesus asked him if he wanted to be made well. At first glance that seems like a foolish question that the Son of God asked him. Jesus asked no foolish questions; so there must have been a good reason why He asked it. I believe it was to test this man's heart. It is obvious that He wanted to be healed because he was sitting by the pool and waiting for the water to be stirred up. What may not be obvious was his realization of his own helplessness. He recognized that he was helpless to be healed based on his own abilities. He knew that without help there was going to be no possible way for him to get into the water to be healed.

This man had the faith to be healed because he kept coming to the place where he could receive the healing he desired but he lacked the ability.

Jesus asked the question so that he would speak out this helplessness and so that Jesus could show Himself to be his Savior. This is the way that the Lord wants to work in our lives. Jesus wants us to recognize our weaknesses and helplessness. Too many people will daily go to the pool and attempt to get into the pool themselves rather than let Jesus do the healing in their lives that they need. How long will you do that? Will you wait thirty-eight years to be healed or will you let Jesus heal you in an instant? Humble yourself before God and go to the Great Physician to heal every part of your life. Jesus, I want to be healed!

MAY 8
Read: 1 Samuel 2:22 – 4:22, John 5:24-47, Psalm 106:1-12, Proverbs 14:30-31

1 SAMUEL 3:10

And the LORD came and called as before, "Samuel, Samuel!" And Samuel replied, "Yes, your servant is listening."

The story of Samuel the Prophet is an interesting one. He was raised by Eli the priest. His mother Hannah had been praying for a son for a long time and she promised to give her first son to the LORD. God answered her prayers by giving her Samuel. Hannah kept her word to the LORD and He then gave her three more sons and two daughters.

The role of a prophet is to receive messages from the Lord and then to pass them on to the people that they are directed. It seems that one of the main messages that the prophets were entrusted with were warnings against turning away from God. Many of the books of the Old Testament are filled with these warnings.

Samuel was raised in the area of the Tabernacle and in service to the LORD. In our text for today he is sleeping in the Tabernacle when he hears a voice calling out to him. He responds by going to Eli to see if he needs anything. Eli tells him to go back to sleep. This happens three times and then Eli understands that it is the LORD. He tells Samuel how to respond if it happens again. Samuel lies down again and a fourth time he hears the LORD call out to him. That begins a long life of direct communication between the LORD and Samuel. Few people will ever hear the voice of the LORD in this way in this life. It is not a matter of worthiness or ability; it is a matter of God's sovereign choice. For most people He chooses to communicate to them in a different way.

It is pretty common as a pastor to be asked how you know if the LORD is speaking to you about something. That can be a difficult question to answer because the fact of the matter is you can't always know for sure it is His voice. You can run some tests to attempt to verify His voice such as compare what He is telling you to Scripture, to His character, to His previous instructions and the like. But the fact is that you will probably have to exercise some amount of faith to respond to the LORD's voice.

There are a couple of things that we can do to prepare ourselves to hear from the LORD. Samuel was sleeping in the Tabernacle near the Ark of the Covenant. To me this is a picture of living a life of worship. It is more than showing up to church once in a while; it is viewing your whole life as an act of worship to God. Then prepare yourself to respond. The first thing Samuel said was "Yes." For someone that truly wants to hear from the LORD, they must already know that they are going to say "Yes" to whatever the LORD tells them to do. Second, Samuel described himself as a servant. To hear from the LORD, acknowledge that He is the Master and you are a servant. Third, he was listening. The only way to hear from the LORD is to be listening for Him. It took four attempts before the Lord reached Samuel. How many times will He need to call out to you? Jesus, help us to be ready to listen.

MAY 9
Read: 1 Samuel 5:1 – 7:17, John 6:1-21, Psalm 106:13-31, Proverbs 14:32-33

1 SAMUEL 6:6
Don't be stubborn and rebellious as Pharaoh and the Egyptians were. They wouldn't let Israel go until God had ravaged them with dreadful plagues.

The Ark of the Covenant has been captured by the Philistines. They first put it into the temple with their god Dagon but his statue keeps falling over and pieces are breaking off. The people also start breaking out in tumors. These must have been large ugly things growing on their bodies because they will eventually make five gold tumors as part of the offering to appease God.

The leaders decide to send the Ark back to Israel because they are suffering from the plague of tumors. In addition to the five gold tumors they make five gold rats. It appears that they were having a problem with rats that they associated with the presence of the Ark. The leaders determine that the only solution is to send the Ark back to Israel.

They do it in an interesting way; they hook a cart up to two cows that had just had calves. Then they shut up the calves away from the cows. Once released the natural thing for those cows to do would have been to return to their calves. Instead, they walk right down the road toward Israel. The Philistines did it this way to prove whether or not it was God that had inflicted them.

What fascinates me about this account is the fact that the people of Philistia knew about God. They knew about the history of the people of Israel. They knew that God had miraculously delivered them from the mighty power of Pharaoh and the Egyptians. They knew that the God of the Israelites was more powerful than the gods of Egypt. They had also just witnessed that God was more powerful than their god Dagon. They understood that these judgments were coming from God.

Their response is not to worship Him but to appease Him so that He will stop punishing them. Today, people still come to God the same way. They are looking for something from God or they want their suffering to stop. They only want to know God enough to figure out what the formula is for success or peace. Once they have that they go right back to their old life and their old gods. God will send tumors and rats if that is what it is going to take to get you to humble your heart before Him. Once you are humbled before Him it is His love, grace, and mercy that will alter your life. As Christians it is our responsibility to be ready to give that love, to show that grace, to offer mercy to those that come to God for the wrong reasons.

They might know God and they might know that they need God but they probably don't know how to love God. They will learn to love Him by watching His people loving one another. It is a tremendous responsibility to understand that you are a vessel of God's unconditional, sacrificial love. That love has the power to save lives. We need to let God use us to pour that love into the lives of others. Jesus, help us to let You love them through us.

MAY 10

Read: 1 Samuel 8:1 – 9:27, John 6:22-42, Psalm 106:32-48, Proverbs 14:34-35

JOHN 6:27

But you shouldn't be so concerned about perishable things like food. Spend your energy seeking the eternal life that I, the Son of Man, can give you. For God the Father has sent me for that very purpose."

The crowds following Jesus have come to where He and the disciples left. The previous day Jesus had fed the five thousand men plus women and children on five loaves and two fishes. Basically, they want to be fed again. Jesus sensing the intents of their hearts takes the opportunity to teach them a very important truth. That truth was that Jesus did not come to feed their bodies so that they may live but to feed their soul so that they could live eternally.

Jesus came to the earth with a purpose. That purpose was to make a way for sinful man to be saved from the penalty of our sins. The crowds that were following Jesus were more concerned about how He might feed them, heal them, and deliver them from evil spirits than they were about eternity. But because of Jesus' compassion He did heal them, feed them and deliver them. And while He was doing that He was teaching them about the Kingdom of God.

God created you for a purpose. That purpose is to love God and to love others. One of the ways that we fulfill that purpose is to show people the power of Jesus operating in our lives and teach them about Him and share with them the hope of eternal life that is found in Him. How we do that is going to be different for every person. Each of us is different in the way that we will fulfill that purpose.

The more successful we are at doing that, the more likely crowds will begin to gather to see if Jesus will feed them, and heal them, and cast out evil spirits from them through us. Many of them aren't looking for God or eternal life. Many of them just want to see what is going on. Many of them just want to be where the action is. Many will be in the crowds for all the wrong reasons. Jesus didn't rebuke them for their wrong motives; he had compassion upon them because they were like sheep without a shepherd.

When the crowds begin to gather, remember that they are there for reasons that are likely to be everything other than the reasons that you or God intends. If they didn't follow Jesus, God the Son, for the right reasons, why would you expect them to follow you for the right reasons? God expects you to respond like Jesus did; with compassion. He wants you to do what you can to feed them, and heal them, and deliver them from evil spirits; all the while teaching them about who Jesus is and what He offers them. Jesus, thank you that we can know You and follow you. We pray that we are following You for the right reasons and that we are leading others to You through the way that we live and teach.

MAY 11

Read: 1 Samuel 10:1 – 11:15, John 6:43-71, Psalm 107:1-43, Proverbs 15:1-3

PSALM 107:43

Those who are wise will take all this to heart; they will see in our history the faithful love of the LORD.

In this psalm we have a beautiful picture of how the Lord has taken care of the nation of Israel, His special possession. Without fail God has provided for them and protected them from all of their enemies. There were times when God allowed their enemies to punish them because of their unfaithfulness but He was always faithful to save them when they returned to Him. The psalmist in today's verse tells his readers what they should do with this knowledge.

First he says that the wise will take this all to heart. "Take it to heart" is a phrase that most of us are familiar with but probably don't truly understand. To take something to heart is more than just knowing something and understanding it. It means that this knowledge is used to change your life and behavior. To take something to heart is to take something inside of you and make it a part of who you are.

The heart is the center of our attitudes and emotions; the way that we feel and act come out of our heart. It is from the abundance or overflow of our heart that we speak and act. The psalmist is telling us that we would be wise to let the knowledge shared in this psalm change the way that we speak and act.

The psalmist gives justification for that in the end of today's verse; he says that the history of the Jews proves what He is saying. God had indeed been very good to the Jewish people. He had made many promised and then kept every one of them. The Lord faithfully showed His love to the nation of Israel even when they were being unfaithful to Him. The Lord has also faithfully shown His love to us. In each of our history's we can find examples of the Lord's faithful love. For each of us this should give us the hope and faith to endure through all that might lie ahead of us. God wants you to take to heart all the faithful love that He has shown to you and then speak and act on that knowledge.

The nation of Israel was very good at remembering and reciting their history. Sadly, they did not take to heart what God had done for them and they suffered great loss as a result of it. We also have the same opportunity with God. Remember what He has done for you and allow those memories to change the way that you see God and the rest of the world. If you change the way that you view God and the rest of the world it will change the way that you view your circumstances and trials and tribulations. By remembering that the Lord has been there for us in the past we can trust that He will be there in the future. By remembering that our unfaithfulness in the past caused us to be separated from God's blessings and protection will help us to remain more faithful today. Take to heart the things that the Lord has done in your life and allow them to change the way that you look at and relate to God. Jesus, help us to remember all that You have done for us.

MAY 12

Read: 1 Samuel 12:1 – 13:23, John 7:1-30, Psalm 108:1-13, Proverbs 15:4

JOHN 7:5

For even his brothers didn't believe in him.

In Psalm 69:8 it was predicted that this would be true of the Messiah. It seems kind of sad that those that are closest to Him are sometimes the ones that understand the least about what He is doing. Jesus' brothers are trying to goad Jesus into doing something that He doesn't want to do; to go to Jerusalem for the feast of Tabernacles.

The gospels don't elaborate of this conversation that Jesus had with His brothers and I have wondered what Jesus was feeling at a time like this. Was He sad because His own brothers wouldn't believe in Him? Might He have had doubts and questions in His mind wondering if anyone else would believe in Him? I believe the answer is no. I don't believe that He felt sadder regarding His brother's unbelief than He was about any others that would not believe. I also know that He knew they weren't going to believe right from the beginning; that's why He inspired the Psalmist to write Psalm 69:8.

The lesson that we should take from this is that just because we have accepted Jesus and believe Him and seek to follow Him doesn't mean that our family is going to also. Statistically, we have seen that once one member of the family accepts Jesus that others are likely to follow but it is not guaranteed. Everyone will ultimately have to make their own decision about Jesus. We know that at some point at least one of Jesus' brothers did come to believe in his older brother but we don't know if they all did.

What we need to focus on is our own relationship with Jesus and our witness to the rest of the world, including our family. Too often people get consumed with the fact that their family members are not saved and it actually draws them away from an intense focus on Jesus. The best way to lead someone to Jesus is to let Jesus shine so brightly from your life that they can't help but see Him. It is Jesus in your life that will be attractive to them. It is Jesus working through the issues of your life that will teach them. It is Jesus carrying you through the trials and tribulations of your life that will cause them to desire what you have. Leave their salvation in the hands of their loving Savior Jesus. You focus on living the life that Jesus died to give you and then allow Him to use you as a witness of His grace, mercy, and power.

You can't drag someone into salvation; they must be lead there. For you that means that you need to be walking in your salvation making it as attractive as you know how. Once the Holy Spirit has done His work in their hearts then you can come along beside them to help them understand their faith better. Until then you just keep walking with Jesus being a beacon of hope. Jesus, help us to follow You and allow You to shine forth from our lives.

MAY 13
Read: 1 Samuel 14:1-52, John 7:31-53, Psalm 109:1-31, Proverbs 15:5-7

1 SAMUEL 14:6
"Let's go across to see those pagans," Jonathan said to his armor bearer. "Perhaps the LORD will help us, for nothing can hinder the LORD. He can win a battle whether he has many warriors or only a few!"

Jonathan takes his armor bearer and goes over toward the camp of the Philistines. It is just the two of them and they approach this army that is enormous. With chariots alone the Philistines had a larger army than Israel. In the previous chapter we are told that the people of Israel when faced with this terrible army ran and hid in caves and holes. This left Saul with only six hundred men.

So Jonathan takes his armor bearer to check out this army. And then Jonathan proposes this wild idea to his armor bearer. He suggests that they go and show themselves to the army of the Philistines and see what they do. And he makes this radical statement: "Perhaps the Lord will help us." Jonathan was going to face this incredible foe and he wasn't even certain that God was going to go with him.

But Jonathan was certain of something; he was certain that if God wanted him to fight the Philistines, that there was nothing that the Philistines could do to stop him. Jonathan had the faith to believe that if God revealed to him that he was to fight the Philistines that God would win the victory. Jonathan knew that it would not be him that was doing the fighting but it would be God and nothing could hinder God in His victory.

That is the kind of faith that allows God to do the incredible things that He wants to do around us. All of us are faced with an army of Philistines; an enemy too great for us to defeat. While it usually isn't a physical army, it is some kind of hindrance to the life that God intended for you to have.

In our ministries and churches, the thing that prevents us from achieving great things for God is our lack of faith when faced with an overwhelming opponent. And often that opponent doesn't even exist; it is something in our minds. We have been asked to do something that is far beyond our abilities or God has revealed to us or our leaders a vision that is impossible. Impossible for whom; you or God?

It was impossible for Jonathan to defeat thirty thousand chariots, six thousand horsemen, and countless foot soldiers. But it wasn't impossible for God. All Jonathan needed was one little confirmation from God to convince him to attempt the impossible. Jonathan was risking his life. Usually when God leads us to attempt the impossible, He is not asking us to risk that much. And if God is telling you to do something, where is the risk? Remember, "nothing can hinder the Lord." Jesus, help us to go boldly where You lead.

MAY 14

Read: 1 Samuel 15:1 – 16:23, John 8:1-20, Psalm 110:1-7, Proverbs 15:8-10

1 SAMUEL 15:22

But Samuel replied, "What is more pleasing to the LORD: your burnt offerings and sacrifices or your obedience to his voice? Obedience is far better than sacrifice. Listening to him is much better than offering the fat of rams.

Samuel came to King Saul with instructions from God. Saul was to utterly destroy the nation of Amalek because of the things that they had done to Israel. God, through Samuel, told King Saul that everyone and everything was to be destroyed. The army of Israel was victorious in their battle against Amalek and destroyed all the people and most of the things.

However, they spared the king and brought him to King Saul. And they kept all the finest of the animals. The text says that they were unwilling to destroy them. Samuel confronts Saul and asks why he didn't do what God told him to do. Saul then starts making excuses and blame-shifting. He tells Samuel he did what God said and also that he was afraid of the people so he didn't make them do what they were supposed to do.

Saul was selected as the leader of the nation of Israel and God's expectation of the leader he appointed was that he would be obedient to him regardless of the consequences. Saul's failure here reveals his true nature and could be used to teach us much about leadership. But the main point of this text is that obedience is more important than any sacrifice that we could make to God.

Saul said that the people intended to sacrifice the animals that they kept to the Lord. Whether or not that was true doesn't change the fact that they were likely doing it for selfish reasons because seldom was the entire animal burned up. Usually the person making the sacrifice would keep a portion of the sacrifice for themselves and some would be given to the priests as their food. Saul allowed the desires of the people to sway his judgment and this cost him everything.

God expects His leaders to obey His voice implicitly, without hesitation and without compromise. God took the kingdom away from Saul because he chose to disobey God and then justified his actions by making a sacrifice to God. Our sacrifices are meaningless if we aren't being obedient. As God's leaders we are called to sacrifice much, and if we want those sacrifices to be of any worth we must be obedient. Obedience becomes difficult when it means it is going to cost us something or like with Saul, it means that we will experience conflict with those that want to do it a different way. Jesus, help us to respond to your voice without looking to the left, right, or behind.

MAY 15

Read: 1 Samuel 17:1 – 18:4, John 8:21-30, Psalm 111:1-10, Proverbs 15:11

JOHN 8:21

Later Jesus said to them again, "I am going away. You will search for me and die in your sin. You cannot come where I am going."

The Jewish leaders were pretty regularly harassing Jesus. They would challenge His teaching. They would scoff at His miracles. They would challenge Him to prove that He was who He said that He was. Jesus would usually respond to them but never in the way that they expected. In yesterday's reading these same Jewish leaders had brought a woman that had been caught in the very act of adultery (Where is the man?) to Jesus to have Him determine what should be done to her. Jesus' response was to confront each of these Jewish leaders with his own sin. The Jewish leaders are back again and Jesus makes this proclamation to them in our verse for the day. First Jesus tells them the He is going to be leaving. That is not news to us; we have read that He has been telling His disciples that for a while. It is news to the Jewish leaders. If Jesus had stopped there, the Jewish leaders could have probably gone away happy thinking the problem was soon going to take care of itself. But Jesus had much more to say to them.

Jesus told them that after He was gone that they would be looking for Him but they wouldn't be able to find Him. Understand that Jesus knew that He was going to be going to the cross and it was these Jewish leaders that were going to see that it happened. They would see Jesus die. When Jesus said that they would be looking for Him, He was not referring to the person that He was but what He represented. Jesus was the Messiah that the Jews knew was coming to save them. After Jesus was gone they would still be looking for the Messiah but because they had missed Him while He was there they will die in their sins.

People are still looking for the Messiah. They are looking for someone to save them from the life they are living or the mistakes they have made. People still want to be rescued. But just like the Jewish leaders they will refuse to see the truth as it is laid out before them. The hard reality of life is that there are many people that will go through their entire lives searching for the answers to their life but will reject the truth that is found in Jesus because it doesn't fit in with their view of how it should go.

The Jewish leaders were waiting for a Messiah to deliver them from the oppression of the Roman government. They were waiting for a king. Jesus didn't fit the job description that they had developed for the person that would fill this role. We have got to be so careful not to do what the Jewish leaders did; putting God into a box that He must fill so that we will believe. We must get to know God and let Him teach us how we should think about Him and view Him. And then we must teach others to do the same thing. The Jewish leaders were the leaders of the people and many people followed them. The people that follow you will perceive Jesus the way that you lead them. Jesus, teach us to see you as you are and not as we think you are.

MAY 16
Read: 1 Samuel 18:5 – 19:24, John 8:31-59, Psalm 112:1-10, Proverbs 15:12-14

PROVERBS 15:14

A wise person is hungry for truth, while the fool feeds on trash.

The book of proverbs is filled with amazing things that can speak to our hearts if we will but let them. It is often difficult to pick out just one verse because so many of them have something to teach us. Today's verse struck me very powerfully and in some respects convicted me as well. It is possible that you may have read this verse and not sensed the Spirit say anything to you about it. That's OK! Maybe this one wasn't for you. At least, not today!

Proverbs spends much of its time comparing the wise person to the foolish one. Within these proverbs we can find a complete and elaborate description of a wise person. By applying these truths to our lives we can become wise. By ignoring them we automatically group ourselves with the fools. In today's verse we see a description of the spiritual diet and its effect on our lives. A wise person has a spiritual hunger for the truth. A wise person feeds their spirit things of truth.

The opposite is true of the fool; they feed their souls trash. A quick scan of the popular television shows is all the evidence that we need to prove that this is true. The shows that are popular are teaching or feeding our souls anything but truth. Many of them glorify sinful lifestyles or degrade the roles that men and women play in the home and family.

The effect of these shows is that they are feeding trash into the souls of those that are watching them. Anyone that says that these shows are harmless fun are buying into the lie of the enemy and allowing poison and garbage into their lives and the net result is that we are seeing an erosion of marriage and family. It is a very simple equation; if you pump trash into your mind, the things that come out in your marriage and family are also going to be trash.

Instead, we should have a hunger and a passion for the truth. If we will feed truth into our mind, then what comes out in our marriage and family is the fruit of that truth. Feed your spirit truth and fruit of truth comes out. Feed your spirit trash and fruit of trash comes out. We can look into our own lives and see the fruit of our lives and determine whether or not we need to examine the things that we are feeding our spirit.

One of the most difficult decisions that I made in my family was to disconnect the cable television. It was the most unpopular decision that I have ever made and still regularly is challenged by my teenage children. Not all television is trash but sadly there is a lot more trash than there is truth. And it is not just television but also movies and the internet. For us to be counted among the wise we must have a hunger for and search out the truth and the trash must disgust us. Jesus, let us hunger and thirst for righteousness.

MAY 17
Read: 1 Samuel 20:1 – 21:15, John 9:1-41, Psalm 113:1 – 114:8, Proverbs 15:15-17

1 SAMUEL 21:13

So he pretended to be insane, scratching on the doors and drooling down his beard.

David will some day be one of the greatest kings that the nation of Israel ever had. During his rule, he will conquer almost all the enemies of

Israel. When his son Solomon takes over the kingdom, he will experience a lifetime of peace and prosperity because of David's efforts before him. But here we see David acting insane, scratching at the door like a dog and drooling down his beard. How did that happen?

Partly we can understand; he is running away from King Saul who is trying to kill him. King Saul wants to kill him because the people like David more than him, or at least that is what his paranoia is telling him. Because of King Saul's disobedience the LORD has taken the kingdom away from Saul and given it to David. It will still be many years before David sits as king.

In the meantime he is in Gath acting insane. The main problem with this picture is where David is. Gath is enemy territory. King Achish is a pagan king whose kingdom is in conflict with the nation of Israel. David's reputation has preceded him and King Achish's officers are not happy about David being there. David is famous for killing Philistines and where is he but in Philistine territory. It was a foolish decision for David to go to Gath and so now he must act foolish to try to get back out of Gath.

As Christians we can do the same thing. We might find ourselves in a place where we have to leave a circumstance because it is uncomfortable or possibly even dangerous but don't consult the LORD about what it is that He thinks we ought to do. Then we find ourselves in a place that might be just as bad as or worse than where we were. To escape this new situation we must do something that under normal circumstances we would never even consider. David didn't consider that where he was headed to might be worse than from where he came. God had a different plan for David and as soon as David was following that plan God started blessing him.

The LORD didn't want David in Gath and so wouldn't bless him there. God will not bless us while we are wandering around in enemy territory acting insane. If you want to experience the blessing and promises of God fully, you must determine where He wants you and go there. For some people that means simply a change of perspective. For David, he had to go somewhere but went the wrong direction. For some God might want them to stay where they are and stop looking for something different.

Spiritually, Gath is any place that you go or desire to go that is outside of God's will for you. If you insist on going, you will find yourself doing something foolish to try to save yourself. It is so much better to go where the LORD wants you to or to stay where you are until He moves you. Jesus, help us to stay out of Gath.

MAY 18

Read: 1 Samuel 22:1 – 23:29, John 10:1-21, Psalm 115:1-18, Proverbs 15:18-19

JOHN 10:4

After he has gathered his own flock, he walks ahead of them, and they follow him because they recognize his voice.

In this section of scripture Jesus describes Himself as the Good Shepherd. Any leader of God's people would do well to study this section of scripture well; it is rich with truth and instruction. In today's verse we find several truths described for us. First we see that the Good Shepherd has gathered His own flock. Jesus is the one that gathers together the flock of God. As a leader in ministry or in a church we might sometimes fall prey to the thought that we need to be gathering God's flock together. This typically appears as church-growth materials or teachings. As leaders we have a role to play but it is the Good Shepherd that will ultimately gather His flock; leave it in His hands.

Then we see next that the Good Shepherd walks ahead of them. As the shepherd of the flock Jesus walks ahead of us to lead us and guide us. It also means that He is watching out for danger and looking for places where there is food and water. As leaders it is our responsibility to be out in front of the flock that Jesus has entrusted to us. We are to be the ones that show them the way to live by living that way ourselves. We need to show them how to stay out of danger by staying out of danger ourselves. This means staying away from things and places that can harm our spirits.

Our verse goes on to say that the flock of God follows the Good Shepherd because they recognize His voice. This part of the verse spoke the most powerfully to me personally as a leader of a part of God's flock. God's flock will only follow the voice of the Good Shepherd. For me that means that as a leader people need to recognize the voice of Christ when I speak. If they don't then they won't follow. This is true of anyone that God has called to fill any kind of role as a leader. Can they hear the voice of Christ when you speak? Do they see Christ in your life? If they don't then you are not leading them and they will not follow. And if you are called to lead them and they don't follow you because they don't see and hear the Good Shepherd in you then you are leading them astray.

As leaders our first and primary responsibility is to follow closely to the Good Shepherd. You can't lead someone to a place that you are not going yourself. You begin by learning to recognize the Shepherd's voice. Hear His voice and then obey Him. As you do that you will find yourself closer and closer to Jesus. Each step closer to Jesus brings you closer to being the kind of leader that He created you to be. Whether you are called to lead a single person or a marriage or a family or a ministry or a church, all of this applies; get close to Jesus. If you walk right behind Him you are exactly where you need to be to lead others. Those you lead will only recognize the voice of the Good Shepherd to the level that you recognize His voice. Jesus, help us to hear You.

MAY 19

Read: 1 Samuel 24:1 – 25:44, John 10:22-42, Psalm 116:1-19, Proverbs 15:20-21

1 SAMUEL 24:5

But then David's conscience began bothering him because he had cut Saul's robe.

King Saul is pursuing David in hopes of killing him and eliminating him as a threat to "his" kingdom. He pauses to relieve himself in a cave which just happens to be occupied by David and his men. David is encouraged by his men to kill Saul. Instead, he sneaks up and cuts off a part of his robe. As soon as he does, his conscience starts to bother him. He knows that he shouldn't have done it and recognizes that it was not pleasing to the LORD.

We might look at a story like this and wonder what the big deal is. Why would God be upset with David for simply cutting his robe? A study of David can teach us a lot about how God wants us to relate to our leaders. David looked at King Saul as his leader; placed in the position of leadership by God Himself. David trusted God to deal with Saul when He was ready to and in the way that He wanted.

David did not feel free to do or say anything he wanted to as far as King Saul was concerned. Even though Saul was seeking his life and slandering him, David refused to speak against or attempt to harm Saul. The leaders in our life should be respected even when they are not worthy of respect. The Bible teaches that those leaders were placed there by God Himself. To speak against them is to question God's wisdom. To attempt to harm them is to fight against God.

We live in a country that promotes the exercise of "free speech." This means that no one can prevent us from speaking as our heart leads us to speak. For Christians, that should mean that we are free to speak about our faith without fear of repercussion. It should also mean that we speak with a fear of God that causes us to respect the leaders that He has allowed to lead us.

Because of Saul's sin, David had to flee and hide. There might come a time in your life where God calls you to depart from where you are because a leader's actions are harmful to you or to others. Until then, you are called by God to support your leaders to the best of your ability. This is true in your family, ministry, church, work, and country.

Attacking the leaders that God has placed in their positions above you is against God and will result in God's hand of judgment in your own life. God doesn't need our help dealing with His leaders. God wants followers that will do everything in their ability to bring a godly influence into even the most wicked of environments. There are no perfect leaders and once we get into the habit of attacking our leaders because of their weaknesses, it is very difficult to stop. We start looking for weakness, instead of looking for their strengths and looking for ways to cover over their weaknesses. To the best of your ability pray for your leaders, encourage them, and look for ways to help them. Then trust them to God for everything else. Jesus, teach us to look up to our leaders, rather than down upon them.

MAY 20

Read: 1 Samuel 26:1 – 28:25, John 11:1-54, Psalm 117:1-2, Proverbs 15:22-23

JOHN 11:51

This prophecy that Jesus should die for the entire nation came from Caiaphas in his position as high priest. He didn't think of it himself; he was inspired to say it.

All the religious leaders of the nation of Israel come together to discuss what they are doing to do about the "Jesus problem." They are concerned about Jesus' ability to draw the common people to Himself. They are concerned that if something isn't done the whole nation is going to follow Him and then they will be in trouble. In the reading it says that they were concerned that if everyone did follow Jesus that the Romans would come in and destroy them. This is further proof that they had no idea what Jesus was about and what He was teaching to the people.

Then Caiaphas speaks up and tells them that the solution is easy; Jesus needs to die for the people. This was a beautiful thing that He says here. In fact, Caiaphas tells the religious leaders of the nation of Israel exactly why Jesus came to the earth; He came to die for the people. Without knowing it Caiaphas tells the religious of Jesus' plan to save the world.

In today's verse we are told that he didn't think of it himself; he was inspired to say it. Here we see the work of the Holy Spirit in the life of an unbeliever. The Holy Spirit planted the idea into Caiaphas' mind. Because of his sinfulness, the idea appealed to him and so he spoke it out. Jesus came to the earth to die for the sins of the whole world and God had a plan of how he was going to do that. The Holy Spirit didn't make Caiaphas say it; He just gave Him the thought knowing that it was the kind of thing that he would be willing to do.

The Holy Spirit is active in the world and He is the primary person at work in the execution of God's plan here. He is active not just in the lives of believers but also with unbelievers. This is probably not one of the ways that we think about when we think about the work of the Holy Spirit but there is a great truth hidden in this verse.

We know that the Holy Spirit is working to draw others to Christ but in this verse we also see that He is also working for the good of others. The Holy Spirit is God and is not limited to whom He interacts with. If you have something going on in your life, the Holy Spirit is not limited to working with people that want to help you or that love God. The Holy Spirit can inspire someone to do something that helps in whatever circumstance you are in. That is very encouraging.

Don't limit God's influence in you life. There is no limit to which the Holy Spirit can reach out to influence those that God loves and wants to bless. Our responsibility is to believe, pray, and obey. Jesus, thank you for the gift of the Holy Spirit in our lives.

MAY 21

Read: 1 Samuel 29:1 – 31:13, John 11:55 – 12:19, Psalm 118:1-18, Proverbs 15:24-26

1 SAMUEL 30:6

David was now in serious trouble because his men were very bitter about losing their wives and children, and they began to talk of stoning him. But David found strength in the LORD his God.

David is in trouble again. King Saul is still hoping to catch him and kill him so he has fled to the Philistines. The Philistine commanders do not trust him, so they send David away from the upcoming battle. And when David and his six hundred men get back to their town, they find it burned to the ground by the Amalekites. All their wives and children and possessions are gone. This is too much for David's men and they turn on him and are talking about stoning him.

Among those taken away were David's two wives. Everything that they had was gone. They were in a foreign land and everything had been taken away from them. The text tells us that they grieved until they had no more strength to grieve.

As we lead God's ministries and churches, there are going to be times when we feel like David did here. Even as we attempt to lead our families we can feel as David did. On every side are enemies and everything that is important to us or has value has been taken away from you. And then even those that are closest to you, that you have fought and battled with, have turned on you. You feel incredibly, painfully, desperately alone. It is at those moments that we need to turn our eyes, as David did, to God.

David found strength in the Lord "his" God. At that moment of his most desperate need David reminded himself that the awesome Creator of the universe was his God and that knowledge brought him the strength that he needed. David realized that his strength wasn't enough, because he didn't have any left.

Too many men and women of God forget this principle at just this time. God is our strength! Because David turned to God for strength and then for guidance, God helped David and his men get back everything that had been taken from them. It also appears from the text that they actually ended up with more than had been taken from them.

There will come a time in every leader's life, in every person's life when he or she will feel as David did. You will feel surrounded by enemies and everything that you treasure is gone. Will you do as David did? Will you get your strength from the Lord "your" God? I pray that you will! Jesus, help us to look up every time things around us are looking down.

MAY 22
Read: 2 Samuel 1:1 – 2:11, John 12:20-50, Psalm 118:19-29, Proverbs 15:27-28

JOHN 12:37

But despite all the miraculous signs he had done, most of the people did not believe in him.

Jesus did things that were absolutely amazing. He healed people of every kind of sickness or disease; nothing was too difficult for Him to heal. He raised a number of people from the dead; which no one had ever seen happen before. He cast out demons of every type and number. Jesus had power over every one of the things that came as a result of sin in the world. It is hard to imagine that people watching these happen could not or would not believe but our verse for the day tells us that very thing. With all of the miracles that Jesus did, MOST of the people did not believe.

Jesus knew that was going to be the case because He inspired the prophet Isaiah to write about their unbelief hundreds of years before He showed up. Since man first walked upon this earth he has been resisting the evidence of God's love, grace, and power to follow his own selfish way. For those of us that believe it can be impossible to comprehend why others do not believe. It can also be very frustrating when we see our own witness of Jesus being rejected and not believed.

We should never be discouraged or frustrated by this. If they didn't believe Jesus while He was on the earth in their very presence, what makes you think people are going to believe you? To be discouraged or frustrated by that is an indication of pride; it is thinking that you could accomplish something that Jesus Himself could not do. Discouragement or frustrations are not the right emotions to feel over the hardness of hearts of others.

The right emotions would be sadness and determination. It should sadden us that they have chosen to reject Jesus. That sadness is born out of the knowledge that they are choosing to be separated from God for all of eternity. That sadness is also because they are missing the power of God in this life to give them the life that they are so desperately seeking on their own.

We should also be determined to be a living witness of that power in our own lives. We should continually be looking for a deeper relationship with Jesus so that the light from our life might break through the darkness of their hearts. We should be determined to allow the Holy Spirit to daily soften our heart so that the hardness of their hearts does not infect ours. Jesus wants everyone to choose to believe but the truth is that most will choose not to believe. Be diligent to pray and ask God to soften their hearts and ask Him to use you to draw them to Himself. Until He does, you just stay close to Him. Jesus, help us to look to our own hearts first.

MAY 23

Read: 2 Samuel 2:12 – 3:39, John 13:1-30, Psalm 119:1-16, Proverbs 15:29-20

PSALM 119:11

I have hidden your word in my heart, that I might not sin against you.

This is one of the first verses that I memorized after I discovered it while reading the Bible. Something about it has always spoken to my heart about what God desires of me. This psalm has also been one of my favorites because of its emphasis upon the word of God. Even very early on in my walk, God has helped me to develop a love for His word. It was His Word and the testimony of my wife's life that drew me to Jesus in the first place.

Our verse for the day tells us that we should hide God's word in our heart. That is a fascinating way to describe how God wants us to treat the things that are contained in the Bible. The idea of hiding something implies that it is placed someplace where it can't be seen or touched by someone else. This is a wonderful picture of what God is asking us to do.

God's word should be locked away deep within your heart. It should not be seen by anyone. That sounds odd doesn't it? You could see the word of God in the Pharisees and the religious leaders of Israel but their hearts were far from God. If the word of God is buried deep within us, far from the sight of others, what will be seen is the fruit of a godly life. People need to see the fruit of the word in your life; they don't need to know how many verses you can quote. They want to see how many of them you are living out in your life; that's all that matters.

By hiding the word deep in your heart, it is also out of the reach of those that might touch it. God's word is perfect and holy. Anyone that might touch God's word within your heart can only soil it with their imperfection. All of us fall short of the glory of God and our hands are dirty with our own sin. We have no right to touch the word as it is in the heart of another believer. This also keeps it far away from the enemy who desires to steal that word from your heart.

There is a result that we should expect from hiding God's Word within our heart; it will keep us from sinning. God's Word is a fire that purifies and cleanses us from sin. It gives us the strength and ability to resist sin through the help of the Holy Spirit. God's Word is powerful and leads us to repentance and forgiveness as we discover the wonder of God's love for us and grace toward us. That doesn't mean that we will never sin again; I wish that were so. It means that we will sin less as we fill our hearts with the Word of God.

Fall in love with God's Word. It is appropriate that our verse tells us to hide God's Word within our heart because that is the seat of love in our lives. Hide God's Word where you keep love and that will help you to live a life that glorifies God and pleases Him. Jesus, fill our hearts with a love of Your Word and then teach us to hide it there.

MAY 24

Read: 2 Samuel 4:1 – 6:23, John 13:31 – 14:14, Psalm 119:17-32, Proverbs 15:31-32

JOHN 13:35

Your love for one another will prove to the world that you are my disciples.

Jesus is preparing His disciples for His imminent departure. Before He leaves to go to the Garden of Gethsemane and then to the cross Jesus gives His disciples a new commandment. That commandment is that they should love each other. He then tells the example that they are to follow; they are to love each other just like He loved them. This love for each other would be the proof to the world that they were Disciples of Christ.

Two thousand years have not changed that commandment; Jesus still wants His disciples to love one another as a proof to the world. Sadly, this is lacking greatly within the church and the church is suffering because of it. Jesus gave this commandment because this was to be one of the greatest evangelistic tools available to the church; Christ's love. Nothing will draw people to Jesus like His love being manifested to the world and especially to other believers.

It is appalling the kinds of things that immature believers will do to one another. They lie to one another. They will gossip against each other. They will sue one another. They will harbor resentment and bitterness to other believers. They will hate each other and attempt to drive people out of the church. I say that these types of people are immature because if they weren't they wouldn't do these kinds of things.

Selfishness and self-centeredness run rampant within the modern church. Self-love is a poison that will kill the best of churches. That is not even the worst part. The worst part of this self-love cancer is that unbelievers will look at what goes on in the church and it will drive them away from God and salvation in Jesus.

People need the love of God in their lives. They don't need to hear about the love of Christ; they need to see the love of Christ. If an unbeliever looks into your life and doesn't see the love of Christ being manifested toward other believers they will not believe that you have the love of Christ and therefore you have nothing to offer them that can help them.

Nothing could be more important in our lives than having the love of Christ in our lives and allowing that love to be revealed to the whole world through the way that we love other believers. The way that the love of Christ is most powerfully manifested is through forgiveness and reconciliation. Nothing communicates the love of Christ like repentance and forgiveness. Repentance and forgiveness are the cure for the cancer of self-love in the church. Jesus, teach us to love others just as You do.

MAY 25
Read: 2 Samuel 7:1 – 8:18, John 14:15:31, Psalm 119:33-48, Proverbs 15:33

2 SAMUEL 7:5

Go and tell my servant David, "This is what the LORD says: Are you the one to build me a temple to live in?"

David is now well established on the throne and God has brought peace to the land. David looks around and recognizes that he is comfortably in a palace of cedar while the Ark of the Covenant is housed in a tent. He decides that this is not appropriate and so he talks to Nathan the prophet about it. Nathan says go ahead and build a temple to replace the tent. God then speaks to Nathan and tells him to go back to David and tell him not to build it.

David's response to God telling him no is a great lesson for all of us. God is a great and awesome God. And as we draw nearer and nearer to God we realize the great things that He has done for us. It is very natural for us to want to do something great for God. The more we love Him, the greater the thing that we want to do for Him.

Just because we want to do something for God, doesn't mean that He wants us to do it for Him. God is sovereign; which means that he gets to decide who does what and when. It was for God to decide who would build Him a temple and when it would be built.

God told David no and David's response was to begin to prepare for the construction of the temple. God told him that it would be his son that would be the one to fulfill this dream that he had. Rather than abandoning the idea of the temple, David did all he could to make sure that his son, Solomon would have everything that he would need to build a great temple for God.

David would not live to see the temple built. He spent years preparing for something that he would not get to see completed. If God tells you no, it doesn't mean that He doesn't want you to work on it. Your responsibility might be to prepare the great work for someone else to do. Solomon got all the credit for building the temple and yet it was David that did much of the preparation.

The great work that God might call you to do is to prepare the way for someone else to do a great work for God. Your love of God will determine whether or not you can live with that. Jesus, help us work as servant/leaders willing to do anything the Master tells us to do even if it means that we don't get to do the great things that we want to do for You.

MAY 26

Read: 2 Samuel 9:1 – 11:27, John 15:1-27, Psalm 119:49-64, Proverbs 16:1-3

JOHN 15:19

The world would love you if you belonged to it, but you don't. I chose you to come out of the world, and so it hates you.

Jesus is spending His last few hours with His disciples. Judas has already left to betray Him to the religious leaders of the Jews. He is taking this time to teach the remaining disciples as much as He can. Few sections of scripture are as rich in spiritual truth as the things that He has been saying here.

In the text for today Jesus is preparing His disciples for the way that they will be treated when He is gone. He wants them to be as prepared for what is coming as they can be. The world will hate them and will treat them all very badly. Most of the disciples died as martyrs and Jesus didn't want that to be a surprise to them.

Having an idea how things are going to go in any circumstance allows you to prepare yourself for that. It also allows you to respond appropriately. Jesus told them that they would be hated so that it would not shake their faith when it happened. He also told them why they would be hated; because they belonged to Jesus and not to the world.

We live in a culture that is very tolerant of our Christian faith. I know that as you read this you are thinking that our society is doing everything it can to remove God from schools, government, and public venues. While that may be true; they aren't crucifying any Christians in the town square. There are countries around the world where being a Christ-follower can result in death. There are places where it is illegal to own a Bible or preach anything other than the state religion.

Jesus told us that we would be hated because we belong to Him. And while we may live in a country where that hatred is pretty tame in comparison to other countries, it is still there. As we approach the Lord's return we will see that hatred increase. We need to be prepared for that and you do that by getting to know Jesus better and better. The better you know Jesus the easier it is to withstand the pressures that will come against you. But the other side of that statement is that the better you know Jesus, the more pressure there will be against you.

With this knowledge, the disciples were able to do and accomplish incredible things for the Kingdom of God. With this knowledge, we can be disciples of Jesus Christ that can do and accomplish incredible things for the Kingdom of God. We lack nothing that prevents us from seeing the same things that the Church in the book of Acts saw happening in their midst. There is nothing that prevents us from seeing the same results except our love of Christ and our faith in Him. Jesus, help us to understand that we are no longer a part of the world but that we are ambassadors for You to this world.

MAY 27

Read: 2 Samuel 12:1-31, John 16:1-33, Psalm 119:65-80, Proverbs 16:4-5

2 SAMUEL 12:13

Then David confessed to Nathan, "I have sinned against the LORD. "Nathan replied, "Yes, but the LORD has forgiven you, and you won't die for this sin.

Here in today's reading we see David's darkest hour. King David was the best leader that the nation of Israel had and yet here we see him falling into sin and then hiding it and ultimately murdering one of his own

"Mighty Men." Nathan the prophet confronts David and lets him know that he has not hidden his sin from God.

David's response is the main thing that we need to see in this text. It is not that he sinned; everyone does that. It is not the sins that he committed; they are no better or worse than any other sin that we could commit. It is the manner in which he responded that gives us all a picture of how God wants us to respond when we are confronted with our sins.

David was the king; the leader of the nation of Israel. David didn't hesitate when confronted with his sin to confess and repent. And David knew that his sin was against God first and primarily. David didn't try to justify his sin. He didn't try to make excuses or try to shift the blame. He had sinned and he knew it and he admitted to it immediately.

As leaders in our families, ministries, and churches we need to follow the example of David. David wrote the incredible Psalm 51 as a result of God confronting him with is sin. Study this psalm to discover the true depth of David's remorse over his sin. And not just the remorse that he felt but also the hope that he had in God's graciousness and mercy. David knew that even though his sin was ugly in the sight of God, that God still loved him and still had a plan for his life.

Nothing will separate us from our God like our "hidden" sins. And nothing will draw us near to God like the confession and repenting from those sins. God is not looking for leaders that don't sin. There aren't any! What God is looking for is leaders that can see their sin the way that God sees it and the sight is repulsive to them.

Your response to the sins in your life will determine whether or not God can use you in the future. Because David responded with brokenness and contrition, God used David mightily later in his life. The instant God reveals one of your sins to you is the time for you to confess it and repent of it. The longer you fight with God about your sin, the longer and harder it will be for you. Your family, your ministry, and your church need leaders that don't hesitate to repent of their sins. Only a repentant leader can truly lead. Jesus, teach us to see our sins quickly and to repent even quicker.

MAY 28

Read: 2 Samuel 13:1-39, John 17:1-26, Psalm 119:81-96, Proverbs 16:6-7

2 SAMUEL 13:15

Then suddenly Amnon's love turned to hate, and he hated her even more than he had loved her. "Get out of here!" he snarled at her.

King David had many sons. Solomon is probably best known and would ultimately succeed David as king of Israel. Absalom and Amnon are not as well known but through them we see God's prediction of unrest within David's family fulfilled. One of the consequences of David's sin with Bathsheba was that there would be conflict within his home for the rest of his life. Much of it will be centered on Absalom.

Absalom had a beautiful sister, Tamar, and she caught the attention of Amnon. Amnon was her half-brother. King David was their father, but they had different mothers. Amnon saw her and fell in love with her; in fact, he became obsessed with her. Amnon conspires to have Tamar come and tend to him and then rapes her. Our verse tells us that once he had his way with her, his love turned to hatred and he rejected her.

The account doesn't tell us their ages but it is not hard for me to imagine them both in their late teens. If you have ever raised teenagers, then you know how this could have happened. This is a time of life when passions run wild and make radical swings from hot to cold in a moment. It certainly doesn't justify Amnon's actions but it is easy enough to see how it might have occurred.

What I think is the greater lesson in this is the effect that a father can have in a child's life. Fathers have been endowed with a supernatural ability to influence their children. If used properly, meaning as God directs, they can help their children grow to healthy, productive maturity. If neglected or abused, the children will follow the influence of their peers or their own selfish desires.

Of course, just because we use our influence as well as we can doesn't guarantee that our children won't make foolish decisions, but it certainly improves the odds in your favor. It should be our goal as parents to give our children the best chances we can in life to make the best possible choices. To do otherwise is to condemn them to a life of pain and suffering.

As a result of Amnon's selfish, undisciplined actions Tamar lived as a "desolate woman" in her brother Absalom's house. This meant that she did not marry, because no man would have her after having been raped. Two years later Absalom schemed against Amnon and murdered him. This resulted in Absalom running away from Israel to escape the consequences of his actions.

In one event we see the lives of many people of one family altered forever. As fathers we need to do everything we can to prevent these kinds of things from happening. We do that by leading our family as the LORD directs and by using the supernatural influence that He has given us to help them grow to maturity in the LORD. Jesus, teach us to lead them to You.

MAY 29

Read: 2 Samuel 14:1 – 15:22, John 18:1-24, Psalm 119:97-112, Proverbs 16:8-9

2 SAMUEL 14:1

Joab realized how much the king longed to see Absalom.

Absalom has been banished from David's presence because he killed David's son Amnon, Absalom's half-brother. Amnon had raped and then rejected Absalom's sister Tamar. Two years after the rape, Absalom took revenge upon Amnon. David was reconciled to the death of Amnon and was now missing his son Absalom.

Joab recognized this state of mind in his king and decided to do something about it. He brought a woman in to make a request of the king that caused him to look at the matter of Absalom's banishment from a different perspective. David did and allowed Absalom to return to Jerusalem and ultimately their relationship was restored, at least for a little while.

Joab knew his king well enough to see that there was something that David needed that he couldn't provide for himself. David had banished Absalom and this decision was causing him much pain. Joab knew that David was a man of integrity and would not readily reverse his decision. Joab, through this woman, brought the matter before David so they he could see it from a different perspective.

In this Joab showed two characteristics that every person that follows a leader must exhibit. The first is awareness. You must be aware of the needs and emotions of your leader. He or she may not be able to express what is going on inside of them and they may not be able to even see the source of their pain or discomfort. For our leaders to be effective, we must love them enough to care about what is going on in their lives.

The second characteristic of a follower that will help his leader is courage. Joab showed great courage when he brought this matter before the king. Joab couldn't have known how the king might respond to his approach but he cared enough about David to risk it. We must have the courage to go to our leaders in love and humility to help them to see the matter from a different perspective.

Leaders are not perfect and they are not invincible. All leaders will go through times when they are not sure about themselves or their decisions. All leaders will have circumstances that challenge them. A good leader has good people that are there to lovingly help them through their times of need. In fact, without good people fulfilling that role, it is difficult for a leader to achieve success. For a leader to be a leader, they must have people following them. Those people have the responsibility to love that leader and to help him or her through whatever they might be going through. Jesus, teach us to be good followers.

MAY 30

Read: 2 Samuel 15:23 – 16:23, John 18:25 – 19:22, Psalm 119:113-128, Proverbs 16:10-11

2 SAMUEL 15:26

But if he is through with me, then let him do what seems best to him.

Absalom has incited the people to revolt against King David and make him king instead of his father. David in response to this rebellion packs up his household and family and leaves Jerusalem. David's concern was for the people and city of Jerusalem. He knew that if he stayed there that Absalom would bring an army to destroy the city to get to him. David decided quickly to move away from the city so that it and its people would be saved.

The Ark of the Covenant was sent back to Jerusalem so that it would also remain safe during this time of unrest. David knew that Absalom only cared about finding and killing him, so by removing himself from the city he was protecting it and everything in it. For many this seems to be an unusual strategy by David. He was the king and had been anointed by God to be the king of Israel. Absalom was a usurper; he had no right to the throne. Many would think that the right strategy for David would be to mobilize the army and fight Absalom.

David was the king but did not cling to his rights as king. David knew that he was king because God had made him the king. He also knew that it was God's place to remove him as king if that was His wish. In our text for today, David is putting his life and future into the hands of the Lord. What a beautiful picture of leadership for us to learn from.

As leaders, there are going to come times when someone comes along and takes our "position" away from us. It is at those times that we need to respond like David did. He stepped aside to see what it was that the Lord wanted to do. What he didn't do was attempt to defend his "position" and fight to keep it. A great deal more harm would have been done to those that David was to protect, if he had resisted this coup. David trusted God with his "position" and trusted God to deal with him justly and fairly. David knew that God had every right and justification to remove him from the throne.

In tomorrow's reading we are going to see that God returns David to the throne and to Jerusalem. David trusted God to do that and we need to trust God to do that in our lives, ministries, and churches. If a usurper has come in and taken your "position" then step aside without defending your position. If you have found favor in God's eyes, He will return you to that place or someplace better. But if He is through with you in that place, it is His right and prerogative to remove you and do with you as He pleases.

David trusted God when he made him king and David trusted God if He wanted to remove him as king. We need to also trust God in our "positions." Jesus, help us to have hearts as David, that desire You to do with us as You please.

MAY 31

Read: 2 Samuel 17:1-29, John 19:23-42, Psalm 119:129-152, Proverbs 16:12-13

2 SAMUEL 17:14

Then Absalom and all the leaders of Israel said, "Hushai's advice is better than Ahithophel's." For the LORD had arranged to defeat the counsel of Ahithophel, which was really the better plan, so that he could bring disaster upon Absalom!

Absalom, King David's son has rebelled against his father and is attempting to take David's throne from him. So far he has been pretty successful. David has evacuated the City of David so that Absalom will not come and besiege it. To cement his hold upon the throne, Absalom must destroy his father. So he calls in his advisors.

Ahithophel is loyal to Absalom and suggests that Absalom attack David immediately before David has a chance to gather troops or get into a fortified city. Hushai is loyal to King David and suggests that Absalom wait and gather the whole army of Israel together before attacking David. Absalom rejects Ahithophel's plan and accepts the plan that Hushai proposed.

All of that seems like pretty normal stuff until you get to the verse for the day. According to today's verse Absalom picked the wrong plan, and not because he wasn't wise enough but because God had arranged it so he would choose the wrong plan. God had determined to "bring disaster upon Absalom." Part of God's plan to accomplish that was to defeat Ahithophel's advice.

We sometimes forget that God is God and that there is nothing that He can't do. There are some things that He chooses not to do but there is nothing that He can't do. We often think that God is not going to make my choices for me; He leaves me the freewill to choose for myself. That is true but that doesn't mean that God can't cause us to choose what He wants rather than what we want.

Today's text is a great example of that. Absalom was outside of the will of God. Absalom wanted to destroy his father and the best plan presented to him was Ahithophel's. God's plan was to bring disaster upon Absalom and He caused Absalom to pick Hushai's plan which was the inferior plan. The LORD influenced Absalom's decision to accomplish His plan.

We might wonder why God doesn't do that all the time so that we are always doing what He desires rather than making some of the foolish decisions that we do. If He did do that our will would not come into the picture and we would not have the kind of relationship with Him that He desires. It is often because of the poor choices and bad decisions that we grow to recognize our great need for a close relationship with Him. If the LORD always influenced us to make only the right choices, then there would be no choice at all. God chooses to let us choose, but there are times when God influences the choice according to His will and plan. Understanding when that is happening is one of the great mysteries of life. Jesus, teach us to look for You in all of our choices.

JUNE

JUNE 1

Read: 2 Samuel 18:1 – 19:10, John 20:1-31, Psalm 119:153-176, Proverbs 16:14-15

PSALM 121:2

My help comes from the LORD, who made the heavens and the earth!

The psalmist in our reading for today started this psalm by asking a rhetorical question; "Where does my help come from?" And then here in our verse for the day he answers his own question. This psalmist knew where his help was coming from and he knew something about the ability of that helper.

First, the source of his help was the Lord. Knowing the source of where your help is going to come from will give you a sense of comfort and peace. Too often people are looking to things and people other than the Lord for their help. Our help comes from the Lord. He might use some of these other things or people but they are still coming from Him.

This requires faith! To believe that God is the source of our help is a step of faith. It means that we may not be able to see how the help is going to come to us and we may not understand how God is going to help us. But by faith we must believe that he is the source of our help and we must wait for Him to do it. But as we wait we must also be listening for the leading of the Holy Spirit in case there is a step that God is asking us to take before He helps us.

This is the part that a lot of people miss. They believe that God is the source of their help and they believe that God will help them. What they are not doing are the things that God wants them to do first. God will often require a step of faith before His helping hand reaches out. We need to be listening for our part, and in faith and obedience do it, so that we can see God's part.

Second, the psalmist knew something about the source of his help. He knew that the Lord had made the heavens and the earth. The psalmist knew that the Lord, the source of his help was powerful enough to create everything that we see. This brings with it a great confidence as we wait. If God is great enough and powerful enough to create the heavens and the earth, then He is great and powerful enough to help me.

As we wait for the Lord to help us, we can do so in comfort and confidence. We are at peace because we know that the creator of everything, including us, is able to help us. This should bring peace even in the midst of the greatest of trials and tribulations; our help comes from the Lord. Have faith that the great God that created the universe and everything in it is the source of your help and look for what it is that He might be asking you to do before He helps you. Sometimes it is just to wait and believe. Jesus, help us to believe that you are the source and power of our help.

JUNE 2

Read: 2 Samuel 19:11 – 20:13, John 21:1-25, Psalm 120:1-7, Proverbs 16:16-17

2 SAMUEL 20:3

When the king arrived at his palace in Jerusalem, he instructed that the ten concubines he had left to keep house should be placed in seclusion. Their needs were to be cared for, he said, but he would no longer sleep with them. So each of them lived like a widow until she died.

David returns to Jerusalem after Absalom's rebellion has been ended. One of the first things that he does is to put away the ten concubines that he had left behind to take care of the palace. Because of the culture that we live in we can't begin to fathom what David is doing or why he did it. These ten women were made to stay and because of their obedience to the king they no longer are allowed to be a part of the king's life.

A concubine had many of the duties and responsibilities of a wife but she didn't have the same rights or status as a wife. Often concubines were obtained so that a man could have more sons which brought him status and sometimes wealth and position. When Absalom came into the city of Jerusalem during his rebellion, the first thing that he did was to sleep with all ten of his father's concubines. This was done to humiliate and insult David and to show that he was victorious over him. It was a serious thing that Absalom did and David's response was to put these ten women away from his presence because they were in the eyes of that culture no longer David's concubines but Absalom's.

We look at an incident like this and think that it is terribly unfair and in reality it is. Because we don't understand the culture we will always struggle with things like this but there is a lesson for us in this. Absalom was a bad leader that did bad things and as a result innocent people were harmed. The harm that was done to these ten concubines was not fatal; but their lives were diminished. All of their needs were met but their position and status was that of a widow.

In life things happen that sometimes cause us to be left in a similar kind of place as these ten concubines. Through no fault of our own we have been diminished in our roles or positions in life. When that happens we need to trust that God is going to meet our needs and we will be taken care of. But we need to also recognize that we may not ever get back to the position that we once had. Our text doesn't tell us how these ten concubines responded to this. It doesn't really matter; they didn't have a choice, this was to be their lot in life.

Your lot in life is what God allowed it to be or caused it to be. Who are you to question what He is doing? Our role is to fulfill our role and let God fulfill His, which is to be God and run the universe including your life. If something bad happens, trust that God is still in control and that His plan is still in effect even if it means that you are being put away. Jesus, help us to rest in Your hands and help us to not try to take matters into our own hands.

JUNE 3

Read: 2 Samuel 20:14 – 21:22, Acts 1:1-26, Psalm 121:1-8, Proverbs 16:18

2 SAMUEL 21:17

But Abishai son of Zeruiah came to his rescue and killed the Philistine. After that, David's men declared, "You are not going out to battle again! Why should we risk snuffing out the light of Israel?"

David is out in a battle with the Philistines again. During this battle David becomes weary and is cornered by one of the descendants of the giants who is about to kill him. One of David's men, Abishai, comes and kills the giant to save David. The men then all agree that David should not come out to battle any longer. They are concerned that he will be killed.

David was a warrior-king. He had fought in many battles and been victorious. Some of those accounts, like the one with Goliath, are the best known stories in the Bible. But things have changed. The biggest thing that has changed is David; he is a lot older than he was when he fought Goliath. David's men see that age has caught up to their king and so they discourage him from joining them in any future battles.

It is not difficult to imagine that David resisted this suggestion at first but ultimately saw the wisdom in it. There is a lesson in this for us as well. As we go through life there will be a few things that will be the trademarks of our life. They are the things that people know about us when they look at our lives. In David's life it was his skill in battle. In Sampson's life it was strength. In Solomon's life it was wisdom. We can often find some one thing that defines our lives.

The problem arises when the circumstances of our life change. Sometimes the very thing that we are best known for becomes a liability. In David's life his prowess in battle could not be carried by his physical body; he was no longer able to fight like his reputation. He could have tried to continue but it ultimately would have cost him his life. His men were not willing to sacrifice David on the battlefield.

His men were not being cruel or prideful; they cared about their king. They believed he was of more value in the palace than on the battlefield. David could have let his pride get in the way in this but it appears that he did not and this was the last battle that David fought.

As the circumstances of our lives change we must be prepared to change along with them. It was as a warrior that David ascended to the throne but once there God wanted him to be a king. The warrior would never be totally gone from David but his role needed to change to match his circumstances. The pathways of life are not straight, well-lit, and filled with signs directing us. That is why it is so important for us to have an intimate relationship with our God. The closer we are to Him, the fewer times we will find ourselves backed into a corner with a giant trying to kill us. Jesus, teach us to stay close.

JUNE 4

Read: 2 Samuel 22:1 – 23:23, Acts 2:1-47, Psalm 122:1-9, Proverbs 16:19-20

2 SAMUEL 22:36

You have given me the shield of your salvation; your help has made me great.

Second Samuel 22 and Psalm 18 are both songs of praise and thanksgiving. God had done amazing things for David during his life and so he composes this song that tells God how he feels. David had experienced all sorts of trials and circumstances in his life. Some of these were because of the sins and mistakes of others and some were by his own hand. But all through his life, David never lost sight of God. There were times where he was a little out of focus but he quickly returned to where he needed to be when he was confronted with his sin.

David was the king of all Israel. He was victorious over every enemy that he faced. David was a humble man even though he had plenty of reasons to be proud. He ruled over one of the greatest nations in the world at that time. There is a saying that says: "Power corrupts and absolute power corrupts absolutely." David was a man with great power and he did not let that power corrupt him.

He accomplished this by remembering where that power came from. David knew that it wasn't his abilities that had made him king; it was God's plan. David knew that is wasn't his strength that had brought him the great victories that he had won; it was God's power.

David was a great man and he knew exactly how he had become great. In our verse for the day, David gives God the credit for making him great. Out of the entire nation of Israel, God had selected David to be great. It was because of God's help that David is the king of Israel and it is because of God's help that he was successful.

It is not likely that God is going to make any of us king, but He does want to do great things with us and through us. To be used by God in some great way we must be like David. We must be humble and know that God is the one with the plan and the power. If we have a tendency toward prideful thoughts and actions, it will hamper our ability to be great for God.

David was an ordinary kid when God took him from tending the sheep and anointed him as king of Israel. God can also take any of us and anoint us to do tremendous things for the Kingdom of God if only we will give God the glory for it. God wants us to fully and completely embrace the truth that without Christ we can do nothing and with Christ we can do anything. The only way that we can achieve greatness is by being ready to lay that greatness at the feet of Jesus. Only then are you ready to be "king." Jesus, help us to be great so that we can bring great glory and honor to You.

JUNE 5

Read: 2 Samuel 23:24 – 24:25, Acts 3:1-26, Psalm 123:1-4, Proverbs 16:21-23

ACTS 3:6

But Peter said, "I don't have any money for you. But I'll give you what I have. In the name of Jesus Christ of Nazareth, get up and walk!"

Peter and John are on their way to the temple to participate in the afternoon prayer time. On the way they encounter a man that has been lame since birth. For his whole life this man has not been able to walk. In these times this meant that he was not able to provide for himself except by begging for the generosity of others. This lame man had a special place that his family or friends would bring him in the morning.

Peter looks intently at the man and realizes that God intends to heal him. God is also going to use this man to proclaim the power of God to others. Peter then makes the statement in the verse for the day and the man is instantly healed and gets up and walks.

It is within this statement that Peter makes that we find an important lesson for anyone that is called to minister to others. In case you are wondering who that might be it is only required of people that are Christians. As Christians we are all required to show love to others. We do that by ministering to their needs as we can.

All around us are people that have needs. Some of these people have small needs and some, like the lame man, have great needs. God is going to arrange it so that the people with needs and the people that He is going to use to meet those needs come together. If there are people around you that have needs, physical, emotional, spiritual, relational, He may have put you there to help them.

In Peter's statement he tells the lame man that he doesn't have any money for him. Too often we think that the answer to meeting someone else's need is money. Peter realized that the lame man's need was not money; he needed to be able to walk so that he could work and provide for himself. Offering money to a person's need might be the last thing that they need. Let the Holy Spirit guide you in what the right way is to minister to others. In the second half of Peter's statement he tells the lame man that he will give him what he has. In that is another powerful lesson for us. God has given you what you have so that you can use it to minister to other people. Our attitude must be like Peter's; he was willing to give what he had. We can't be stingy with the things that God has given us. If we are stingy, we limit the continued blessings and empowerment of God. God won't give us more if we won't use what he has already given us.

It is a lack of faith to refuse to help others with what you have. It proves that you care more for your life and for your stuff than you trust God to provide for your own needs and desires. All we have is from God and He desires that we would use all that we have to minister to those that He puts around us. The greatest blessings in life come when we give all that we have to God. Jesus, let us live our lives trying to give away to others all that You have given to us.

JUNE 6
Read: 1 Kings 1-53, Acts 4:1-37, Psalm 124:1-8, Proverbs 16:24

1 KINGS 1:5

About that time David's son Adonijah, whose mother was Haggith, decided to make himself king in place of his aged father. So he provided himself with chariots and horses and recruited fifty men to run in front of him.

This is one of those odd accounts in scripture that you might wonder what the point is. Adonijah decides that he wants to be king in the place of his father King David. The problem with that idea is God has already selected Solomon to be the next king and David has already announced that to the whole world.

There is a sense in the text that Adonijah was spoiled as a child; David never disciplined him in any way. That might explain his actions; he might have just decided one day that he should be king rather than Solomon and so he acted upon his desires. There is a message in that alone about men fulfilling their role as fathers to their children; especially to their sons.

The thing that struck me about this text is that Adonijah managed to get Joab and Abiathar to agree to his plan. Joab was David's army commander and Abiathar was one of the chief priests. Joab had been with David from very early in his time as king. It is difficult to understand fully why these two men would do something like this. King David was close to death and a new king was going to be selected; it is possible that they thought Adonijah would be a better king than Solomon.

In life, ministry, and church there will come times when there is a need for a change in leadership. Life happens and things change! This is one of the must vulnerable times for ministries and churches and any other organization because it is then that the people looking to advance themselves are most likely to act. As is the case with Adonijah, they can act very foolishly. He had no chance of success and yet he acted anyway

This can create great strife and division. From our text, we know that Nathan handled it very well and there was very little fallout from it. As we approach the inevitable changes that must take place within our ministries, we should do so upon our knees. We should be praying that God's chosen people will be raised up to the places that he wants them and those that would try to take advantage would be held back from acting. This is not likely to prevent it from happening but it will prepare your heart for it when it does.

Ministry and life is about people and people have a tendency to do the wrong things. As leaders, we should be ready for that through an active prayer life and because of a sincere desire to shepherd the flock of God that has been entrusted to us. Sheep have a tendency to wander wherever they want to and sometimes it is the sheep that are closest to you that wander the farthest. We don't need to fear it; we need to expect it and prepare for it. Jesus, help us to stay close to the Good Shepherd as we shepherd Your flock.

JUNE 7

Read: 1 Kings 2:1 – 3:2, Acts 5:1-42, Psalm 125:1-5, Proverbs 16:25

1 KINGS 2:3

Observe the requirements of the Lord your God and follow all his ways. Keep each of the laws, commands, regulations, and stipulations written in the law of Moses so that you will be successful in all you do and wherever you go.

King David is now very old and will die soon. Before he dies he calls his son Solomon to himself and gives him some last minute instructions. He tells Solomon to take care of some people for him. Some he tells him to be kind to and others he instructs Solomon to arrange for a bloody death. In this short section of scripture there is an interesting study in the contrasts of David's life. But that is for another time.

His first instruction to Solomon has to do with the Law of Moses. David is very specific about what he thinks Solomon should do with these laws. David told Solomon to observe, follow, and keep them. And seemingly to make sure there were no loopholes in his statement David told Solomon to do these things with the laws, commands, regulations, and stipulations.

To observe carries with it the idea of studying. The kings of Israel were told to write out a copy of the Law of Moses when they took the throne and they were to keep the Law with them. This personally hand-written copy was to be a continual reminder of who they were to answer to; God. Only as we study God's Word can we truly get to know the God that we serve. Our studies of His Word form the basis of all our understanding of life and this world that we are in.

David told Solomon to follow all of "his ways." This means that Solomon was to obey what was written within the Law of Moses. It is not enough to know God's Word, we need to obey it. If we are not following the Lord's directions as found in His Word we can be sure that we are going the wrong way. Sadly, this is what happened to Solomon.

Solomon is also instructed to keep these laws as well. The word "keep" carries the idea of guarding and protecting. God's Word is a precious thing and should be guarded, first in our hearts and then in our lives and in the lives of those around us. Frequently in Scripture we are counseled to guard our hearts. This is because where our heart dwells is where our love is. God wants us to love Him and that is more easily done as we guard God's Word within our hearts.

David ended this verse with a promise. If Solomon would observe, follow, and keep the laws, commands, regulations, and stipulations he would be successful in everything he did and everywhere he went. That is a promise that I can really embrace; I want to be successful in everything and everywhere. For that to happen I simply need to observe, follow, and keep. Jesus, help me hide Your Word in my heart.

JUNE 8
Read: 1 Kings 3:3 – 4:34, Acts 6:1-15, Psalm 126:1-6, Proverbs 16:26-27

ACTS 6:2

So the Twelve called a meeting of all the believers. "We apostles should spend our time preaching and teaching the word of God, not administering a food program," they said.

The early church faced many challenges. Sometimes the challenges were from within and sometimes they were from outside influences. We are told in our reading for today that the disciples are multiplying; that is the sign of a healthy church. Later in the reading we find that they were experiencing persecution; that is another sign of a healthy church. The growth of the church seldom comes without some form of opposition.

A growing church also has challenges that are directly related to growth. In our reading for today we see that the church was taking care of the widows in the church. One group was not being ministered to and so a complaint was raised. What we can infer from this verse is that the apostles were doing a lot of the work of the ministry.

The apostles had reached their limit of how much of the work that they could do themselves. To do any more they were going to have let something else go. Speaking to the congregation they tell them to bring them seven men. Three characteristics were to determine who they were to be. They needed to be men of good reputation, men filled with the Holy Spirit, and filled with wisdom. These were the qualifications of the men that were selected to "wait on tables." We ought to keep these standards in mind as we are selecting people to be in the ministry as well. Just because someone wants to serve in the church doesn't mean that they should.

The apostles determined that they couldn't meet all the needs of the ministry by themselves and so they humbled themselves to ask for help. Too many pastors and ministry leaders fail in this area; and it cost them and their ministry dearly. We can't do it all; and if we try to, it will lead to frustration and harm. By humbling themselves they make it possible for all the needs to be met and the church continues to grow.

Another key point of this verse is that the apostles make the right choice to deal with this situation and they give us a model to follow in similar circumstances. They devoted themselves to prayer and to the ministry of the Word. That is what they were called to do. That was the one thing that they could do exceptionally well for the church. God would have us make the same kind of decisions.

Look around you, there are capable men and women with good reputations, full of the Holy Spirit and wisdom. Invite them to come alongside of you to help you in meeting the needs of the ministry or church. You should focus as much of your attention as you can onto your calling. Then you will be amazed at how the Lord will add to the church daily. Jesus help us to focus on the main thing and invite others to help us with the other stuff.

JUNE 9

Read: 1 Kings 5:1 – 6:38, Acts 7:1-29, Psalm 127:1-5, Proverbs 16:28-30

PSALM 127:1

Unless the LORD builds a house, the work of the builders is useless.

Unless the LORD protects a city, guarding it with sentries will do no good.

King Solomon built more things than probably any other king in Israel. We are told in scripture that he built to his heart's content. Anything that he wanted to build he did. Many great structures and palaces and fortified cities were built during the reign of Solomon. And in our text for today Solomon makes this fascinating statement about building.

What Solomon is telling us is that unless God is the architect and construction supervisor that the project will be useless. We all know that if you wanted to, you could have a house built and live in it and it would be just fine. But Solomon is making a spiritual statement, not a practical one.

Whether you are in a church, ministry, or family you are building something; you are building a spiritual house. God has a perfect design for that house and it is found in the Bible. As we study scripture it gives us a good picture of what God intends for His church, for ministries that bear His name, and for the families of children of God. It is our blueprint and if we will follow it, we will end up with something that matters; something that is useful.

The Holy Spirit stands ready to supervise the construction. We will encounter challenges during the construction project (sometimes referred to as trials) and the Holy Spirit can help us to overcome these obstacles and complete the project before us. Too often we try to jury-rig a solution to a problem that ends up having to be torn out and redone. The Holy Spirit will direct our paths if we will just listen to Him.

If we were just talking about building a house, it would be bad enough that it might end up as useless. But when we are talking about a family, or a ministry, or a church it is a much more serious matter. A useless family, ministry, or church is a tragedy. They are especially tragic because they don't have to be that way. By simply following the blueprint and listening to the supervisor anyone can build a spiritual house that is used by God to change the world.

All God needs is laborers; men and women that desire to be used by God. Solomon used over 150,000 people to construct the temple and his palace. Not one of those people could imagine themselves building that massive structure by themselves. It was only through the combined effort of them all could such a thing be done. It is no different when building a spiritual house; it will take all of us to accomplish the task. Jesus, help us to follow the plan and the Planner.

JUNE 10

Read: 1 Kings 7:1-51, Acts 7:30-50, Psalm 128:1-6, Proverbs 16:31-33

1 KINGS 7:1

Solomon also built a palace for himself, and it took him thirteen years to complete the construction.

Any time that I read about Solomon I find myself asking questions. There are some things about his life that do not make sense. It seems that he often did things that were out of character with the picture that I have of him in my mind. Solomon was selected by God to be the successor as king of Israel after his father David died. God told Solomon that he could ask God for something and that He would give it to Solomon. Solomon asked for wisdom to rule the great nation of Israel. God gave him wisdom and wealth and power and long life. And Solomon did receive all those things.

It occurred to me today while I read today's text why I am troubled by the life of Solomon. Solomon built himself a palace. That is not a huge surprise, nor is it alarming. What caught my attention is that it took thirteen years to complete it. Solomon also built the temple to the Lord. Building the temple took seven years to complete. It took twice as long to build Solomon's palace as it did to build the Lord's temple.

Solomon was the wisest man to live with the exception of Jesus. And my assumption was that this somehow meant that He was godly. In my mind I assumed that the wisest man on earth would naturally be drawn to God. The obvious truth from Solomon's life is that great wisdom, power, and wealth do not lead you to God. In fact Jesus taught that it has the opposite effect. Solomon's wisdom, power, and wealth led him to do some of the very things that God had forbid the kings of Israel from doing. Rather than drawing Solomon to God, these things drew him away from God. It wasn't until late in his life that he started to realize the mistake that he had made. We see his failure in the legacy that he left behind; a divided kingdom and nearly perpetual conflict.

None of us will ever experience even a fraction of the power, wisdom, or wealth that Solomon had. But all of us do have some power, wealth, or wisdom. If we are not careful, that little bit that we have can be twisted by our sinful nature or by our enemy to cause us to behave just like Solomon. Which is more important to you; building the kingdom of God or a palace for yourself? Only your heart knows for sure.

Solomon had it all and yet if you read the book of Ecclesiastes, you get the strong sense that Solomon felt that much of what he did in his life was futile and meaningless. That is a perfect description of any activity that is not led by the Lord and meant to honor and glorify him; futile and meaningless. Jesus, help us to use all the wealth, power, and wisdom that you give us to bring glory and honor to you.

JUNE 11
Read: 1 Kings 8:1-66, Acts 7:51 – 8:13, Psalm 129:1-8, Proverbs 17:1

ACTS 8:4

But the believers who had fled Jerusalem went everywhere preaching the Good News about Jesus.

Stephen has just been martyred, killed by the Jewish religious leaders because of his faith in Jesus. This begins one of the first great persecutions of the Christian faith. The result is that Christians are dispersed all over the known world. Each time the Church has been persecuted, the result has been the same; it is spread even further. Each time it grows even stronger. In some respects I think that is one of the reasons why the church in the United States is so weak because it encounters very little persecution. Sadly most Christians in the United States don't even realize how weak the church is here because they have never experienced the refining fire of persecution.

As the persecution heated up the Christians fled so that they would not all be destroyed. But instead of going into hiding to protect themselves wherever they ended up they preached the Good News to anyone that would listen. Oh how I pray that we had this same zeal for the gospel of Jesus Christ! Even though they were persecuted in one town, they went to the next and shared the truth of Jesus with others.

It is God's desire that the Good News of Jesus go everywhere. I believe that He wants us to do it obediently and out of a great love for Him and for what Jesus has done for us. Because it is His plan He will carry it out even if that means that He needs to compel us to do what He wants. If we will not obediently share the gospel with others He might allow some trial or tribulation in our lives to get us to a point where we do what He wants.

This doesn't mean that all trials, tribulations, or persecutions are because we are not sharing Jesus with others but it should be considered as we encounter those things. Persecution, trials, and tribulations can also come because we are sharing Jesus with others and the enemy of our souls and theirs doesn't like it. The point is not why those things happen but what we should be doing through it all; sharing the Good News of Jesus with others.

God never promised us a life free from attacks or persecutions. In fact, Jesus said that as Christians we should expect tribulations for as long as we are in this life. Only once we have begun our eternity in heaven with Jesus should we expect peace and tranquility. Until then it is a daily battle against our sinful desires, the ways of the world, and the schemes of Satan. Let your life be a living testimony of the Good News of Jesus Christ. Let every breath that you take point others to Him and the hope that He provides. Even in the midst of your darkest hours, you can know the brightness of His glory. Jesus, help us to speak about you often.

JUNE 12

Read: 1 Kings 9:1 – 10:29, Acts 8:14-40, Psalm 130:1-8, Proverbs 17:2-3

1 KINGS 10:8

How happy these people must be! What a privilege for your officials to stand here day after day, listening to your wisdom!

The queen of Sheba pays a visit to King Solomon because she has heard in her country about the amazing wisdom that Solomon has. When she comes she brings a great caravan of wealth as a gift to Solomon. When she left Solomon gave to her gifts that were greater than she gave to him. The queen of Sheba had come to witness what God had done and was astounded by the things that Solomon had accomplished.

This account has always fascinated me because this queen left her own country for what must have been a relatively long period just so that she could see what was going on in Israel and to witness to herself what people were saying about the Wisdom of Solomon. She came not only with gifts but also with questions. And that is one of the lessons of this account. God gave the gift of great wisdom to Solomon. This gift attracted the queen of Sheba to Solomon to have her questions answered.

God has also given you gifts that He expects you to exercise. It is during the exercise of those gifts that the rest of the world sees the power of God at work. Eventually word will get out to people that need to have that power or gift in their lives and they will bring to you their needs in the hopes that you might be able to meet them. That is exactly the reason why God gave you the gifts in the first place.

The queen's response to Solomon's wisdom was to comment on how fortunate Solomon's officials were for being able to stand there in his presence and listen to Solomon all day long. It is true that those that God surrounds us with will also benefit and be blessed by the gifts that God has given to us. There is one thing that makes this account so beautiful and such a powerful lesson for us.

The queen goes on to recognize that Solomon's wisdom and success are because God has blessed Solomon. This came from a woman that did not believe in the God of Israel and probably believed in many gods, which was common during that period. Because of the way that Solomon used the gift that God had given him, God was glorified and His name was magnified.

When the queen of Sheba returned to her country she would take back a report about the amazing things that the God of Israel was doing through King Solomon. Her whole country would likely hear about the God of Israel. This is one of the main reasons that God gives us gifts and abilities and why he will choose to bless us; so that the rest of the world can hear about Him. We must never fail to remind those that see God at work in us or through us that it is God at work and not us; that way they will leave and tell others about the Jesus that gave us the ability. Jesus, help us to give you all the credit.

JUNE 13

Read: 1 Kings 11:1 – 12:19, Acts 9:1-25, Psalm 131:1-3, Proverbs 17:4-5

Fire tests the purity of silver and gold, but the LORD tests the heart.

By using fire gold and silver is tested to determine the purity of the metal. It is heated to the point of melting. If there are any impurities they will rise to the surface of the metal. This process may be repeated several times to get the metal to as pure a state as possible.

In our verse for today we are told that the Lord tests the heart. Within each of our hearts are impurities that God wants to remove from us. His desire is to get our heart to be as pure as possible. Purity in this case means holiness; or the absence of sin. It is God's desire that we allow Him to purify our hearts to the point that there is no sin found there. This is a lifelong process because we are in a fallen world and we all have this sin nature that will not die until our flesh dies.

The Lord tests our heart by allowing circumstances and situations to come into our lives that reveal the impurities in our lives. I have often remarked half kidding that this is the reason that God allows teenagers to live with us. If anything can test what is in our heart it is the natural instincts of a teenager.

But all they or any other circumstance is revealing is the sin that already exists in your heart. And once that sin or impurity is revealed God expects us to come to Him and ask Him to help us get rid of it. Usually we blame our circumstances for the way that we feel and/or react. Your behavior is a choice that you have made in response to the circumstance.

Every action, thought, behavior, attitude, or feeling that you experience is a programmed response to circumstances or situations in your life. Your whole life goes into creating the way that you respond to things. God through the testing process wants to reprogram you to respond like Jesus would respond. God will turn up the heat and an impurity will rise to the surface. This will be a wrong action, thought, behavior, attitude, or feeling. God then wants you to allow Him to scoop that impurity out of your life. But we often don't do that; instead we will push that impurity back down into our lives. God will then have to turn up the heat again to bring that impurity back up again. And He is patient; He will keep doing it until you allow Him to cleanse you of it.

Every time that we allow God to scoop some of the impurities from our lives we become purer; more holy. That is God goal; to make us holy as He is holy. We have to allow Him to do that and we need to understand that He will not stop testing us until He has achieved His goal; our holiness. Jesus, help us to stand in the heat of your testing and be willing to be cleansed of anything that is not of you.

JUNE 14
Read: 1 Kings 12:20 – 13:34, Acts 9:26-43, Psalm 132:1-18, Proverbs 17:6

1 KINGS 12:15

So the king paid no attention to the people's demands. This turn of events was the will of the LORD, for it fulfilled the LORD'S message to Jeroboam son of Nebat through the prophet Ahijah from Shiloh.

Rehoboam has just become king over all of the twelve tribes of Israel after the death of his father Solomon. The people come to Rehoboam and ask him to lighten the load that was placed on them by his father and in exchange they promise to be loyal subjects to him. Solomon had been very strong with the people. For forty years he has put a difficult burden upon them so that he could experience the comfort and success that he desired. The kingdom was prosperous and successful beyond most people's imagination. Rehoboam inherited the greatest kingdom on the planet. He inherited from Solomon wealth beyond measure. The kingdom was safe and secure from his enemies. It would have made perfect sense for Rehoboam to give the people what they wanted and he could have lived in great comfort and security for his entire life. There was just one little obstacle to that life; God had made a promise to Solomon and Jeroboam.

God is always faithful to His promises; nothing in life is as sure as the promises of God. Because Solomon was unfaithful to God, he was told that most of the kingdom would be taken away from his son. At the same time Jeroboam was told that ten of the tribes would be given to him to rule. God then orchestrated things so that His promises would be fulfilled. I think this is something that we sometimes forget about God; that He can cause to happen whatever He wants. God caused Rehoboam to reject the council of King Solomon's advisors which would have been the correct way to go. Instead Rehoboam used the foolish council of his friends. By following that advice, Rehoboam succeeded in accomplishing God's promise of splitting the nation of Israel into two parts.

This is an important truth for us to understand as we go through this life. As we follow leaders we must remember what God did through Rehoboam in this text; He caused him to make a foolish decision so that His plans could be completed. There are going to come times when God will direct our leaders to make decisions that are perplexing to us so that He can accomplish a greater goal. When that happens we need to determine what our responsibility is in that. In the case of the people of Judah they were to continue to follow Rehoboam. In the case of the ten tribes, they were to split and follow Jeroboam.

By following Rehoboam, the tribe of Judah was being obedient to God even though Rehoboam had made a foolish decision. Don't let a single bad decision by your leader cause you to desert him; seek to determine what the Lord is trying to do and then do it. Jesus, help us to follow where You are leading our leaders.

JUNE 15

Read: 1 Kings 14:1 – 15:24, Acts 10:1-23, Psalm 133:1-3, Proverbs 17:7-8

ACTS 10:14

"Never, Lord," Peter declared. "I have never in all my life eaten anything forbidden by our Jewish laws."

Peter is on the roof of the house where he is staying while he waits for a meal to be prepared. While waiting, he falls into a trance and God gives him a vision. The vision of a sheet being lowered from heaven and within this sheet is every kind of unclean animal. These are the animals that according to Jewish laws that he is not allowed to eat; even touching most of them will defile him.

God was sending a message to Peter which he would soon understand to mean that the Gentiles were to be included in the kingdom of God and that he was not to think of them as unclean. Up until this point Peter believed that Jesus had come to save only the Jews even though Jesus had made it pretty clear that everyone was welcome into the kingdom of God.

It was Peter's response to the voice of the Lord that we will press in upon. The voice told Peter to kill and eat the unclean animals that were represented in the vision. Peter's response was "Never, Lord." What the Lord had asked Peter to do was against everything that he had been taught since he was a child. He had lived his whole life staying away from certain kinds of animals so that he might remain ceremonially clean. It was unthinkable for him to actually kill and eat any of the animals that he saw in the vision. Peter's response is exactly the same response that we would give if the Lord asked us to do something that was contrary to something we have always done.

In fact, we often give the Lord the same response to many things that the Lord tells us to do. The Lord tells us to forgive that person that has wronged us and our response is "Never." The Lord tells us to help that person in need and our response is "Never." We may not actually say it out loud but our actions say clearly what is going on in our hearts.

There is a contradiction in terms in Peter's response to the Lord. If Jesus is Lord than a response of "Never" or "No" is inappropriate. As Lord, Jesus has the right to direct our lives; every part of our lives. He has the right to ask us to do things that are opposed to everything that we learned as children. We have no right to refuse Him in any request or command that He makes of us. We can trust that He will never ask us to do something that is wrong or sinful because He will never ask us to do something that is contrary to His nature or in contradiction to His word.

If Jesus is Lord, then our only response to Him is "Yes, Lord." We may not understand why He is directing us in one direction or another and we have the liberty to ask for understanding and wisdom but we have no right to refuse to obey. Jesus is Lord and as Lord my life is His to direct any way that He desires. Jesus, teach me to obey.

JUNE 16

Read: 1 Kings 15:25 – 17:24, Acts 10:24-48, Psalm 134:1-3, Proverbs 17:9-11

1 KINGS 17:16

For no matter how much they used, there was always enough left in the containers, just as the LORD had promised through Elijah.

This is one of the accounts of scripture that I have enjoyed since I first read it. God supernaturally takes care of Elijah by taking care of this widow and her son. They have just enough food for one last meal when Elijah shows up and asks the widow to make him some bread. She tells him that she is about to cook up her last meal and then she and her son are going to die. Elijah tells her not to worry because God is going to provide for her. Then no matter how much food she prepares she has enough for her "last meal."

In faith this widow prepared the bread for Elijah, trusting God to do what Elijah had said that He would do. She couldn't have known for sure that there was going to be enough food for them to eat more than one more meal. There was a famine in the land and she had no one else that she could depend upon. The widow's circumstances were desperate. But, in faith she put her own needs aside to meet the needs of Elijah and God blessed her because of it.

All of us will encounter circumstances that cause us to think we are having our "last meal." For each of us the circumstances will be different. For some it might be financial desperation. Others could be struggling in their jobs or relationships and feel that there is just enough left in them to go one more day. Or it could be that the consequences of sins that have been allowed into their lives are weighing so heavily upon them that they feel that they will be crushed. Our verse for the day should give all of us hope that regardless of our circumstances we can make it one more day if we will just have faith in Jesus Christ and go about our life as best we can.

After each meal that the widow prepared she had left just enough for one "last meal." God did not give her an abundance that she could depend upon. After each meal her situation was just as desperate as it was before the meal. Too often we want God to deliver us completely from the desperate situations that we are in. He would remind us that He has provided for us this far; He will continue to provide for us.

Don't expect more than what you need for this moment; that's all that you need. Be content that you have enough for this moment and trust God for what you need next. Don't worry about your "next meal;" let God worry about that. Have faith, believe that God loves you and will never leave you nor forsake you. Believe that He will continue to provide for you just as He has up to this point and then go about this day as best as you can. The text of our reading tells us that God provided for the widow and her son for several months in this way. Be patient; trust God. Jesus, thank You that You never fail to provide for those that trust You.

JUNE 17
Read: 1 Kings 18:1-46, Acts 11:1-30, Psalm 135:1-21, Proverbs 17:12-13

1 KINGS 18:21

Then Elijah stood in front of them and said, "How long are you going to waver between two opinions? If the LORD is God, follow him! But if Baal is God, then follow him!" But the people were completely silent.

Elijah is confronting the people of Israel. They have been following the example of King Ahab as he leads them to worship Baal and other false gods. They are also still worshipping the True God. Elijah confronts them and tells them to decide for themselves who the one and true God is and worship him only. God is telling them through Elijah that there room in their hearts for only one God. It is up to them which one they will pick.

God then gives them a very powerful proof that He is the one and only God by burning up the sacrifice that Elijah has prepared after the prophets of Baal failed to cause their sacrifice to be burned. The people seem to turn to God but it is unfortunately short-lived.

To most of us, God would say the same thing: "How long will you waver between two opinions?" We have allowed something else to come in and divide our heart in two. In one breath we say that we are Christians and in the next we are worshipping the gods of this world; money, possessions, success, beauty, positions, and the like. There is only room in your heart for one God. Which one will you pick; the one that satisfies your flesh or the one and true God? The choice is yours and your actions and life will reveal your choice to God and to the world.

King Ahab had the choice of leading the people of Israel to God or away from God. He chose poorly! As a leader in your family, ministry, or church you have the opportunity to make the same choice that King Ahab did. Your choice affects not only you but all of those around you. One of the rules of leadership is that where the leader goes, the people follow. Where are you going? Are you going to God?

Later in our text we see God supernaturally delivering King Ahab and the people of Israel from the hand of the king of Aram. He will do this so that Ahab will realize that there is only one God and turn back to Him. God will do amazing and incredible things to remind His children that He alone is God. And incredibly, we miss those tremendous events and look at them as coincidence or as ordinary.

It is our role as leaders to draw people to God. It is our responsibility to first empty our hearts of all the gods of this world that do not belong there. And then we are to teach the people who are following us to do the same. We must first choose and help them to make the right choice as well. As a leader you have a tremendous influence on those around you. Use that God-given influence to direct people to the Lover of their souls. Jesus, help us to choose well and to lead others to the right choice also.

JUNE 18
Read: 1 Kings 19:1-21, Acts 12:1-23, Psalm 136:1-26, Proverbs 17:14-15

ACTS 12:12

After a little thought, he went to the home of Mary, the mother of John Mark, where many were gathered for prayer.

Herod Agrippa has begun to actively persecute the believers. James, the brother of John, has been killed and now he has arrested Peter.

Herod's plan is bring Peter out for a public trial and then to execute him. One of his primary motivations for doing this is because it pleases the Jewish leaders. Herod is not very popular with the Jews because he represents the Roman government that rules over them. He will do anything to keep the Jews happy so that they will continue to pay their taxes and to keep peace in his province. The Christians are of no concern to Herod. If exterminating them will help him to accomplish his plan, Herod has no hesitation in wiping them out.

What Herod hasn't taken into consideration is God's plan. It does not fit into God's plan to allow Herod to execute Peter and so He miraculously delivers him from the prison where Herod placed him. God sends an angel to bring Peter out of the prison. Can you imagine the surprise of the two guards that Peter was chained to when they woke and realized that Peter was gone? Peter thought he was dreaming until he was outside and the angel had departed. Then he took a moment and thought about what his next move should be. After he thought about it he went to where he knew that people would be praying for him. As soon as they heard that Peter was thrown in prison they started to pray for him. Peter's first move after being released miraculously from prison was to let those prayer warriors know that God had answered their prayers.

As Christians we are taught that God answers our prayers. And as our spiritual eyes open we see more clearly how and when He does answer our prayers. Even the most experienced of prayer veterans can get discouraged if they do not see or hear the results of their labors of prayer. After a little thought, Peter's first act was to encourage those that had played such a vital role in his release.

Nothing encourages a prayer warrior like knowing that their prayers have been answered. Hearing that God has acted in a powerful way is the stuff that fuels the fires of the prayer warrior. As a leader in the church, Peter knew that by encouraging them with the report of his supernatural delivery would do much to keep them going and build their faith. After telling them what happened, Peter told them to tell others what had happened. These prayer warriors were excited about what God had done and they would be great messengers to the others. Take a moment and think about those that have been praying for you and then let them know what God is doing in your life. Jesus, help us to think a little.

JUNE 19

Read: 1 Kings 20:1 – 21:29, Acts 12:24 – 13:15, Psalm 137:1-9, Proverbs 17:16

1 KINGS 20:28

Then the man of God went to the king of Israel and said, "This is what the Lord says: The Arameans have said that the Lord is a god of the hills and not of the plains. So I will help you defeat this vast army. Then you will know that I am the Lord."

King Ben-hadad is determined to defeat King Ahab and conquer Israel. God previously had defeated Ben-hadad's forces and sent them packing. The king's advisers explain why a smaller Israelite army had been able to defeat a stronger military force. They told the king that it was because the battle had been fought in the hills and the Israelite gods were stronger there. Their suggestion was to move the battle down onto the plains where the Israelite gods would be weaker.

It is fascinating to see the unbelieving mind at work in a text like this. As believers we might even scoff at the ignorance of comments like these. For some, myself included, I can still remember thinking thoughts that were similar to the suggestions of Ben-hadad's advisers. To them the Lord was similar to the gods that they worshipped, which means they weren't gods at all. Because these gods were not all-powerful, there were places where they were weak or unconcerned. They believed that by changing the circumstances they could change the outcome.

People still think and act the same way. If some plan or desire is not fulfilled in the way that they think it should be, they will change the circumstances thinking that something new will change the outcome. The problem with that type of thinking is that it takes God out of the equation. The most important part of the verse that we are looking at today is the last part. God's reason for giving King Ahab the victory in this battle that was coming was so that he would "know that I am the Lord," says God. God does the things that he does in our lives so that we will come to know Him better and better.

It is through an intimate knowledge of God and His will that we know how to live this life. There may be times that God wants us to change the circumstances so that we can experience a different outcome in our lives. More often I think God wants us to change the outcome we desire so that

He can change the circumstances. Many people have the wrong understanding of God and His will and this misunderstanding is reflected in the way that are living their lives. They will change spouses, jobs, churches, or friendships every time something doesn't go the way they want it.

God is at work in your circumstance attempting to show you more of who He is. Until you recognize this and submit to His plan in your life, you will continue striving after one thing or another and never find what you are seeking. Get to know Him better through your particular circumstances and then ask Him what, if any, changes you should make in your circumstances. Jesus, help us to let You be God in our life.

JUNE 20

Read: 1 Kings 22:1-53, Acts 13:16-41, Psalm 138:1-8, Proverbs 17:17-18

1 KINGS 22:14

But Micaiah replied, "As surely as the Lord lives, I will say only what the Lord tells me to say."

King Ahab and King Jehoshaphat are trying to decide if they are going to go to war against the Arameans. King Ahab's "prophets" are encouraging him telling him he will have a glorious victory. King Jehoshaphat has suggested to Ahab that they inquire of a prophet of the Lord. Ahab tells him that there is only one, but he hates him because he always gives him bad news. That speaks a lot about the character of Ahab and the condition of the nation of Israel.

A messenger is sent to Micaiah to have him come and prophecy for the kings. He is instructed to agree with the other prophets and say to the king what he wanted to hear. Micaiah, being a true prophet of God, told the messenger that he would not do that; he was going to tell the king only what God told him to say.

Upon getting to the king he begins by telling the king what he wanted to hear. There must have been something in the way that he said it because the king recognized that he was not telling the truth immediately and challenged him. Micaiah then tells him what God has revealed is going to happen; King Ahab is going to be killed and Israel scattered on the hills.

King Ahab responds to Micaiah by having him arrested and thrown into prison. He was to be fed bread and water until King Ahab returned from the battle. King Ahab never returned from the battle and the Bible does not tell us what became of Micaiah. He may have spent the rest of his life in prison eating nothing but bread and water.

Micaiah knew that telling the truth could cost him everything. He knew what the likely response of King Ahab was going to be. And yet he spoke only as the Lord directed him. How many of us would have the faith to do that? How many of us would believe God and obey God even if it meant that we would be thrown into prison? Sadly, most Christians believe God for far less than this.

God wants us to say only what He tells us to, no matter what the potential consequences might be. God is responsible for the consequences when we are being obedient to Him. Too often we don't trust God enough to trust him with the consequences of our obedience. In my heart I believe that God acted on Micaiah's behalf and rescued him from that prison but I have no proof of it. It doesn't matter anyways because even if he didn't he was right where God allowed him to be. Micaiah's reward in heaven will be great. Jesus, help us to have the faith of Miciah to obey even when it might cost us greatly.

JUNE 21
Read: 2 Kings 1:1 – 2:25, Acts 13:42 – 14:7, Psalm 139:1-24, Proverbs 17:9-21

They replied, "A man came up to us and said, 'Go back to the king and give him this message from the LORD: Why are you sending men to Baal-zebub, the god of Ekron, to ask whether you will get well? Is there no God in Israel? Now, since you have done this, you will never leave the bed on which you are lying, but you will surely die.'"

King Ahaziah has fallen and seriously injured himself. He can tell that he may be dying and he wants to know if he is going to live. The king of Israel sends some messengers to enquire of Baal-zebub, the god of Ekron. Baal-zebub was said to have the power of prophecy. Ekron was one of the cities of the Philistines. God sends an angel to tell Elijah to intercept the king's messengers and to give them a message for the king. The message is that because the king did not inquire of Him that Ahaziah would not survive his injuries.

In the message the Lord asks the question: "Is there no God in Israel?" By going to the god of their enemy, Ahaziah was totally rejecting the only True God. By going to ask of Baal-zebub he was rejecting the God that could actually help him in his time of need. God had proved Himself time and again to the ancestors of Ahaziah and yet he turned to some other god. One of the sad things about this is that Ahaziah didn't even believe that Baal-zebub could heal him; he only wanted to know whether he was going to live or not.

Because of Ahaziah's lack of faith God sent him a message that he wasn't going to live much longer. Before we are too quick to judge Ahaziah we should examine our own lives to see if we have done the same thing. It is amazing how often we will turn to the gods of this world when we should be turning to the True God. The Bible teaches that God has supplied everything we need for life and godliness and yet we will often turn to the world for its wisdom and help.

God allowed Ahaziah to fall and become critically injured. He probably wanted Ahaziah to turn to Him and ask for His help. God may have even planned to use this to turn Ahaziah back to Him by healing him from this injury. We often miss the radical things that God wants to do because we fail to go to Him in our times of need. Instead we will turn to gods that neither see nor hear and cannot help us.

Go to the Lord for everything that is going on in your life. Seek the counsel of the godly but trust God only for true wisdom. There is no way to imagine the blessings that God would bestow upon the person that will live their life like that. Trust God and give no place in your life for the gods of this world. Jesus, teach us to see You as the only true source of wisdom and power in this life.

JUNE 22

Read: 2 Kings 3:1 – 4:17, Acts 14:8-28, Psalm 140:1-13, Proverbs 17:22

ACTS 14:22

...where they strengthened the believers. They encouraged them to continue in the faith, reminding them that they must enter into the Kingdom of God through many tribulations.

Paul and Barnabas are traveling to many of the cities that they had visited on previous journeys. In these cities they had visited were churches that had sprung up as a result of the work that Paul and Barnabas had done. Paul and Barnabas had also experienced a fair amount of persecution and tribulation on these journeys and in some of these cities. Paul was even stoned in the town of Lystra.

This is did not stop Paul and Barnabas from returning to these to strengthen and encourage these new believers in their faith. Paul and Barnabas took this opportunity to remind the people that their entry into the kingdom of God was going to be through many tribulations. As their spiritual leaders, Paul and Barnabas did not hesitate to tell them the truth about what the future held for them. They were going to experience persecution and tribulations similar to what Paul and Barnabas were experiencing.

As Christians trials and tribulations are a part of our lives; just like eating and breathing. Nothing we do is going to change the fact that the world and the enemy are out to make our way very difficult. But we should be encouraged because that tells us that we are on the path that leads to the Kingdom of God.

As leaders of families, ministries, or churches this can be one of the hardest things to do; to encourage someone that is in the midst of a severe tribulation. It can be hard to tell someone that is going through cancer; either in their life or the life of a loved one that this is a part of the tribulations that Jesus told us to expect and that we should be encouraged.

What we must do to help those people is not to try to cause them to look at their circumstances as a proof of their faith but to get them to look at their faith as the strength of their lives. Too often we forget to point people to Jesus in their times of need. People don't need psychology or therapy; they simply need Jesus. In the midst of trials, tribulations, or persecutions we need to believe that God is still on the throne and that He loves us with an unending love. We need to believe that He has allowed this thing into our life for a reason and that He is strong enough to fix it and to carry us through it.

That is how we should be encouraging our people; by encouraging them to look up into the loving eyes of Jesus. He is not just the Savior of our souls but He is also the Savior of our lives. If we would just trust Him with more of our lives we would realize that more deeply every day. Jesus, teach me to surrender more of my life to You every single day of my life.

JUNE 23

Read: 2 Kings 4:18 – 5:27, Acts 15:1-35, Psalm 141:1-10, Proverbs 17:23

2 KINGS 5:13

But his officers tried to reason with him and said, "Sir, if the prophet had told you to do some great thing, wouldn't you have done it? So you should certainly obey him when he says simply to go and wash and be cured!"

Naaman is the commander Aram's army. He is well admired by his king. He has been very successful for the king of Aram but he has contracted leprosy. A slave girl from Israel informs Naaman's wife that there is a prophet in Israel that can heal him. So Naaman comes to Elisha in Samaria to be healed of leprosy, a very contagious skin disease.

When Naaman shows up at Elisha's door, he sends a messenger out to tell Naaman to go to the Jordan River and wash himself and be healed. Naaman gets very upset; this was not how he expected to be treated. He expected to be shown a great deal more respect and he expected some kind of ritual that led to his healing. In our verse for the day, his officers attempt to reason with him. They point to the error in his logic. Naaman believed he was a great man and so believed he should be treated in some great way including in the manner in which he was to be healed. To go and wash in the Jordan River was simply too simple.

There is a great picture of salvation here, in that salvation is simply accepting what Jesus did for us at Calvary. It is not involved in some great ritual or process; simply believe in Jesus. That bothers some people, and some people try to add to it to make it seem more important. Salvation is simple enough for a child to understand it and accept and I thank God that it is.

Some people approach serving God in the same way that Naaman approached being healed by God. They expect that their importance will determine where and how they serve God. Their problem is that they are comparing themselves to the people they are serving instead of the God they are serving. People that are important in the world sometimes expect to have important positions in serving God.

When we come to God and tell Him that we are ready to serve Him we must be ready to serve wherever He might direct us. As a pastor people regularly come to me and tell me that they believe that God is telling them that they should be serving Him in some way but they are not sure how. I can always tell if they have a heart like Naaman's when I suggest they do something small or simple. If they are upset because they were not given a task as great as they are, it is proof that the pride of Naaman lives in their heart.

The only way that they can be healed of that is through obedience and the washing of the blood of Christ. Naaman did as Elisha instructed and was healed and he came back to Elisha a changed man. We must never think ourselves so great that there is any task that is below us, especially when it comes from a God that is so much greater than us. Jesus, teach to gladly do the simple tasks for our great God.

JUNE 24
Read: 2 Kings 6:1 – 7:20, Acts 15:36 – 16:15, Psalm 142:1-7, Proverbs 17:24-25

ACTS 15:39

Their disagreement over this was so sharp that they separated. Barnabas took John Mark with him and sailed for Cyprus.

This text that we read today is one that has always comforted me when I see or experience division in ministry. Division within ministry seems to be unavoidable; it shouldn't be that way but that's how it seems. In today's reading we have an example of division within the ministry of Paul and Barnabas. Barnabas has the idea of going back to all the churches that they had started and visiting them to see how they are doing. Paul agrees but doesn't want to bring John Mark with him. Paul feels that John Mark had abandoned them earlier in their ministry.

The question that we might ask here is whether or not Paul was in sin in this matter. It seems based on the text that Paul was having a problem forgiving John Mark and allowed his flesh to get in the way. It could also be a matter of Barnabas' plan being outside of the will of God. God may not have wanted them to go back to the churches that they had previously visited but to go out to start other churches in new areas.

It has long been my opinion that God allowed this division to take place so that the ministry of Paul and Barnabas could increase. By separating they could cover more ground. Barnabas could go back to the churches that they had already started and Paul could continue with the ministry that God had called him. We don't hear much about Barnabas after this event but we will near the end of Paul's life he calls for John Mark to be sent to him. At some point they were reconciled to one another.

God is at work in everything that is going on in our lives; even the difficult circumstances that come along. Even though this disagreement between Paul and Barnabas was wrong, God used it to increase the amount of ministry that was taking place. There is a lesson in that for all of us that are called into any kind of leadership within families, ministries, and churches. God wants unity; He doesn't want division and strife. But if it does happen, God wants to use it to do greater works. Sometimes God uses the sinful striving of men to move them into places where He can use them more effectively for His glory.

Don't let the natural tendencies to divide discourage you. Do what you can to encourage unity in the body. If division occurs, do what you can to minimize the damage that it might cause to your family, ministry, or church. Then pray that God would use this situation to bring more glory to His name. We must remember that just because someone has left our ministry or church doesn't mean that God can't use them to do radical things in the world. That is true even if the reason why they left was sinful and a move of the flesh. Trust God with them and His reputation; you just do your part and leave the rest to God. Jesus, help me to keep unity and peace.

JUNE 25

Read: 2 Kings 8:1 – 9:13, Acts 16:16-40, Psalm 143:1-12, Proverbs 17:26

2 KINGS 8:5

And Gehazi was telling the king about the time Elisha had brought a boy back to life. At that very moment, the mother of the boy walked in to make her appeal to the king about her house and land. "Look, my lord the king!" Gehazi exclaimed. "Here is the woman now, and this is her son—the very one Elisha brought back to life!"

Gehazi is Elisha's servant. He has just been telling the king of Israel some stories about Elisha. He chooses as one of the stories of Elisha's displays of God's power the account of raising a boy from the dead. As he is reaching the climax of that account, in walks the woman. At first read this might seem like an amazing coincidence. I have grown to recognize that there is no such thing as a coincidence in the things of God.

Seven years earlier, this woman, who is not named in Scripture, is told by Elisha that there is going to be a seven-year famine and that she should leave. She packs up her family and leaves to live in the land of the Philistines for seven years. What is not obvious from the text is that someone has moved into her house and been using her land while she was gone. That is the only reason she would have to the king to ask for his help.

God has blessed this woman before by raising her son from the dead. This son was a gift from God to her, as her husband was old and not able to produce children. The reason that He has done this is because she has been helping Elisha for years. Every time Elisha would pass through, they would give him a place to sleep and feed him. She eventually had a room prepared just for him. God's sovereign power is at work in this account. He put it into the mind of the king to ask Gehazi to share some of the stories of the power of God being used through Elisha. The LORD put it in the mind of Gehazi to share the account of raising this woman's son from the dead. And He coordinated all of these things to happen just as she is approaching the king to make a request of him to get her land back.

The king responds by doing exactly what she wants. We might think, "Well, of course he did! That was the right thing to do!" If you read about the kings of Israel, they were not famous for doing the right things. It is very likely that this king would have sided with the current possessors of the land and not with this woman. God supernaturally intervened so that He could bless her because she had blessed His servant, Elisha.

This woman is a great example of the maxim that no good deed goes unrewarded. This is especially true of the good things that we do for God's people. We have to be careful not to presume upon God some reward for our efforts because God will be a debtor to no man. But it fills my heart with joy to know that God can not only move heaven and earth to bless me, but He can also influence the hearts of men in my favor. Jesus, give us eyes to see Your hand of providence in all things.

JUNE 26
Read: 2 Kings 9:14 – 10:31, Acts 17:1-34, Psalm 144:1-15, Proverbs 17:27-28

ACTS 17:16
While Paul was waiting for them in Athens, he was deeply troubled by all the idols he saw everywhere in the city.

Paul is waiting for Silas and Timothy to arrive from Berea. It appears from the text that Paul is alone while he is waiting for them to join him in Athens. Even though Paul is alone he stays busy about the work that the Holy Spirit has given him. As he looks around Athens he sees that there are idols everywhere in the city. The Athenians had idols to deal with every aspect of their lives. This greatly troubled Paul. Paul knew that there was great emptiness and futility in the worship of idols.

Idol worship in its most innocent state is worshipping something that is inanimate and totally without life or power. In effect it is giving your power to something that is powerless. Not only are idols powerless but they incapable of receiving or utilizing the power that their worshippers give to them. At the worst, idol worship is actually the worship of Satan and his demons.

We don't hear much about idol worship in the United States because to us idol worship is making sacrifices and bowing before an image or statue of something or someone. There is a lot more idol worship going on around you than you think there is. You don't notice it because it is being done in a way that is different than you think of as idol worship. You might even be guilty of it yourself.

Anything or anyone that we place above Jesus is idol worship. It doesn't matter what or who it is; if it or they hold a place in your life that is greater than Jesus, it is idol worship. One of the ways that you can tell if something is an idol in your life is whether or not you would sacrifice it to Jesus. If you can't lay it down on the altar for Jesus then there is a good chance that it is an idol in your life.

This isn't just things; it also applies to positions, careers, fame, and prestige. It applies to all of your relationships, including your most intimate relationships. You might be willing to sacrifice your relationship with your in-laws but would you be willing to sacrifice your relationship with your children. Could you, like Abraham, lay your child on the altar for Jesus? It is God's desire that we would have nothing in our lives that we would not lay on the altar.

We need to understand that just because we would be willing to do something doesn't mean that the Father is going to make us do it. Just because I would be willing to lay my wife on the altar for Jesus doesn't mean that the Father is going to ask me to do it. In fact, I believe that it is our willingness to sacrifice everything that is the sacrifice that God desires most. True worship of God will require some amount of real sacrifice and a willingness to sacrifice everything. Jesus, teach us to hold nothing back from You.

JUNE 27

Read: 2 Kings 10:32 – 12:21, Acts 18:1-22, Psalm 145:1-21, Proverbs 18:1

PSALM 145:18

The LORD is close to all who call on him, yes, to all who call on him sincerely.

There are going to be times as we step out for God that we find ourselves in a place where we feel very alone. A verse like this can be very comforting. And I particularly love the complex system that we must use to bring the Lord near to us. We must call on Him. There is no formula, no liturgical process, and no penance that needs to be paid for us to be near our Lord. All we need to do is call.

Calling my mother is more difficult than this is. I have to go to the phone, pick it up, dial the number and then hope that she is there to answer. If she isn't, I have to leave a message and wait for her to call me back. It is not this way with the Lord. He is always there waiting for us to call. And when we do, He is right there.

Hebrews tells us to come boldly to the throne of grace. Because of God's great love for us and because of Jesus' work on the cross at Calvary for us we can approach God with confidence and boldness. Not in a disrespectful, arrogant way but from the understanding that He wants us to come to Him. God will never refuse our call. That same verse in Hebrews says God will help us in times of need.

Our verse today tells us that we need to call on Him "sincerely." The New King James Version for this verse says "in truth." When we call upon God, it must be with an understanding of whom He is and who we are. He is the Almighty God and we are His creation. He deserves our reverence and awe. He is The Father and we are His children. He loves us and wants us to love Him back.

As we step further out of our comfort zone, take comfort in the fact that you are not alone. As long as you are in Christ, you can never be alone, for He lives within you. He is right there with you and He is waiting for your call. Jesus, help us to know Your presence.

JUNE 28

Read: 2 Kings 13:1 – 14:29, Acts 18:23 – 19:12, Psalm 146:1-10, Proverbs 18:2-3

ACTS 19:9

But some rejected his message and publicly spoke against the Way, so Paul left the synagogue and took the believers with him. Then he began preaching daily at the lecture hall of Tyrannus.

As was his custom Paul began to minister in the city of Ephesus to the Jews that he found there in the synagogue. Paul was a Jew and had a heart to reach the Jews, so every town that he visited he started by trying to minister to the Jews. Ephesus was a large important city. For over two years Paul stayed and preached to the people here in Ephesus.

Paul's calling was to the Gentiles; he was appointed by God to reach the non-Jews for Jesus Christ. Even though the Jews of the synagogue rejected the message and began speaking against the Way there were some that believed. The church of Ephesus was founded with converted Jews. Only after the harvest field was no longer ripe with the Jews did Paul leave to go the Gentiles.

We should learn from Paul in his example of ministering to the lost. God wants us in fields that are ripe. In this we can learn a great lesson from the farmer. When he harvests a field, he leaves it lie for a period of time. He will then plow it under and plant more seeds. He will then leave that field until time has passed and the plants have grown up and a new crop has been produced.

We need to be careful not to be trying to harvest dead fields. Once we have shared the truth with someone, we need to allow the Lord time to plow up the ground and water the hearts of those that have heard it. That might include leaving someone alone with God for a period of time for Him to do His part. It is my belief that we sometimes get in the way of that when we are continually trying to harvest where the crop has not sprung up. The farmer is patient; he waits for the signs that the harvest is ready and then he gets to work. The former doesn't pester or prod the plants until they produce fruit; he just lets it grow until it is ready.

We need to be patient with the harvest of people's souls. You can't poke and prod a person until they are saved. You might be preventing the harvest from happening by doing that. You might need to move away from that field and go to one that is ready for harvest and then come back to this field when it is ready.

Paul went to preach to the Gentiles after the Jews rejected the message. If someone rejects your message go to someone else with the message. But before you leave, plant some seeds of the loving truth of the gospel of Jesus Christ and then trust God to bring about the harvest. God didn't call Paul to save all the Jews; he called him to preach to the Gentiles. Your greatest success as a Christian will come as you realize who God has called you to and you go there. Jesus, lead us to those You have called us.

JUNE 29

Read: 2 Kings 15:1 – 16:20, Acts 19:13-41, Psalm 147:1-20, Proverbs 18:4-5

2 KINGS 16:10

King Ahaz then went to Damascus to meet with King Tiglath-pileser of Assyria. While he was there, he noticed an unusual altar. So he sent a model of it to Uriah the priest, along with its design in full detail.

King Ahaz is the king of Judah. While he is king, the kings of Israel and Aram declare war on him. Judah and Israel are relatives and Aram should be a common enemy. King Ahaz hired the king of Assyria to come and save him. After saving him, King Ahaz goes to visit the king of Assyria. While there he sees an altar that catches his attention. He then sends the plans for that altar back to Uriah the priest, who promptly duplicates it for the king.

Ahaz is not a good king in the eyes of God. He did not do things that were pleasing to God. He even sacrificed his own children in the fire. His religious practices were very much like the people of Canaan before God drove them out. God had warned the people not to look at or study the way that these people worshipped. He warned them because He knew that there would be things about the way that they worship that they would find attractive. He knew that this would begin a process of them turning away from the LORD.

As soon as Ahaz got his new altar built, he started changing the way the people worshipped in the temple. God had given very clear and specific instructions as to how He wanted His people to worship Him. Ahaz substituted his own form of worship.

As God's people, we need to be so careful not to fall into this trap. It can be so subtle but it is so dangerous. There are some fascinating things being done today that are being called worship. That is not to say that everything that is different is evil. God has led some to worship Him in ways that are different.

It is impossible to say what the motives of King Ahaz were as he had this altar built and then worshipped at it. We cannot presume to know where his heart was because the Scriptures do not tell us. All the Scriptures say is that he did evil in the sight of the LORD. He had access to the same five books that make up the first books of our Bibles. He could have and should have known how God wanted to be worshipped. It appears that He had no desire to please God in his worship.

Being New Testament Christians, we are not bound by the Law. But we also have clear instruction regarding what will please our Lord in worship. And where the Scriptures are not clear or silent, we have the Holy Spirit to guide us. True worship begins not in the way that we worship but in the desire of our heart to please our Savior and Creator. Be careful not to let the world's ways of worship to distract you from a pure and undefiled worship. Jesus, you are worthy of our worship.

JUNE 30

Read: 2 Kings 17:1 – 18:12, Acts 20:1-38, Psalm 148:1-14, Proverbs 18:6-7

ACTS 20:20

Yet I never shrank from telling you the truth, either publicly or in your homes.

Paul is making his way to Jerusalem where he knows that he will eventually be arrested. He doesn't know the details of how it is going to happen and he doesn't know how it is going to turn out, except that it is going to be hard. And yet he is hurrying along his way to Jerusalem. But he doesn't want to miss an opportunity to minister to the people of Ephesus so he calls for them to meet him. When they arrive Paul pours his heart out to them.

The elders of the church of Ephesus had witnessed many of the things that had happened to Paul as he was ministering to them in and around Ephesus. Paul had experienced much opposition and persecution. He had suffered many trials and tribulations as he helped this now flourishing church get on its feet. Then Paul makes the statement in our verse for the day as a punctuation mark to his experiences with them; he never shrank back from telling them the truth.

Paul didn't hesitate to tell the people the truth regardless of what was going on in his life. He told them the truth when things were going well and when it was difficult. Paul in this text is exhorting the elders of the

Ephesian church to do the same thing. Paul wants them to never hesitate to share the truth of the Good News of Jesus to others. Sadly the book of Revelation in Jesus' letter to the church in Ephesus it appears that they did not follow Paul's direction.

It is my opinion that one of the reasons that Paul was so effective in ministry was this very thing. It didn't matter who he was talking to or where he was, the gospel was proclaimed with boldness. It didn't matter if he was meeting privately in a person's home or out on the streets or in the temple or other gatherings, Paul never shrank from telling the truth about Jesus. It didn't matter if everyone loved him and wanted to hear what he had to say or if they hated him and wanted to stone him; Paul told the truth.

Paul could do that because he trusted God with his life. Later in our reading Paul says that his life is useless if he is not doing what the Lord appointed him to do. We were created with a purpose, and that purpose was appointed by God and it is for God. If we shrink back from doing it because of external circumstances then our lies are meaningless and useless. Even though Paul experienced all sorts of difficult things in his life because of his divine calling, God carried him through safely in each one of those things. The same is true of your divine calling. That calling may lead through some very difficult things, but if God is leading you through them, He will also make sure that you get through to the other side. Trust God with your life and follow your calling without shrinking back from anything the world or Satan might throw at you. Jesus, lead on!

JULY

JULY 1

Read: 2 Kings 18:13 – 19:37, Acts 21:1-17, Psalm 149:1-9, Proverbs 18:8

2 KINGS 19:31

For a remnant of my people will spread out from Jerusalem, a group of survivors from Mount Zion. The passion of the LORD Almighty will make this happen!

God has allowed the enemies of Israel to come in and punish them for their unfaithfulness to God. Many people have been killed and many more have been led away as captives to foreign lands. This is how God typically will punish His people for disobedience; through their enemies.

God's desire is that He be their God. As God of the Israelites He had promised to provide for them and to protect them from their enemies. This was a conditional promise though; it required their obedience. Because of their disobedience God withdrew His hand of protection and they were nearly destroyed. But God is rich in mercy and would not allow them to be completely destroyed; He left a remnant alive. This remnant was sent to distant lands and thus spread the knowledge of God to a much greater area than just Israel.

As Christians we are also in a covenant relationship with God. He has agreed to be our God on the condition that we obey Him. When we disobey Him we break our part of the agreement and open ourselves up for God's punishment. God will send us warnings and try to woo us back to Himself before He punishes us but we must be very clear that God will punish us if we don't repent.

As modern Christians we don't need to worry too much about the Assyrians or the Babylonians; that is not the kind of enemy that God is likely to send our way to punish us. The enemies that He sends now might look like your boss or the IRS or sickness. It could be a financial setback or strained personal relationships. Whatever it is it will have the effect of feeling like a part of your life is being torn apart and sent off in all directions. It is a painful and terrible experience that will likely change your life forever.

A verse such as todays should give hope to those that might be in the midst of being cast out of the Promised Life. God will not allow the enemy to completely destroy you; He will leave a remnant of your life. From that remnant He desires to raise up a new and better life. Every time the Israelites humbled themselves and repented of their disobedience God sent a rescuer to save them. If you are experiencing the punishment of God because of your own disobedience, turn back to God in repentance and then wait for your rescue to come. Trust God that he will not allow you to be destroyed and that He can restore back to you everything that you have lost and even more. Jesus, teach us to turn from our disobedience back to You before You have to spank us.

JULY 2

Read: 2 Kings 20:1 – 22:2, Acts 21:18-36, Psalm 150:1-6, Proverbs 18:9-10

2 KINGS 20:3

"Remember, O LORD, how I have always tried to be faithful to you and do what is pleasing in your sight." Then he broke down and wept bitterly.

There is something fascinating about this account of when Hezekiah became deathly ill. Hezekiah was one of the best kings that Israel ever had. He instituted a great many reforms and did a great job of drawing the people back to the worship of God. At this point in his life he becomes very ill. God sends the prophet Isaiah to him to let him know that he will not recover from this illness. We see Hezekiah's response in our verse for the day. He is very upset and weeps bitterly.

First, I would like you to recognize Hezekiah's faith; he believed the report of Isaiah. This is one of the things that made Hezekiah such a good king; he believed the things that God told him. We would do well to follow Hezekiah's example in this area of our lives. We may not have a prophet like Isaiah around but we do have the Bible, the Holy Spirit, and those that have been appointed to teach and disciple us. Start believing what they say and do what the Bible and Holy Spirit are telling you to.

Hezekiah also reminds God of all the things that he had done for God. There was one word in this reminder that really caught my attention and I believe bears reflection upon; "tried." Hezekiah did not say that he had always been faithful or that he had always done what was pleasing; he said that he had tried to do those things. As we continue to read this account we see that God answers Hezekiah's prayer almost immediately and sends Isaiah back to the king with the news that God has decided to extend his life by fifteen years.

God will never ask us to be perfect; because He knows that we can't be perfect. He asks us to try to be perfect. Our goal in life is to try to be faithful to God and to try to always do what is pleasing to Him. Our problem is that our ability to achieve that is limited by our sinful flesh. God knows that we are going to blow it occasionally; but He wants us to keep trying.

God gave King Hezekiah an extra fifteen years to live. This was partly because Hezekiah had the faith to ask God to intervene on his behalf but we need to be careful not to create a theology that claims enough faith can extend your life. God extended Hezekiah's life because He wanted to and because Hezekiah asked in faith. Your faith is irrelevant if it is outside of God's will. What would you do if you knew that God had extended your life by fifteen years? What would you do with those fifteen years? Remember that every day that you are alive is a day that God extended to you. Live it as though it were your last. Jesus, help us to thank you for every day that we are here and to live each day faithfully and in a way that is pleasing to You.

JULY 3

Read: 2 Kings 22:3 – 23:30, Acts 21:37 – 22:16, Psalm 1:1-6, Proverbs 18:11-12

2 KINGS 23:3

The king took his place of authority beside the pillar and renewed the covenant in the LORD'S presence. He pledged to obey the LORD by keeping all his commands, regulations, and laws with all his heart and soul. In this way, he confirmed all the terms of the covenant that were written in the scroll, and all the people pledged themselves to the covenant.

King Josiah had been made king at the age of eight. The kingdom was well established and everyone was living their lives as they thought was the best way to live. As Josiah grew up he began leading the people back to God by first having the priests repair the temple. During this process they discovered the scroll of the Law of Moses. Upon reading it, Josiah knew that they were in trouble. He knew that God was upset with the nation of Israel and that He was going to judge them for their sins of idolatry.

Josiah's response was repentance. This is amazing! Josiah inherited the kingdom the way that it was. It was his ancestors, starting as far back as King Solomon that had allowed the sins of idolatry to defile the people. But Josiah is repentant and goes to God to seek His will. Josiah found out that the prophecies of impending doom for the nation of Israel were true but because of his repentance it would not happen in his lifetime.

Josiah then did what every leader should do in a time of crisis; he "took his place of authority." Josiah knew that it was his place to lead the people, especially in their relationship with God. Josiah was not responsible for the past but he knew he would be responsible for the future. He went to great lengths to bring the people back to God.

Some of us will have the opportunity to start ministries and churches but more of us will inherit ministries and churches that are already established. We may go into those situations and see as Josiah did a temple that is run down and neglected and determine that there are serious problems including sin and idolatry throughout the ministry and church. Your role is to take your place of authority and bring people back to God. That may involve tearing down idols and shrines to other gods and removing the priests of those gods. You can probably imagine that many of the people of Josiah's time were wondering what he was doing because that was the way that they had always worshipped. Josiah used his authority to drive the sin from the land and to draw the people back to God.

The very first thing that Josiah did after he "took his place of authority" was to renew his covenant with the LORD. He started the process of cleansing the land by cleansing himself. Nothing that you do "for God" will matter as much as what you do "with God." Begin by cleansing yourself and letting Jesus do the work in you before you try to do it in others. Jesus, help us to see your church the way that you see it and give us the courage to take our place of authority.

JULY 4

Read: 2 Kings 23:31 – 25:30, Acts 22:17 – 23:10, Psalm 2:1-12, Proverbs 18:13

ACTS 22:21

But the LORD said to me, "Leave Jerusalem, for I will send you far away to the Gentiles!"

Paul has been arrested by the Romans because a mob of Jews are beating him in the temple. Some Jews from Asia had come and incited a mob by making false accusations against him. Before the Romans take him into the fortress Paul is given an opportunity to speak to his fellow Jews. Paul shares with them the experience that he had on the road to Damascus. They listen intently until Paul shares with them the mission that Jesus sent Paul on; to preach to the Gentiles. At this the crowd erupts and wants him dead.

As far as they were concerned Paul had just spoken blasphemy. Most Jews believed that the Gentiles, which is anyone that is not a Jew, were beyond salvation. They believed that Gentiles were so far from God that is was impossible for them to be saved. This was also a problem in the early church which was largely converted Jews in the beginning. That was never God's viewpoint of Gentiles. A careful study of the Old Testament finds numerous references to God's plan to save the whole world; Jew and Gentile alike.

Paul had been given a very specific mission and ministry; to preach to the Gentiles. He didn't abandon his Jewish heritage or people but he recognized the new covenant that Jesus had established in His blood and on the cross. The problem was that other people couldn't see or understand what his mission and purpose were. Others understood it but didn't agree with it.

There will come times as you lead your family, ministry, or church in which you are called to do something that others don't understand. God is going to give you direction that He will confirm through prayer and His Word that others will look at and not understand. Be careful not to fall into the same trap that so many people do; listening to men rather than God. Paul's upbringing and training all told him not to go to the Gentiles. All of his friends and associates would likely have told him not to go to the Gentiles. Paul chose to obey God rather than men. The result was miraculous; God did a tremendous work through the missionary trips of the apostle Paul.

God is probably not asking you to abandon everything that your life currently is to follow His direction like He did with Paul. But the work that He desires to do through you and your family, ministry, or church is no less tremendous. God has a mission and purpose for your life that only He understands fully. Our responsibility is not to understand what God wants us to do, but to simply obey and do it. We don't need to convince others about the God-given purpose of our lives, that is the responsibility of the Holy Spirit. Besides the fruit of your obedience is all the proof that they should need. If God says do, then do it; nothing else matters. Jesus, help us to follow where you lead regardless of the mobs that don't understand your purpose for my life.

JULY 5

Read: 1 Chronicles 1:1 – 2:17, Acts 23:11-35, Psalm 3:1-8, Proverbs 18:14-15

1 CHRONICLES 1:10

Cush was also the ancestor of Nimrod, who was known across the earth as a heroic warrior.

Reading through the genealogies can sometimes be a laborious and difficult thing. The names are sometimes hard to pronounce and there is a drone to the rhythm of the text that can lull you to sleep. Over the years as I have become more familiar with the Scriptures, the genealogies have become more interesting. Now as I read each name, the story of this person's life as it is revealed in Scripture also pops up.

Nimrod in our verse is described as a great warrior. His fame was so great that everyone in the whole world knew about him. That is a pretty amazing statement considering there was no news coverage on television. Elsewhere Nimrod is described as a mighty hunter. He is also given credit for building a number of cities.

The most famous of the cities that Nimrod built was Babel. We are familiar with Babel; that is where the people decided to build a tower to reach up to God. They were attempting to elevate themselves to be equal with God. It is not certain that Nimrod was responsible for starting that project but it would not be a surprise if he was. God came and saw what they were doing and confused their language and dispersed the peoples to the ends of the earth.

Babel was later renamed Babylon and was a center of pagan worship practices. Babylon would later become a great world power that would be used by God to discipline His Chosen People, Israel, when they were disobedient. Babylon will also play a role in the end times as the Antichrist rebuilds it and uses it as his capital during the seven-year Tribulation period.

All of this started with a man by the name of Nimrod. As I grow in knowledge of the Scriptures my love of them grows. They are beautiful, not just in the content, but also in the way that they are put together. As time goes by and I grow in my understanding of this amazing book, I find myself more awe-struck by how wonderful it truly is. Only God could create something this beautiful and detailed.

The Bible teaches that man is God's highest creation. We were made in the image of God so that we could fellowship and commune with Him. His Word is given to us so that we might know how to do that. As my love of God grows, so does my love of His Word. As my love of the Bible grows, so does my love of God. I am convinced that someone that does not love God's Word cannot truly love God.

Choose to Love God more fully by choosing to love His Word. Not just the interesting stories, but every single word. Even the genealogies are given for a reason. Don't skip over them. Ask God to speak to you through the genealogies and through all the more difficult texts. You'll be amazed by what might come out. Jesus, help us to love You more by loving Your Word more.

JULY 6

ACTS 24:5

For we have found him to be a troublemaker, a man who is constantly inciting the Jews throughout the world to riots and rebellions against the Roman government. He is a ringleader of the sect known as the Nazarenes.

Paul is in Caesarea on his way ultimately to Rome. He is standing before Governor Felix who is being told the charges that the Jews are bringing against Paul. The Jews were hoping that their charges would be sufficient to convince Felix to have Paul executed. Their accusations against Paul were weak right out of the gate and Paul quickly and easily refuted them and then he took the opportunity to speak to everyone listening about the gospel of Jesus.

If we are faithful to do the work that the LORD appoints us to do we can also expect to be accused by those that oppose the work of Jesus in the world. The world system that was engineered by Satan will do anything it can to quench the work of the Holy Spirit in the world. The only thing that prevents that from happening is that faithful men and women continue to allow the Holy Spirit to work through them.

Paul's response to their accusations was not to get angry and explode all over them and the governor. Paul's response was calm and well spoken. This is a testimony of his faith in the saving power of Jesus Christ. Paul knew that Jesus could save him from his accusers and the governor and so he had nothing to worry about. When we get angry and attempt to defend ourselves strenuously, it is because we lack the faith to trust God to protect us and save us.

Paul also took advantage of his circumstances to share the gospel of Jesus with others. Because of these false accusations Paul is standing before the governor; one of the most powerful men in the nation. Paul didn't waste this opportunity by thinking about himself; he took this opportunity to share Jesus. We also may through false accusations and trials will be allowed to meet with people that we wouldn't ordinarily be able. God allowed it and orchestrated it so that you would be there for the reason of revealing Jesus to them.

Paul had the courage to fight past his fear of death and the boldness to speak to powerful people because he knew that nothing else mattered. He knew that his life was only important if he was a vessel for revealing Jesus to others. He knew that his life was in the hands of God and not the governor and so that helped to strengthen and encourage him.

Our God is the same God that stood with Paul in the governor's court. Just because you have been falsely accused doesn't mean that God has abandoned you. What is going on is a part of His grand plan and you have a role to play. Don't worry about the results; just tell them the truth and let them see Jesus. Jesus, give us courage and boldness.

JULY 7

Read: 1 Chronicles 4:5 – 5:17, Acts 25:1-27, Psalm 5:1-12, Proverbs 18:19

1 CHRONICLES 4:10

He was the one who prayed to the God of Israel, "Oh, that you would bless me and extend my lands! Please be with me in all that I do, and keep me from all trouble and pain!" And God granted him his request.

This little prayer that is recorded in the middle of the genealogies has become pretty famous. Books have been written about it and countless sermons have been preached on it. It is commonly referred to by people that proclaim certain types of theologies that suggest that God will give you anything you ask for. It is often associated with the belief that if you have enough faith you can ask God for the moon and He will give it to you.

It is placed here in the Scriptures for a reason; it is there to teach us something. The challenge as always is to try to figure out just what that is. One of the clues that we need to look at is context. In this case this account gives us very little to go on. Jabez was more distinguished than his brothers and his birth was difficult. Neither of those facts give us that much to go on. Other men in Scripture were very distinguished and did not have their prayers answered like this. Other people were born through difficult births. Neither of those facts warrant the kind of response that Jabez received here.

The danger we run into with a verse like this one is that we attempt to discover a method hidden in the request. If we can figure out what Jabez did than we can pray like this and get the same results. There is one little problem with that, God doesn't work that way. God works outside of our understanding and comprehension. We cannot put methods on our relationship with God.

God is absolutely faithful; He will never deviate from His character. In those areas where He has spoken on a subject, we can be absolutely certain how things are going to happen. The Bible tells us that if we confess our sins that God will forgive us. That is an absolute guarantee. If the Bible has not spoken clearly on a subject God is free to operate any way that He chooses, within the confines of His character. People are looking for a formula to getting everything they want from God. He is not a genie in a bottle. That is approaching God with the wrong attitude. There is no clear explanation as to why God answered this prayer of Jabez so completely. We only have two verses to tell us about the man, the prayer, and about God's response.

God granted Jabez all of His requests. We don't know any more than that. The prayer of Jabez can then be used to teach us about what God can do. It cannot be used to teach us about what we should do to get our prayers answered. God chose to grant all of the requests that Jabez laid before Him. It is not important why God did that; he simply did! God may grant all your requests and He may not. That is His choice. He is God after all! Approach Him as though He can answer any and every request that you have. But understand that He is God and it is His will that determines what He will do, not your method or process, or even how much "faith" you have. Jesus, teach to believe that you answer every prayer.

JULY 8

Read: 1 Chronicles 5:18 – 6:81, Acts 26:1-32, Psalm 6:1-10, Proverbs 18:20-21

1 CHRONICLES 6:49

Only Aaron and his descendants served as priests. They presented the offerings on the altar of burnt offering and the altar of incense, and they performed all the other duties related to the Most Holy Place. They made atonement for Israel by doing everything that Moses, the servant of God, had commanded them.

Aaron and his descendants were chosen by God to perform the most sacred of duties within the tabernacle and ultimately the Temple. This was a position of great authority and responsibility. Even the clothes that they were to wear while on duty set them apart from the people. They had the immense responsibility of going before God to make atonement for the people.

This was no small thing. God commanded that they be purified first before they entered into the Most Holy Place. If the High Priest was not purified and came before the LORD in an incorrect manner it would cost him his life. Two of Aaron's sons were killed because they burned a "strange fire" before the LORD. It was no small thing to be a priest of the LORD. A careful study of the priestly responsibilities will point you to the work of Christ on behalf of fallen man. Each sacrifice and each element of the rituals is a picture of some characteristic or pattern of Christ's work and sacrifice. The role and responsibility of Aaron and his sons was a shadow of the perfect High Priest, Jesus.

The Bible teaches that, as believers, we are being raised up into a holy priesthood. We have the unique responsibility of performing priestly duties before the LORD. While we are not involved in many of the rituals and sacrifices we still perform duties that carry the same spiritual significance before the LORD.

This is especially true if we are in some position of leadership within our family, ministry, or church. One of the roles of men is to be the priest of his family. One of the problems of great responsibility and authority is the temptations that come along with them. Over a period of time, the role of High Priest became a coveted position of great power. It became a source of pride.

To be called to lead people is one of the noblest efforts a person could ever aspire to, especially in service to the LORD. We must always remember the significance of our role. We are not to build a kingdom of our own but to lead people to the kingdom of God. As leaders we will be called to a greater accounting than those that follow. Aaron and his descendants were expected to be more holy and righteous than others. They were held to a higher standard. We also, as leaders, are to be held to a higher standard. Your position does not mean that you are more holy and righteous, but that you should be allowing the Holy Spirit to make you that way. Jesus, help us to take our responsibility seriously.

JULY 9

Read: 1 Chronicles 7:1 – 8:40, Acts 27:1-20, Psalm 7:1-17, Proverbs 18:22

ACTS 27:3

The next day we docked at Sidon, Julius was very kind to Paul and let him go ashore to visit with friends so they could provide for his needs.

Paul is on his way to Rome. He is in the custody of a Roman officer by the name of Julius. Little is known of Julius except that he was a captain of the Imperial Regiment. It was his responsibility to get Paul and the other prisoners to Rome so that they could stand trial before Caesar. Failure to complete this mission could cost him his position and possibly his life.

At the first stop that the ship makes Julius allows Paul to go ashore to visit with his friends. Have you ever wondered at that? This Roman soldier lets one of his prisoners go ashore so that Paul's friends could provide for his needs. The Romans are not known for their compassion and gentleness. We don't know if Paul asked to go ashore or if one of his traveling companions made the request. It is very likely that Luke was there and others could have been there as well. A typical suspicious guard probably wouldn't be too keen on letting a prisoner out that had the support of companions to facilitate an escape.

Something caused Julius to trust Paul. The text doesn't tell us whether Julius sent a guard with Paul or not but the implication in the text is that he did not. That fascinates me and causes me to desire more information about this account. It is also not easy to determine how long Julius has been assigned to this task; though the text infers that it has been short. In a very short period of time, Paul had earned the trust of this hardened Roman army officer to the point that he would allow him to walk off the ship with his friends. This is just one more testimony of the amazing character of Paul.

Julius was confident that he could trust his prisoner Paul because Paul had in a very short period of time proven to Julius that he could be trusted. People will trust us when we prove ourselves to be trustworthy. The world usually wants it the other way; it wants you to trust before there is any proof that they are trustworthy.

It is especially important for us as leaders of families, ministries, and churches to be trustworthy. So much depends upon it. If you are not trustworthy the people that are called to follow you will struggle to do that. You should not expect them to trust you until you have proven yourself to be trustworthy.

We prove ourselves trustworthy by saying what we mean and then do what we say. Being trustworthy is also proven when we are where we are expected and needed to be when possible. Nothing will limit your ability to lead God's people like losing their trust because of unfaithfulness or neglect. Remember, they are God's people and they deserve a leader that they can trust. Jesus, teach us to be faithful.

JULY 10

Read: 1 Chronicles 9:1 – 10:14, Acts 27:21-44, Psalm 8:1-9, Proverbs 18:23-24

1 CHRONICLES 10:13-14

So Saul died because he was unfaithful to the LORD. He failed to obey the LORD's command, and he even consulted a medium instead of asking the LORD for guidance. So the LORD killed him and turned his kingdom over to David son of Jesse.

Saul's rule of Israel was hardly something to brag about. He was disobedient to the LORD right from the beginning. The prophet Samuel tried to warn him and teach him the right way to go but Saul insisted on doing things his own way. The LORD sent a number of things into Saul's life in an attempt to turn him back to the LORD. Saul was determined to be his own man.

Saul's life was ended at the hands of the Philistines over twenty years after David had been anointed to be the next king of Israel. It is not clear why the LORD waited so long before making the transition to David as king of Israel. It could have been to give David time to become more mature and gain experience. It could also have been to give Saul time to repent and turn back to the LORD.

Saul failed to respond and so the LORD killed him in battle with the Philistines. This verse reminds us that God is in control of everything. As those arrows were flying in the battle, the LORD directed one to fly to the target He had placed on King Saul. He had no chance of escape. His fate had been sealed.

What is tragic about this is the two things that Saul depended upon became trophies of his enemies; his armor and his head. Saul's armor was placed in the temple of their gods and his head was placed on the wall of the temple of Dagon. Saul depended upon his own strength which is pictured in his armor and his own wisdom. The enemy took both and mounted them on their walls like they might the head of an animal they had hunted. It was a way of saying that our gods are stronger than yours.

All of this happened because Saul was unfaithful to the LORD. As leaders of families, ministries, churches, or in industry we need to take careful note of what happened to Saul. Because he was unfaithful, the LORD took him out. In this case, He did it literally by taking his life. There are other ways that the LORD can take you out. He can take away your position or authority or ability. Humble your heart before you find yourself hanging on some enemy's wall as a trophy.

God will be patient, desiring that you would humble your heart before Him and repent. But don't think even for a second that a rebellious leader is going to get away with his sins forever. In His time, the LORD will act. If you find yourself under the leadership of a leader that is rebelling against God, remember to let Him deal with that leader. It is your responsibility before the LORD to follow as if He were the LORD until the LORD acts or causes you to move on. Jesus, help us to be faithful to you whether we are leading or following.

JULY 11

Read: 1 Chronicles 11:1 – 12:18, Acts 28:1-31, Psalm 9:1-12, Proverbs 19:1-3

ACTS 28:15

The brothers and sisters in Rome had heard we were coming, and they came to meet us at the Forum on the Appian Way. Other joined us at the three taverns. When Paul saw them, he thanked God and took courage.

Paul is on his way to Rome. It has been a difficult trip, which included a shipwreck and a winter on the little island of Malta. It is not clear how this happened but the brothers and sisters from Rome heard that Paul had arrived and went to meet him. They traveled between 35 and 45 miles to meet Paul on the final leg of his journey to stand before Caesar in Rome. Our verse says that Paul thanked God and took courage as a result of the visit of the brothers and sisters from Rome.

Paul was not certain what awaited him in Rome. He knew that he would stand before the emperor and that he would share the truth of Jesus before great and powerful people but he did not know what would ultimately come of his life. And then to get to Rome had been very difficult. Things like that can have the effect of draining your courage and joy. It is very likely that was where Paul was at this time.

Knowing this God motivated the believers in Rome to come and encourage him along the way. When Paul saw these brothers and sisters, he felt the love of Jesus pour forth from them and into himself. Even as great as Paul was spiritually he needed the fellowship of other believers to refill his joy and courage.

People don't often think about that with their spiritual leaders. There are times when their spiritual tank is emptied by the seemingly endless needs that they are called to minister to. God is so gracious and never fails to fill the leader with what they need to do that ministry but there are times when the leader needs someone to meet their needs. It encourages me that Paul needed that occasionally. It reminds me that it is OK if I occasionally have needs that I can't meet through my relationship with Christ; that I need others to encourage me. It fills my heart with joy to think of those people that God has brought into my life to meet me along the way to encourage me. They may never know what a vital role they play in my life and in my ability to minister to others. It fills my heart with joy to think of them.

Is there someone in your life that is serving the LORD that God would call you to go to and encourage? If so, do it. You are not just serving them by doing that but you are also serving others. Your words of encouragement might be just what that leader needs so that he can minister to the rest of the flock that God has entrusted to him (or her). It is amazing what kind of fruit can be born from just a few words of encouragement. Jesus, help us to meet those weary servants that are on their way to serve you.

JULY 12

Read: 1 Chronicles 12:19 – 14:17, Romans 1:1-17, Psalm 9:13-20, Proverbs 19:4-5

1 CHRONICLES 12:40

And people from as far away as Issachar, Zebulun, and Naphtali brought food on donkeys, camels, mules, and oxen. Vast supplies of flour, fig cakes, raisins, wine, olive oil, cattle, and sheep were brought to the celebration. There was great joy throughout the land of Israel.

David is finally king of Israel. People come from all over Israel to celebrate the rise of this new king. Somehow the people knew something about David that they did not know about Saul. They were celebrating the fact that there was a new king with great enthusiasm. Somehow they knew that God was going to bless Israel because David was now king. Somehow they knew this was God's perfect plan at work and it filled them with joy.

This is not the way people usually feel when there is a significant change taking place. More often than not, there is fear or concern whenever a change is coming. There is uncertainty about what the future holds and questions about how the change will affect them personally.

It would be great if we could all face change the way that Israel faced this change of leadership. The people may not have known exactly why they had joy; it just welled up within them. The same can be said of us in our own walk with the LORD. There are times when joy seems to flow like a rushing river and there are other times when it is glaringly absent.

Joy is not easy to manufacture. It can be done but it is difficult to maintain. Joy is a fruit; one of the fruits of the Holy Spirit. As a fruit it grows spontaneously from the source that produces it. Joy springs forth from faith and trust. When faith and trust are nurtured in your life, joy is the natural byproduct. Obviously our faith and trust must be in something that can generate joy for it to produce any. I can believe and trust an apple tree will produce oranges but it never will; it can't.

When we put our faith in God's Word and trust Him implicitly, we are in the fertile ground that produces healthy fruit, including joy. As we nurture and tend to our faith and trust we will see fruit to grow naturally. We will experience joy in our lives without effort. Even in normally stressful or difficult times, there will be an underlying sense of joy in the faith and trust you have in the LORD.

If there is no joy in our lives it is often an indication that we need to tend to our faith and trust. The Holy Spirit might be trying to show you an area of your life that you have not fully surrendered to the LORD. Humble your heart and ask the Spirit to show you clearly what you are holding on to. Then lay it down at the feet of Jesus. Open up your Bible and find something that speaks to that subject and then choose to believe it.

Joy is a choice; it is a choice to believe God's Word and trust in Him. After you have made the right choice, celebrate. Jesus, strengthen our faith and trust.

JULY 13
Read: 1 Chronicles 15:1 – 16:36, Romans 1:18-32, Psalm 10:1-15, Proverbs 19:6-7

PSALM 10:11

The wicked say to themselves, "God isn't watching! He will never notice!"

It is amazing to think that some people can imagine that God doesn't see the things that they are doing. They even think to themselves that God doesn't care about the wicked things that they are doing. It is as though they think that God is off somewhere and can't be bothered to pay attention to them as they do their evil little things.

God is everywhere and nothing escapes his notice. The reason that some people develop the attitude that God won't notice their wicked deeds is because He doesn't judge them right on the spot as they are doing them. They imagine in their minds that God didn't notice the last time because if He had He would have done something.

It is just like our kids. If they "get away" with doing something they are not supposed to they are more likely to think they can get away with it again. One of the reasons that our children will behave is because they fear the consequences of getting caught and punished.

God doesn't usually punish us as soon as we sin against Him. Often when He does, we don't make the connection between our sin and His punishment. God has given us the Holy Spirit to help us to recognize His work in our lives. The wicked tend to ignore the warnings of the Holy Spirit. If they ignore Him long enough their hearts can become so hard as to not even notice Him any longer. Their consciences can become seared to the point that they do not even feel that there is anything wrong with the evil things that they do.

God never sleeps and He never gets tired. He never stops watching what is going on in this universe that He created. He is still in control of everything except our free will. Nothing happens that He doesn't notice and make note of. There will come a day when all things will be revealed and judged. The wicked may think that He doesn't notice but He will notice and then He is going to hold them accountable for every wicked thing they have done.

They may think they are getting away with something but there is no way to get away with anything with God. If they will repent of their wicked ways and confess the evil things that they have done, they will be forgiven. If they don't, God will take care of them in His timing.

We as Christians don't need to concern ourselves about how the wicked seem to mock and scoff at God. Sometimes I think we forget that God doesn't miss anything and that He doesn't forget anything. Trust God to deal with the wicked in the way and time that He decides. Jesus, help us leave the future of the wicked in Your hands.

JULY 14

Read: 1 Chronicles 16:37 – 18:17, Romans 2:1-24, Psalm 10:16-18, Proverbs 19:8-9

ROMANS 2:7

He will give eternal life to those who persist in doing what is good, seeking after the glory and honor and immortality that God offers.

Paul writes to the Christian church in Rome this powerful exposition on the faith. Few works in the Bible compare to this masterpiece on Christian beliefs. One could easily spend a considerable amount of their life studying this book and still find that there is much to learn from it. In our reading for the day Paul is discussing the judgment of God as it relates to the Jews and the Gentiles and the Law and circumcision. Paul goes to great lengths to show the differences between the two groups but also to show that God is just. The word that jumped out at me this morning was "persist."

Paul is telling his Christian readers that God gives eternal life to those that persist in doing what is good. There is an obvious implication concerning the theology of once-saved-always-saved but that is not the focus of today's devotional. Paul is exhorting his readers to persistence. Persistence is the steady following of a single course or direction.

To be persistent we must have a goal that we are hoping to achieve. Paul is telling us that our goal should be the glory and honor and immortality that God offers. Immortality is life without death. Paul could mean a couple of things by using that word. He could mean that we should have as a goal eternal life. That seems redundant based on the context. Paul combines immortality with glory and honor. He could also mean something different from a physical never-ending life; he could be referring to a legacy.

A legacy is something that is handed down from an ancestor. A legacy can be a material possession or property or it could be a tradition or history. A legacy is something that can long outlive us. A legacy is a form of immortality. The legacy that we are being told to leave is that of doing what is good. We are to persist at doing good works with the goal of receiving from God a legacy that will outlive our physical lives.

Our problem is that we are often looking for glory and honor and immortality from the wrong place; from men. The problem with receiving glory, honor, and immortality from men is that men are very fickle. The only source of glory, honor, and immortality that is worthwhile and lasting is that from God. Glory and honor and immortality from men is like a bunch of cut flowers; they are beautiful and smell great but in a week they are going to be wilted and dead. Seek what God offers by steadily following a direction of doing what is good. The glory and honor and immortality are the rewards of doing what is good. Seek after them as evidence that you are doing what God desires you to be doing. Jesus, help us to seek after Your rewards and not the rewards of men.

JULY 15

Read: 1 Chronicles 19:1 – 21:30, Romans 2:25 – 3:8, Psalm 11:1-7, Proverbs 19:10-12

1 CHRONICLES 21:1

Satan rose up against Israel and caused David to take a census of the Israelites.

In our culture a census is not that big of a deal; every ten years a census is taken. It seems odd to us that a census would be something that God would call a sin. The thing was that God had promised David and the nation of Israel to multiply them until their numbers were like the sands of the seashore; meaning too great to count. For David to do a census was to test God to see if His promise had come true or not. God also had a concern that this census would provide a source of pride and independence in the heart of the king and the people.

God had caused David to be very successful. David had taken control over the nation of Israel and it was prospering under his leadership and control. David had done a pretty good job of depending upon and following the will of God in his life. But David slipped into that dangerous phase of a leader's life; comfort. David had become comfortable and nothing is more dangerous to a leader's ability to lead than to become very successful and becoming comfortable in that success.

Satan used David's success against him and the nation of Israel by planting the idea of a census in David's mind. This is the place that David could have had the victory; if he had only rejected the idea while it was still in his mind. David was given another opportunity to do the right thing when Joab tried to talk him out of it. David allowed his pride to get in the way of the right decision.

Too many leaders within God's churches, ministries, and families fall into the same kind of traps. God blesses them and they become successful. They then fall into the trap of being comfortable in that success and forget who made them successful. Then Satan very gently plants the seed of an idea in their minds. That seed is then fed and nurtured by our pride and selfishness and before long they find themselves involved in some kind of sin. The sad thing about that is that it is not just the leader that suffers from sin. When David sinned, the whole nation suffered as a result of that. The same is true in the churches, ministries, and families of God; when the leader sins it is not just the leader that pays for that sin.

God wants us all to be successful; though we need to understand and accept His description of success. God doesn't want us to allow our success to open a door into our lives for sin. The best way to defend ourselves from this is to keep our focus on God and to continually point to God as the source of any good thing in our lives. This must be done in the heart before it is done with the mouth but both must take place if you desire to see God's continued blessings and protection. Jesus, help us to only look at our successes as a way of glorifying and praising You.

JULY 16

Read: 1 Chronicles 22:1 – 23:32, Romans 3:9-31, Psalm 12:1-8, Proverbs 19:13-14

1 CHRONICLES 23:1

When David was an old man, he appointed his son Solomon to be king over Israel.

David is getting old and he is nearing the end of his life. God has already told him that Solomon is to replace him as king of Israel. David has been preparing for this transition in leadership for some time. He had been preparing the materials to build the temple and teaching Solomon everything he needed to know so that he could build the temple. He had also been preparing the people that would assist Solomon.

We see also in our text for today that David is preparing and assigning the people that will minister in the temple once it is complete. David is doing everything he can to get everyone ready for the change in leaders.

It was common in these times for the king to rule until he died and then their heir would assume the throne. While it was common, it also led to many challenges in the transition. Often there were conflicts over who should be king and sometimes wars would break out over the issue. David showed great humility and wisdom by preparing for and appointing Solomon to be king before he died. We will see in a few chapters that David will step down from the throne and make Solomon king in his place. This puts David in the unique position of being able to help Solomon as he assumes the responsibility of king.

David loved God and God's people so much that he worked to make sure that the transition would be smooth and that Solomon would have the greatest chance of success. In life and ministry we will have opportunities to act as David has acted here. We will regularly be faced with transitions that will test our humility and wisdom. Changes in jobs, homes, schools, family, ministry, and churches all provide opportunities for us to show the same humility and wisdom that David did.

We should prepare for the transition so that the person that is replacing us has the greatest chance of success. This is easier to do when we are being promoted or moving to something better but the real test comes when we are losing our job or ministry or it is a "negative" move. This is the time that God will test your humility. Will you show your love for God by preparing for your replacement so that they will succeed? And even more than that, will you help them to be more successful than you were? God would call you to do this in all areas of your life. The humility and wisdom that David showed here is available to everyone that trusts in Jesus. He is the source and the reason for both. Jesus, help us to show our love for you by trying to make this a better place after we move on.

JULY 17

Read: 1 Chronicles 24:1 – 26:11, Romans 4:1-12, Psalm 13:1-6, Proverbs 19:15-16

1 CHRONICLES 26:8

All of these descendants of Obed-edom, including their sons and grandsons—sixty-two of them in all—were very capable men, well qualified for their work.

Several times during our reading today the author of Chronicles comments that the descendants of Obed-edom were exceptional men. They were assigned the duties of gatekeepers and it appears that this duty required men of exceptional ability. It has been said that God doesn't call the equipped, He equips the called. However you might interpret that saying the fact is that it is God that is doing the equipping. The descendants of Obed-edom were equipped before they were called.

Some people are under the false impression that God can only use simple people that God must work through supernaturally to accomplish His tasks. God also equips some to have natural abilities so that they can accomplish much of what He wants done in the world. There are some that have a natural gift to teach before they ever teach a single thing. Those gifts are obvious to everyone.

As leaders in families, ministries, and churches we ought to be looking for those that God has equipped so that they can be assigned to tasks that allow them to fully explore and exercise those gifts and abilities. Yesterday we saw that it is the heart that determines a person's usability by God, but God wants to use every gift that He has placed in the body.

This becomes difficult when there are people around us that are better qualified and equipped than we are. This can create a sense of fear with leaders to try to block a well-qualified person from using their gifts for fear that they themselves might be replaced. This is a selfish and self-centered attitude that does not bring glory to God. You should rejoice if God brings someone into your midst that is better than you.

Never forget that if it was God that put you into the position of leadership, than it is His place to replace you if He so chooses. To be afraid that might happen is a lack of trust that God has something better for you. And after all, it is not all about you; it's about God, it's about the ministry, it's about His church. Who God uses to do what is His part; our part is to do our part, which is what He tells us to do.

As leaders we should be praying that God would bring people into our ministries and churches that are better than we are so that our ministries and churches can be better than we are. And then we should rejoice when God answers those prayers by helping those people find the place that God can best use their gifts and abilities. God is looking for leaders that are humble enough to encourage people better than they are to be a part of what God is doing around them. Jesus, help us to see your church, as your church.

JULY 18

Read: 1 Chronicles 26:12 – 27:34, Romans 4:13 – 5:5, Psalm 14:1-7, Proverbs 19:17

ROMANS 5:3

We can rejoice, too, when we run into problems and trials, for we know that they are good for us - they help us learn to endure.

Rejoice in your problems and trials! Celebrate when you experience tribulations and suffering! That is probably not our first response to things like that in our lives. Typically, if there is going to be a party during those times it is a pity party. Paul is suggesting that during our times of distress that we rejoice and thank God for those times. Before we label Paul as a nut-case we ought to look closer at who is saying this and who he is saying it to.

A close study of Paul's life which you can read in the New Testament will tell you that he was a man that well-accustomed to trials, tribulations, and suffering. He had experienced more really difficult things than most of us ever will. Most of us have never been stoned (with rocks), flogged, or ship-wrecked just to name a few of the things that happened to Paul. He also lived with some kind of a physical ailment that he begged God to take away and was told by God, "My grace is sufficient for you."

This letter was written to the church in Rome that was experiencing great levels of persecution. Each new Caesar that came to power stepped up the pressure on the Christians. It was becoming increasingly difficult to be a Christian. Most of us have no idea what it is like to experience that kind of life. It was to a people that were in the midst of great problems and trails that Paul, a man well-acquainted with problems and trails, wrote this epistle.

Sometimes it is a good idea for us to remember that our problems and trials are not as big as we might think they are. Granted, to us they are very big but in proportion to what others are experiencing they are not so huge. It is also always good for us to remember that God has a plan in those problems and trials that is meant to move us closer to being conformed to the image of His Son Jesus.

We see one of the end results that God is looking for through our problems and trails; endurance. Endurance is the ability to continue or last until the end of the race. It is God's desire that we would be able to run the race to the very end. The only way that we will be able to do that is if we are strengthened in those areas where we are weak. God allows problems and trials to come into our lives so that we will see where we are weak. As a loving Father, He will help us through those times but His desire is that we would build strength of our own. The reason why He wants us to have strength is so that we can help others through similar kinds of times in their lives. In the midst of your problems it is probably difficult to rejoice but you should recognize that it is not made as a suggestion but we obviously have a choice. It is also difficult to look at our problems and trials and see them in light of how they will help others; that also is a choice. Jesus, teach to see the goal that you have for us in our problems and trials.

JULY 19

Read: 1 Chronicles 28:1 – 29:30, Romans 5:6-21, Psalm 15:1-5, Proverbs 19:18-19

1 CHRONICLES 29:14

But who am I, and who are my people, that we could give anything to you? Everything we have has come from you, and we give you only what you have already given us!

David has been preparing all the materials for the building of the temple of the LORD. David's desire is that this temple be magnificent and spectacular. Out of his own resources David provides over 100 tons of gold and even more silver and other precious items. He then encourages the other leaders of the nation of Israel to donate to the project as well. These leaders contribute almost two hundred tons of gold. Just the gold collected in this single offering would be valued at over two billion dollars in today's money.

David then breaks out in a song of praise over the willing generosity of the people. David rejoiced over the fact that the people had given so much without any reason except that they had a loyal heart. The people wanted to bless God and their king and so they gave great amounts for the construction project that was on David's heart.

God had blessed the nation of Israel with great abundance. And He was not through blessing them as we will see as we look at the reign of King Solomon. In David's song he recognized that God was the one that had blessed them. He reminds the nation of Israel and us that it is through God's provision that we have everything that we have. David marvels over the fact that the things that the people give to God are His in the first place.

It is an interesting truth in the Kingdom of God that there is nothing in this world that we can own. Everything that comes into our lives was given to us by God. Even the ability to go to work and earn money so that we can buy things comes from God. The best we can be is good stewards of the things of God. And the things of God include all the things that we think are ours.

In the church we can easily be distracted from this truth and think that as leaders we are giving everything to God. Are we really? Too often within the ministry, the ministry can become a self-propelled machine that seems to have a mind of its own. And this machine can become an extension of its leaders. The church and ministry ought to be an extension of only one person; Jesus Christ.

As leaders we need to be bringing our families, ministries, and churches and offering them to God to do with as He pleases. And we need to do this willingly and generously; remembering that our families, ministries, and churches were given by God. What David and the leaders gave was built by them into a marvelous temple used to be focal point of worship for the entire nation. What does God want to build through your offering?

JULY 20

Read: 2 Chronicles 1:1 – 3:17, Romans 6:1-23, Psalm 16:1-11, Proverbs 19:20-21

2 CHRONICLES 2:6

But who can really build him a worthy home? Not even the highest heavens can contain him! So who am I to consider building a Temple for him, except as a place to burn sacrifices to him?

Solomon is about to undertake his first major project since he has become the king replacing his father King David. This project is to build a temple for the LORD. His father had wanted to build this temple but God told him no because he was a man of war. God had told David that Solomon would be the one to build this temple and so David spent the rest of his life preparing the materials and plans for building the temple.

Today's verse is found in the middle of a letter that King Solomon has written to King Hiram of Tyre. It is as though right in the midst of writing this letter that Solomon gets a glimpse of God. And when Solomon sees Him, he is awed by the sight. At this moment, Solomon doesn't see the temple as a magnificent place that he will build for his God to live in but simply as a place where he can come to make sacrifices. Solomon sees the temple as a place that he will come to worship his God.

God is bigger than anything that we could ever build. We will never be able to build something that God could be contained in. This is so important for us to understand as we attempt to build things for God. And God does call us to build. He calls us to build our families, to build ministries, and to build churches. But we need to always remember that these things that He will invite us to build are not places for Him but places for us.

The temple was the focus of Hebrew worship for over a thousand years. It was there that the whole Hebrew race would come to seek the presence and atonement of their Mighty God. Even during the times that the temple was destroyed, the Jews would still pray toward the temple.

As God calls us to build, we need to have the same heart that Solomon did. He desired to build a magnificent structure for God but he understood that God could not be contained within it and that ultimately it was just a place that he would go to make sacrifices to his Awesome God.

We can build awesome ministries and magnificent churches but ultimately they only serve to provide us a place to make sacrifices to our God.

Solomon sacrificed animals to make atonement to God for the sins of the nation of Israel. Jesus forever took care of that for us. Today we sacrifice ourselves by serving others for God and by leading them to Jesus. Jesus, help us to be more concerned about building temples of the Holy Spirit than temples of wood and stone.

JULY 21

Read: 2 Chronicles 4:1 – 6:11, Romans 7:1-13, Psalm 17:1-15, Proverbs 19:22-23

2 CHRONICLES 5:11

Then the priests left the Holy Place. All the priests who were present had purified themselves, whether or not they were on duty that day.

Solomon has completed the construction of the temple. They have moved the Ark of the Covenant into the Most Holy Place and also brought all of the furnishings and the tent that the Ark was housed in into the temple. It seems from the text that there were a lot of priests present for this event. The priests had the responsibility and duties within the temple. Back in 1 Chronicles 24, David had divided the descendants of Aaron into 24 divisions. Each division had an assigned time to serve in the temple. Many priests were present that were not on duty.

What caught my attention here in this text is not that they were there, but that they had purified themselves. For the Hebrew priest this was a ritual act of cleansing that would make them presentable and acceptable to God. There were also certain things that they had to stay away from so that they would not become defiled which would prevent them from serving for a period of time.

Even though these priests were not going to be serving in the temple they had prepared themselves as though they were. What a great lesson for us to keep in mind. We also need to be prepared for what God might want to do through us. Too often people think about their relationship to God and their service to Him in relation to when they are going to church.

Our time of service is not limited to once or twice a week when the church meets to hold services. Our time of service to God is 24 hours a day and seven days a week. We need to be ready whenever He might call.

The priests got ready by going through a cleansing ritual and by staying away from things that would defile them. We stay ready the same way but using different methods. We are cleansed by the blood of Jesus as we go to the LORD and seek forgiveness of our sins. We also need to stay away from things that defile us. Things like sexual immorality, drugs, alcohol, and pornography just to name a few. By staying away from these things we keep ourselves ready to serve the LORD when He wants to use us.

It doesn't matter who you are or where you are, as a Christian you have a responsibility to serve God when He says that he wants you. That could be in a ministry, or a church, or a home Bible study, or in your family. Wherever it is, you must be prepared to serve; you must keep yourself ready. Your opportunity to serve might happen at the gas station, grocery store, at work, at home, and of course at church. We are not on a rotating schedule of service; we are on call all the time. Jesus, help us to prepare ourselves so that we can serve you when you want us.

JULY 22

Read: 2 Chronicles 6:12 – 8:10, Romans 7:14 – 8:8, Psalm 18:1-15, Proverbs 19:24-25

PSALM 18:6

But in my distress I cried out to the LORD; yes, I prayed to my God for help. He heard me from his sanctuary; my cry reached his ears.

David wrote this psalm as a result of his joy over being delivered from the many enemies that surrounded him. Just recently he has been delivered from his own son Absalom who attempted to steal the kingdom away from him and kill him. Psalm 18 is a beautiful picture of how David was feeling during the times of distress and his wonder at the way that God took care of him and protected him from his enemies.

There is something that is very special and comforting about our verse for the day. David was in distress in many times during his life; most especially while Saul was trying to kill him. This was a difficult time for David because Saul was after him because of jealousy; not because of anything that David had done wrong. Saul knew that the kingdom had been taken away from him and was going to be given to David by God. Rather than submitting to God and turning the kingdom over to David, Saul sought to destroy David.

During those lonely times in the wilderness you can probably imagine David's distress. Here he was doing what he believed that God would have him to do and he is being persecuted. He knows that God has called him to be the next king of Israel and yet he doesn't know if the next day brings death at the hands of Saul. That had to be a very difficult time for David. So in desperation David cried out to God for help. And in our verse today we are told that God heard his cries.

It is an amazing thing that our cries and prayers ascend into heaven and enter into God's sanctuary and touch His ears. It is a thing of wonder that our cries and prayers actually are heard by God. It is too great to truly comprehend that even if every person on earth at the same instant cried out to God that He would hear my prayer and yours as though they were the only ones. Our God is truly an awesome God!

David believed that God heard His prayers. That is how we should pray and live. We need to believe beyond the shadow of a doubt that our prayers are instantly in the ear of our Heavenly Father. What a comfort that is and what peace it should bring to our souls.

When God hears, He responds. God does answer our prayers; every last one of them. We may not always see the answers to our prayer or at least recognize that they were answered. And there are times when God does answer and we don't like the answer, but He always answers. And because of His great love for us, the answer is always the right one for us and for the circumstances we are in, even if we don't see that. God hears your prayers. Let that comfort your soul during the times of distress and trials. Then you will rejoice about what God has done in your life just as David did in this beautiful psalm. Jesus, teach us to pray with confidence and security.

JULY 23

Read: 2 Chronicles 8:11 – 10:19, Romans 8:9-25, Psalm 18:16-36, Proverbs 19:26

ROMANS 8:18

Yet what we suffer now is nothing compared to the glory he will give us later.

Paul is well acquainted with suffering. He experienced persecution at the hands of the Jews and Gentiles. He was jailed on several occasions. He was beaten many times. He was even stoned once and left for dead. He was also shipwrecked and adrift at sea. Paul also suffered from some sort of malady that most people believe had something to do with his eyes. There are few people that could say that they had suffered as much as Paul.

With all that Paul suffered he was able to make statements like the one that he made in our verse for the day. To truly grasp the significance of what Paul is saying here you need to study all that he experienced in his life after he met Christ on the road to Damascus. Few of us will ever experience anything even remotely as intense as what Paul experienced in his life serving Christ.

With that in mind Paul says that these sufferings are nothing when they are compared to the glory that Jesus will give us later. In the very next verse of today's reading we learn when later is; it is when God reveals who His children really are. We know from other places in scripture that will be when we all have our glorified bodies and "we know just as we are known." At that time Jesus is going to give us glory. It is impossible to say what that fully means, "the glory he will give us," but we do know from our verse today that it is going to pretty incredible.

If you could add up all the pain and suffering that you have gone through and will experience in your life it does not compare to the glory that you will receive. Imagine if all of your pain and suffering could be measured in drops of water. Some would be able to fill a water glass, while others might be able to fill a large bucket. There are some people that could fill a swimming pool with all the pain and suffering that they have experienced. But even the largest swimming pool is nothing compared to the Pacific Ocean. That is the picture that Paul is trying to paint for us.

We will experience pain and suffering in this world; it is promised in Scripture. We should be able to endure it because of the hope of the other promises of Scripture such as the verse for the day. We are promised a glory from Jesus that causes our pain and suffering to seem absolutely insignificant in comparison. This will not make pain and suffering any more enjoyable; but we should be able to endure because of the hope that it provides us. The next time you find yourself holding a cup full of pain and suffering just compare it to the ocean of glory that Jesus is preparing to give you. Jesus, help us to endure the tough days of our lives with the hope that you provide in your Word.

JULY 24
Read: 2 Chronicles 11:1 – 13:22, Romans 8:26-39, Psalm 18:37-50, Proverbs 19:27-29

2 CHRONICLES 12:8
But they will become his subjects, so they will know the difference between serving me and serving earthly rulers.

King Rehoboam of Judah was the son of Solomon and grandson of David. King David was described as a man after God's own heart. This means that he followed God in all his ways. It doesn't mean that he was perfect, but he lived a life that was centered imperfectly around the LORD. His grandson Rehoboam was not that way; he went his own way and turned away from the law of the LORD.

The LORD then sent King Shishak from Egypt to punish Rehoboam for his unfaithfulness. Upon seeing Shishak come and his huge army destroying everything in their path Rehoboam and the leaders of Israel humbled themselves and confessed their sins before the LORD. That was what the LORD was hoping would happen.

God gives us the choice; humble your heart before Him or He will send a destroyer that will force you to humble your heart. If we would just logically examine this choice we would quickly recognize the foolishness of many of our actions. God is a loving, generous Father who cares for us and protects and provides for us. The destroyer seeks only to destroy some part or all of our life. Which does it make more sense to humble your heart before? And yet all too often we resist God and refuse to humble our hearts before Him.

When I was in boot camp as a young man I quickly realized one of the objectives of the instructors was to break our will to teach us how to follow commands. This is necessary in a military unit; it can mean life and death, not just for the one following the commands but for their entire unit. I learned quickly that by humbling myself before these instructors that I would be more successful. I saw that some men resisted the leadership and instruction and paid a price in various forms of discipline or punishment.

God's purposes are the same in my life. He wants me to learn to follow His commands quickly and without question. I have come to recognize the direct connection between a humble heart and God's blessings. The more quickly I respond, the more successful I am in this Christian life. This is so important to God that if we do not do it, He will send someone or something into our lives to teach it to us. The problem with that is that other "instructor" doesn't love us or desire to see us prosper as God does. But if that is what it will take to teach us how to serve God with a humble heart, God is willing to let us endure it.

The choice is ours; serve God with a humble heart or endure the forced humbling of our heart by an unloving destroyer. If you are in the hands of the destroyer now, simply humble your heart before God and ask Him to help you to learn to serve Him. God may not deliver you until you have done that, because that may be exactly why you are in the hands of the destroyer. Jesus, teach us to serve with a humble heart.

JULY 25

Read: 2 Chronicles 14:1 – 16:14, Romans 9:1-24, Psalm 19:1-14, Proverbs 20:1

2 CHRONICLES 16:7

At that time Hanani the seer came to King Asa and told him, "Because you have put your trust in the king of Aram instead of in the LORD your God, you missed your chance to destroy the army of the king of Aram."

King Asa was one of the better kings of Judah. He spent most of his life doing what was pleasing to the LORD. Here we have an account of King Asa missing the mark in God's opinion. Because of King Solomon's sin, the nation of Israel is split in half and they are in constant conflict for hundreds of years. Wars rage on and off between Israel and Judah even though they are both the children of God and part of the nation of Israel. That is an interesting study all unto itself.

King Baasha of Israel has attacked again and taken Ramah. Asa's response is to bribe Ben-Hadad the king of Aram (Syria) to break his treaty with Baasha. Asa's plan works; at least in his eyes. Ben-Hadad attacks the territory of Baasha and so Baasha withdraws from Ramah. Then the seer Hanani comes and tells Asa that he has made a mistake.

The problem is that Aram is an enemy nation and God had told the nation of Israel not to make any treaties with them. It was God's desire to give the land of King Ben-Hadad to the nation of Israel. And to do that they would have to destroy the king and his army. God wanted Asa to come to Him with this problem and allow Him to solve it for Asa. This was an ongoing weakness of Asa. As this chapter ends we are told that Asa had a disease in his feet that he would not go to the LORD about and so he died.

Asa missed an opportunity to do a great work for God. He missed it because he trusted in something that he could see and understand rather than going in faith to God. Because of his lack of faith he missed an opportunity to win a great victory for God. How many of us have done the same thing? As we look at a situation, we determine how to deal with it without ever even consulting the LORD. We might even do something like Asa did and work out a deal with the enemy to help us.

Twice in this chapter it is mentioned that Asa did not trust fully in the LORD and it cost him something. Trusting in the LORD means that we go to Him with absolutely everything and ask for His wisdom and direction. And while you wait for a response from God you keep working on plans and strategies, but you must trust the LORD to direct your path because that is exactly what He wants to and will do.

As leaders in families, ministries, and churches we must trust God with all of our decisions. If we don't, then we risk missing an opportunity to something tremendous for God. God wants to use us, no matter how insignificant we might think we are, to do mighty miraculous things. Jesus, help us so that we don't miss an opportunity that You set before us to change someone's life or to change the world.

JULY 26

Read: 2 Chronicles 17:1 – 18:34, Romans 9:25 – 10:13, Psalm 20:1-9, Proverbs 20:2-3

PROVERBS 20:3

Avoiding a fight is a mark of honor; only fools insist on quarreling.

In the Sermon on the Mount Jesus said blessed are the peacemakers for they shall be called sons of God. It seems that in this life that fights and quarrels are inevitable. It seems like there is always someone at odds with someone else. And it is no different in the church than it is in the world. Are fights and quarrels inevitable? The answer is no!

Don't get me wrong, as long as there are fools in the world, the opportunity exists to have fights and quarrels. But we can make a choice not to participate in those fights and quarrels. A fight or a quarrel is a situation in which two or more people disagree on some topic or issue. This disagreement in itself is not a fight or a quarrel. It is how we respond to the disagreement that creates the fight or quarrel.

As long as we are in these imperfect sacks of flesh and bones we will disagree with others. But we can make a choice not to fight or quarrel about those disagreements. Fights and quarrels almost always result in foolish things being done and said. And fights and quarrels always have at their center pride and self-centeredness. And the remedy for the problem is humility and an other's focus.

It takes at least two people (or as the text says: "fools") to fight and quarrel. The honorable person will choose not to be one of those two people. The honorable person will choose to throw water on the fire rather than gasoline. The honorable person will care more about keeping peace than about winning the fight; even if that means sacrificing something of themselves. The foolish person only cares about winning; no matter how much it costs. No one ever "wins" a fight or a quarrel; everyone loses.

As leaders in our families, ministries, and churches it is absolutely required that we take the honorable road. If there is fighting going on in your home, ministry, or church you have got to be the one that chooses to stop it. You stop it by choosing not to participate and by helping others to see the foolishness of fighting and quarreling.

Our enemy will use fighting and quarreling to destroy or at least weaken otherwise strong families, ministries, and churches. Churches have fought over and split up because of the most foolish things. And all the while the devil is laughing in the background.

God calls us to be one flesh in our marriages and one body in our ministries and churches. Fights and quarrels are tools of the enemy to divide us and make us weaker. We must decide today to be men and women of honor that choose to fight our true enemy, Satan, and not each other. Jesus, teach us to love peace more than ourselves.

JULY 27

Read: 2 Chronicles 19:1 – 20:37, Romans 10:14 – 11:12, Psalm 21:1-13, Proverbs 20:4-6

2 CHRONICLES 20:33

During his reign, however, he failed to remove all the pagan shrines, and the people never fully committed themselves to following the God of their ancestors.

King Jehoshaphat was a pretty good king in Judah. For the most part he did what was pleasing to the LORD. He did make some mistakes that the Bible declares. That is one of the amazing things about Scripture; it doesn't hide the mistakes of the children of God. And for one, I am very happy about that. Because if all we ever saw in the Bible is people that were very pleasing to the LORD it would cause all the rest of us normal people to feel like we could never possibly measure up.

But the Bible reveals that many of God's people made mistakes and sometimes did things that displeased Him and resulted in punishment or loss of reward. That should give the rest of us hope in the knowledge that God uses imperfect people to get His work done on the earth. After all, that's all that He has to work with.

In our text for today we see this comment during the summary of Jehoshaphat's reign in Judah. He failed to do something that God wanted him to do and there was a consequence to Jehoshaphat's failure. God wanted His land cleansed of all the pagan places of worship. This is not a new request of God. When God led them into the Promised Land He told them to drive out all the nations that were living there and to utterly destroy their idols and places of worship.

God knew that if the people of Canaan, their places of worship, or their idols remained in the land that the children of Israel would be drawn to them. God knew that as long as those pagan shrines remained that it was just a matter of time before the Israelites turned away from God and to the idols.

Johoshaphat was the leader of the nation and he was in a place where he could have had a tremendous effect on the people towards God. It was his responsibility to lead the people toward God. Too often leaders define their role based on some task that they are trying to accomplish. As leaders, our first and most important priority is to lead people to Christ. And that is not completed once they come to Christ, but when they become like Christ.

Everything else that we do as leaders must be secondary to that. As leaders of families, ministries, or churches we must see our most important task as helping people to follow their God, Jesus Christ. The other things that we do are just tools and techniques for doing that. Helping them to follow Jesus means helping them tear down the pagan shrines that are in their lives. Jesus, help us to follow you so that we can lead others.

JULY 28

Read: 2 Chronicles 22:1 – 23:21, Romans 11:13-36, Psalm 22:1-18, Proverbs 20:7

ROMANS 11:33

Oh, what a wonderful God we have! How great are His riches and wisdom and knowledge! How impossible it is for us to understand his decisions and his methods!

The apostle Paul has been talking to the church in Rome about God's great mercy to them when he stops and bursts out in praise toward God. This is a good lesson for all of us to model. As we meditate on the things of God and the attributes of God (which we should do regularly) it should result in spontaneous praise. This is one of the ways that we know that our hearts are in a right place with God. If you don't find yourself thanking God and praising God periodically throughout the day, then God may not be where He belongs in your life. Start by deliberating picking one or two things every day to praise Him about. If you make a habit of this it will eventually become natural.

In addition to praising God for some of His attributes Paul praises God because He is beyond understanding. This is another of those things that does not come naturally to most people; I know it didn't for me. I am one of those types that believed that everything in the world could be understood. That is one of the reasons why it took me so long (40 years) to come to the LORD; I couldn't understand God. It wasn't until I grew to recognize that I didn't need to understand God to believe that He was real. I have since grown to rejoice in the fact that God is greater than I can understand. It is a fact that if God was small enough for me to understand He wouldn't be big enough to deal with the things in my life that I don't understand.

The other side of this understanding is that there are going to come times when God is going to make a decision for my life that I don't understand. It is one thing to know that God is big enough to handle all the troubles of your life; it is quite another to understand that He will make decisions that you don't understand that have an impact on the way that your life is lived. God is a wonderful God and He is rich in wisdom and knowledge. All the knowledge and wisdom of the world is poor in comparison to God. It makes good sense to let someone that has infinite knowledge and wisdom make decisions for my life.

The problem is that the natural part of me wants to make decisions and control my life. And so a battle rages within us that wrestle over the control of our lives. True victory in the Christian life comes as you allow God to make the decisions of your life and resist the temptation to fight against Him. God's methods are almost always different than the way that we would decide to do things. To gain the victory in this area of your life just start by rejoicing in that fact just as the apostle Paul did in our verse for the day. Recognize that is part of the nature and attributes of Almighty God and praise Him for those qualities. As you grow in your ability to praise God for His unique attributes you will learn to live within them more successfully. Our natural desires can only be overcome by replacing them with spiritual desires. Jesus, help us to fill our lives with You.

JULY 29

Read: 2 Chronicles 24:1 – 25:28, Romans 12:1-21, Psalm 22:19-31, Proverbs 20:8-10

2 CHRONICLES 25:9

Amaziah asked the man of God, "But what should I do about the silver I paid to hire the army of Israel?" The man of God replied, "The LORD is able to give you much more than this!"

King Amaziah of Judah was a king that was pleasing to the LORD for most of his life. He usually did what he was supposed to do. In our reading for today we saw that Amaziah built up a large army. Amaziah also used a large amount of silver to hire troops from the nation of Israel. An unnamed man of God comes to Amaziah and tells him that God is not pleased with him hiring the troops from Israel and that if they stay in his army that God will defeat Amaziah every time he goes into battle. The only solution is to send the troops from Israel back to their homes.

In our verse today Amaziah asks a practical question that many of us would probably ask, "What about the silver that I paid for those troops?" It had been a mistake on Amaziah's part to hire those troops and sadly it doesn't look like that bothers him as much as the fact that he is going to be out all of the silver that he paid. To his credit Amaziah did send the troops home.

The man of God told Amaziah not to worry about the silver because God is able to give him much more silver than he spent on those troops. As we go through this life we will make mistakes in our relationship with God. Nothing that we do is ever going to prevent that. How we respond is absolutely critical. Our mistakes should bother us because they are against God not because it costs us money, or time, or prestige, or position. When we are concerned about those things it shows that we don't fully trust God. If we did, we would be concerned about how our mistakes affect our relationship with God. We would know that God is fully able to give back to us anything we have lost or wasted; in fact He can give us a lot more.

This lack of faith is something that will also prevent us from dealing with our mistakes the way that we should. When we make a mistake, we should respond immediately. Too often we allow fear to prevent us from doing the right thing when a mistake is discovered in our lives. The fear is that we will lose something that we can't get back; that is a lack of faith. God is able to give us anything and everything and He is more interested in our immediate obedience than in what will be wasted. There is no waste in the life of a person that is obedient to God. This begins with humility; we must believe that God's interests in our life are more important than our own. Then we must believe and trust God for everything. There is no mistake in our lives that God can't redeem and bring good out of. Jesus, teach us to trust You and Your ability to bring good even out of our mistakes.

JULY 30

Read: 2 Chronicles 26:1 – 28:27, Romans 13:1-14, Psalm 23:1-6, Proverbs 20:11

2 CHRONICLES 28:19

The LORD was humbling Judah because of King Ahaz of Judah, for he had encouraged his people to sin and had been utterly unfaithful to the LORD.

Judah is experiencing oppression and persecution because God has withdrawn His hand of blessing and protection because of the sins and unfaithfulness of King Ahaz. The sins of King Ahaz are also leading the people to commit those same sins. So God is allowing enemies to come against Judah and to defeat them.

King Ahaz had every opportunity to do the right thing. And we have already seen in many other accounts that when the king does what God wants them to, when they follow the LORD, that He protects and prospers them. Each time they fail to follow the LORD, He withdraws His hand of blessing and protection. It sometimes amazes me how the kings of Israel and Judah could have been so blind to this truth. But then I just need to look into my own life to see how easy it is to fall into sin and to stop wholly following the LORD.

Few of us will ever be in a place of King Ahaz's power and authority. We cannot possibly understand the things that were influencing him and distracting him from wholly following the LORD. It is not possible for us to feel the temptations that he was faced with. Because we can't relate to what he experienced we shouldn't judge him; we may have done exactly the same thing if we had been in his place.

What we can do is look at his life and see his mistakes and attempt to inoculate ourselves from the same disease that he suffered. This was a disease of the eyes; King Ahaz didn't keep his eyes on the LORD. God attempted to get Ahaz's attention by allowing an enemy to come against him. Instead of looking to God, Ahaz turned to the gods of the nation that came against him. We can be tempted to do exactly the same thing. The world throws some attack our way and instead of turning to God we turn to the world to try to save ourselves and protect ourselves. There is nothing in the world that can protect or save you. In fact the world is designed to entrap you and destroy you.

This is especially true of those that have been called to lead within their families, and within ministries and churches. You can't take you eyes off the LORD for a second. If you do, you will find yourself stumbling down the same path that King Ahaz did. Attacks from the enemy will come because God will allow them. God wants you to keep your eyes on Him, not upon the enemy, even in the midst of the attack. Do that and you will always sense God's hand of blessing and protection, even in the darkest times. Jesus, help us to focus on the source of our blessings and protection; You.

JULY 31

Read: 2 Chronicles 29:1-36, Romans 14:1-23, Psalm 24:1-10, Proverbs 20:12

2 CHRONICLES 29:3

In the very first month of the first year of his reign, Hezekiah reopened the doors of the Temple of the LORD and repaired them.

Hezekiah takes over the kingdom after his father Ahaz dies. The very first thing that he does is open the doors of the temple which had been closed for some time. This is just the first of many things that Hezekiah did as he was king to bring the people of Israel back into a right relationship with God.

The temple was the focal point of all Jewish worship. When the nation of Israel wanted to worship God it was supposed to be at the temple in Jerusalem. Because it had been closed, the people were not able to worship God as they had been instructed and raised. Instead they started turning to the pagan idols of the nations that surrounded them.

This verse spoke to me about the importance of the role of leader in the worship of God. God places leaders over us to lead and guide us so that we don't wander from the path that he has set before us. God sets them up and then tells us to follow them. Their role is to lead us to God and His plans for our lives. What we have that the Israelites lacked was the Holy Spirit living within us. He now leads us as we become attuned to His voice. There are still leaders in our lives and we are still to follow them but now we don't need to depend upon them as we follow God.

Some people have not attuned their ears to the voice of the Holy Spirit and there are those that sometimes "tune out." At those times the leader is the one that should be leading us back to the "temple" to worship God. The leader has the responsibility of opening the doors to the temple. Once the doors are open it is up to each person whether or not they go into the temple and worship God.

As leaders, everything that we do should be drawing people closer to God. We must be very careful not to close the doors to God through our bad or sinful behaviors. God will hold us to account for the times that we have allowed that to happen. Everything that we do should open the doors and clear the way for people to enter into an intimate relationship with Jesus.

As followers, we should be doing everything we can to learn to hear from the Holy Spirit as He leads us to that relationship. To help us learn to do that God has given us godly leaders to follow. We need to faithfully pray for them as they work to open the doors to worship, not just for you but for everyone they are called to shepherd. And if God has called you to follow Jesus by following their example; then do it. That means when they open the door for you that you go through it into the place that has been prepared for you. Jesus, teach us to listen and obey.

AUGUST

AUGUST 1

Read: 2 Chronicles 30:1 – 31:21, Romans 15:1-22, Psalm 25:1-15, Proverbs 20:13-15

ROMANS 15:7

So accept each other just as Christ has accepted you; then God will be glorified.

In the last few chapters of Romans Paul has been writing about not allowing our freedom in Christ to be a stumbling block to other Christians. Just because we have the liberty to eat or drink or do certain things doesn't mean that we should if it means that a fellow Christian is going to struggle in their walk with the LORD. Ultimately it comes down to our unselfish desire to please God and to love others and not ourselves. Paul wraps up this thought with today's verse. In it he tells us to accept each other. Because people had different viewpoints as to what was allowed and what wasn't in the Christian faith, people were dividing and not fellowshipping with each other. Paul wants us to know that we shouldn't be doing that.

There are things that the Bible says very clearly should be reasons for dividing. An example of that is when people say they believe in God but do not believe the gospel of Jesus Christ. We cannot have unity and true fellowship with someone that doesn't believe that Jesus Christ is God. We are also told to break fellowship with Christians that choose sin in direct disobedience to God until they repent.

Just because someone doesn't interpret certain aspects of scripture the same way that we do is not a cause for division. An example of this is the doctrine of the Rapture. There are several different viewpoints as to when the Rapture is going to take place in relation to the Tribulation period. These viewpoints do not affect salvation and so they can peacefully coexist. Paul's point is that things like our viewpoint on the Rapture should be accepted as different and they should not be a cause of division.

Paul goes on to say that it is the Holy Spirit that will tell us if we are wrong or not. Often division comes as we try to play the role of the Holy Spirit and try to convince someone that their viewpoint on a non-salvation issue is wrong. In those issues that are not critical to salvation, we need to accept one another. Let people worship God the way they feel is the proper way and show them that you have the love of God by loving them; in spite of their differences.

Paul tells us that if we will do that, we will be glorifying God. It brings glory to God when two people that have nothing in common, except faith in Jesus Christ, accept one another in spite their differences. More harm is done in families, ministries, and churches because we fail to obey this instruction. For some bizarre reason we believe that we have a monopoly on truth and wisdom. That is the pinnacle of arrogance and pride. And we are all probably going to be embarrassed in heaven when we find that we were probably wrong too. Jesus, help us to see You in others and not differences.

AUGUST 2

Read: 2 Chronicles 32:1 – 33:13, Romans 15:23 – 16:9, Psalm 25:16-22, Proverbs 20:16-18

2 CHRONICLES 32:25

But Hezekiah did not respond appropriately to the kindness shown him, and he became proud. So the LORD'S anger came against him and against Judah and Jerusalem.

Hezekiah, the king of Israel, had become deathly ill. Isaiah the prophet comes and with great bedside manner tells Isaiah that he needs to get his stuff in order because he is about to die. Hezekiah wasn't happy about that prognosis and so he went to God in prayer and asked God to heal Him. God responds to Hezekiah and heals him and adds another fifteen years onto his life. To prove to Hezekiah that God is going to keep His promise God causes the shadow on the sundial to move backward "ten steps."

Then something terrible happened; God begins to prosper Hezekiah greatly. We might think that is a good thing but in fact it turns out be Hezekiah's downfall. God blessed King Hezekiah with great abundance and then Hezekiah allowed that abundance to influence him. Hezekiah became filled with pride. This is seen in the way that Hezekiah showed the envoys from Babylon all his stuff. Even after Isaiah came and tried to correct him, Hezekiah's response is selfish and prideful.

In our text we are told that Hezekiah did not respond appropriately. God had shown Hezekiah great kindness by sparing his life and by blessing him greatly. We must be very careful also about the blessings of God.

Everything that the Lord gives us whether good or bad (in our eyes) should cause us to respond to God in worship and adoration.

Often that is easier when the things that God is allowing to happen in our lives are bad. It is easy for us to depend upon Him and seek His face and wisdom. But when things start going good, we will sometimes forget that it is God that has provided these good things and claim some of His glory as our own. That is a very dangerous place to be.

Some people will be blessed tremendously in their families, ministries, or churches. They may need your prayers and encouragement more than those that are experiencing trials and difficulties. With success and achievement come pride and temptation. If God is blessing your life, family, ministry, or church your response should be to praise God for those blessings. With your next breath you should be crying out to God for His protection from your own sinful nature and asking for His help to keep your heart humble.

God wants to bless us, our families, and our ministries and churches. He will do that only as long as we respond appropriately to His blessings. With appropriate responses God's blessings and protection continue. Jesus, help us to never lose sight of the fact that absolutely everything that we have came from you and teach us to respond appropriately.

AUGUST 3

Read: 2 Chronicles 33:14 – 34:33, Romans 16:10-27, Psalm 26:1-12, Proverbs 20:19

2 CHRONICLES 34:33

So Josiah removed all detestable idols from the entire land of Israel and required everyone to worship the Lord their God. And throughout the rest of his lifetime, they did not turn away from the Lord, the God of their ancestors.

Josiah was one of the good kings of Israel. From early in his reign he sought to follow the LORD. In the eighteenth year of his reign, one of the priests found the Book of the Law in the Temple. This in itself is a sad testimony to how far Israel had drifted from the LORD. It took over a decade to uncover God's instructions to the people of Israel. Once Josiah heard the words that the scroll contained he realized that God was going to judge Israel for her sins of rebellion and idolatry. His response was to humble his heart before God and repent for the whole nation.

Josiah had been trying to seek the LORD for the last decade, but he had been doing it without God's written word. Once he heard God's word Josiah realized that his best efforts still left the whole nation under the impending judgment of God. Man's best efforts or best intentions will never substitute for obeying His word. Doing what we think God wants will never replace what God's says that He wants.

Even though Josiah was seeking the LORD, there were still things in his kingdom that were offensive to God. Without God's word Josiah did not know that the idols that were everywhere in the land was one of the key things that God was about to judge the nation for. He didn't see anything wrong with them until God's word was presented to him.

This is why it is so important for leaders of God's people to be in the Word of God often. They should have an intimate knowledge of what God says and wants from His people. When they counsel others it should be from God's Word and not from man's opinions. It is only as the Word of God comes to life within them that they will see the idols that litter their lives and set them up as targets of God's judgment.

It is also important for God's leaders to be in God's Word so that they can see the idols in their own lives. Josiah didn't see the idols in his kingdom as idols until God's Word revealed them as idols. Up to that point, they were just places where people worshipped whatever god they believed in. He didn't see that as sin until God's Word helped him to see it as sin. Just because we are seeking the LORD, doesn't mean that we can see every area of sin in our lives. As leaders seeking to serve God and please Him, we need to invite the Holy Spirit to use the Word of God to illuminate all the dark areas of our lives, especially all the areas that are hidden even to us.

Only God's Word has the power to change our lives to the level of perfection that God desires for us. Our best efforts are not good enough. Our best intentions will always fall short. Only the Holy Spirit quickened Word of God is able to bring about that kind of change. Jesus, help us to make Your Word a greater part of our lives.

AUGUST 4

2 CHRONICLES 36:14

All the leaders of the priests and the people became more and more unfaithful. They followed the pagan practices of the surrounding nations, desecrating the Temple of the LORD in Jerusalem.

Nebuchadnezzar, king of Babylon, has conquered Jerusalem and taken much of the treasures and people back with him to Babylonia. He appointed Zedekiah to be king over Israel. Zedekiah was part of the royal family and a descendant of King David. Nebuchadnezzar left Zedekiah to rule over Israel so that he could get tribute from Israel. There was a benefit in this for the Israelites. They did not have an oppressing government ruling over them. One of their own people was placed to lead them. God did this so that the national identity of Israel would not fade away.

Zedekiah had the opportunity to be a good or an evil king. He chose to do what was evil in the Lord's sight as did many of his ancestors. The really tragic part of all this is that it didn't have to happen. God had warned them through the prophets for a couple hundred years that this was going to happen. Both of the prophets Jeremiah and Ezekiel spoke very clearly to the people that this was going to happen soon and why it was happening. God told them that He was going to kick them out of the land because they were worshipping idols instead of Him.

Even with all the warnings and then the prophecies being fulfilled in their very presence the people did not respond. Many of these prophecies and warnings were spoken directly to the king and the leaders of the people and priests. But even with this mountain of evidence our verse for the day says that they became more and more unfaithful.

It is no wonder that the people were doing the wrong things. They were doing what they saw and heard. While this is no excuse, they should have also known to do the right thing but where the leaders go, so go the people. A leader's role is to go somewhere or do something and have other people follow. A leader can have tremendous influence upon those that are following him.

God doesn't call us to be perfect; He calls us to follow Him as well as we are able. Then He calls us to lead others to follow us as well as they can. It is an enormous responsibility to assume the role of leader. Often we don't choose the role of leader; God does. Zedekiah was appointed by Nebuchadnezzar to be king. It was Zedekiah's choice of what kind of king he was. We also may not get to vote on whether we are to be leaders or not, but we do get to choose what kind of leader that we will be. Choose to follow Christ with your whole heart, soul, mind, and strength. That's all God needs to make you into a leader. Jesus, help us to choose you.

AUGUST 5

Read: Ezra 1:1 – 2:70, 1 Corinthians 1:18 – 2:5, Psalm 27:7-14, Proverbs 20:22-23

EZRA 1:2

This is what King Cyrus of Persia says: "The Lord, the God of heaven, has given me all the kingdoms of the earth. He has appointed me to build him a Temple at Jerusalem, which is in Judah."

As I reflected upon this verse there were so many different things that I could have touched on. This proclamation by King Cyrus of Persia was the fulfillment of a prophecy given by Jeremiah. The prophecy was so specific that it mentioned Cyrus by name before he was born. The previous verse mentions that God stirred Cyrus' heart. We sometimes overlook the fact that God can touch the hearts of those that are not believers. What struck me about this verse is what God stirred Cyrus' heart to do; to build God a temple.

The first temple was built by Solomon. Cyrus is here ordering the construction of the second temple. This temple was later renovated and the temple mount was built around it by Herod the Great. This second temple is the one that Jesus visited some 500 later. The second temple was destroyed by the Romans in 70 AD. A third temple is predicted in Scripture to be built in the end days in a terrible period of time known as the Tribulation.

As a pastor of a small church that currently meets in an elementary school, this verse encourages me. From a human standpoint it is impossible for us to buy a piece of land and build a church. There simply is not enough money. The Jews coming out of the exile were in exactly the same position. There were not very many of them and they did not have a lot of resources to work with. They had to rebuild their whole country. Without God's intervention, the temple might never have been built.

It is going to take God's direct intervention in the hearts of people with resources for our church to find itself in a building that it can call its own. As most people would do I would pray and ask God to send someone, a Christian, to the church that would catch the vision of what we are doing and want to help see it come to life. I was praying too small. God has the sovereign ability to control anything and anyone. My prayer is now that God would send whoever He is preparing to do this work.

God can operate through unbelievers just as easily as He can through believers. We need to trust Him to accomplish His work using His methods and not our own. What great thing has God called you to do? Maybe God is preparing a Cyrus to help it to happen. We need to keep our eyes open and be prepared to work even when the work seems impossible. It is impossible to you but it is not impossible to God. Jesus, help us to learn that Your power is greater than our ability to dream.

AUGUST 6
Read: Ezra 3:1 – 4:23, 1 Corinthians 2:6 – 3:4, Psalm 28:1-9, Proverbs 20:24-25

EZRA 3:3
Even though the people were afraid of the local residents, they rebuilt the altar at its old site. Then they immediately began to sacrifice burnt offerings on the altar to the LORD. They did this each morning and evening.

About fifty thousand Israelites return to Judah from their exile in Babylon. Once back they begin to rebuild the towns and cities where they had lived. They also begin to rebuild the temple. Part of rebuilding the temple was rebuilding the altar so that they could reinstate the sacrificial system that God had instructed Moses to teach the people. It has been a long time since they had been able to perform these sacrifices.

After the Israelites had been exiled, the Babylonians had moved other people into the land to farm it and to live in it. These foreigners had settled into the land and made homes and livings there. In many respects they would now look upon the Israelites as foreigners.

Our verse for the day gives us an idea that there was a tension that existed between the two groups. The Israelites were afraid of the people that were living in the land. This could be for many different reasons but it was real enough to get into scripture. One of the likely things that would have created a tension between the two groups was their religions. What people worship and the way that they worship can be a very divisive force.

The returning Israelites wanted to return to the manner of worship that Moses had taught them; they had to build a large altar and started the sacrifices again. The Israelites were obeying God by doing this. This verse is a testimony of their faith; even though they were afraid, they rebuilt the altar and began making sacrifices upon it. What an important lesson for all of us to learn. God expects us to be obedient regardless of the external circumstances. God had exiled the Israelites because they had turned away from Him. They were determined to start over again, the right way.

We are also surrounded by people that desire to worship their gods in ways that are contrary to what God would have us to do. That will create a tension between you and them. It may also create a fear in you because of what they might be able to do to you. This is not referring just to other religious groups but also to people that worship themselves or some other idol like money or position. They are in our neighborhoods, at work, where we play, even at church. We need to have the faith to believe that if God wants us to do something that He is also strong enough to help us to accomplish it. Too often we let fear stop us from worshipping God the way that He desires. When we do that we are robbing God of His glory and ourselves of His blessings. Fear should never stop us from acting, it should teach us to depend upon God as we act. Jesus, help us to do what You want even when we are afraid.

AUGUST 7

Read: Ezra 4:24 – 6:22, 1 Corinthians 3:5-23, Psalm 29:1-11, Proverbs 20:26-27

The Passover meal was eaten by the people of Israel who had returned from exile and by the others in the land who had turned from their immoral customs to worship the LORD, the God of Israel.

Many of the Hebrews have returned from exile to Jerusalem. One of the first things that they did upon returning was to rebuild the temple. They initially encountered opposition but because God was in the project the opposition was turned to support. Once completed, the temple was dedicated and the people prepared to celebrate their first Passover in a long time.

What caught my attention about this verse is who ate this Passover meal. Not only did the Jews eat the Passover but also people from the land. These would have been the nations that had remained in the land when the children of Israel conquered the land as well as people that the Babylonians would have brought in during their conquests. These were non-Jews eating the Passover meal.

God's plan for the Jews had always been to make them a separated people so that the rest of the world could see God and be drawn to Him. God's plan has always been to redeem the world through the Jews and we see a beautiful picture here of that happening after the exile. The Passover meal was a celebration of the salvation of God. God's plan of salvation includes everyone that will believe. No one is to be excluded from that plan. Regardless of their background or experiences or sins, everyone has a place at God's table of salvation. We as a people too often stereotype people as being worthy or not of God's salvation. Or we will determine in our minds that someone is beyond saving. There is no one that is beyond the reach of God. There is no one that is not invited to the table of salvation.

However, we should be selective about who we allow to share this meal with us. The Hebrews allowed only those that had turned from their immoral ways to follow God. Those that we allow to get close to us must be described the same way. Only those that have turned away from their immoral ways and idolatry should be invited to be in close fellowship with us. That is the only condition that we should put on our relationships with others; nothing else should matter.

It shouldn't matter how much they can do for you or how much they can give to your ministry or church. The only thing that should matter is whether or not they have turned from their sin to follow God. And it doesn't even matter how well they are doing that; just that they are. Jesus, help us to offer a seat at your table to any that would follow You.

AUGUST 8
Read: Ezra 7:1 – 8:20, 1 Corinthians 4:1-21, Psalm 30:1-12, Proverbs 20:28-30

1 CORINTHIANS 4:1
So look at Apollos and me as mere servants of Christ who have been put in charge of explaining God's secrets.

The letter from the Apostle Paul to the church in Corinth was written to deal with some questions they had and more importantly to deal with some wrong thinking that had crept into the church. Paul is dealing with one of those wrong ideas here in our verse for the day. The Corinthians had begun quibbling over who was the spiritual leader of the church. They were dividing over who was the disciple of whom. Some were saying that they were the disciple of Apollos. Others were saying they were of Paul. Others were saying that they follow only Christ.

Paul makes it very clear to the Corinthians that they were not to be put on this high plain with Christ. They were in fact servants and should be treated as such. As servants Christ had assigned them a responsibility to share the secrets of God with those that do not know them. This task does not make them greater than anyone else. It only means that they have a task that is different from the other servants in the household of God.

People are no different today. Given an opportunity they will find someone to elevate to a position higher than themselves that they might look up to them. Today it would be Billy Graham or Chuck Smith or Greg Laurie or Rick Lancaster (heaven forbid). There is only one person that we should ever look up to and that is Jesus Christ. God calls us to look at others the same way that He looks at us; as equals to each other. We shouldn't look up to others because that places them in a position superior to ours and us in an inferior place. We also shouldn't look down on others for the same reason.

Paul boldly said elsewhere that people should follow him as he follows Christ. He meant that we should follow his example of following Christ. To follow someone you don't look up or down; you look out or upon. It's all about your perspective. We need to look upon other servants so that we can see them accomplishing their tasks for the Lord. Whatever their tasks are does not change their spiritual position in the body of Christ.

In the instructions to the priests of the Old Testament, they were told to wear special undergarments as they served at the altar. You see the altar was at the top of a set of stairs. The instruction for undergarments was to prevent people from seeing their nakedness while performing their duties. If we elevate someone or allow someone to elevate us, we run the risk of them looking at our nakedness; our faults. These faults may be no different than theirs but because of our perspective they look worse. When we and those that are called to follow us look up, all they should see is Jesus. Jesus, teach us to look up only to You, to look out for our fellow servants, and to look down upon sin.

AUGUST 9

Read: Ezra 8:21 – 9:15, 1 Corinthians 5:1-13, Psalm 31:1-8, Proverbs 21:1-2

PROVERBS 21:2

People may think they are doing what is right, but the LORD examines the heart.

Today's verse is one of those ones that may cause you to scratch your head and wonder what it means. It doesn't seem to make sense. It seems to say that just because it seems right to me doesn't mean that it is. In fact, you almost get a sense from the verse that there might be something wrong with your heart even though you think something is right. That is precisely what this verse is telling us.

The longest and most difficult distance to travel is the eighteen inches between a person's head and their heart. It is amazing how we can think something and feel something else and they are in absolute opposition with each other. In our minds we can convince ourselves that something is true and right and yet our hearts tell us that something is wrong. And for some reason we will tolerate that disconnection in almost every aspect of our lives.

The question is what do we do about it? Our verse gives us the answer. First, you should note that it is the heart that the Lord examines. It is the heart that drives everything else in our lives. Our minds interact with the physical world, but it is our hearts that interact with God. What we tend to focus on is the way that we think and there is some validity to doing that; but not at the expense of allowing God to work on our heart.

This demands humility and vulnerability before God. It takes humility to acknowledge that God knows something about you that you do not know about yourself. It takes humility to acknowledge that God has a right to look into your heart and disapprove of what He finds there. It takes humility to allow God to tell you that you are thinking wrong because your heart is wrong. You must make yourself vulnerable before God by offering him your heart for examination and correction.

This verse challenges us to question the motives of our hearts. I recently experienced this challenge as I was sharing with someone how much that I love to preach. I was sharing that one of the reasons that I do it is because I love to feel the power of God working through me. They challenged me to search the motives of my heart; was I teaching for me or for the people or for the Lord? Of course the right motive is that I must be doing it for the Lord and then for His people. What I get out of it is irrelevant.

Even in the things that it seems that God is blessing should be open for Him to examine and make adjustments if necessary. The moment that we begin to close off our heart to that kind of review and adjusting is the beginning of walking away from intimate fellowship with God. Allow God to search every last part of your heart, and don't hesitate to go to the Lord and ask Him to search your heart and reveal anything that needs to be changed. If you do that you will see radical transformation in your walk with the Lord. Jesus, shine your light into our hearts that we might see.

AUGUST 10

Read: Ezra 10:1-44, 1 Corinthians 6:1-20, Psalm 31:9-18, Proverbs 21:3

EZRA 10:4

Take courage, for it is your duty to tell us how to proceed in setting things straight, and we will cooperate fully.

Ezra was a prophet that had come with a remnant of the Jewish people back from the exile. God had sent conquering nations to drive the people from their land because they had been unfaithful to Him. As was the custom of many of these conquering nations, they brought people from other nations they had conquered to maintain the land so that it wouldn't go wild.

When the remnant of Jews returned from captivity, the land was once again occupied by people from pagan nations. It wasn't long after they returned that the Jewish men, including many of the leaders of the nation and priests were marrying pagan women. God had chosen the Jewish people to be a separated people. He commanded them not to marry pagan women. The reason was simple; they would lead the nation of Israel into the sin of idolatry. Israel's own history proved God to be right in this. When Ezra found out that this was going on he was greatly upset. He tore his clothes and went before God in an attitude of confession and mourning. He knew that the people were sinning and that God would end up judging them again for their sin. Ezra's heart was broken and everyone around him could see that. Shecaniah seems to speak for all the people to confess that they had indeed acted shamefully in marrying pagan women.

In today's verse, Shecaniah tells Ezra three things. First, he tells Ezra to "take courage." Ezra was discouraged. They had just been delivered from captivity and had a chance at a fresh start with God. Now here the people were committing a sin against the simple word of God. The people knew they weren't supposed to marry these women but they did it anyway. Shecaniah tells Ezra to "get up," he has work to do.

The second thing that Shecaniah tells Ezra is that it is Ezra's duty to tell them how to do things that correct the mistakes of the people. One of the reasons that Ezra is in such deep mourning over this is not just because the people are now subject to God's punishment but because they are not in the place that God can bless them. God had been blessing them since they had returned and Ezra wept because he knew that would not continue while they were in rebellion and sin. One of the roles of the leader of families, churches, or any organization is to tell people how to move from rebellion against God, disobedience to His Word, and His curses to a place of surrender, obedience, and blessing. That is our duty; if we don't tell them then we are in disobedience.

The third thing that Shecaniah told Ezra was that the people would all listen and do what he told them to do. It would be great if that was the way it always worked, but the reality of things is that it doesn't. Sometimes people don't want to know what God wants and have no intention of turning away from their sin and rebellion. That is not your problem. Tell them the truth and tell them what they need to do to get right with God. The rest is up to the Holy Spirit. Trust Him to deal with them. Jesus, help us to tell them what they need to hear.

AUGUST 11

Read: Nehemiah 1:1 – 3:14, 1 Corinthians 7:1-24, Psalm 31:19-24, Proverbs 21:4

NEHEMIAH 3:1

Then Eliashib the high priest and the other priests started to rebuild at the Sheep Gate. They dedicated it and set up its doors, building the wall as far as the Tower of the Hundred, which they dedicated, and the Tower of Hananel.

The wall around Jerusalem was destroyed when Nebuchadnezzar conquered Judah and exiled its people. The fact that the wall is down is a reproach to the Jewish people and Nehemiah sets about to do something about it. In our verse for the day we see that the high priest is one of the first ones mentioned as taking part in the reconstruction. Whether or not he was physically involved is impossible to tell but the text suggests that he was. The high priest was one of the highest positions in the nation of Israel.

The fact that the high priest and the other priests were the first ones mentioned speaks of a spiritual principle that we all should be sensitive to. As spiritual leaders we ought to be the first ones on the wall to do the work that needs to get done. We need to set the example of what is expected. We should never fall into the trap of believing that we are someone important and therefore above certain activities. The moment that we do, we have disqualified ourselves from our "greater" positions.

God can only use us while we realize that we are where we are because God placed us there. He placed us there to do a certain type of task but that does not elevate us above other necessary tasks. To accomplish the task of rebuilding the wall it was going to take everyone's efforts. It encourages me that the high priest was right there in the midst of the work.

Often as I go about working around during the time that we set up the church on Sunday morning someone will see me doing something and will come over to take it from me and do it. I am one of those types that can't sit still while others are working. When they do that I go and find something else to do. My goal is to set the example that the work that needs to get done can be done by anyone and that no one is above any kind of work.

This applies to all aspects of our lives, not just at church. At home, in our neighborhoods, at work, and at play we can set the example of a people that don't think too highly of ourselves and do what we can to help other people wherever we can. Even little things like picking up trash in the parking lot at the grocery store can make a tremendous difference. There are so many little things that we could do to make life a little easier for someone else that cost us virtually nothing; except our pride.

We need to humble ourselves and actually want to find things to do that show the world that Christians care about someone or something other than themselves. We can say it and we can preach it but until we practice it, it means nothing. Jesus, help us to help.

AUGUST 12

Read: Nehemiah 3:15 – 5:13, 1 Corinthians 7:25-40, Psalm 32:1-11, Proverbs 21:5-7

NEHEMIAH 5:9

Then I pressed further, "What you are doing is not right! Should you not walk in the fear of our God in order to avoid being mocked by enemy nations?"

Nehemiah has done a great job of getting the returned exiles organized and the wall around the city of Jerusalem is being rebuilt.

Then Nehemiah finds out that the wealthy Jews are taking advantage of their poorer relatives. They are charging interest on loans and even taking their children as slaves to pay for food. Both of these things are against the law of God and Nehemiah is very upset about it. Nehemiah rebukes the nobles and officials and then tells them to return everything that they took.

In our verse he tells them why they should do this. Nehemiah asks them a rhetorical question. This means that the answer is obvious in the manner that the question was asked. He asks them, "Should you not walk in fear of our God...?" The obvious answer is, "Yes!" To walk in fear of God, means that we humbly obey all of God's commands. We do this because we recognize His ultimate authority and power in the universe and our lives.

Nehemiah goes on to explain why they should walk in fear of God; to avoid being mocked by enemy nations. The Jews are surrounded by the nations that the Babylonians moved into Israel after they exiled the Jews. These conquering nations would often bring other conquered nations in to maintain the land to provide food and other resources to the capitals of the conquering nations. These nations were watching what was going with the rebuilding of the wall and seeing what the nobles and officials were doing to their own people. Their poor behavior was causing these enemy nations to mock Israel and God and this upset Nehemiah.

We should take a lesson from this account as well. The way that we treat other Christians is being watched by the enemies of God. We must be so careful not to give them reason to mock God. The New Testament has over fifty "one another" verses. These are Scriptures that specifically deal with how Christians relate to one another. If we disregard these instructions and do things the way we think we should or the way the world would, we are giving the enemies of God the opportunity to make fun of God.

Obeying God will cost us something that we think is fair or right for us to have. The nobles and officials felt that is was fair to collect interest on the money that they loaned to their relatives. God said it wasn't. Trusting God means that we believe that God will give us what He thinks is fair. God promised to bless the Jews if they obeyed Him completely. That promise applies to us as well. Jesus, help us to walk in the "fear of God."

AUGUST 13

Read: Nehemiah 5:14 – 7:73a, 1 Corinthians 8:1-13, Psalm 33:1-11, Proverbs 21:8-10

1 CORINTHIANS 8:1

Now let's talk about food that has been sacrificed to idols. You think that everyone should agree with your perfect knowledge. While knowledge may make us feel important, it is love that really builds up the church.

In his epistle to the church in Corinth the apostle Paul deals with a number of issues that they are struggling with. Here in chapter eight it is the matter of food that has been offered to an idol. The city of Corinth was, like many cities of this age, steeped in idol worship. Pagan temples were everywhere and for various and assorted gods. Regularly animals were brought to these temples and sacrificed on the altars. These animals were then often eaten by the people that sacrificed them. Sometimes they would take the animal after the sacrifice to a butcher and its meat was sold in the market.

The issue that the Corinthians were dealing with was whether or not they were sinning against God by eating meat that was sacrificed to idols. Paul deals with this matter beautifully in chapter eight of the reading for today. But, in today's verse is something that all Christians, especially mature Christians should take note of. As we mature in Christ our knowledge increases. That is how you mature in Christ by coming to know Christ and His word better and better.

A problem arises as we grow in knowledge; we begin to recognize that there are people that do not have the same knowledge that we do. The Bible even warns us against being puffed up by knowledge. The temptation here is that our "superior" knowledge causes us to start thinking more highly of ourselves than we ought to; pride begins to grow in our hearts.

Paul corrects that thinking by telling us in our verse for the day that it is love that really builds up the church not knowledge. An ignorant church that loves God and each other is much better and stronger than a church that knows "everything" but has no love. Christ would look at a church without love as a dead church. This makes sense because God is love and if there is no love in a church then God is not in that church.

There are lots of things in our lives that might raise questions and issues like those raised in the church of Corinth. What we do with those things is what really matters in life. We should never allow those things to create division within the church unless there is blatant sin that is leading others astray. Our goal should be to foster love and unity. Issues like whether or not Christians should watch "R" rated movies or whether or not Christians should drink beer or wine will probably be discussed and argued until the Lord returns to tell us absolutely what He thinks. Until then we need to let people wrestle with those questions and issues with the Lord. We need to love rather than trying to make everyone agree with our "perfect knowledge;" only God has perfect knowledge. Jesus, teach us to know You and Your love above all else.

AUGUST 14

Read: Nehemiah 7:73b-9:21, 1 Corinthians 9:1-18, Psalm 33:12-22, Proverbs 21:11-12

NEHEMIAH 8:8

They read from the Book of the Law of God and clearly explained the meaning of what was being read, helping the people understand each passage.

Nehemiah gathers all the people together and then the leaders have Ezra, the priest, bring out the Book of the Law of Moses. Ezra stands before the people and reads it to them. Other priests and Levites were scattered throughout this large crowd to explain to the people what was being read. For about six hours straight Ezra reads from the Book of the Law of Moses and explains to the people what it means to their lives. This is a preacher's dream, several thousand people standing eagerly waiting to hear what God's word has to say. And they stood there for six hours. That is incredible.

This has a tremendous effect on the people as they weep after hearing what the word of God says and after hearing what it means to each of them individually. Nehemiah tells the people not to weep but to celebrate. They are to rejoice in their knowledge of God, not weep.

Nothing in this life is as powerful or wonderful as the word of God. It has the power to free people from lives of bondage and misery. It has the ability to bring sight and hearing to the spiritually blind and deaf. God's word is the source of joy and joy in the Lord is our strength as it says a couple of verses after our verse of the day.

As leaders of families, ministries, or churches it is our responsibility to help people discover this joy just as the priests and Levites did in Nehemiah's day. God's word has the same power today as it did then. It still has the power to bring people down from their prideful towers and to bring people up from their pitiful dungeons. We need to help them to hear and to understand. Of course not everyone wants to hear or understand but we need to try to help them to anyway.

This means that we need to have a deep love for and desire to learn about the word of God. God doesn't need us to be experts in His word for us to share with others. He doesn't need us to be theologians. He doesn't need us to have memorized the entire New Testaments. All He needs are students. All God needs is for you to desire to learn about God's word and then He will even help you to do that. Then He is going to ask you to share what you are learning with others. The others that He wants you to share it with are all those that can hear you. Wherever He has placed you is where He wants you to share what He is teaching you. Only Ezra got to share from the pulpit, all the rest were amongst the people. Jesus, help us to love what you are teaching us so much that we must share it with those that you have surrounded us with.

AUGUST 15

Read: Nehemiah 9:22 – 10:39, 1 Corinthians 9:19 – 10:13, Psalm 34:1-10, Proverbs 21:13

Even strong young lions sometimes go hungry, but those who trust in the LORD will never lack any good thing.

David wrote this psalm when he was in a pretty desperate time in his life. Saul has just rocked his world. David has been a faithful servant of King Saul and done everything that has been asked of him and then some. Saul has become increasingly jealous of David's success at everything he does. Finally Saul determines that the only thing to do with this young man is to kill him.

Saul's son Jonathan helps David to determine Saul's true intents and then helps him to escape. David is now on the run. He leaves his own country and goes to Gath, in enemy territory. He realizes that this was a mistake and feigns madness so that they won't kill him.

David is now a man without a country. His own king is trying to kill him out of jealousy and the enemy wants to kill him because he has been so successful against them. This is a time when David's emotions and feelings must be all over the place. And yet in the midst of these very difficult circumstances he writes this beautiful psalm. Just a couple of verses before this one he wrote, "Taste and see that the Lord is good." Even in the midst of these difficult circumstances David can turn his eyes to the Lord and see past these "things" and see the Lord and His goodness.

In your life, ministry, or church there is going to come a time, or maybe you are in that time now, when it seems that everyone and everything is against you. The people that should be protecting you are attacking you, possibly for no good reason. And your enemies seem to be multiplying faster than you can count them. It is at those times when we feel the most alone and dry and empty that we need to do as David did and turn to the Lord. Jesus told the woman at the well that He could give her water that would make it so that she would never thirst again.

In Jesus we have everything that we will ever need. But often we will only turn to Him when our need becomes desperate. He wants us to come to Him daily to supply every need every day. If we will do that we stand a better chance of not getting to a place of desperation. Life is hard and it is impossible without the power of the Holy Spirit providing for your every need. Ministry and church can suck the life out of you if you are trying to do it by your own power. Allow God to fill you and daily return to the source for refilling by staying in prayer and in the Word. Trust in and seek the Lord and you will not lack any good thing. Jesus, teach us to come to you before we run out of gas.

AUGUST 16

Read: Nehemiah 11:1 – 12:26, 1 Corinthians 10:14-33, Psalm 34:11-22, Proverbs 21:14-16

NEHEMIAH 11:2

And the people commended everyone who volunteered to resettle in Jerusalem.

The people of Israel are re-establishing themselves in the land. They have been returning from exile in waves. In Jerusalem, the temple has been rebuilt and the walls of the city have recently been rebuilt. The city itself does not have a lot of people living in it. Most of the people that have returned have returned to the land that was their ancestral inheritance.

Jerusalem was the center of Hebrew worship. It was there that the temple of God was located. It was there that the only altar for making sacrifices to God was found. Jerusalem was the city that God said that he would live in among the children of Israel. Jerusalem was and still is a very important city to the nation of Israel.

The leaders determined that there were not enough people living in the city to maintain it and the temple of God and so they determined that some people would need to leave their ancestral homes to come and live in Jerusalem. They determined that one out of every ten would come and live in Jerusalem. To determine who would make the move they cast sacred lots to determine God's will in the matter.

There were some that willingly volunteered to make this move. They could see the need and decided to meet the need. This was a sacrifice. It meant giving up their ancestral home to go and live in the city of Jerusalem. It is not possible to know the level of significance of this sacrifice but it was enough that the other people recognized it and commended those that would do such a thing.

Life is filled with opportunities to sacrifice something that is important or valuable to you for the needs of others or the greater good. As leaders of families, ministries, or churches sacrifice should be second nature to us. It should be something that we do almost without thinking. But there will come times when there is a need to give up something very valuable to us. And the question will be; "Will God have to tell you to give it up or will you volunteer to give it up?"

Some of the people were told to leave their homes and move to Jerusalem. Others went voluntarily. Those that chose to move to Jerusalem received the commendation of their peers. We don't do our deeds to be seen by men but you should note that the only people that were recognized by God by being recorded in scripture were the ones that volunteered to move to Jerusalem. Men noticed their choice but that is recorded so that we know that God noticed their choice. Life is all about our choices. Jesus, help us to move toward You with all of our choices.

AUGUST 17

Read: Nehemiah 12:27 – 13:31, 1 Corinthians 11:1-16, Psalm 35:1-16, Proverbs 21:17-18

1 CORINTHIANS 11:2

I am so glad, dear friends, that you always keep me in your thoughts and you are following the Christian teaching I passed on to you.

There are few things as precious to a Christian leader as knowing that those that he has been called to lead are thinking about him and following the Christian principles that he has been teaching. Paul encourages the church of Corinth for their care for him. He goes on through the remainder of this chapter to rebuke them for wrong thinking in another area but begins with a compliment that would have likely built them up greatly.

Paul begins this verse sharing with them the joy that he has in them. He calls them his friends. Just yesterday, God impressed upon me and I shared with the church how cool it was that all of my friends gathered together every weekend to join me as I worshipped God. I know it is not about me, they are coming to worship God themselves. But there is a sense of gladness as I look around and see all those that I love and cherish as friends there fellowshipping and rejoicing in their relationship with the Lord.

For me and I know for anyone that has been called to shepherd the flock of God, there is nothing like seeing the power of God changing people's lives. We baptized ten people from the church yesterday and the joy and power of that moment was radical. With some, you could see a transformation taking place in their hearts and lives almost immediately from coming up out of the water.

If you are a Christian leader and especially if you are starting a new work of any kind, just love people and teach them the word of God. That is the most powerful and effective thing that you can do. Learn to love people, let them know that you love them through your words and deeds, and teach them to love God and other people. If you do that you will sense, as Paul does in our verse for the day, the love that they have for God, for you, and for others. It will fill your heart with a joy that is impossible to describe fully.

Everyone has a Christian leader that God has placed in their life; even if you are a Christian leader yourself. Do they know that you love them? Do they know that you are praying for them? Can they see that you love God and them and others through your words and deeds? One of the most precious gifts that you could give to the Christian leader in your life would be the ability to answer "yes" to all of those questions.

This is more important than anything else that you could be doing in your life. In chapter 13 of First Corinthians we are told of the importance of love. Love is the form of measurement that determines the value of your life and service. Nothing that you give, say, or do matters if it is not motivated by love. Without love it is all useless and meaningless. Jesus, help us to do everything out of a deep abiding love for you and for others.

AUGUST 18

Read: Esther 1:1 – 3:15, 1 Corinthians 11:17-34, Psalm 35:17-28, Proverbs 21:19-20

He sent letters to all parts of the empire, to each province in its own script and language, proclaiming that every man should be the ruler of his home.

King Xerxes was the most powerful man in the world at this time. The Persian Empire stretched across much of the known world. King Xerxes had little to concern himself with and so threw a huge party that lasted six months. After that party was over, the king threw a feast for all the servants and officials of the palace. While half drunk he decided to parade his beautiful wife before everyone to show off. She refused to come and Xerxes flew into a rage. Xerxes' counselors told him that if he didn't do something, all the wives in the kingdom would soon rebel because of her actions. The beautiful Queen Vashti was forever banished from the king's presence and Xerxes sent a decree throughout his kingdom.

This decree, as our verse for the day tells us, was that every man should be ruler in his home. This meant that husbands were given the power to treat their wives the same way that Xerxes had just treated Vashti. Husbands now had ultimate, unquestionable authority over their wives. It is not hard to imagine the abuse that was spawned by this sinful decree. This may also be the source of the idea that "a man is the king of his castle."

Xerxes' mistake is the same mistake that men have been making for thousands of years; believing that they are superior to women. There is no question that God made men different than women. Generally speaking men are stronger physically than women. They also respond differently in certain situations causing men to attribute superiority over women. What these men fail to recognize is that women excel in areas that men are weak. These same men don't recognize this because they perceive those areas to be unimportant.

God's view of men and women are as equals. Neither is superior over the other. Both are uniquely designed to complement one another to accomplish something miraculous; living together in marriage and raising children. Unhealthy views about our roles in marriage and family is the source of many of our society's woes and struggles. If more men stood up to be who God created them to be, our world would be radically different than it is today.

God didn't create men to the rulers of their homes; He created them to lead their homes. The distinction might appear to be small but is, in fact, enormous. A ruler has absolute authority. No one has permission to question or challenge his authority or rule. A leader uses influence to guide people toward a desired objective. A man that is fulfilling his God-given roles as a husband and father is not so much a ruler as he is a servant, steward, and shepherd. That kind of a man will enjoy blessings beyond his imaginings as God rearranges heaven and earth to pour out his grace upon him. Jesus, help men to be real men, not as the world says but as You say.

AUGUST 19

Read: Esther 4:1 – 7:10, 1 Corinthians 12:1-26, Psalm 36:1-12, Proverbs 21:21-22

PSALM 36:5

Your unfailing love, O Lord, is as vast as the heavens; your faithfulness reaches beyond the clouds.

The love of God is truly an awesome thing. In this psalm of David he attempts to paint a picture of just how amazing God's love is. It is good for us regularly to stop and meditate on the love and faithfulness of God. God's love and faithfulness should often fill our minds with wonder and awe. Our hearts should regularly rejoice over the knowledge of this amazing love that God directs to His creation; His most precious creation, man.

David's first description of God's love is that it is unfailing. God's love cannot fail. It cannot be hindered or restrained in any way. Just as the world turns without failing; God's love will also continue. In fact, the world will some day pass away but God's love will endure. This is very encouraging as we live in a society where love is such a variably commodity based on the whims and external conditions of people's "stuff." It gives me great comfort that nothing I do or say can change the fact that God loves me.

David goes on to say that God's love is as vast as the heavens. Humanity has yet to measure the universe. With all of our vast "knowledge," we don't know how many stars there are or where the universe ends. The Bible teaches us that God knows every star and that He has assigned them names and has set them upon their courses. When David penned this psalm the universe was beyond measuring. Three thousand years have passed and the universe is still beyond measuring; giving us a great picture of the vastness of God's love.

David also points to the faithfulness of God as being beyond the clouds. At the time David wrote this psalm man was not able to reach beyond the clouds. To me David is saying that God can go where I cannot. God can reach beyond my fears, worries, and concerns and because of His infinite love; He is faithful to do so. No matter what comes into our lives God is able and willing to do something about it.

What is our role and responsibility in relation to the love and faithfulness of God? Believe it, receive it, and live it! Believe that God's love is beyond anything and everything that will come into your life. Receive this fact as a truth of your life; let it settle deep into your heart. Then live like you believe this truth. If we would recognize God's great love for us as the incredible thing that it is we would be less prone to feel sorry for ourselves or be wrapped up in depression.

A true understanding of the immensity and faithfulness of God's love can be a source of tremendous encouragement and strength. Let it seep into your very soul that God loves you with an infinite love that cannot be altered or diminished. Let the joy of that knowledge saturate every part of your life. Then walk in the knowledge of the faithfulness of God. Jesus, help us to know You.

AUGUST 20

Read: Esther 8:1 – 10:3, 1 Corinthians 12:27 – 13:13, Psalm 37:1-11, Proverbs 21:23-24

ESTHER 8:8

Now go ahead and send a message to the Jews in the king's name, telling them whatever you want, and seal it with the king's signet ring. But remember that whatever is written in the king's name and sealed with his ring can never be revoked.

There are many parts of the book of Esther that are difficult for modern readers to relate. The whole process that led to Esther becoming queen is certainly pretty strange. When we think of the ancient kings we usually picture in our minds men that did pretty much whatever they wanted. King Xerxes was the ruler of the Medes and the Persians, one of the largest empires ever formed. From our text we see that Xerxes wasn't free to do whatever he wanted. There were rules that he had to abide by, even though he was the most powerful man in the world at that time.

The main message of the book of Esther is God's providential care for His people. Haman had planned to destroy the Jews but God frustrated his plan by placing Esther, a Jew, in the palace as queen. As a little side-note, Haman is an Agagite, his ancestor was King Agag the Amalekite. King Saul had been commanded by God to utterly destroy the Amalekites from the face of the earth. King Saul rebelled against God and spared some of the Amalekites. Haman and his treachery are the result of King Saul's rebellion.

King Xerxes gives Esther permission to do whatever she wants to but she cannot reverse what has already been ordered. King Xerxes is a symbol of the world and the flesh. Queen Esther is a symbol of God's people. God's people are in close proximity to the world. In the New Testament we are told that we are in the world but not of the world. There is a fascinating lesson in this verse for all of us.

The king of this world, Satan, has instituted things that are designed and determined to destroy God's people. Many of those things we have no power to alter or change. While we have no power to change the way things are, we do have power to act to try to produce a different outcome. Esther and Mordecai sent a decree in the king's name and sealed with his signet ring telling the Jews to defend themselves and attack their enemies.

We also have received a decree that has the same purpose. The Bible's primary purpose is to teach us how to know, love, and worship God. It points us always to His Son Jesus. This decree is written in King Jesus' name and is sealed with the Holy Spirit. Nothing within this decree can ever be revoked. Jesus referred to God's Word as eternal. But it is also a powerful tool to teach us how to defend ourselves from our enemies and how to attack his spiritual strongholds. To do that we must know, believe, and obey God's Word. Jesus, teach us to go to Your Word for our defense.

AUGUST 21

Read: Job 1:1 – 3:26, 1 Corinthians 14:1-17, Psalm 37:12-29, Proverbs 21:25-26

1 CORINTHIANS 14:1

Let love be your highest goal, but also desire the special abilities the Spirit gives, especially the gift of prophecy.

Paul has just spent the last two chapters describing the gifts of the Holy Spirit. In chapter thirteen Paul reminds us that while spiritual gifts are important, love is more important. The reason love is more important is because when we receive our glorified bodies, we will no longer have a need for the other gifts. Three things will remain after we have our glorified bodies; faith, hope, and love.

The reason why Paul is making this statement is because the Corinthians were desiring the manifested gifts of the Holy Spirit but there was no evidence of love. Paul's letter was to help them to put these things in the proper order. In our verse today, Paul is telling them it is OK to desire those gifts but only as they are secondary to their pursuit of love.

This is an important message for us as well. We can easily fall into the trap of desiring to do certain things for God or to be done for God's people that are born out of the wrong motivation. Our motivation should be love. Your love for God and for others will determine how effective you are in ministry or in life. If you want to be successful in the things that you do, then you need to be loving people.

If you don't love people then your ability to serve, pray, teach, and minister to others is going to be seriously hampered. Everything we do is going to be tested to see if it was done the way that God wants. You might have a form of success but it will not survive the testing by the fire of the Lord if you do not have love.

Our verse for the day gives us the first step towards loving others. If you want to love others more than you do today, you start by making that a goal; and not just any goal, but your highest goal. Too many of us put others things as our highest goal. We might make our highest goal being the best preacher that has ever lived so that many will be saved. We might say that we want to make a bunch of money so that we can give it to the church or to the poor or to some mission or ministry. If anything is a higher goal in your life than love than you are not obeying God. The Great Commandment tells us that the two most important things that we can do with our lives is to love God and to love others.

It is OK to desire to do great things for God and to desire that you be given the necessary things to cause those great things to happen; just as long as love for God and love for others is your great motivation. God is looking for people just like that so that He can show Himself to be strong on their behalf. A person whose highest goal is to love God and others is obvious for the world to see because they are modeling a life that looks like Christ's. Jesus, help to put all our goals at Your feet and teach us to desire love above all.

AUGUST 22

Read: Job 4:1 – 7:21, 1 Corinthians 14:18-40, Psalm 37:30-40, Proverbs 21:27

JOB 6:10

At least I can take comfort in this: Despite the pain, I have not denied the words of the Holy One.

Everything that Job had has been taken away from him. All of the wealth that he had acquired and his children have been taken away from him by Satan. God had previously referred to Job as a man of complete integrity. Satan, the constant accuser of the brethren challenges God by saying that Job worships God only because of what God has given him. God allowed Satan to test Job. Not only does God allow Satan to take everything from Job but He also allowed Satan to strike Job with boils all over his body. They say that a boil is excruciatingly painful. Try to imagine the pain of having boils all over your body.

Most of us will never experience what Job experienced. Praise God! Most of us will not have great wealth and lose it in an instant. Hopefully, none of us will have a large family and lose it in a moment of time. Most of us will not be stricken with a terrible disease. And certainly none of us will have all of these things happen to us at once.

Here in Job 6 we have Job defending himself against the words of the first of his "friends" that have come to "comfort" him. Job is maintaining his innocence while his friends tell him to confess his sins and get right with God. It has grieved my heart on more than one occasion to hear a Christian tell another that the reason why they are experiencing trials and tribulations is because they have unconfessed sin in their life. How arrogant and presumptuous.

God allows trials and tribulations in our lives for all sorts of reasons. Only one of those reasons is as punishment for our sin. We cannot possibly know why God allows trials and tribulations into the lives of others. We often can't understand why it happens in our own lives. Our role must be to always point people to the Lord.

Job responds to his friend by saying that even in the midst of the great anguish and suffering that he is in, He still believes God. He says that He will not deny the words of the Holy One. Earlier Job said that God gave him everything that He had and it was God's to take away. In responding to his wife Job said that they should accept both the good and the bad (our interpretation of bad) that comes from God.

In life and in ministry there will come times of great anguish and suffering. These things are a part of being in this world. Are you prepared for when those days come? Will you be able to say as Job did in chapter one: "The Lord gave, and the Lord has taken away; blessed be the name of the Lord." Do not hold on too tight to those things that are not yours to keep. The Lord might have need of it.

AUGUST 23
Read: Job 8:1 – 11:20, 1 Corinthians 15:1-28, Psalm 38:1-22, Proverbs 21:28-29

JOB 8:6

If you are pure and live in complete integrity, he will rise up and restore your happy home.

As we continue to read through the book of Job, we will be seeing these exchanges between Job and his "friends" increase in intensity. His friends are convinced that Job had been judged by God as having been unrighteous and Job resolutely maintains his innocence. And while Job's friends are arguing from the wrong assumption of Job's guilt, they do speak on many occasions things that are true about God.

And here Bildad tells Job that if he is righteous that God will give Job back everything that he lost. Well, that is exactly what God is going to do. In the last chapter of Job we are going to see that God blesses Job with twice as much as he had lost.

While Bildad was correct in what God was going to do with Job, we can't build a theology out of this text. We can't believe that if we are pure and righteous that God is going to bless us with great wealth. Will He bless us? Absolutely! But his blessings are not necessarily with material things.

God in His sovereignty chose to bless Job with great wealth. Someone else might be blessed with influence, or health, or long life, or special gifts and abilities. Or you might be blessed with a more intimate walk with

God. But the qualifier for this blessing is the same for everyone. We must be pure and upright. To receive this blessing, we must cleanse ourselves from the sin that separates us from God and we must walk in righteousness. Job's friends are judging Job's relationship with God, when theirs is questionable. They are looking at the circumstances of his life and assuming that they know what God is doing in his life.

And we do the same thing in ministry and church. We see something that is going on with a person in ministry or within a ministry or church and assume that we know what God is doing there. We automatically judge that person or ministry or church and suggest that sin must be present. We might not call it sin but we will imply that unrighteousness is present. And while that might be true, you need to be careful that you are not allowing their sin to cause you to sin.

God was doing a work in Job to be sure. But the greater work that God was doing was through the life and trials of Job. Because of these events in Job's life, millions of people have learned to understand God better and learned how to stand during the inevitable trials of life. If God did it with Job, isn't it possible that He could be doing it again today with you or someone around you? Job needed comfort and support, not judgment and condemnation. Is that true of someone around you? Lord, help us to see them like You do.

AUGUST 24

Read: Job 12:1 – 15:35, 1 Corinthians 15:29-58, Psalm 39:1-13, Proverbs 21:30-31

JOB 12:13

But true wisdom and power are with God; counsel and understanding are his.

Job stands firm to his claim of blamelessness before God. God Himself called Job blameless. But even so Job doesn't understand that the things that are happening to Him were caused by the enemy of his soul. There is a difference between what God allows to happen in our lives and what He does in our lives. God allowed all of the things that are happening to Job to take place; He didn't cause them to happen.

Job views all these calamities that have taken place in his life as some form of judgment by God. His friends say that it is an indication of sin which Job steadfastly denies. Job is disturbed by these circumstances in his life because he can see no reason for them. Because he doesn't attribute them to Satan, it gives Job a distorted view of God. Then Job makes the statement we see in our verse for the day.

Job recognizes that God is the ultimate source of wisdom and power in the universe. Even though Job doesn't understand why things are happening the way that they are he knows that only God has true wisdom. Job wants to meet with God and argue his case but he knows that to do so would only prove his ignorance.

We do the same thing with God. When we look at our circumstances and see something that we don't understand, we automatically determine who is to blame and decide who the source of our circumstances is. The problem is that only God is a true source of wisdom and there will be times such as in the life of Job when our circumstances are what they are for reasons that are a mystery to us.

One of the great lessons of the book of Job is that you don't need to understand everything that is happening in your life. In fact, you never will understand why all the circumstances of your life are the way that they are. We are to simply rest in the knowledge that God knows what our circumstances are and He has the power to change them.

Our verse for the day goes on to say that counsel and understanding are God's also. During those times when you don't understand why your circumstances are as they are, it is OK to ask God for understanding and counsel. We are told in the book of James to ask for wisdom if we need it and God will give it to us. That doesn't mean that He will explain everything that is going on in our lives just as God will not fully explain to Job why he went through the things that he did. Sometimes God will just let us know that He is there and He knows what is going on. Then all we can do is wait for Him to finish the work that He is doing in our circumstances. Jesus, give us the strength to wait for You to act in our circumstances.

AUGUST 25

Read: Job 16:1 – 19:29, 1 Corinthians 16:1-24, Psalm 40:1-10, Proverbs 22:1

1 CORINTHIANS 16:9

...for there is a wide-open door for a great work here, and many people are responding. But there are many who oppose me.

Paul is bringing his first letter to the Corinthians to a close. As he does he shares with them his desire and plans to come visit them. His plan is to stay for a while and it is believed that he did stay about three months. But Paul also inserts a statement in our verse for today that is interesting. Paul is in Ephesus when he writes to the Corinthians. He has been there for some time.

Paul is saying that in Ephesus there is an open door for the gospel of Jesus Christ to be shared. Not only is there a door but many people are responding to this message and being saved. Paul is being sensitive to the moving of the Holy Spirit. He is making plans but he is also allowing God to set the path and the timing of his life.

We need to take a lesson from Paul in this. Just because we have a plan doesn't mean that God has to follow it. Paul had his eyes open for where God was at work and he was determined to go where God was working; even if that meant throwing his plans out the window. How many of us would be willing to throw our plans out the window so that we could be where God was working? You need to know that the opportunity to do that happens more often than you are probably aware. We need to start looking for them with much greater diligence.

Paul also states in today's verse that there are many that oppose him. In fact, shortly after writing this letter to the Corinthians there was a riot in Ephesus because of the Christians. It was at that time that Paul perceived that the door was closing and he left and eventually made his way to Corinth. We also need to be looking for the closing of doors. In churches all over America, maybe even yours, God has closed doors that people are still trying to go through. The way that we know the door is open is because people are responding. If no one is responding to the things that are being done, than the door is closed to that and God is at work in something else.

What has God closed the door to in your life, ministry, or church? Are there areas where no one is responding but you are still doing it because "that's what we've always done"? It takes more courage to turn from a closed door than it does to go through an open door. God wants us to be watching for where He is working and then coming alongside of Him. If God has closed a door to something, than you are wasting God's resources that He placed in you if you continue to try to keep the door open. It doesn't matter how much you enjoy doing that thing. It doesn't even matter if you are really good at it. If God has closed the door and is working somewhere else, you need to turn from the closed door and go to where God is working. The sooner you do that the better. Jesus, teach us to watch for Your movements that we might always be right where You are.

AUGUST 26

Read: Job 20:1 – 22:30, 2 Corinthians 1:1-11, Psalm 40:11-17, Proverbs 22:2-4

JOB 22:21

Stop quarreling with God! If you agree with him, you will have peace at last, and things will go well for you.

Eliphaz the Temanite has just really let Job have it with all sorts of suggestions as to why Job is experiencing this great trial in his life. It is funny how people will create things to explain why something is the way that it is. We will often see this in ministry. If someone cannot understand why something is the way that it is, they will create in their minds a scenario that fits the evidence that they have. The problem with this is that they often don't have all the information that they need to create an accurate scenario. And this is very dangerous and divisive to a ministry or church.

After Eliphaz has spent some time creating this fantasy world that he believes that Job lives in he makes a statement that everyone should take hold of. Eliphaz tells Job to stop arguing with God and be at peace. And then says that if Job will do that, good will come out of it for Job. While the statement doesn't really apply to Job's current situation, it is a true statement that we should look at.

Too often in life, ministry, or the church we find ourselves arguing with God. He has made something clear to us and yet we think we know better and tell God that. As servants, our only response should be to obey. We have no place instructing the Master in how our lives or ministries should run, especially a Master that is the Almighty God, and is omniscient, omnipresent, and omnipotent.

As children of God, our role is to be obedient. Our loving Father knows just what we need when we need it and we are to trust Him with our lives. Too often, like we were when we were teenagers, we think we know everything. We especially know more than our parents did. But compared to God we are not teenagers, but toddlers. We are not capable of surviving on our own. And seeing ourselves as toddlers we must stop arguing with God.

Eliphaz says that two things will result from not arguing with God; peace and good. When we are being the faithful servants and obedient children that God desires us to be, it results in peace in our lives and ministries. And when we are at peace with God, He is inclined to bring good into your life, ministry, and church. If there is not peace in your life, ministry, or church it is a sign that you or someone else may be arguing with God. And if you are in a leadership position, which you probably are to some extent, than you have a responsibility to bring peace to the situation. You do this by starting in your own heart and asking God to reveal to you where you are arguing with Him. And then you ask Him to help you to cleanse that rebellious attitude from your life. And then with others, do not do as Eliphaz did by creating reasons for the situation, but by praying for those involved and by comforting, encouraging, and exhorting those that are involved. Jesus, help us to see things like you see them.

AUGUST 27

Read: Job 23:1 – 27:23, 2 Corinthians 1:12 – 2:11, Psalm 41:1-13, Proverbs 22:5-6

JOB 27:6

I will maintain my innocence without wavering. My conscience is clear for as long as I live.

Job's friends have been relentlessly trying to get Job to confess that it is because of some sin in his life that all of his misfortune has befallen him. They persist with this desire for a confession from Job because they believe that is the only reason that God would allow this to happen to him. They believe that a righteous person is blessed and never experiences any calamities such as those that have happened to Job. Job at no time during his conversations with his friends gives in to their request for a confession. He states emphatically in our verse for the day that he has no reason to confess. We know from reading this far through the book of Job that he was right to do that; even God called him blameless.

What an amazing testimony about Job; God says that he was blameless. We need to understand that this does not mean that he was perfect. As we have read thus far through the book of Job we have seen that Job does not have a correct view of God. This incorrect viewpoint will lead him to make some statements that he is going to need to repent of later in the book. The second half of our verse for the day is the key to Job's relationship with God and the reason why he could "maintain my innocence without wavering."

Job's conscience was clear! That means that in his heart, Job had no unfinished business with God. It was one of Job's habits to make sure that his heart was right before God. That meant that he did what he needed to so that there was nothing interfering with his relationship with God. He would even intercede on behalf on his children in case they had committed a sin that they were not aware of.

Our conscience tells us when we have business to do with God. The things of God are written on our hearts and our conscience will tell us when we are doing things that are right or wrong. Job made it a habit in his life to deal with all of the things in his life that his conscience told him were wrong by repenting of them to God.

We also have the same conscience within us to tell us when we are out of alignment with God; He is the Holy Spirit. When our conscience is bothering us; that is the Holy Spirit telling us that it is time to get right with God. God will judge us for what we know; not for the things that we did not know. God is going to rebuke Job later in this book for the things that he says in ignorance but he does not judge him because of his ignorance. Every time something showed up on Job's conscience he cleared it out through repentance; that is how he got the description of blameless. We also can be described as blameless if we will simply repent every time something shows up on our conscience. Jesus, help us to be sensitive to what the Holy Spirit is telling us.

AUGUST 28

Read: Job 28:1 – 30:31, 2 Corinthians 2:12-17, Psalm 42:1-11, Proverbs 22:7

PSALM 42:1

As the deer pants for streams of water, so I long for you, O God.

The Bible has many parables and word pictures that are designed to help us to understand how we should be relating to God. These are very helpful to me. I am one of those types that need to see something to understand it. That may be part of the reason why it took me so long to come to the Lord; I couldn't see God and so I couldn't accept what it said about Him. Thankfully, God found a way to deal with that in my life.

Today's verse is one of those word pictures. In this verse we are given a description of one of the ways that our attitude toward God should be described; we should long for Him. The dictionary defines the word "long" as: "to earnestly yearn or desire." This means that we should be determined in our desire for God. Too often I think we tend to act in a very lazy manner toward God. We long for the grace of God. We long for the mercy of God. We long for the blessings of God. But do we long for God?

God's grace, mercy, and blessings are born out of the relationship that God desires to have with us. It is God's longing that we long for Him, not for what He can give to us. The picture that is painted is of a deer panting for water. We live in a desert area of Southern California and it is close to or over 100 degrees every day this time of the year. Our animals that spend the day outside tend to pant and enjoy it greatly when we provide them cool fresh water.

It is God's desire that we would desire Him just as we would that cool drink of water on a hot day. He provides us so much out of His great love and the abundance of His grace. Let us not get tangled up in the blessings and forget the God that gives them to us. Too often that is what happened to the Israelites of the Old Testament; they would be enjoying the fruits of their relationship with God and then turn away from Him

We should be daily looking to refresh ourselves in the streams of His goodness and greatness. We should regularly be looking for a fresh approach to our relationship with the Lover of our souls. We need to frequently check our hearts to make sure that we are longing for a closer relationship and walk with God. In the Revelation Jesus told one of the churches to return to their first love. They had stopped longing for a close relationship with God.

Just as a deer draws that cool fresh water into itself, we need to be looking to draw more of God into our lives. To do that requires that we allow the things that are not of God to be pushed out of our life so that we can be refreshed by His Spirit. The more we allow this to happen the more we find that we desire it. The more that we desire this refreshing by God, the more room that we make for it. The more room that we make for God in our lives, the more we desire that He would fill that space. When we long for Him, He will fill us. Jesus, help us to pant for You alone.

AUGUST 29

Read: Job 31:1 – 33:33, 2 Corinthians 3:1-18, Psalm 43:1-5, Proverbs 22:8-9

2 CORINTHIANS 3:5

It is not that we think we can do anything of lasting value by ourselves. Our only power and success come from God.

For most people there is a deep-seated need to do things that are important. Everyone wants to believe that the things that they are doing matter and that there is a reason and purpose for what we do. Unfortunately most people look at that from the perspectives of what they can do and what it means to them. Paul points us to the right perspective.

Perspective is absolutely critical to us having joy and contentment in our lives. The reason that a lot of people have the kind of lives that they do is because they have the wrong perspective. Perspective is the way that we look at things. Only when we look at things from the correct perspective can we truly appreciate them. Take the painting of the Mona Lisa for example. Viewed from the front it is a masterpiece. If you were to be able to change your perspective so that you could view the painting from behind; what you would see is a rectangular object that is very unappealing in appearance. If you had never seen the Mona Lisa from the correct perspective, from the front, your viewpoint would be that the Mona Lisa is not a masterpiece at all.

This is true of every aspect of our lives. If you are viewing life from the wrong perspective, not only will you not be able to see life as you should, but nothing that you try to do will be of any lasting value. If you wanted to paint a picture that looked like the Mona Lisa but have never seen it from the front, the right perspective, you would not be able to be successful.

We try to do that with our lives. We want to do something that is meaningful and of lasting value but we are looking at what we are trying to do from the wrong perspective. In our verse for the day, Paul is telling us that we need to see that power and success come from God. If we want the things of our lives to be of any lasting value then we must first start by viewing those things through God's perspective as well as we can.

We do that by acknowledging our own inability to do it ourselves. This is called humility and it is the greatest key to doing something of lasting value. We also must acknowledge that what we are doing is God's and is for God. If we are doing it because of what we are going to get out of it, we have the wrong perspective. We need to understand that if we get anything out of what we do is up to God and then we need to be content whether we get anything out of it or not. Finally, we need to trust the results to God. It is His and for Him; only He can determine what lasting value looks like. Jesus, help us to look at the God-given desire to do something of lasting value, something eternal from Your perspective.

AUGUST 30

Read: Job 34:1 – 36:33, 2 Corinthians 4:1-12, Psalm 44:1-8, Proverbs 22:10-12

JOB 36:15

But by means of their suffering, he rescues those who suffer. For he gets their attention through adversity.

Here is a verse that none of us truly want to embrace until we are in a place like Job is in the account. Elihu continues to proclaim the amazing attributes and character of God and makes this fantastic statement in our verse for the day. Elihu tells Job and us that God uses the suffering that comes into our life to rescue us and to get our attention.

The image that comes into my mind is of a parent crying out to a child that is about to do something that is very dangerous and likely to cause them harm. To the child being yelled at might be as bad as a spanking. The parent uses that momentary pain to prevent the child from suffering even greater pain. That is what Elihu is describing here in our verse. God knows everything about what is going to happen in the future. He knows that the path that we might be on could be very dangerous for us spiritually, physically, or emotionally and so He may rescue us from that danger by allowing some other suffering to come into our lives.

That suffering and pain that He allows is often meant to get our attention drawn back to God. It is often during times of pain and suffering that we tend to draw nearer to God. That's what He wants; God wants you to draw nearer to Him. If the only way for Him to do that is to allow pain and suffering in your life, than that is what He is going to do.

He would prefer that you not need pain and suffering to draw nearer to Him. God's desire is that your love for Jesus would be the driving force for you to continually be working to be nearer to Him, but if you need pain and suffering to motivate you, then God will give it to you. God's primary concern in your life is to see that Jesus is at the core of your life, marriage, family, work, and church. If He needs to allow pain and suffering so that you can get there He will do that.

If we would just learn this truth we would experience so much less pain and suffering. It wouldn't eliminate all pain and suffering but I believe that it would greatly reduce it. Some pain and suffering is allowed for reasons that we may never fully understand. No matter how close you get to the Lord, you are not guaranteed to be free from suffering. God uses the suffering in our lives to reveal Himself to others. One of the ways that people come to know Jesus is when they see how Jesus helps us through our suffering. God may allow suffering in your life because someone around needs to come to know Him and this is the only way that it can happen.

It has been said "God doesn't waste pain." If God has allowed some pain or suffering into your life, marriage, family, work, ministry, or church then He has a plan to rescue someone. Jesus, help us to pay attention when God knocks through pain and suffering.

AUGUST 31

Read: Job 37:1 – 39:30, 2 Corinthians 4:13 – 5:10, Psalm 44:9-26, Proverbs 22:13

JOB 38:2

Who is this that questions my wisdom with such ignorant words?

Job has been laying out his case before God and Job's "friends" have been trying to get Job to see what they think that they see. God responds to Job from the whirlwind, not with answers but with questions. Why didn't God answer Job's questions? Because Job's questions were based out of his ignorance of God and the ways of God!

Like the toddler asking questions about why things happen the way that they do, there comes a point as a parent that we tell them: "Because I said so!" Or, "that's just the way that it is!" The toddler's mind cannot possibly understand why things are the way that they are until their mind gains an understanding of the world around them.

God's ways and thoughts are so much higher than us that we are barely equivalent to the toddler. There is no way that we can understand God's ways or thoughts. There is no way that we can totally or completely understand why things happen the way that they do. And so that leaves us with a choice. Either we whine and complain and question God. Or we can totally and completely trust Him.

Everyone, at some point in your life, ministry, or church, will come to a place where you are tempted to question God. God, why did you allow this to happen? God, I thought you said… God, why didn't you… And when that temptation comes, resist it! The problem is not with God, it is with you. Your understanding is incomplete. And because your understanding is not complete, you cannot understand the reasons for what is happening.

Our response to God in these kinds of circumstances is not to question God, but to go to Him and beg Him for His mercy and grace. Pray that He will increase our understanding and help us to understand His purposes in whatever is going on. Believe God when He says that He will never leave us nor forsake us. Believe Him when He says that he has a plan and a purpose for your life.

It all comes down to trust and faith. Do you trust God? Do you believe God? Not just with your life, but with your ministry, and church as well? If you are questioning God, you are doing so from a position of ignorance. Before you ask God any questions, you answer the ones that He asked Job. Jesus, help us to rest in the truth that we know almost nothing compared to you and that you have our lives in your hands.

SEPTEMBER

SEPTEMBER 1

Read: Job 40:1 – 42:17, 2 Corinthians 5:11-21, Psalm 45:1-17, Proverbs 22:14

JOB 42:17

Then he died, an old man who had lived a long, good life.

Job lived 140 years after he went through his time of great trials. It is estimated that Job may have been as old as 240 years old when he finally died. God allowed him to live for a very long time. The book of Job is a snapshot of a brief period of Job's life. That snapshot is a picture of great trials and tribulation. It is bleak picture of a very difficult time in Job's life. It is a dark image of the wrong ways that Job was picturing God.

The last verse of this book paints a different picture of Job's life. When we think of Job, we think of someone that suffered and struggled through something that most of us will never come close to experiencing. The picture that today's verse paints of Job's life is that it was long and good. The events and circumstances that are recorded here in the book of Job were not the defining moments in Job's life; they were just some of the moments of his life.

No one moment makes our lives. Every moment is a stroke in the painting of our lives. Some of those strokes are vivid and striking; others are subtle and gentle. The painting that is our life is not done until every day of our lives has been recorded. These events in Job's life are just a few of the many thousands of strokes that represent the totality of his life; they were not the defining moments of his life.

All of us will have both good and bad moments that go into the creation of the painting of our lives. In the last words of this book that describes one man's great struggles and trials it is said that Job had a "good life." Just because there were some bad moments, those moments did not comprise a bad life.

No matter how bad your circumstances are right now, they do not have to result in anything other than a few more strokes in the painting of your life. We are the ones that determine the impact that any single moment has on our lives. We can allow the Job-like circumstances to cripple us or we can allow the Holy Spirit to use these circumstances to add depth and beauty to the image that He is trying to create out of our lives.

When it comes time to write the last verse of your life, what will it say? Will the last verse of your life say that you had a good life or something less than that? The choice is yours. A good life is not one that is free from bad things. A good life is one that takes the bad things with the good and uses them to draw a person toward God and uses them to allow the Holy Spirit to shape them into the image of Jesus Christ. Ultimately, a good life is one that has allowed God, the Master Artist to use the colors, strokes, and textures that He chooses to paint an image that pleases Him. Jesus, help us to be a willing canvas that You can use to create a masterpiece that pleases You.

SEPTEMBER 2

Read: Ecclesiastes 1:1 – 3:22, 2 Corinthians 6:1-13, Psalm 46:1-11, Proverbs 22:15

ECCLESIASTES 1:2

"Everything is meaningless," says the Teacher, "utterly meaningless!"

Ecclesiastes is believed to be the last book written by King Solomon and it is believed to have been written near the end of his life. Upon first entering into this book it can be very depressing. It speaks of futility and vanity. Today's verse tells us that everything is meaningless. As you read things like that you can come away with a belief that there is no point to human existence.

It would be a mistake to take that outlook from this fascinating book. What Ecclesiastes does is take our eyes off of the things that we think are important and places them on the things that God says are important. Solomon was the wisest man to ever live. Sadly, his wisdom did not keep him from disobeying and turning away from the LORD. King Solomon had everything and he was the world's greatest example that "having it all" is not enough.

At the end of his life when he had experienced "everything that his heart desired" he uttered the statement above; it was all meaningless. Throughout the rest of this book he qualifies this statement and gives us a picture of how to bring meaning to our lives but the point is that meaning is not found in the things that most of us think or what the world promotes as bringing meaning and purpose to life.

Solomon had wealth, great wealth and learned that it did not bring meaning to his life. He had power and it did not fulfill him the way that He hoped that it would. Solomon was king so he had position, the highest position there was, and it brought him no satisfaction. Solomon enjoyed any kind of pleasure that he desired and it left him empty and wanting. Solomon had all the things that the world tries to tell you will make you happy and fulfilled and discovered that they did not.

At the end of Solomon's life he discovered or realized that even with all the things that should make him happy he was not. It was at that realization that he uttered the words above; "it is all meaningless." And understand that Solomon is not saying that any of those things are bad; though some of them were forbidden by God and thus were bad. It was the pursuit of those things that was meaningless. To make the driving force of your life the pursuit of the things that Solomon had and enjoyed; that is meaningless.

It is pointless and meaningless to spend your life going after something that will not satisfy you and bring meaning to your life. As you read Ecclesiastes you will learn what it is that will bring meaning to your life and you will learn that it is probably not what you think it is. If you will keep your spiritual eyes and ears open to what the Spirit would say to you, you will learn how to have a life of meaning and fulfillment. Jesus, help us to see where true meaning and fulfillment can be found in this life.

SEPTEMBER 3

Read: Ecclesiastes 4:1 – 6:12, 2 Corinthians 6:14 – 7:7, Psalm 47:1-9, Proverbs 22:16

2 CORINTHIANS 6:14

Don't team up with those who are unbelievers. How can goodness be a partner with wickedness? How can light live with darkness?

In our reading for the day Paul gives an exhortation that must have come as a shock to his readers. Paul was telling the Christians in the church in

Corinth that they were not to partner with people that were not believers. As the living temple of God, they are being told to keep themselves away from things that will defile that temple. Elsewhere Paul said "Bad company corrupts good character." That was two thousand years ago; nothing has changed. We are still the temple of the living God and we are still being called to stay away from things that might defile our temples.

In our verse for the day, Paul is using contrasts to make his point. These things that he is contrasting cannot exist together without conflict. At some point one of these two will win out over the other and dominate the relationship. You might think that goodness will win out every time. Paul wouldn't have given us this warning if that were true. If goodness and light would win every time then we would be encouraged to form these partnerships. Because we are being warned against them ought to indicate to us that these partnerships with unbelievers are dangerous; not for them but for us.

This doesn't mean that we shouldn't be involved with unbelievers; it means that we shouldn't form close relationships with them. The verse for the day talks about partnering. Anyone that has ever had a partner knows that can be a lot like a marriage in the way that the relationship functions. That kind of relationship cannot function if the two, or more, partners are not in unity in their beliefs. The same thing is true of a marriage. A marriage between a believer and an unbeliever is more likely to fail than it is to succeed. The believer in that relationship will struggle and is the most likely to be swayed from the beliefs that they took into that relationship.

The Bible warns us about things like this so that we will avoid some of the pain and suffering that our natural decisions would lead us into. Partnering with an unbeliever might make great business and financial sense. But because the Bible warns you not to do so, you need to trust that God knows best. If you decide to do it anyway, you need to understand that God considers that disobedience and He doesn't like that.

If you are already in an unequally yoked relationship, our reading tells us to get out of it. You need to separate yourself from that partnership as soon as is possible. In the case of a marriage God would tell you to stay in it in the hopes that your good witness might win your spouse to the LORD. If you are in an unequally yoked relationship focus your heart more fully on the LORD. He can carry you and help you through whatever hard things might come as a result of partnering with an unbeliever. Trust in Him completely and do not allow the darkness to settle in your life. Jesus, may Your light so shine in me that the darkness around me flees from it.

SEPTEMBER 4

Read: Ecclesiastes 7:1 – 9:18, 2 Corinthians 7:8-16, Psalm 48:1-14, Proverbs 22:17-19

PROVERBS 22:18

For it is good to keep these sayings deep within yourself, always ready on your lips.

Within the book of Proverbs are great pearls of wisdom. They are stated in very simple ways so that virtually anyone with a mind seeking after God can understand them. Many of them are given in small morsels that are easy to chew but they contain within them the power to radically alter the way that we view God and other people and ourselves. These words have the power to change lives.

In our text for today we are told that we should keep these sayings deep within us. And if we do that they will always be ready on our lips. As I thought about this verse it occurred to me that elsewhere in scripture we are told to feed upon the word of God.

When we eat something, our body draws nutrients from the food and it nourishes us. Many of us have probably heard the saying: "You are what you eat!" The things that we eat have a tremendous impact on our health and strength. I recently read that 8 out 10 of the serious health risks that Americans face could be avoided or minimized if we just ate better foods.

Our soul also requires nourishment. And if we feed it the wrong things it will become sick and weak and vulnerable to attack. There is also spiritual junk food that tastes good and makes us feel good but provides no nourishment to our soul. Our soul is nourished only by the word of God. Only the word of God can provide our souls with the things that it needs to be strong and healthy.

We feed our soul by being in God's word; the Bible. And we need to be doing so on a very regular and consistent basis. Your soul needs to be fed regularly, just like your body does. We need to read and study the Bible.

We need to talk to God (pray) about what His word says and meditate on what it means to you, your family, your ministry, and your church. We need to memorize those scriptures that God has spoken to us about, which plants them deep within us.

And ultimately God wants us to share these words with those around us. It is amazing how the Holy Spirit will bring just the right verses to your mind as you need them to minister to someone. But He can't do that if you haven't planted them there for Him to bring back to your remembrance.

It has been said: "You can't give what you ain't got!" For you to be effective in your family, ministry, or church in ministering to others you must have been nourished by God. And because you are not a baby, God expects you to feed yourself by daily feeding upon His word. Jesus, teach us to have a hunger for Your word.

SEPTEMBER 5

Read: Ecclesiastes 10:1 – 12:14, 2 Corinthians 8:1-15, Psalm 49:1-20, Proverbs 22:20:21

ECCLESIASTES 12:11

A wise teacher's words spur students to action and emphasize important truths. The collected sayings of the wise are like guidance from a shepherd.

As the book of Ecclesiastes comes to a close, Solomon reminds us of the purpose and objective of the book and ultimately of his life. God had blessed Solomon with incredible wisdom. His wisdom was greater than that of anyone that had lived. And Solomon knew as his life was drawing to a close that his purpose in life was to share that wisdom with others.

Here in our verse for the day Solomon tells us that the wise teacher's words will create a reaction within those that hear them. They will also deal with important truths. How important that is for us as we strive to build godly homes, ministries, or churches. God's desire for all of His children is that they be conformed into the image of His son Jesus. The only way that can happen is if people change from the way that they are to the way they should be. And the only way they can do that is if people teach them how to do that.

As we teach those people that God has placed around us, we must stick to the important things and teach in such a way as to show them the way to change to be like Jesus. If we aren't doing that, then we are not being wise teachers. It has been said: "Major in the majors and minor in the minors." We must not allow ourselves to get caught up in the insignificant issues of the day but must stick with the issues of eternity.

Our verse for today ends by reminding us that these wise sayings will guide us like a shepherd. They will keep us from danger and lead us to safety. They will nourish our souls and fill us with the good things of God. They will mend our wounds and heal us when we are sick. They will lead us back when we have gone astray. Within the word of God resides all that we need for life and happiness.

Whether or not you have the position of teacher or shepherd, if you are in a family, ministry, or church, you have a responsibility to share the wise sayings of scripture with those around you. You do that through your words and your actions. God calls all of His children to share His truths with others and to live out those truths in their lives. Our lives should be living examples and illustrations of the truths of God.

Look around you! Are the words that you are speaking and the behaviors of your life spurring people to action? Are they moving to become more like Jesus? Jesus, teach us to teach them to love You and to be like You.

SEPTEMBER 6

Read: Song of Songs 1:1 – 4:16, 2 Corinthians 8:16-24, Psalm 50:1-23, Proverbs 22:22-23

PSALM 50:9

But I want no more bulls from your barns; I want no more goats from your pens.

Asaph is inspired to write this psalm or song about what God wants from us. He starts by speaking about the greatness of the LORD Almighty and His power. And then in verses 8 to 15, Asaph speaks about the sacrifices of the people of Israel and how God feels about them.

First, God reminds them that everything that exists is His. Everything that they bring to God is His already. Nothing that we have or will ever have belongs to us. It was all given to us to care for and to use for God's glory and honor. This means that anything that we could possibly give to God already belongs to him.

Asaph then says that God would not tell us if He was hungry. The things that we bring to God are not things that He needs. He is complete; that means that He needs nothing at all. There is nothing that we could do or bring to Him that would add to Him. The things that we do for God or bring to God should be done not because He needs it but because we need it. We need to give to God some of the things that He has given us.

In verse 14 God calls us to "offer to God thanksgiving." Our offerings to God should be because we are thankful. It is not because God needs it and it is not because we have to. God's word tells us that He doesn't want our offerings unless they are given with a thankful heart.

God has given us so much. He has given us much more than most of us appreciate. He has given us life and everything that we have. He sent His Son Jesus to die for our sins and, through Christ, God has given us eternal life. Everything that we have, including our families and careers, were given to us by God. We should be thankful for what He has done.

In ministry and church, we can sometimes be distracted from the fact that our service to God is an offering and that we are to do it with thanksgiving. God doesn't need us! It is a gift to us that we get to be used by God to minister to His people. Jesus, help us to never forget that what we do for you, we do because we are thankful for all that you have done for us.

SEPTEMBER 7
Read: Song of Songs 5:1 – 8:14, 2 Corinthians 9:1-15, Psalm 51:1-19, Proverbs 22:24-25

SONG OF SONGS 8:6

Place me like a seal over your heart, or like a seal on your arm. For love is as strong as death, and its jealousy is as enduring as the grave. Love flashes like fire, the brightest kind of flame.

Here is one of the most beautiful pieces of text in all of scripture. Solomon writes this love story to describe the way that he feels about his young bride. His description of her is wonderful and romantic. It is difficult to come away from this text without feelings of love stirring deep within you.

When I first read this book I wondered why it was in the Bible. Then God revealed something to me that has radically changed the way that I think of my wife. Solomon was describing the way that he viewed his young wife. There is no way of knowing what she looked like but Solomon saw her the way that he describes her in this book.

In our verse for today the young woman asks the man to place her as a seal over his heart. A seal was used to close a letter and keep it that way until the person that it was addressed to opened it. A seal was also used to let the reader know who sent the letter. By placing her as a seal over his heart he was sealing his heart from all others.

God's plan for my marriage is that there is only one woman that He has chosen for me. And I get to choose how I view her. I can choose to view her as the perfect wife for me or I can choose to see her imperfections. Years ago I determined in my heart to view my wife as the perfect woman for me. And in my heart I view her just as the young man in our text for today views his lover. I have placed her as a seal over my heart; only she can open it. It was a decision and a choice that has kept me faithful and in love.

As Christians we are described as the bride of Christ. As a man this is a little difficult to embrace, but embrace it we must. Christ asks us to place Him as a seal over our hearts. Only Christ should have a position higher in our hearts than our spouses. And no one else should have a position higher than your spouse. It is your choice to make; Christ first, spouse second, and all others after.

God sees us as a beautiful masterpiece of His creation. We need to view our spouses the same way. Stop looking at flaws and start looking at them through the eyes of Christ. He gave His life for them and He thinks they are beautiful. Read Solomon's Song of Songs again and picture you and your spouse as the two main characters in this story. Let the descriptions of the characters be descriptions of you and your spouse. Jesus, help us to choose to put a seal over our hearts that only You and our spouse can open.

SEPTEMBER 8

Read: Isaiah 1:1 – 2:22, 2 Corinthians 10:1-18, Psalm 52:1-9, Proverbs 22:26-27

ISAIAH 1:27

Because the LORD is just and righteous, the repentant people of Jerusalem will be redeemed.

Much of the book of Isaiah is a call for the nation of Israel to come back from its sin and idolatry to worship the One True God. There are many words of impending judgment and imminent disaster. Here in the very beginning of the book we see that it is not all about doom and destruction. The book of Isaiah is a call to repentance and here in our text for today there is a promise.

That promise says that the repentant people of Jerusalem would be redeemed. This means that God is going to buy them back from their sins and unfaithfulness. In that period and culture, if someone had to sell themselves into slavery or servitude, a kinsman redeemer could come and pay for them to be released.

God is telling the people of Israel that if they will just repent that He will redeem; He will buy them out of the bondage of their sin and rebellion. It is a part of His character. Because of that character, He can't help but redeem the repentant.

God's great complaint against Israel was that they knew God and felt no shame in their sins. They sinned and knew that what they were doing was against God and did it anyway. Theirs was deliberate sin and in their rebellion God still reached out to them to warn them of the impending disaster in the hopes that they might still be saved from it.

As humans, we all sin. The sin nature within us guarantees that. We are going to sin, no matter how good we are and how hard we try not to. God knows that! He knows that eventually all of His children are going to make a mistake. God will not judge us for our mistakes; He is going to judge us for our hearts. Judgment comes to those whose hearts are hardened to their sin and don't care that God is angry about their sin.

The heart of a repentant person hurts when God's heart is hurt by our sin. Child of God, your Father in heaven wants your heart to hurt so much at your sin that it keeps you from sin in the first place. That is the kind of person to which this verse refers.

God's great plan is to redeem everyone from the bondage of sin and rebellion. However, in His great love for us, He has given us the choice. We must choose to be redeemed. To be redeemed we must allow God to develop a repentant heart within us. We must learn what hurts God's heart and we must allow the Holy Spirit to conform our heart so that it hurts in the same way. We must deliberately seek out the sin in our lives and completely and utterly destroy it from our lives. Jesus, soften our hearts to be like yours.

SEPTEMBER 9

Read: Isaiah 3:1 – 5:30, 2 Corinthians 11:1-15, Psalm 53:1-6, Proverbs 22:28-29

2 CORINTHIANS 11:2

I am jealous for you with the jealousy of God himself. For I promised you as a pure bride to one husband, Christ.

Paul's second letter to the church in Corinth has some very strong language in it. The tone of it in some sections sounds like a father reprimanding a child. We have one such section in our reading today. Paul is upset because some men have come into the church and disturbed the work that Paul had done here. Paul refers to them as "super apostles" in an obvious voice of sarcasm. The "super apostles" are apparently taking advantage of the flock of Corinth and teaching things that are contrary to the things that Paul taught.

In our verse for the day we see why Paul was writing this letter and using such strong language; he was jealous for the church in Corinth. When we think of jealousy, we usually think of the green-eyed monster that poisons our heart. That is not the kind of jealousy that Paul is talking about. Paul is not jealous because someone is in Corinth and getting better press reports than he was. He was not jealous because these "super apostles" were being wined and dined while he had worked his way through the ministry.

Paul was jealous for them with the jealousy of God. The Bible teaches that God is a jealous God. He will not share our affections with anyone or anything else. Nothing can come between God and us. Paul is saying that his heart toward the Corinthians is just like God's. His great desire is that nothing would come between them and their God. We see that more clearly in the second part of our verse for today.

Paul played a major role in starting this church and ministering to its people. He felt a responsibility to them and viewed his role with them as that of preparing a bride for her groom. The church of Corinth was engaged to Jesus and Paul was concerned that the Corinthians might be drawn away to another. God considers it adultery when we give our love to anything or anyone other than Him. This is what Paul is jealous about. He has been working to prepare this bride and it bothers him that there are people within the church that are trying to draw her away from her intended groom, Jesus.

As leaders of God's families, ministries, or churches we are to have this same jealousy for the work of preparing the bride of Christ. Whatever group of people that God has called you to minister to, part of your role is to prepare the bride so that she can be presented to God pure and undefiled by the things of this world. This should burn as a passion within you. It should cause you great pain to see sinful behavior and unrepentant hearts. The purity of the bride should be something that you are jealous for and focused on achieving. Paul wrote this letter and he intended to visit Corinth to further explain the need for purity to the church in Corinth. I pray that you also are doing what you are called to so that the bride of Christ is being prepared for her Groom. Jesus, give us Your jealousy for the Church.

SEPTEMBER 10

Read: Isaiah 6:1 – 7:25, 2 Corinthians 11:16-33, Psalm 54:1-7, Proverbs 23:1-3

ISAIAH 7:9

Israel is no stronger than its capital, Samaria. And Samaria is no stronger than its king, Pekah son of Remaliah. You do not believe me? If you want me to protect you, learn to believe what I say."

The kings of Syria and Israel have come against Ahaz, the king of Judah. Isaiah, the prophet, comes to Ahaz and gives a prophecy from the

LORD. He tells King Ahaz that he doesn't need to worry about these two kings because in 65 years that both of these nations will be gone. That prophecy comes true when the Assyrians come in and lead the nation of Israel into captivity. Unfortunately, it is not much after that the nation of Judah is also led into captivity.

Obviously, King Ahaz didn't believe what Isaiah said. Isaiah then makes this amazing statement to King Ahaz. He tells him that if he wants God to protect him, he is going to have to learn to believe what God says. This statement carries much power for the child of God that wants more from God.

One of the benefits of our relationship with God is that He will protect us. God will supernaturally keep us from harm and suffering. Not all harm and suffering; some of that is needful for our growth. But He will keep unnecessary suffering from our life. Our text tells us that we play a role in that protection. We have to want that protection! It is amazing to say that we can actually decide that we don't want God to protect us. Most of us wouldn't actually say that but our behaviors and attitudes communicate that clearly. To receive God's protection we must act like we want Him to protect us.

The way that our text tells us to act like we want God's protection is to learn to believe Him when He tells us something. In other words we need to learn to have faith. Faith is: believing that what God said is true and acting upon that knowledge. In Hebrews we are told that it is impossible to please God without faith. If you don't believe God or what He says then you cannot please Him and He does not need to protect you.

Our text also tells us that we need to learn to believe God. Faith grows like a tree. It starts small and then as it is fed and nourished it grows stronger. Each time we find ourselves in a place where we decide to believe God or not, our faith is strengthened or weakened.

God's protection is a byproduct of our relationship with Him. As faithful children, God will keep us from all unnecessary suffering and pain. To experience His complete protection, we must completely believe what He says. If you feel like you are outside of God's protection, ask God to reveal to you if what you are experiencing is unnecessary suffering. If it is, then ask Him to reveal to you where you need to learn to believe Him. Jesus, teach us to believe You so that we can rest under the shadows of His wings.

SEPTEMBER 11

Read: Isaiah 8:1 – 9:21, 2 Corinthians 12:1-10, Psalm 55:1-23, Proverbs 23:4-5

PROVERBS 23:4

Don't weary yourself trying to get rich. Why waste your time?

Today's verse speaks about a topic to which most people can relate. We live in a culture that glorifies the rich and famous. Subconsciously, we desire to be like the people that we see on the news, television, or movies. We want the fame, possessions, and wealth that the world is continuously parading in front of us. Today's verse tells us to rethink what we are doing.

It is not saying that we shouldn't be rich or even that we shouldn't desire to be rich; it is telling us not to chase after riches. Whether or not we become rich is part of God's plan; not ours. Just because you desire to be rich doesn't mean that God intends to make you rich.

Our verse tells us not to try to get rich. That means that our efforts in this life to work and invest should not be with the goal of becoming rich. God wants us to work and He wants us to be good stewards of the resources that He gives us, but He doesn't want us to do that just so that we can be rich.

Too many people are living this verse out in the negative way that it is stated; they are wearing themselves out chasing after something that God is not going to give them. That is like a two-year-old asking for candy for breakfast; mom keeps saying no and the child keeps asking. People all around us are wasting their time and lives chasing after something that they can't have.

Instead, God would have us work faithfully and diligently at whatever job that He has provided for us. He would also call us to live within our means and not get over-extended. He would also call us to be good stewards and make wise investments. God calls us to do the work; He is the one that will cause the crop to grow. If it is His will He will make you rich and no amount of chasing after it is going to make any difference.

Life is too short to be wasting it chasing after something that we can't have. People that chase after riches are often very unhappy and unsatisfied. Even if they find riches; it is never enough and it is not as satisfying as they thought it would be. It is God's desire that we would be happy with whatever He has given us. It is an absolute fact that if you can't be happy with what you have now; you won't be happy even if you get what you think will make you happy.

All of this depends upon our trust that God is going to provide for our every need. Scripture is filled with people that God chose to make rich. It is also filled with people that lived humble lives. Trust God to decide which is best for you, your family, your ministry, or even your church. Jesus, teach us to chase after You and not riches.

SEPTEMBER 12

Read: Isaiah 10:1 – 11:16, 2 Corinthians 12:11-21, Psalm 56:1-13, Proverbs 23:6-8

ISAIAH 10:15

Can the ax boast greater power than the person who uses it? Is the saw greater than the person who saws? Can a whip strike unless a hand is moving it? Can a cane walk by itself?

God is describing how He is going to use the king of Assyria to punish His people for disobedience and rebellion. He then goes on to say that He is going to then punish the king of Assyria because of his pride and arrogance. It was God who gave the Assyrian king his power and it was the LORD who gave him the victory over His people. Isaiah accuses the Assyrian king of boasting of his power to overcome the people of God.

Isaiah then asks the rhetorical questions above. The answer is the same in all four questions; "No!" The point is simple, the king of Assyria may boast of his great power and accomplishments but it is God that used him as a simple tool to accomplish His will in the world and in the lives of His Chosen People.

There is an important lesson in this for modern-day Christians, especially those that are leading families, ministries, or churches. Don't look upon the things that God is doing through you as "your accomplishments." This devotional is close to the 600th one that I have written. It would be very easy to be impressed with myself for having accomplished something like this. Then I remind myself that I am not the writer, but only the conduit through whom the Holy Spirit has chosen to flow to produce this devotional.

If it ever becomes something that might be considered great, it is only because God has chosen to do so. I am simply the pen that God chose to write it. Without His hand holding the pen, it would never have happened. I am a tool in the hand of the Master.

It is this understanding that positions us to be of even greater use to God. When we understand and acknowledge that He is in control and is controlling everything, we are then in a position to be used to an even greater degree. Our next choice must be to let Him use us when He wants to and in the way that He wants. A pen cannot tell the person holding it what to write.

Nothing will remove you from a place of usefulness to God like pride and boasting. God resists the proud and boasting is stealing God's glory. Instead we should have humble hearts before God and men. I have a goal of writing one of these devotionals for every chapter in the Bible, all 1,189 of them. It will only be possible if I keep my heart right before the LORD and remember who is actually doing the writing.

Whatever you do in this life, whether it is great or small is because God has used you to do it. Give Him the glory and rejoice that He chose to use you. Jesus, help us to be willing tools in the hand of the Master.

SEPTEMBER 13

Read: Isaiah 12:1 – 14:32, 2 Corinthians 13:1-13, Psalm 57:1-11, Proverbs 23:9-11

ISAIAH 13:3

I, the LORD, have assigned this task to these armies, and they will rejoice when I am exalted. I have called them to satisfy my anger.

God is God! That means that He is in control and able to control everything in the universe. But sometimes as Christians we lose sight of the complete control that God has. Many people believe that God only uses those that are His Children. They believe that God just ignores all the rest of them to live their lives any way they wish.

Nothing could be further from the truth. God is active in the lives of believers and unbelievers alike. He is just active in different ways. Here in our text for today God is using these armies to complete a task. He has assigned them the task and called them to it. The task is to go and defeat the Babylonians.

God had used the Babylonians earlier to punish the Israelites for turning away from God to worship idols. However, the Babylonians were too severe in their punishment of the children of Israel and now God is going to punish them with another strong force.

As Christians, we often think that the things in our life that we describe as attacks all come from our enemy, Satan. What we need to understand is that God will sometimes assign the task and call an enemy to come and discipline us if we have been disobedient or rebellious. We might even find ourselves asking God to protect us from an enemy that He has sent to discipline us.

God in His divine sovereignty will allow some attacks so that we will be conformed more into the image of His Son Jesus. Others, like today's text come as a result of our not being where He told us to be. God doesn't want to punish us; He wants us to obey Him. When we don't and we refuse to respond to His warnings He is left with no option but to send someone against us to force us to a place of complete surrender to God.

God had told the Israelites how they could have a blessed and fruitful relationship with God. He sent them the prophets to warn them when they wandered away from the way that God wanted them to live and ultimately sent enemies against them to get their attention.

God is still doing that in the lives of His children. He still wants to have a relationship with His children that is marked by fellowship, communion, blessings, and abundance. But that can only happen if we are living our lives the way that God desires. If we choose to live our lives the way that we want to, He will do whatever He has to do to get us back, including sending enemies to punish us. Whenever we find ourselves faced with an enemy we need to ask God to reveal to us if that enemy is there to teach us, to test us, or to punish us. That will help us to respond the correct way to the attack. Jesus, help us to see every enemy attack as an opportunity to be more like you and to draw closer to God.

SEPTEMBER 14

Read: Isaiah 15:1 – 18:7, Galatians 1:1-24, Psalm 58:1-11, Proverbs 23:12

Then at last the people will think of their Creator and have respect for the Holy One of Israel.

In our verse for the day Isaiah gives us an explanation as to why God sends punishment into our lives when we rebel against Him. He wants us to think about Him and respect Him. This is a beautiful picture of God and the way that He would like us to relate to Him. It is found in the two descriptions of God and our response to those descriptions.

First, we are told that God is our Creator. For us to truly interact with God the way that He desires we need to begin with an understanding that He created us. Not only did He create us but He determined exactly how we are going to turn out. He has a master plan that determines the ideal manner in which we develop and grow and function in this world that God created.

Our response to that knowledge is that it should cause us to think about God. If we spent more time thinking about the God that created us we would think less about ourselves and our circumstances. We would also be less likely to sin because we are focused on our Great Creator instead of the things that we want or could be doing. This doesn't mean that we should run away to some retreat and become a monk or something. It means that we should allow everything in this world to cause us to think about God. The sunrise, the birds chirping, the song on the radio, a child's smile, everything should cause us to think about our Creator.

Second, we are told in our verse that God is the Holy One of Israel. Holiness describes who and what God is. Holiness is the absolute absence of sin. God is absolutely perfect. He never makes mistakes and He never does anything that is wrong. He is also in complete control over all of His creation. Because He is holy, that means that everything that happens has happened according to His perfect plan. Free will comes into play here but the main thing we need to understand is that what God does is perfect.

Our response to God's holiness is to respect Him and His ways. To show respect is to indicate through our actions that we believe that what

God has done or is doing is right. This can be hard when our circumstances are unfavorable but those are the times when we need to do it the most. Because God's ways are perfect we need to behave as if we believe that what God has allowed in our lives are the perfect circumstances to accomplish His plan. When we try to take the matter into our own hands we are being disrespectful of God. We need to trust God and believe that what is going on is for His purposes. Trust in Him and respect His ways. Jesus, teach us to love and respect you.

SEPTEMBER 15
Read: Isaiah 19:1 – 21:17, Galatians 2:1-16, Psalm 59:1-17, Proverbs 23:13-14

ISAIAH 19:13

The wise men from Zoan are fools, and those from Memphis are deluded. The leaders of Egypt have ruined the land with their foolish counsel.

Isaiah is prophesying about Egypt. Egypt as a nation had been one of the richest and most powerful nations in the world. Few nations could compare to the things that they had accomplished. One of the things that they prided themselves on was their wisdom. They did have a lot to be proud of. Things like the pyramids are still marvels of engineering and construction. But with all of their great accomplishments, they confused intelligence for wisdom.

Wisdom is a very precious thing. The Bible teaches us that we should search it out like we would gold or precious stones. Where we go to look will determine how successful we are at finding wisdom. If we go to the wrong source what we may find is knowledge but knowledge alone is not enough to produce wisdom. In fact, history has proven countless times that knowledge by itself will usually lead to foolish decisions.

There is only one source of wisdom and that is God. He is the source of both wisdom and knowledge. Amazingly we will gladly receive knowledge from Him and then reject wisdom from Him. That is the height of foolishness. It is sad when someone is foolish due to ignorance. But it can be disastrous when someone claiming to be wise makes foolish decisions.

The leaders of Egypt sought wisdom from every source they could find. They relied heavily upon "wise" men to counsel them and to make their decisions. Often these men would be the descendants of men that had proven themselves wise in the past. This became a position of great influence and people desired the position not because they wanted to share the wisdom they had but because they wanted the power that came with the position.

The Bible teaches us to get the counsel of others before we make decisions. As leaders in God's families, ministries, and churches we must be looking to the right source of that counsel. Wisdom comes from God and so we need to be seeking people that have a relationship with God for our counsel. Seeking counsel from ungodly sources can be disastrous. While the secular world has an incredible wealth of knowledge, we must not let that replace the counsel of God's word and those of God that have been given the gift of wisdom.

The world seeks counsel from people that they hope are wiser than they are. But no matter how "wise" someone in the world is, they cannot know the mind of God. And without knowing the mind of God, the "wisest" of counselors may lead you to do the opposite of what God would tell you to do, and that would be disastrous. Jesus, teach us to seek You where we can find all wisdom and knowledge.

SEPTEMBER 16

Read: Isaiah 22:1 – 24:23, Galatians 2:17 – 3:9, Psalm 60:1-12, Proverbs 23:15-16

ISAIAH 24:14

But all who are left will shout and sing for joy. Those in the west will praise the LORD'S majesty.

Many of Isaiah's prophecies are terrible and depressing. You can easily come away with a view of God that is dark and angry. But to do that would be to miss the whole point of the book of Isaiah and most of the Old Testament. As we read the Old Testament and especially books like Isaiah we must keep in mind that God is love. Everything that He does is motivated by an infinite love. That love is directed at His special creation; man.

Anything that separates God from the object of His love is apt to receive His anger and judgment. When sin entered the world through Adam, mankind was separated from its loving creator and God. Through Christ's work on the cross, a bridge has been built that allows sinful man to get back into fellowship with the Father.

Many people choose not to cross over that bridge and would rather stay in their fallen state as an enemy of God. Despite everything that God has done for them and His numerous attempts to woo them back through the work of the Holy Spirit, they choose to stay in their sins. Because of His righteousness, God must judge sin. But His motivation never changes; He punishes us because of His incredible love for us.

When we come back to God like the people in the text today, there is a joy that is difficult to explain. Even though we have experienced God's punishment, we can sense His unending love for us and we burst forth with shouts of joy and in songs of praise. When any of God's people get a sense of that love and His grace, the response will always be rejoicing and praise.

It is an amazing thing that people can praise God in the midst of serious trials and tribulations. Despite attacks and struggles, God's children can know a peace and a joy that the world has no way to understand. When we recognize the perfect faithfulness of God, we are brought to a place where worship springs forth spontaneously. I was reminded of this recently as we were studying about the Triumphal Entry of Jesus into Jerusalem. The people burst forth with praise and worship. When challenged about that Jesus said if they didn't cry out that the very stones of the road would.

Even in the midst of the judgments of God there are going to be those that have the awareness of God's presence, grace, and mercy to praise and worship Him. We need but to look about and look for Him and there He will be. Our response should then be to shout for joy and sing praises to His name. If we don't someone or something else will and we will lose the blessing that was intended for us. I don't want any of my blessings to be given to anyone else and I especially don't want to see them being given to rocks. Jesus, give the eyes to see You in the midst of the battles and to sing praises to Your name.

SEPTEMBER 17

Read: Isaiah 25:1 – 28:13, Galatians 3:10-22, Psalm 61:1-8, Proverbs 23:17-18

ISAIAH 26:12

LORD, you will grant us peace, for all we have accomplished is really from you.

O ur verse for the day is found in a song of praise and thanksgiving for God's salvation. A day is coming in which the nation of Israel will sing this song because God has restored them to their place as His special people. Until that day this song is a testimony of what God has done for all those that have turned to Him for salvation through His Son Jesus Christ.

The verse for the day says that God will grant us peace. Too often we look to other people or things to find peace in our lives. The only true source of peace is God. The only way to achieve true peace in your life is to look to Jesus and trust in Him alone. The only kind of peace that the things of the world can provide is weak and temporary compared to the peace that God provides. In Philippians we are told that there is a peace that surpasses understanding; that is the peace of God.

One of the evidences of your relationship with God is peace; it is one of the fruits of the Holy Spirit. When we are at peace with God, He produces peace in our lives. This is the time that we need to be the most careful as Christians, when we have peace in our lives. For some reason when we have peace in our lives we tend to take our eyes off God and start to focus on ourselves. We can even begin to take credit for creating the peace in our lives.

We need to do as Isaiah suggests; we need to recognize how it is that we have accomplished all that we have. Everything that we have and everything we have done has been done by God. Any success that we have is a result of God working in our lives. Any things that we have acquired are a result of His blessing our lives. Any skills or abilities that we have are a result of His empowering us to do what He wants us to do.

To achieve and maintain peace in our lives, we need to fully embrace the knowledge that without God we are nothing and can do nothing. This goes against our sinful tendencies and against what the world teaches us to believe. It requires that we humble our hearts before the LORD and acknowledge that He is Master of everything in our lives.

There would be so much more peace and success in our lives if we would just surrender to this truth and stop trying to find peace and success through the world. It is also a truth that the further that we surrender to this truth, the more peace and success we experience in our lives. In my own life, marriage, family, and church I am trying desperately to daily achieve new levels of surrender in all those areas I might experience new levels of peace and success. God is looking to bless His people; all we have to do is let Him by surrendering to the truth that He is God. Jesus, thank you for all that You do for us every day.

SEPTEMBER 18

Read: Isaiah 28:14 – 30:11, Galatians 3:23 – 4:31, Psalm 62:1-12, Proverbs 23:19-21

GALATIANS 3:28

There is no longer Jew or Gentile, slave or free, male or female. For you are all Christians – you are one in Christ Jesus.

It is interesting how easily we label people and develop pre-conceived notions about them and the way that they are. We label people based on their race, religion, national origin, profession, and endless other things. Once we have placed a label on someone it has an effect on the way that we think about them and act toward them. In our verse for the day the Apostle Paul is teaching us that there is only one label that matters; that is the label of Christian.

Not only is it the only one that matters it is the only one that we should use in relation to other Christians. When we look at and interact with other Christians it ought to be regardless of who they are and what other labels the world might place on them. This can be very difficult because our natural man is all about labels and trying to determine where we fit in with others. Without even thinking about it we want to know if we are esteemed higher than someone else around us. This is one of the main reasons why we label people.

Jesus taught a new way to look at people; in comparison to Himself. If you look at the three comparisons that Paul refers to in our verse for the day you will notice that these are comparisons that have dramatic differences. Especially in Paul's day the gap in between each of these three groups socially and economically was great. Even between men and women there was a great divide of social and economic difference as women were often treated like property.

Paul tells us in our verse that we are all one in Christ and that there is no longer this great divide. When Jesus died on the cross He not only destroyed the separation between God and man but He also destroyed the division between man and other men. This is especially important to those that lead families, ministries, and churches. We must be so careful not to judge people based on the natural titles the world would give them. Only one title matters and that is whether or not they are a Christian. That title is the one that should determine your behavior toward them.

We must do everything in our power to prevent other titles influencing our behavior towards the people that we are called to lead. Titles like rich or poor, president or janitor, salesman or hippie must be ignored and treated as things of the world. If they are Christians treat them as one in Christ. If they are not Christians treat them as someone that needs to know Jesus. You will find this difficult to do and the people will struggle with understanding it but it is worth the effort. Jesus wants us all to be in unity in our faith and one of the ways that we get there is by doing our part to break down the barriers that separate us from other people. Jesus, teach us to treat every Christian as a child of God.

SEPTEMBER 19

Read: Isaiah 30:12 – 33:9, Galatians 5:1-12, Psalm 63:1-11, Proverbs 23:22

ISAIAH 31:7

I know the glorious day will come when every one of you will throw away the gold idols and silver images that your sinful hands have made.

God can foresee a day when we will choose to throw away all of the idols that we have made. Most people that read this will probably say that they don't have any idols in their lives to throw away. There might actually be some that don't, but probably not. Most people probably have more idols in their lives than they are even aware of. Anything that takes any place in your life that Jesus should have is an idol and God is not happy about it. But God knows that some day we will throw them all away and our worship of Him will be pure and undefiled.

In our verse for the day we are told that gold idols and silver images were made by our own hands. These things that we are worshipping were made by our hands. To worship something is to give it some power to control and provide for your life. I don't think we understand just how foolish it is to think that something that we made with our own hands can take care of us or provide for us. We will sometimes give control of our lives to something that has no power other than what we have given it.

Not only did we make these things with our hands but we made them with our sinful hands. That means that the things that we can make with our own hands can be no more holy or righteous than we are. The things that we make with our own hands can have no more power than we do. Something that is imperfect cannot make something that is perfect. The only way that we can make anything with our hands that is of any value in our lives or the lives of others is to remove the idols of gold and silver from our lives and let Jesus take His rightful place in our hearts.

To throw these idols away we might need to literally remove things from our lives that distract us from God. That is not what is required if you can simply eliminate its importance from your life. It has to be okay with you if God wanted to remove it; your relationship with Him should be the most important thing to you. It must be more important to you than the things you have or your position or fame or any such thing. If Jesus is the most important thing in your life then there is nothing that God will deny you. It is when our things possess us that we become entangled in them and our sinful hands fashion them into idols for our worship.

God can see a day when each of us will throw away our idols and worship Him the way that we should. Today we should be striving towards achieving that level of worship by systematically asking God to reveal in our lives anything that hinders our walk with Him and then taking radical steps to discard them from our lives. Jesus, help us to take out the trash.

SEPTEMBER 20

Read: Isaiah 33:10 – 36:22, Galatians 5:13-26, Psalm 64:1-10, Proverbs 23:23

ISAIAH 35:3

With this news, strengthen those who have tired hands, and encourage those who have weak knees.

In this chapter of Isaiah, the prophet, speaks about the future glory of Zion. God has a special plan and blessing for the nation of Israel and its capital Jerusalem that at some future date will be made to be glorious again. But what does that have to do with us? These promises are specific for the nation of Israel and those that are not of Israel will not partake of them. They give the nation of Israel hope of a future salvation and the abundant blessings of God.

We, as Christians, also have the hope of salvation and promises of blessing. We have the hope of eternal life and the blessings of an abundant life while we wait for His return. We also have the gospel message that promises, to anyone that will receive it, the same things for them. Jesus Christ came that everyone would not have to be eternally separated from God. God gave us this good news to share with others.

Our verse for the day tells us how that good news can help others. First we are told that this good news will strengthen those who have tired hands. This speaks of the things that we do with our lives. People all around us are tired. They are tired because they are doing everything they can to get by in this world. The problem is that they are trying to do it without God or without His help. It is possible for us to do that for a while but there comes a time when we all get tired. We must surrender our will to God and let Him do for us what we can't do. We need to stop trying so hard and start letting God be God in our lives. Part of the abundant life that Jesus promised is rest from our labors.

Second, we are told that this good news will encourage those that have weak knees. The word "encourage" means "to fill with courage." This world does a great job of creating fear in the minds and hearts of people. When we are afraid of what the world thinks or what it might do or what could happen we are showing a lack of faith in the God that is in complete control over everything. If we will just get to know the good news as it is revealed in God's Word, it will cast out all fear.

What we do and what we think are the ways that God is revealed to the world around us. The good news of Jesus Christ is given so that we can have strength and be fearless. The good news is also given to us so that we can share it with others because they are weak and afraid. To not share the good news with others is to deprive them of hope and peace. Some day all of us will stand before God and give account for how we shared the good news with others. The gospel of Jesus Christ is a precious gift that is more valuable when you give it away. That doesn't mean that you need to preach at them; just love God and love others, God will do the rest. Jesus, teach us to be generous givers of the precious gift of Your good news.

SEPTEMBER 21

Read: Isaiah 37:1 – 38:22, Galatians 6:1-18, Psalm 65:1-13, Proverbs 23:24

ISAIAH 37:4

But perhaps the LORD your God has heard the Assyrian representative defying the living God and will punish him for his words. Oh, pray for those of us who are left!

Isaiah is relating in our reading for today about the time that the king of Assyria came to attack Israel. He sent a representative to Jerusalem to let King Hezekiah know that he was coming and that surrender was their only option. In his message he spoke boastfully about his prior conflicts and said that Israel's God was no match for his gods. Hezekiah's response is to go to the temple and cry out to the LORD for help.

What caught my attention in today's verse was the word "perhaps." With a casual reading of the verse you might think that Hezekiah is saying, "maybe God will hear him." I don't believe that is the correct interpretation. God hears everything; nothing escapes his gaze or ears. There is no question that the LORD heard the boastful words of the Assyrian representative. The word "perhaps" would be better placed with God's possible response to the representative. I believe that what is being said here is, "perhaps God will punish him for his words."

That is where we sometimes struggle with God. Our sense of justice expects God to punish evildoers quickly and decisively. This is especially true when we are truly doing our best to be right with God and do the right things with those around us. We feel that in our righteousness that God should act immediately to defend His name and our cause.

In His sovereignty, he doesn't always do that. Sometimes He does nothing, at least from our perspective. But then that is our problem. We can only see what God is doing from our perspective. God's ways are so far above our ways! Our perspective is limited by our limitations as humans. Only God can see everything, everywhere, and at all times.

From our limited perspective we expect God to work in a certain way within our circumstances. Perhaps He will but there is also a chance that He won't. He is always at work and in control of all situations and circumstances and His way of dealing with your particular circumstance might be radically different than what you might want or expect.

It wasn't long after this that the angel of the LORD descended upon the camp of the Assyrians and killed 185,000 in the night. The king took his army and left Israel and was soon after killed by two of his sons. We get no word in Scripture about what happened to the representative. That means that it is not important for us to know what happened to him. God did what he wanted to do and that should be enough for us.

Trust God to act on your behalf within your circumstances. And trust God enough to not be concerned about how He intends to do it or about the results. Those are all His responsibilities. Jesus, help us to pray and then leave it for You to handle.

SEPTEMBER 22

Read: Isaiah 39:1 – 41:16, Ephesians 1:1-23, Psalm 66:1-20, Proverbs 23:25-28

PSALM 66:18

If I had not confessed the sin in my heart, my LORD would not have listened.

In our verse for the day, King David touches on one of the most important things that we can do to have a successful Christian life, ministry, or church; confess our sins before God. In fact, David also tells us that there is a cost to our resisting this work going on in our hearts; God will not listen to our prayers. I don't know about you but I know that I want God to be listening to my prayers because that is the only way that they can get answered.

David also wrote that the heart is deceitful and wicked and that the only person that truly knows our hearts is God. We don't even know the true state of our hearts. We might look at our hearts and see that everything is OK, but then have our prayers go unanswered. I just heard a recording of Alan Redpath where he stated that repentance is a forgotten art in the church and it shows in the church's lack of power and impact on the world.

Repentance and prayer are two sides of the same coin. Repentance places us into the forgiveness, grace, and mercy of God and permits us to enter into His presence and petition Him for anything and everything in our lives. It is through prayer that the "dunamis," supernatural, miraculous power of God is released into the world. God chooses to release that power through repentant hearts.

As children of God that truly seek to see God work powerfully in our families, ministries, and churches we must begin by asking God to search our hearts and reveal any wickedness that He finds there. We can't do that without the Holy Spirit actively at work in our hearts. This takes humility and a sincere desire to draw nearer to God. If we will allow Him to do it, the Holy Spirit will reveal the sins that dwell in all of our hearts. We have but to confess those sins as He reveals them to us and then we are free to pray without any concern about our prayers bouncing off the ceiling.

God invites us to come into His Almighty presence and ask anything that we want or need. The Bible teaches that God is able to give to us more than we could ever ask or even think of. The Bible also teaches that God will give us the desires of our hearts. But all of that is only available to the person whose heart is open and tender to the Holy Spirit. As we allow the Holy Spirit to do His work in our heart, He takes away the wicked desires of our heart and replaces them with good desires that are pleasing to God. God then joyfully gives us those things that our hearts desire. The vast storehouse of God's good blessings is opened up to the person that quickly confesses and repents of the sins that the Holy Spirit reveals. Jesus, help us to have soft and humble hearts before You.

SEPTEMBER 23

Read: Isaiah 41:17 – 43:13, Ephesians 2:1-22, Psalm 67:1-7, Proverbs 23:29-35

ISAIAH 42:20

You see and understand what is right but refuse to act upon it. You hear, but you don't really listen.

The prophet Isaiah is speaking a prophecy against the nation of Israel. The LORD spoke through Isaiah to tell them in no uncertain terms that He did not approve of their continued rejection of Almighty God as their God. They persisted in turning to worthless idols rather than to the One True God.

Often as we read texts such as this one today, we can't relate to how it might apply to us. What does Israel's turning from the LORD to idols have to do with modern-day Christians? Quite a bit more than you might think! Not much has changed in the last 2,500 years as it relates to the way people respond to God. We may not be Jews, God's Chosen People, but we are God's children. As such we do many of the same things that the Jews did. Many of the warnings and exhortations to the Jews apply directly to the 21st Century Christian.

Today's verse tells us that the Jews were guilty of not paying attention to God. They knew about Him but they did not listen to Him or do what He told them to do. They had the Law given to them by Moses to teach them how to live with God in fellowship and communion. They had the prophets to help them understand the world around them and to point them back to God whenever they wandered away from Him.

Even though this verse was written more than two thousand years ago it could easily be spoken to many of the Christians that sit in churches today. For years they have heard the truth about God and how He wants to work in our lives. Sermon after sermon has described to them the life that Jesus died to give them. Message after message has instructed them in the pathway to the abundant life that Jesus promised to His people. And just like the Hebrews of Isaiah's time they refuse to act upon what they know.

This was very frustrating to Isaiah. He knew that the Jews were headed for disaster because they refused to do what God wanted them to do; because they refused to go where He wanted them to go. As a pastor, I can feel that same frustration as I preach week after week knowing that many people are there because a sense of obligation and not so they can know Christ.

Going to church is meaningless if you are not going to meet with Jesus. Showing up on Sunday will not please God if you do not come with a heart to please God in your worship. Attending services is a waste of time if you have no desire to serve God. God has no interest in people filling churches; He wants churches filled with people that are coming to be filled with His Spirit. Don't come so that you can say you did; come so that you can do what He tells you to do. Jesus, give us Your heart of obedience.

SEPTEMBER 24

Read: Isaiah 43:14 – 45:10, Ephesians 3:1-21, Psalm 68:1-18, Proverbs 24:1-2

EPHESIANS 3:2

As you already know, God has given me this special ministry of announcing his favor to you Gentiles.

Paul, writing while he was imprisoned in Rome, writes to share with the church in Ephesus of the riches that they have in Jesus Christ. The church in Ephesus was founded by Paul and was comprised almost exclusively of Gentiles. In our verse for the day Paul lets them know that this was part of the "special ministry" that God had given him; to preach the gospel to the Gentiles. Paul describes this ministry as that of announcing God's favor to the Gentiles. It was because of Paul's special ministry that the Gentiles first heard that they were to receive an equal share in the Kingdom of God.

Our verse also tells us that this "special ministry" was given to Paul by God. Paul would never have asked for this assignment. Paul was previously called Saul. He was a devout Jew and believed as most Jews did that the Gentiles were beyond saving. Paul's special ministry took him someplace that was beyond where he was comfortable; to a place where he needed to depend upon God.

God would also like to give to each of us a "special ministry;" a ministry that is beyond your normal area of comfort and influence. God created you for a very specific purpose to fulfill a special mission and ministry that was appointed to you. All of us have purposes that revolve around areas of our lives. We have ministries to our spouses and families. We have ministries at work and in our neighborhoods and with our friends. But each of us also has a "special ministry" that is very unique to the way that God created us. That "special ministry" might be used in some of those previously mentioned areas but more than likely God wants you to take it out of where you are comfortable to use it.

Our "special ministry" is one that God will use to spread the gospel beyond where it reaches today. This doesn't necessarily mean that you are going to go to the ends of the earth and share the gospel with the "Gentiles" of the world but there is a unique way that God would use you to spread His saving gospel to those that need it. In fact, your special ministry may have nothing at all to do with talking to anyone about Christ; it may have to do with supporting others that do.

It is up to each of us to determine what the "special ministry" is that God has appointed to us. We do that through the Bible, prayer, and the leading of the Holy Spirit. As you seek the LORD in this He will speak to your heart and give you a passion for something. Then God would have you begin to explore just how that "special ministry" would be carried out. Speak to your pastor and he can help you to discover your "special ministry." Don't stop searching until you know you have found it; then watch the amazing things that God will do in your life. Jesus, lead us to our "special ministry."

SEPTEMBER 25
Read: Isaiah 45:11 – 48:11, Ephesians 4:1-16, Psalm 68:15-35, Proverbs 24:3-4

ISAIAH 47:6
For I was angry with my chosen people and began their punishment by letting them fall into your hands. But you, Babylon, showed them no mercy. You have forced even the elderly to carry heavy burdens.

The LORD gives Isaiah another prophecy against the nation of Babylon. This verse is rich in spiritual application. God was angry because the nation of Israel rejected Him, their God and Savior to chase after false idols. God is displeased when we choose anything or anyone over Him. After all He has done for us, He expects us to worship only Him. If we refuse, we should expect to experience His displeasure.

This verse also tells us that God punishes His people when they are disobedient or rebellious. We like to believe that God only punishes "bad people." Compared to God, we are all bad people and deserve far more punishment that we get. It is God's incredible mercy that keeps Him from giving us all the punishment we deserve. We also learn that God punishes the nations that mistreat His people. Over and over prophets of God spoke of the destruction of the nation of Babylon. The nation of Babylon was destroyed just as the LORD predicted. Babylon also represents the evil world system that we see today and includes all false religion. The book of Revelation speaks of the ultimate fate of this world system; total destruction.

What was of particular interest to me was that God told the nation of Babylon that he had began the punishment of His people by allowing them to fall into the hands of their enemies, the Babylonians. God is saying clearly that the reason why Babylon was able to defeat the Jews was because God allowed them to be defeated. God had withdrawn His hand of protection from His Chosen People.

There is a tremendous lesson in that for all of us whenever we find ourselves in the hands of our enemies; God has allowed them to prevail over us. Any time the enemy has victory in our lives we must understand that it was allowed by the LORD. Until the LORD withdraws His protective hand from us, it is impossible for the enemy to prevail in our lives. Our enemy can take no ground that the LORD hasn't given him permission to take.

Israel was being punished for disobedience and rebellion. That is one of the primary reasons why God withdraws His hand of protection but it is not the only reason. Sometimes He will allow an enemy to gain ground so that we will draw nearer to the LORD and grow in our faith. It may also be to prove our faith.

Our response should be the same regardless of why we think the enemy is prevailing; run to the LORD and humbly seek His presence more fully. Do all that you can to obey God completely and trust Him with your whole being. Ultimately your enemy cannot prevail against you if you will seek God in this way. God always protects His faithful people. Jesus, help us to run to You whenever we see the enemy on our borders.

SEPTEMBER 26

Read: Isaiah 48:12 – 50:11, Ephesians 4:17-32, Psalm 69:1-18, Proverbs 24:5-6

Don't let those who trust in you stumble because of me, O Sovereign LORD Almighty. Don't let me cause them to be humiliated, O God of Israel.

David was a king of great power and ability. He had done amazing things while king of Israel. But he was also a humble king. He recognized his weaknesses and wasn't afraid to confront his sins and unrighteousness. It was this that earned him the title of: A man after God's own heart. And here in our verse for the day we see another example of a heart that seeks to be like God's heart.

David's prayer here is that he not be the cause of any that follow him from falling away from the LORD. David is concerned that his own foolishness and sins might be the cause of someone else stumbling and falling. And he has good cause to be concerned about that. After David's son Solomon dies we will see a whole series of kings that do what is evil in the sight of the LORD and they lead the people of Israel to follow them into sin.

As a leader, you have the ability to influence people toward God or away from God. And it doesn't matter what you are leading; your family, in your neighborhood, at your workplace, a ministry, or a church. As a leader at any level or place you will be influencing people, that's what leaders do. And your heart should burn like David's did to lead well.

Knowing that your actions, attitudes, behaviors, sins, or foolishness could be the stumbling block that prevents someone from coming to Jesus should cause pain to your heart. It should create within you a passion to control your members so that the only thing that anyone around you sees in you is Jesus.

Knowing that you are leading others which means that they are following you to where you are going should give you a burden to always be checking your compass to make sure that you are headed toward Jesus. If God has called you to lead He expects you to lead people to His Son.

All of us have the responsibility to lead people to Jesus. Our lives should be living signposts directing people to the Savior of our souls. And with that responsibility should come the awareness that our lives can also lead people away from Christ.

To be a leader is to bear a burden that is impossible to carry. But if we are doing it in the power of the Holy Spirit and leading people toward Jesus, then it is also one of the greatest joys that you will experience on this earth. Jesus, help me to look back and see who is following me and help me to look forward and make sure that I am leading them to You.

SEPTEMBER 27

Read: Isaiah 51:1 – 53:12, Ephesians 5:1-33, Psalm 69:19-36, Proverbs 24:7

EPHESIANS 5:17

Don't act thoughtlessly, but try to understand what the LORD wants you to do.

In today's verse Paul is giving an admonition to the church in Ephesus about the way that they think. It is great instruction for us as well today as it was nearly two thousand years ago. Paul begins be telling us not to act thoughtlessly. Sadly this is how most people live a good percentage of their lives; they don't think about the things that they do or the consequences of their actions. People will usually do what feels good or satisfies some natural desire. It is God's desire that we think about everything that we do in our lives. He would like us to compare the things that we are thinking about to the filter of His Word. If we would do that more often we would find ourselves making much fewer mistakes than we normally do.

Paul then goes on to instruct the Ephesians and us to "try to understand what the LORD wants you to do." The thing that struck me about this verse is the words "try to understand." To me this says that what Jesus wants us to do is understandable; we can know it and understand it. This is important because one of the things that we should understand about our relationship to God is that He expects us to do what He wants us to do. And because God expects us to do things obediently, it is reasonable to expect that we can know and understand what those things are.

The whole point is that it is not going to be a natural understanding. You are not going to just wake up in the morning and know what it is that the LORD is asking you to do. That is where the relationship becomes so important; it is through our relationship with Christ that we come to understand what Christ wants us to do. As we draw nearer and nearer to Christ in our daily walk with Him we become increasingly aware of what it is that He wants us to do. That is the "try" part of the equation. You must try to get closer to Christ in your daily activities and actions.

There are lots of obvious ways that we can do that. The first is the Bible; if you want a good idea what it is that God wants you to do, read the Bible. The next obvious one is prayer. Prayer is the channel of communication that allows God to speak to our hearts about what it is that He wants us to do. Less obvious might be fellowship; being around other believers is another way that you can try to understand what Jesus wants you to do.

One of the best ways to try to understand what Jesus wants you to do is to read your Bible daily, develop a consistent prayer life where you are listening for His voice, then getting together with other Christians. Then start doing something; it doesn't matter what you do, just do something. If it is not what Christ wants you to do, He will let you know that either directly or through your pastors or leaders. You need to keep trying to understand until you do understand. Jesus, help us to keep trying.

SEPTEMBER 28

Read: Isaiah 54:1 – 57:14, Ephesians 6:1-24, Psalm 70:1-5, Proverbs 24:8

ISAIAH 55:8

"My thoughts are completely different from yours," says the LORD. "And my ways are far beyond anything you could imagine.

God doesn't think like we do. There is no way that our minds can think like God's can. All of human intelligence combined does not impress God because He is far beyond the best that man will ever be. Many people live out their lives trying to prove how smart they are compared to other people. One glimpse of the mind of God would let them know that they don't know that much.

As we go through this life, we need to keep this truth in our hearts. There will be times when we don't understand what is going in our lives. There will be times when things are not going the way that we planned them. Some of these times we will be struggling just to keep our heads above water. It is at these times that we must understand that God's mind is so much greater than ours.

One of the other attributes about God's mind that comforts me is that he is outside of time. He does not view time as one day after another. God sees time like we would look at a picture. He can look anywhere in time that He chooses. It is also stated that He can see all of it at once. Our finite, temporal minds cannot fathom that; it is way beyond us.

The Bible also teaches that God thinks about me a lot. He thought about me before time. He thought about me before I was born. He thought about me while I was in my mother's womb. He thinks about me now. He also has a plan for my life in the future. God's thoughts of me are too great for me to count.

Put all that together with the fact that God loves me with an infinite, never-ending love and I am filled with a great sense of awe and peace. God knows me and loves me. God knows everything that is going on in and around my life. God knows how it is all going to turn out and how things are going to turn out for me. What an incredible thing that is to know. I don't need to know what God knows to know that God knows what is best for me.

Trusting God means that we don't need an answer to the "Why" questions of our life. We might ask them because we can't understand our God's thoughts and ways but we don't need Him to answer them. I am so thankful that God's ways are far above my ways. I want a God that can handle all of those things that are going to come into my life that I can't understand. Only a God bigger, smarter, and stronger than me or anything that this world can throw at me is big enough for me. Jesus, thank you for being a big God!

SEPTEMBER 29

Read: Isaiah 57:15 – 59:21, Philippians 1:1-26, Psalm 71:1-24, Proverbs 24:9-10

ISAIAH 58:2

Yet they act so pious! They come to the Temple every day and seem delighted to hear my laws. You would almost think this was a righteous nation that would never abandon its God. They love to make a show of coming to me and asking me to take action on their behalf.

Isaiah is speaking out against those people that were acting like they believed God. Their worship was not true worship. They were just putting on a show so that others would see them as very spiritual people. Sadly, some of them probably thought that was what God wanted from them.

The people in the church today are no different than the people 2,700 years ago in Isaiah's time. There are still great numbers of people that worship God in a way that is false worship. Their worship is all about what they do and not what God wants. They are putting on a show that will not save them. They come to church and even give the impression that they are growing and maturing from the teaching of the Word.

As leaders of families, ministries, or churches we must be very watchful for people like this. Often these sorts of people will be coming to you looking for a position of leadership because it helps with their act. And some of them come with great gifts, abilities, and resources. The problem is that their motives are all wrong and they are likely to do more harm than good.

As leaders, especially if we are involved in starting a new ministry or church, we must be very watchful for this. God does not look at the outward man and neither should we. If someone comes into your ministry or church that is too good to be true; be careful, they might be! The Bible teaches that we should test those that desire to be in a position of leadership.

The idea of testing is similar to what is done to verify the purity of precious metals. There are tests that prove that the metal is pure. A true servant does not mind being tested. Someone that has a wrong heart or is a false worshipper will object and probably resist or refuse to being tested. That is proving the purity of their heart.

Only God knows the condition of someone's heart. We must be very careful not to judge anyone's heart. But we can test them and we can look for the fruit of their lives. A great test for this is to put that person in a position of humility; a place of service where they are not the leader or the center of attention. A true servant will serve and wait for the LORD to open the doors to allow them to serve where their gifts, abilities, and resources can be used to their fullest. Do not be quick to place someone in a position of leadership just because they look perfect; it could be an act. Jesus, help us to patiently wait for you to reveal to us where you want to place people in service to You in Your church.

SEPTEMBER 30

Read: Isaiah 60:1 – 62:5, Philippians 1:27 – 2:18, Psalm 72:1-20, Proverbs 24:11-12

ISAIAH 62:1

Because I love Zion, because my heart yearns for Jerusalem, I cannot remain silent. I will not stop praying for her until her righteousness shines like the dawn, and her salvation blazes like a burning torch.

Isaiah reveals his heart in today's verse. Throughout this book he has spoken prophecies against the nation of Israel and the city of Jerusalem. But it is not in his heart that he wants to see the things that he spoke about come to pass. He loves Israel and the city of Jerusalem. Because of that love Isaiah feels compelled to speak out and to pray.

Isaiah's goal is not to condemn the nation of Israel or any other nation for that matter, but to warn them away from the danger that they are heading toward. God has given Isaiah visions of the future and told Isaiah to tell the people what he has seen. God doesn't want to destroy anyone and so He warns them of the danger that they cannot see. It is God's desire that everyone would heed His warnings and respond in a way that takes away the need for judgment and punishment. Isaiah goes on to say that he is praying for Zion and Jerusalem. Even while he is speaking out judgments and warnings, he is praying. Prayer is one of the signs of a person that has the love of God in their hearts. Prayer aligns our heart to the heart of God and releases His power in the universe around us.

Isaiah is praying for two things in particular; righteousness and salvation. Righteousness is rightness with God. Isaiah wants the nation of Israel to be so right with God that their behavior lights up the whole world around them. That is precisely what results from righteousness with God. We usually think that righteousness is a very personal thing; it is all about me and my relationship with God. It is never that simple. Your righteousness is a tool that God uses to reveal Himself to other people through your life.

What does your life reveal about the nature, character, and abilities of God? What does your righteousness reveal about the holiness of God? What does your faith reveal about the faithfulness of God? You can be certain of one thing; your righteousness is revealing what you believe to be true of God. It was Isaiah's prayer that his people's righteousness would be so bright that it would rival the brightness of the dawning sun.

Isaiah was also praying for the salvation of Zion and Jerusalem. This was likely a literal salvation from her enemies. Isaiah was praying that God would rescue Zion and Jerusalem from her enemies. That salvation was to blaze like a torch. A torch brings light to the darkness. It is also a symbol of hope and guidance.

If you are reading this you are probably already saved. Your salvation should be a beacon for others, to draw them to salvation. Is your life guiding others to Christ? Can they see the hope of eternity in your eyes? They should! You remain on this earth to be a bright beacon in the darkness of this world to the lost and dying. Jesus, I pray that they will all let their light burn ever brighter.

OCTOBER

OCTOBER 1

Read: Isaiah 62:6 – 65:25, Philippians 2:19 – 3:3, Psalm 73:1-28, Proverbs 24:13-14

PHILIPPIANS 2:21

All the others care only for themselves and not for what matters to Jesus Christ.

Paul is planning on sending Timothy to the church that Paul started in the city of Philippi. Before he does he sends this letter to tell them a little bit about Timothy. It is difficult to say whether or not Timothy ever made it to Philippi but it is likely that he visited there on occasion. Timothy ended up in Ephesus where he was the pastor of its church for some time.

In the midst of the commendation of Timothy we find this negative comment. In some respects it seems out of character for Paul. We need to remember where Paul was when he wrote this letter to the Philippian church; a Roman prison. It is difficult to imagine what that must have been like for Paul to endure that captivity but I believe the behavior of those that professed to be Christians and his friends during this time was more grievous to Paul.

All the others are not named by Paul in this letter but as you read the other epistles you can get an idea of who some of them might be. These people obviously did not respond well to Paul while he was in prison. Paul might have been a little frustrated when he made this comment and allowed that frustration to be vented here in this letter.

Within this verse we also see something that as leaders we need always to remember about people; sometimes they act like sinners. While Paul is suffering in prison he is also doing his best to minister to all the churches that he was involved with. He was also reaching out to everyone that he could in Rome. Paul was working hard even though he was in this very difficult circumstance of life.

Few people will look at life the same way that you do. God has given you a unique perspective on things around you. That perspective is shaped and molded by your experiences and circumstances. Others looking into your life are going to view things differently than you do. They will then need to make their own decisions based on their experiences and circumstances. And often those decisions are made based on their own desires as opposed to what God desires.

As we grow and mature in the Lord (which we should be doing daily) we will have more and more people around us that think more of themselves that what God desires. We should learn to expect it and prepare ourselves so that it doesn't unravel our own faith. There will also be people in our lives like Timothy was in Paul's life. Cherish those that God brings you that care more for what Christ wants than what they want. Encourage and exhort those that think of themselves but don't allow them to discourage or distract you from what God desires of you. Jesus, thank you for the Timothys in our lives.

OCTOBER 2

Read: Isaiah 66:1-24, Philippians 3:4-21, Psalm 74:1-23, Proverbs 24:15-16

ISAIAH 66:1

This is what the LORD says: "Heaven is my throne, and the earth is my footstool. Could you ever build me a temple as good as that? Could you build a dwelling place for me?"

In today's verse we see the immensity of God alluded to. Nothing can contain Him. No structure could ever be big enough for Him to live in. All of creation is not large enough for Him to dwell in. Even David said as he built the temple for God that it was inadequate to house God. It seems kind of foolish for us to think that we can build something for God but that is exactly what we do; especially when it comes to church buildings.

At some point as we lead ministries and churches our minds turn to buildings and other structures. We get it in our minds that we will build this beautiful edifice that will glorify God. I believe God would have us to look at buildings differently than that. A building is a tool; it is something we use as long as it is useful and then we replace it with another that is more useful.

If we would do that there would be much simpler church buildings constructed with a greater focus on use than upon looks. God doesn't care how big your building is or how beautiful it is if people aren't being drawn to His son within it. The purpose of the buildings that we build should be to help people get to know Jesus. You don't need a huge elaborate building to do that.

As Jesus was leaving the last time before He was crucified His disciples were pointing to how amazing the temple was and I can imagine Jesus shrugging His shoulders before He told them that soon this temple that they were so impressed with was going to be torn down. In Israel today you can still see where the stones of the temple were pushed off of the temple mount and created craters in the sidewalk around it.

No building that we build today is likely even to be around in 100 years. Don't build to impress God or men; it is a waste of time and the resources that God gave you to grow the kingdom. We should strive to build buildings that are pleasing but not extravagant. Our buildings should be simple and humble like our Lord was during His ministry upon the earth.

Build buildings that will build people in their relationship with Jesus. Anything else is likely to be arrogance and vanity. You can't build a building that will impress God so build one that will make it easier for people to draw near to Him. God is impressed by churches that reach the lost for Jesus Christ. Jesus, help us to see our buildings as tools that you want to use only as long as they are useful.

OCTOBER 3
Read: Jeremiah 1:1 – 2:30, Philippians 4:1-23, Psalm 75:1-10, Proverbs 24:17-20

Like a thief, Israel feels shame only when she gets caught. Kings, officials, priests, and prophets—all are alike in this.

God sends the prophet Jeremiah to Israel to warn her about the danger they are in. His desire is that they would turn back to the Lord so that He will not need to punish them for their disobedience and rebellion. Sadly, history tells us that they did not do that and God did have to punish them severely. Even then they did not turn back to Him as they should have.

One of the symptoms of a heart hardened toward God is the lack of shame over our sins. The fact that we can sin against God and others and it doesn't bother us is a sign of our depraved state and our rejection of God's place in our lives. In our verse for the day we see a very common trait in people; they were ashamed only when they got caught.

One of the things that really caught me about this verse was that it is directed at the leaders of the nation more than anyone else. Kings, officials, priests, and prophets are all accused in this verse of having hearts that are hardened toward God so that they do not feel shame over sin until they are caught. God is rebuking the leaders here because He knows the people are likely to do what they see their leaders doing.

As leaders of our families, ministries, or churches we need to avoid hardening our hearts toward God. Sin and rebellion in our hearts or lives ought to bring shame and sadness to us regardless if we are caught or not. God sees everything in our lives. It should shame us that God knows about our sins more than it does that other people know about our sins. When we do that we are proving to God that we don't love Him that much and that we don't esteem Him over other people.

As the leaders we ought to striving to soften our hearts. We should be praying daily that God would break down any hard spots that are developing. We should look into our hearts to examine them and determine if there is any sin or rebellion that we should be embarrassed about within our lives. There should be a daily process of examination, repentance, and forgiveness taking place in our lives. We need to allow the Holy Spirit to tenderize our hearts to the point that even the smallest of things contrary to God embarrass us and drive us to the cross for forgiveness.

If we do that as leaders, then we can stand before those we lead and encourage them to do the same thing. We can lead them to a higher place in their walk with Jesus Christ. We need to model the behaviors that God calls for from His children. The people that God has called to follow us will do what they see. Let's set a good example for them so that they can experience all the good things that God has for them. Jesus, teach us to follow You as we lead them.

And I will give you leaders after my own heart, who will guide you with knowledge and understanding.

Most of Jeremiah's prophecies were centered on the unfaithfulness of Judah and Israel and on God's faithfulness to them. As you read through the book of Jeremiah, you will see one prophecy after another beseeching the Israelites to return to their God and to forsake their worship of idols. The book is filled with descriptions of the curses that were going to befall the Israelites if they did not respond. It was also filled with promises of the blessings that God would pour out on them if they would repent from their disobedience.

One such promise is found here in our text for today. God promised to give them leaders that would be able to guide them. They already had leaders that were guiding them. Any leader, by the very nature of the fact that they are a leader guides those that they lead. The question is where they are leading them to. Throughout the books of Kings and Chronicles we see how the king influences the people either toward God or away from Him.

God's promise here in our text is that the leaders that He would provide would lead with knowledge and understanding. The knowledge that these leaders have is of God and of His plan for His people. This knowledge is God-breathed, meaning that we can seek after it, but God has to provide it. This is also true of understanding how to use the knowledge to move people toward God; it must come from God.

Our text for today gives what might be the single most important characteristic of a leader of God's people. Whether you are a leader of a family, Bible study, ministry, church, or corporation having this characteristic will enable you to be an effective leader. God told the Israelites that He would give them "leaders after my own heart."

This word "after" describes the active seeking or pursuing of something. God is telling the Israelites that these leaders would be actively seeking to know and understand the heart of God. And even more than that, they are actively working to conform their own heart into the same shape as that of God's.

As leaders it is not enough just to lead people; we must be leading them somewhere. And as leaders "set apart and appointed" from before the foundation of time to lead God's people, we must lead them to God. To do that our hearts must be soft and pliable so that the Master Craftsman can shape our hearts to look like His. We do that by seeking to know God in a deep and personal way and by seeking to understand His plan for His people. Jesus, change my heart to be like Yours.

OCTOBER 5

Read: Jeremiah 4:19 – 6:15, Colossians 1:18 – 2:7, Psalm 77:1-20, Proverbs 24:23-25

COLOSSIANS 1:29

I work very hard at this, as I depend on Christ's mighty power that works within me.

Paul is writing to the church that he started in Colosse. He is writing from prison in Rome. We should remind ourselves often as we read the prison epistles that these incredible books that bring great freedom and hope in our relationship with Christ were written by a man that was imprisoned for his faith in Jesus. Paul has just told the Colossians in the verse prior to our verse for the day that everywhere they go they tell everyone about Jesus. He also said that he warns them and teaches them and then explains why. It is Paul's great desire to present them to God having been perfected in their relationship to Christ. The word "perfect" carries with it the idea of complete maturity or full development.

Before Christ we are incomplete, lacking the spiritual life that God intended us to have from the beginning. The sin that entered the world through Adam infected us with a disease that makes us less than what we should be. This disease prevents us from growing spiritually into the people that God created us to be. Once we receive Christ the Holy Spirit takes up residence within our hearts and begins the process of leading us to spiritual maturity.

Paul is saying in our verse that He works very hard at this, warning and teaching others so that they can become spiritually mature. As leaders of God's people that is exactly what we are called to do as well. God wants us to work hard at getting the gospel of Jesus Christ out to others so that they can begin the process of becoming whole Christians; not lacking in anything.

What really strikes me about this verse is what Paul says at the end of it; he says that he depends on Christ's mighty power that works within him. In context this means that this power is what helps Paul to do the work that he is talking about. It is Paul's dependence upon Christ's mighty power that makes him able to tell people about Jesus and warn and teach them.

What I think some people forget as they are leading is that while they are working hard at doing these things for Jesus that they cannot neglect working hard at those things in their own lives. Too often we hear about influential pastors or ministry leaders that fall into some kind of sin. I believe that this usually happens because they have been neglecting their own mature relationship with Christ as they have been working hard at exhorting others about this issue. As leaders we must never neglect our own relationship with Christ. Jesus gave us the example as He was often separating Himself from the multitudes to pray and to be with the Father in fellowship. We also need to take the time we need to work hard at allowing the mighty power of Christ to mature our relationship with God. Jesus, remind us often to tend to our own garden.

OCTOBER 6
Read: Jeremiah 6:16 – 8:7, Colossians 2:8-23, Psalm 78:1-31, Proverbs 24:26

JEREMIAH 7:27

Tell them all this, but do not expect them to listen. Shout out your warnings, but do not expect them to respond.

It is difficult to imagine how difficult the ministry of Jeremiah must have been. It is reported that Jeremiah had no visible success within his time of ministry. Not a single person is believed to have responded to the ministry of this man of God. Here in our verse for the day the Lord tells Jeremiah that is exactly what is going to happen; no one will listen and no one will respond.

As a pastor, one of the great encouragements of my life is to see the ministry that I am doing result in the fruit of lives that are changed for God. There are times in my ministry that I wonder if I am having any impact at all in the world. God is always faithful at those times to send someone to me to remind me that God is working through me to reach His children.

Jeremiah lived in a time and place that the people's hearts were hard toward God. They didn't want to hear from God and they had no intention of responding to Him even if they did hear from Him. He was in the most difficult ministry of all; proclaiming the gospel to people that don't want to hear it and don't feel they need it.

Nothing has changed in the world in the last 2,500 years. There are still people that have no desire to hear from God. There are still people that want nothing to do with God or the things of God. Those people are all around us. Some might even be in your own family. They can even be in your church! What should we do with those people in our lives? The very same thing that Jeremiah was told to do; tell them what God wants them to know.

God would tell you the same thing He told Jeremiah, keep telling them the truth. They aren't going to listen and they aren't going to respond but you keep warning them and telling them the truth. We can never fully know the effect we are having on others. Even though it appears that they are not listening or responding, we can't know what is going on in their hearts. The seeds that we plant in their lives may take a long time to sprout and there may not be fruit until long after they are gone from our lives.

God is calling us to be faithful to Him and to the ministry that He has given us. Whether or not we get to see any fruit from that ministry is wholly up to God. We will be evaluated based on our obedience to God's call on our lives, not based on the fruit that we produce. The fruit is God's responsibility, obedience is ours. Jesus, help us to faithfully obey You regardless of the results that we see around us.

OCTOBER 7

Read: Jeremiah 8:8 – 9:26, Colossians 3:1-17, Psalm 78:32-55, Proverbs 24:27

JEREMIAH 8:11

They offer superficial treatments for my people's mortal wound. They give assurances of peace when all is war.

The prophet Jeremiah speaks this prophecy toward the scribes and priests of the nation of Israel. These were the men that were to be teaching the people how to fear and worship God and yet they were misleading them with false assurances. They were treating this mortal wound that they had with a band-aid. The mortal sin that the people were suffering from was idolatry. They had turned away from God and His ways and were following the ways of the wicked nations around them.

The image that I see in this is that the people have cancer and the scribes and priests are giving them aspirin to make them feel better. It might make them feel better but it is doing nothing to heal them of the disease that they have. To be healed they need dramatic, immediate, and strong action. God is warning them that they are close to death; if they don't do something soon it will be too late.

We still see a lot of this in the church. From the teaching to the counseling; people are being given aspirin when they need surgery or radiation. They are just given band-aids when they need amputation. People don't need to feel good, they need to see God. The only way that people can see God is if they deal with the cancer and other diseases that are ravaging their lives. They need to receive radical treatment so that they can be healed.

As leaders of families, ministries, and churches we need to be careful that we are not giving out band-aids and aspirin to our people. We should always, in love, be telling the people the truth about where they stand with God. Sometimes that means saying something that is hard and hurts deeply. Just as a surgeon is not afraid to cause pain to see healing take place in a patient's life, we should not be afraid to use the loving scalpel of truth to remove a soul-threatening disease from someone's life.

In fact, as leaders we will stand before God and give an accounting of how we have done that very thing. We might even try to justify our actions by saying that we didn't want to hurt them. But by our negligence we are allowing them to suffer more than a little pain that might draw them to healing.

This is where the Holy Spirit is so critical in our lives. We should strive to be gentle and meek with those that God has called us to lead. But there comes a time when we need to inflict the pain of truth strongly into a person's life. This is only possible if we are practiced at speaking the truth no matter what the circumstances. We should never hold the truth back from someone that needs to hear it. Their very soul may hang in the balance. Jesus, give us the words of truth to speak and the love to speak them.

OCTOBER 8

Read: Jeremiah 10:1 – 11:23, Colossians 3:18 – 4:18, Psalm 78:56-72, Proverbs 24:28-29

PSALM 78:72

He cared for them with a true heart and led them with skillful hands.

At the end of this psalm Asaph speaks about King David and how God chose him and used him. God called David out of the sheepfold to be the shepherd of the people of Israel. David was one of the greatest kings that Israel ever had and a study of his life can teach us a lot about how to lead the people that God has entrusted to us.

Here in our verse for the day we have two roles that David fulfilled and what was required for him to do it the way that he did. First it begins by saying that David cared for the people of Israel just as a shepherd would care for his flock. This speaks of love and sacrifice. To be an effective leader, you need to love those that you are called to lead. The flock is His and He loves the sheep; He also expects His shepherds to love them. To do that you need to have a true heart. That means that your heart is true to God and His purposes for your life and for the flock that He has entrusted to you. If your motives are wrong than you do not have a true heart and you can't care for your flock. A true heart lines up with God's Word and is obedient to Him.

Our verse goes on to tell us that David also led the people of Israel; God's flock. This one should seem obvious that God's leaders ought to lead the people that He has given them. The thing that may not be so obvious is that David did both leading and caring; both are necessary if we want to be leaders that excel in God's eyes.

Leading is about influencing people to move and change so that their lives line up with God's will and plan. As a leader we are called to follow Christ and influence others to follow Him also. One of most important things that you need to do to accomplish is the first we looked at; care for the flock. If you don't care for the flock it is not likely to follow you very far or very well. A well-cared for flock is much more likely to experience the fullness of its relationship with Christ than is one that is just being led from one place to the next.

To be a good leader is not something that most people can claim is natural. For most people leading is awkward and unnatural; even something to be feared and avoided. If God called you to lead, then you have nothing to fear and God won't let you avoid it easily. To be the shepherd of the flock that God has entrusted to you, you need to be developing the skills that are required to be successful. This doesn't mean that you depend upon yourself for the work but that you allow the Holy Spirit to prepare and equip in whatever is available. A true heart and skillful hands are required to care for and lead God's people. To get these we must make a deliberate decision to be the kind of shepherd that God desires. Jesus, teach us to love and lead Your flock.

OCTOBER 9
Read: Jeremiah 12:1 – 14:10, 1 Thessalonians 1:1 – 2:8, Psalm 79:1-13, Proverbs 24:30-34

JEREMIAH 12:5
Then the Lord replied to me, "If racing against mere men makes you tired, how will you race against horses? If you stumble and fall on open ground, what will you do in the thickets near the Jordan?"

Jeremiah has been whining and complaining to God about what he sees in the world around him. The wicked people seem to be prospering and don't seem to care about what God thinks about their evil behavior.

Jeremiah wants to see justice; He wants God to punish the wicked people around him.

Based on the Lord's response in our verse today we can deduce that Jeremiah was feeling like quitting his ministry for the Lord. He was experiencing what we commonly call "ministry burnout." Ministering to uncaring, rebellious people had left him tired and depressed. It is interesting to me that God doesn't encourage Jeremiah, but instead challenges him.

The Lord asks Jeremiah some questions that cause him to examine himself. It seems as though the Lord is telling Jeremiah that the things that he sees going on around him will in fact get worse than they are now. The Lord asks Jeremiah how he is going to do things in the future, if he is burned-out now. Ministry burn-out is a fact-of-life. At some point in your life in ministry it is going to get so hard that you just want to lie down and quit. You will be tired of ministering to people that are uncaring and rebellious. Or they will betray you and attack you or your character. The thought of another day of ministry will depress you.

Jeremiah was a prophet. His ministry was to relate to the nations around him the word of the Lord as it was given to him. Immediately after our verse for the day God gives Jeremiah more things to say to the nations. God gives him more work to do. There is no sense in the text that God gave Jeremiah any time to get over his burn-out. The prophet Jeremiah had taken his eyes off of the work that God had given him to do and he was looking at his circumstances. He was looking at the results of his labors rather than at the Lord of his labors. Any time we take our eyes off the Lord, we are eventually going to find ourselves tired and depressed. The only solution is to get your eyes back on the Lord and get back to the work that He gave you.

Ministry burn-out is a fact-of-life. This is true because we are weak creatures that are too often distracted away from our source of strength and endurance and we focus on the injustices of the world. If we keep our eyes on the Lord and obey Him implicitly, then we will not burn out in ministry. When you begin to feel tired and depressed, refocus on the Lord and ask Him to remind you of the work that he assigned to you. Jesus, help us to only do what You want us to do.

OCTOBER 10

Read: Jeremiah 14:11 – 16:15, 1 Thessalonians 2:9 – 3:13, Psalm 80:1-19, Proverbs 25:1-5

JEREMIAH 15:19

The LORD replied, "If you return to me, I will restore you so you can continue to serve me. If you speak words that are worthy, you will be my spokesman. You are to influence them; do not let them influence you!

Jeremiah has been complaining to God about how horrible his ministry is. Everyone is against him and hates him. No one has listened to Jeremiah's message and he is questioning why he is even doing it. Have you ever wondered what you were doing in ministry? Have you ever questioned God about what it is that you are doing for Him? Have you ever questioned God about how the ministry was going? That's precisely what Jeremiah is doing and God has a word for Jeremiah and for you; "return to Me."

When we are questioning God and complaining to Him, it is an indication that we have moved away from a total and complete dependence upon and trust in God. Our relationship with God must be based upon the fact that He is God and He gets to decide how my life and my ministry develop. It is not God's job to make me happy and fulfilled in life and ministry. It is my responsibility to stay so close to the Lord that I am filled with His joy and fulfilled by His presence.

Ministry can be very tough; especially if those that you have been called to minister to do not respond. Jeremiah was told three things that he needed to do. The first thing was to return to the Lord. When you sense the frustration that sometimes comes with life and ministry; run back to the presence of the Lord through prayer, His word, and fellowship with other believers. Respond quickly when you sense this happening. The longer you wait to run back to the Lord the harder it is to find your way back.

Second, God told Jeremiah to speak words that are worthy. When we are frustrated with our life and ministry it can come out in the words that we speak. We must tame our tongue and speak only words that edify the body and that bring glory and honor to the Lord. Only then can you be a spokesman for God.

Third, Jeremiah's role was to influence the people around him. He was not to allow them to influence him. Our faith, life, and ministry ought to be built upon the solid foundation of Jesus Christ. If it is, there should be nothing that can move us from that place. It doesn't matter what other people think or say about you; it only matters what God says about you. You are to influence the world around you and draw them to Jesus. There is an implication in this verse that it is imperative that we do these things. Otherwise, we will not be able to serve God. It is certain that if you are not clinging to God, speaking His truths, and avoiding the influences of the world that you will not be very effective at serving Him. Life and ministry can be tough; don't forget to let God do His part. Jesus, help us to stay close to you as we go out into the world.

OCTOBER 11

Read: Jeremiah 16:16 – 18:23, 1 Thessalonians 4:1 – 5:3, Psalm 81:1-16, Proverbs 25:6-8

JEREMIAH 17:8

They are like trees planted along a riverbank, with roots that reach deep into the water. Such trees are not bothered by the heat or worried by long months of drought. Their leaves stay green, and they never stop producing fruit.

Today's verse is one of the thousands of promises found in God's Word. It is a promise that God's people will be able to endure all of the difficult circumstances of life. Even more than that, it promises that they will prosper during the difficult circumstances of life. It doesn't say that they won't be touched by those things but that they will be secure and fruitful during those times.

This is one of the many conditional promises found in the Bible. The preceding verse calls God's people blessed if they trust in the Lord and put their hope and confidence in Him. This means to us that we can be successful and fruitful in the midst of great difficulties by trusting God and putting our hope and confidence in Him.

I found it interesting that the very next verse after today's verse speaks about the wickedness of our hearts and that we shouldn't trust the things of our heart. This speaks to our feelings and emotions. We can't trust our feelings and emotions because they lie to us about what is going on in the world around us. The preceding and following verses are bookends to our verse for the day. What are we trusting in, God or our feelings and emotions? Where is our hope and confidence, in the Lord or in our heart? Your heart is fickle and unreliable. Only God is worthy of trust. Only the Lord is someone in whom we can depend upon regardless of the situation or circumstances.

It is a great encouragement to me that I don't have to depend upon my own heart and what I feel or know. It gives me great confidence to know that God has offered to me all that I need, simply through trusting Him. And then on top of that He promises me that I will be fruitful even in the times of drought or famine. When the world around me is experiencing difficult times, my trust in the Lord will sustain me and cause me to be fruitful.

Promises like this should cause us to examine our lives and evaluate whether or not we see this promise being fulfilled in our lives. If not, we should be asking God to reveal to us any areas where we are not doing our part to meet His conditions for fulfillment. God is faithful; He will always do His part if we do our part. If one of His promises to us is not being fulfilled in our lives it means we are probably not meeting the condition for fulfillment. The solution is simple, humble your heart before the Lord and do what He says. And then you will experience the fullness of His promises. Jesus, help us to appropriate all Your promises.

OCTOBER 12
Read: Jeremiah 19:1 – 21:14, 1 Thessalonians 5:4-28, Psalm 82:1-8, Proverbs 25:9-10

1 THESSALONIANS 5:12
Dear brothers and sisters, honor those who are your leaders in the Lord's work. They work hard among you and warn you against all that is wrong.

Here the apostle Paul exhorts the believers of Thessalonica in the manner in which they should behave toward the leaders of the work of the Lord. As leaders we are likely to wish that all of the people that we have responsibility to minister to in any form of leadership would memorize this verse and the next one. However, I believe there is an important lesson in this verse for leaders and it is found in the description of what the leader does.

First, it says that the leader works hard among them. In context this applies to the Lord's work. By this we should recognize that we should be hard at work for the Lord. Working hard has a couple of meanings; it can mean that we are laboring at the work of the ministry. Leading is in many respects a labor; you can't just cruise through being a leader in the Lord's work, it should make you sweat figuratively and physically. To work hard also applies to our priorities. When we are working hard at something we have raised that thing to a high priority in our lives. If God has called you to lead His people then the work of the Lord should have a high priority in your life.

Second, we are called in our verse for the day to warn them (those that we lead) against all that is wrong. This speaks of two things to me; knowledge of God's Word and knowledge of God's people. To warn someone against all that is wrong you must know right from wrong as God's Word describes it. This means that a leader that is worthy of the honor that Paul is calling the Thessalonians to is a student of God's Word. Only as we spend time in God's Word and learn it and about it can we be equipped to warn the people against all that is wrong.

This leader must also have knowledge of God's people. If you do not know the people that you are leading then you cannot possibly warn them against all the things that are wrong. The only way to do that is to know them well enough to know what is wrong in their lives. We can give them general warnings that might help them but to see them grow to complete maturity, which is our goal, they need to deal with specific things that are wrong in their lives.

This is not an attempt to control them and make them into some kind of Christian zombie; it is meant to help them be conformed into the image of Jesus Christ. Besides this being a commandment of God for all believers it is through this process of being conformed or sanctified that brings people into closer fellowship with the Father in heaven. And it is through that closer fellowship that the grace, mercy, love, and power of God are appropriated and experienced. It is in the best interests of those following you that you become a leader worthy of honor. Jesus, help us to work hard and to grow in our knowledge of You and those that we are leading.

OCTOBER 13

Read: Jeremiah 22:1 – 23:20, 2 Thessalonians 1:1-12, Psalm 83:1-18, Proverbs 25:11-14

PROVERBS 25:12

Valid criticism is as treasured by the one who heeds it as jewelry made from finest gold.

Criticism is something that many people tend to struggle with. The word "criticism" tends to stir up negative emotions in people. Most of us either know someone or are someone that does not take criticism well. Some people would rather you lie to them about something than have you criticize them.

In my own life I have learned that there are two types of criticism; bad and good. Our text refers to the good criticism as "valid." Good or valid criticism is something to be treasured; it should be worn like fine jewelry. Many people would say that there is no such thing as good criticism and there is a reason why they feel that way. Criticism by its very nature is a judgment of you or what you do. It is a critique of who you are or what you do by someone other than yourself. To be criticized means that something about you is not perfect and possibly not even acceptable to the person doing the critiquing. Why do we struggle with that? Because it is an attack against self!

To accept criticism is to say that you know that you are not perfect and possibly not even acceptable. To accept criticism is to deny yourself and admit that there are areas in your life that need to change. It also says that you acknowledge that you don't know what it is that you need to change and that you need help.

As leaders in ministries and churches, you will receive criticism. Your ministries and churches are filled with people that feel they know better than you how you should run your life and ministry or church. Some of those people know how they would run your life or ministry. They know what they like and what they want and that is what they want from you.

There are also people that know what God would like and what he wants. These are the ones that will provide valid criticism. Your goal as a leader is to sort through the selfish criticism and the valid criticism and keep only what is good. The hard part about that is that to do it you must first receive the criticism. The trick is not to receive it fully until you have tested it. Once you have tested it, you throw away the bad criticism and keep the valid criticism like you would a precious treasure.

As a leader you will be criticized! There is no avoiding it. You get to decide how you respond to it. The right choice is to deny yourself and test the criticism so that you can find the gems that will help you to be more pleasing to the Lord. Valid criticism will help you to be more like Christ. Without valid criticism you cannot grow and become the person that God wants you to be. The only person that doesn't need criticism is the person that is perfect. And the last perfect person that the world saw was nailed to a cross at Calvary. Jesus, help us to discern the criticism that comes from You.

OCTOBER 14

Read: Jeremiah 23:21 – 25:38, 2 Thessalonians 2:1-17, Psalm 84:1-12, Proverbs 25:15

PSALM 84:9

O God, look with favor upon the king, our protector! Have mercy on the one you have anointed.

The psalmist writes in Psalm 84 what a great thing it is to be in fellow-ship with God. Even the birds find a place in the house of God where they are sheltered and protected. It is a place of rejoicing and praise.

In out text for today we have a prayer in which the psalmist asks for God's attention. This prayer is that God would look with favor upon the king and show him mercy. This is a fascinating thing and we need to see the great truth that it reveals.

One thing we need to understand is that the person that is in a position to lead us was placed there by God. It is very unlikely that the psalmist had any say in who would be the king during the time this was written. We don't even know if he was happy with who was king when he wrote this. In reality, none of that matters. God appointed and anointed that person to lead and to protect the people.

We don't always get to pick the one that we are to follow. We may get to vote for the President but the one that we vote for may not win. You probably don't a get choice of who will be your supervisor or manager at work. And it is likely that you will not be asked to vote about who will lead the ministry or church that you fellowship at. God appoints them and anoints them for the task of leading and protecting you. How well they do that is their choice and they will answer to God about that.

We must do more that just accept God's choice of who will lead us but we must be proactive at helping them to be successful. The psalmist is praying for his leader and we need to do the same thing. We need to be praying for those that God has placed in leadership of us. That includes those ungodly leaders that God has allowed to be in leadership of us.

What we pray for is just as important as the fact that we pray. The psalmist prays for favor and mercy. He wants God to look with favor upon the king and to show him mercy. The psalmist knew that if the king was being blessed that the people were likely to be blessed. Praying for favor and mercy on the people that lead you will benefit you as you experience some of the blessings that God is pouring out on them.

As leaders appointed and anointed by God we need the prayers of those that God has appointed and anointed to follow us. The very best way that we can see that happen is to model that behavior for them and be praying for those that have been appointed and anointed to lead us. Jesus, teach us to pray for our leaders.

OCTOBER 15

Read: Jeremiah 26:1 – 27:22, 2 Thessalonians 3:1-18, Psalm 85:1-13, Proverbs 25:16

JEREMIAH 27:13

Why do you insist on dying—you and your people? Why should you choose war, famine, and disease, which the LORD will bring against every nation that refuses to submit to Babylon's king?

God is about to punish the nation of Israel because they have been rebellious and turned away from the One True God to worship worth-less idols. To punish them He is going to send Babylon to conquer them and take them away into captivity for a period of time. The false prophets have been telling King Zedikiah of Judah that Babylon will never come. Jeremiah is trying to warn them not to resist God's punishment.

In today's text Jeremiah warns that any nation that resists God's punishment will experience war, famine, and disease. God is saying you are better off to take the punishment than if you are to resist it. God is giving them a choice between life and death. By choosing life they will live out their lives in Babylon. While this is not the life that they would choose for themselves, it is better than the alternative.

They will be choosing the alternative when they resist God's punishment for their disobedience. By resisting they are choosing death through war, famine, and disease. Two simple choices; God's way or your way, life or death. There is no third option.

It is God's desire that He would never have to punish His children. Most parents have no desire to punish their children. The Bible teaches that God chastises or punishes those that he loves. When God spanks His children, it is proof that He loves us. God's chastisement is meant to cause us to repent from our sinful ways and then draw near to Him as we should.

Getting a spanking from God is never going to be fun. But it is proof that God still loves us and wants us to be in close intimate fellowship with Him. But that fellowship is always going to be on God's terms and not ours. The Bible teaches us that God is a jealous God; He will not share us with another "god." If we allow anything to enter our life that takes His place in our lives, we are opening ourselves up to receive His punishment. God will always warn us first and give us a chance to repent, just like He did to the Israelites through the prophets. If we refuse to listen, we are choosing God's punishment.

As uncomfortable as God's punishment might be, it is far better than resisting and experiencing the consequences. Our best response when we suspect that we might be experiencing the punishment of God is humbly repent of any sins that we know about in our lives and ask Him for forgiveness and mercy. And then we need to trust God with whatever happens next in our lives, even if it means a long trip to Babylon. Jesus, teach us follow closely and repent quickly.

OCTOBER 16

Read: Jeremiah 28:1 – 29:32, 1 Timothy 1:1-20, Psalm 86:1-17, Proverbs 25:17

PSALM 86:11

Teach me your ways, O LORD, that I may live according to your truth! Grant me purity of heart, that I may honor you.

King David makes two requests in our verse for the day that could serve as the foundation of any true Christ-follower's daily prayer life. In these two requests we can find the secret to a successful Christian life. We will not be able to fully explore that in this daily devotion and so I would encourage you to spend some time with the Lord on your own to mine out the riches of this verse.

First, David asks that God would teach him the ways of the Lord. In humility David comes to God and says that he doesn't know everything and submits himself to the teaching of the Lord. His desire in doing this is so that he can live according to God's truth. It is a fact that our capacity to be blessed by God is directly proportional to our ability to obey. As we obey God, He more freely pours out His blessings into our lives. Our obedience is linked to our knowledge of the ways of God which we acquire through the teaching of the Holy Spirit of God's word. Fall in love with the Bible and open your heart to the instruction of the Spirit.

Second, David asks that God would purify his heart. David recognized that his heart was not pure and also realized that there was nothing that He could do about it. Our hearts are hopelessly wicked and deceitful; only God truly knows the depth of the darkness of our hearts. Our hearts lie to us and tell us that we are good, but the Spirit reveals to those with open eyes that this is not true. David realized that the only way that he would be able to honor God was to ask God to purify his heart.

David was asking God to show him his sins and then asking God to help him to purge those sins from his heart and life. We all need to do the same thing; we need to pray and ask God to open up our hearts and shine His perfect light into our lives and reveal that darkness that resides there. Then we need to humble ourselves before God and ask His forgiveness for those sins and then we need to turn away from those sins and never return to them.

The only way that we can live a life that is pleasing to God and brings honor and glory to His name is by allowing this heart-work by the Holy Spirit to take place on a regular basis. Daily, we need to go before God and ask Him to teach us and to purify us. This is a scary thing to pray because it means that things in your life are going to have to change. Nobody likes to change but you need to remember that God's plan is to make you better than you are now; it is worth any pain that you might experience. We were created by Jesus for Jesus and He is not going to rest until we are as close to perfect as He can make us. That begins when we humble ourselves before Him and give Him permission to perfect us. Jesus, change us into the people that You created us to be.

OCTOBER 17

Read: Jeremiah 30:1 – 31:26, 1 Timothy 2:1-15, Psalm 87:1-7, Proverbs 25:18-19

JEREMIAH 31:18

I have heard Israel saying, "You disciplined me severely, but I deserved it. I was like a calf that needed to be trained for the yoke and plow. Turn me again to you and restore me, for you alone are the LORD my God."

The nation of Israel had been conquered and much of the population taken into exile. God allowed this for a purpose; He was training His people to follow Him and Him alone. The people had been guilty of idol worship and were following any pagan practice that appealed to them. God had warned continuously that if they did not stop that He was going to drive them from the land. God used the Babylonians, a fierce and vicious people to fulfill this warning.

Today's verse is a prophesy of a time when the nation of Israel will turn away from the idols that they have been worshipping and turn back to God. They will acknowledge that God had to discipline them so that they would be trained to follow God. Throughout much of today's reading are the prophesies about the punishment that God inflicted upon Babylon. How can we tell the difference between God's discipline and His punishment?

As with most things about God, it is a matter of the heart. The nation of Israel knew the God of Abraham, Isaac, and Jacob. They had just taken their eyes off of Him and turned them to worthless, lifeless idols. The Babylonians did not know God, nor did they desire to. The Babylonians were a proud and arrogant people. God disciplines His children and punishes those that will not turn back to Him.

There will probably be times in all of our lives when we are being disobedient or rebellious against God. If we are, we will feel God's hand heavy upon us. It is at times like that, that we might feel that God is punishing us. Punishment is the act of inflicting pain as a result of some offense. Discipline is the act of inflicting pain for the purpose of correction. Scripture is quite clear; God punishes those that will not turn to Him and disciplines those that will.

When we feel God's hand heavy upon us we need to turn to Him and ask Him to reveal where we may be disobedient or rebellious. We need to ask God to reveal to us how He is trying to train us to follow Him more closely. If God is disciplining you it is a sign that He loves you. Allow His discipline to draw you closer to Him. We cannot fight God's discipline; but must embrace it as the training that we need so that we can be more like His Son Jesus.

God doesn't want to discipline us. He would much rather we never wander from the path that He desires us to walk. But we like sheep have gone astray. We will wander and God will correct us. Welcome His correction and respond quickly to it. Jesus, help us to respond more quickly to Your staff so that You don't need to use the rod.

OCTOBER 18

Read: Jeremiah 31:27 – 32:44, 1 Timothy 3:1-16, Psalm 88:1-18, Proverbs 25:20-22

1 TIMOTHY 3:1

It is a true saying that if someone wants to be an elder, he desires an honorable responsibility.

The verse for the day begins a section scripture that is often referred to when appointing elders and deacons in the church. In this section are listed what are sometimes called the qualifications for these offices in the church. Today's verse caught my attention because of something that I remember hearing that might be a real problem in the church. I have heard it said that if you want a position in the church that you probably shouldn't get one. The inference is that to have a position or office such as elder or deacon or pastor, it should be a calling not a desire. It is as thought we should be dragged into a position like these screaming and kicking. The Apostle Paul seems to disagree with that viewpoint.

Here in our verse for the day, Paul says that a person that wants this office desires something honorable. There is no rebuke or challenge in his statement. Paul goes on to give a list of characteristics that you should see in a person that you would appoint to be a deacon or elder. It is not wrong to want to be an elder. The office of elder is an honorable responsibility and to seek it is to seek to bless God's people.

God has given every last Christian gifts, skills, abilities, and experiences that He wants used in the building up of His Church. If a person has been given the specific gifts that would best be used in the office of elder or deacon than they should want that office. That way they can use their gifts to their fullest and the Church can benefit from them.

Calling should always precede appointment. A person should sense a desire within them to be used by God in some particular way before they are appointed to that office. It is God that will place that desire in their heart. Once that desire is recognized you need to let the ministry or church that you are called to know what God is doing inside of you. Then it is up to the ministry or church to determine where that calling can best be fulfilled. That might take some time. They should be looking at your life and looking for the characteristics of an elder or deacon and determining if your life lines up with them or not. I view them as signposts rather than qualifications. Signposts lead and guide me to a desired destination. If I desire to find a Spirit-filled elder or deacon there are certain signs that I want to see so that I know that I have found one.

A Spirit-filled church should only be appointing Spirit-filled elders and deacons. If you are leading a ministry or church be watching for the signposts leading to those people. If you are in a Spirit-filled ministry than you should be checking to see what your signposts are telling your leaders. Jesus, help us to keep our hearts pure and our desires focused on pleasing You.

OCTOBER 19

Read: Jeremiah 33:1 – 34:22, 1 Timothy 4:1-16, Psalm 89:1-13, Proverbs 25:23-24

JEREMIAH 34:16

But now you have shrugged off your oath and defiled my name by taking back the men and women you had freed, making them slaves once again.

The topic of slavery is one that our western sensibilities struggle with. The word evokes some very strong images in our minds. In the culture of Jeremiah's time it was as natural as day-care is for our children today. It was often used to take care of people that couldn't take care of themselves. A person would place themselves into the care of another person. They would lose their freedom but they would gain the security of the homeowner.

God's plan for the Hebrews was that He didn't want them taking advantage of their Hebrew brethren and so He established laws limiting slavery. All Hebrew slaves were to be freed to go and start their own lives after they had served for six years. The Hebrew slave was then given the choice to go or to stay. If he chose to stay, it would be for the rest of his or her life.

King Zedekiah for some reason decided to free all the Hebrew slaves that were in Judah and made an oath before God to treat their Hebrew brethren the way that they should. This obviously pleased God. But the leaders and the people went back on their oath and took the men and women back into slavery that they had freed.

It is probably difficult for us to picture what it would have been like for those people that had freed their slaves. Those slaves would likely have done all the work of the house and field and flocks. They would have taken care of everything that needed to be done. With those slaves gone it would have been very difficult for them to live their normal life. To do what God had called them to do and what they had committed to God to do was going to be hard. Your life is no different than that of the Hebrew homeowners. As your relationship with Jesus grows and matures there are going to come times when God is going to call you to make some kind of a commitment to Him. Fulfilling that commitment might even cost you something or be uncomfortable. It might mean a time of inconvenience or require an adjustment of your lifestyle.

The Hebrew homeowners shrugged off their oath to God and He didn't like it. God wants to bless us more than we can imagine. The only way that we can hope to receive all that God has promised us is to answer when He calls and keep our commitments to Him. Our temporary times of difficulty or inconvenience are nothing compared to the times of refreshing that God wants to give us. Don't run from your commitments to God just because it gets hard. Run to God and let Him help you keep your commitments. Jesus, help us to count our oaths to You as precious and worth keeping.

OCTOBER 20

Read: Jeremiah 35:1 – 36:32, 1 Timothy 5:1-25, Psalm 89:14-37, Proverbs 25:25-27

JEREMIAH 36:24

Neither the king nor his officials showed any signs of fear or repentance at what they heard.

Jeremiah received a word from God which Jeremiah had written on a scroll. Jeremiah then sent his servant Baruch to the Temple to read this scroll to the people. In this scroll were all the prophecies that God had given to Jeremiah concerning Israel and its people. God's plan was that maybe the people would respond and turn away from their sins and turn back to God. One of the king's officials heard what Jeremiah had written on the scroll and so he had the scroll taken to the king. But before he did, he warned Jeremiah's servant to hide and that Jeremiah should hide as well. The king responded to hearing the words that God had spoken through Jeremiah by first burning up the scroll and then ordering that Jeremiah be arrested.

God's desire was that the words on the scroll would bring conviction to the hearts of the people and to that of the king and his officials. God wanted them to fear Him and to repent of their sins. His desire was to heal the land of the sin of idolatry that had so permeated the nation of Israel. But instead of conviction, the king felt contempt for the message and the messenger. King Jehoiakim would suffer the consequences of his faithlessness and sin by being killed and being left unburied.

Two of the most important character traits that God desires in His people, especially His leaders are fear of God and repentance. God wants us to have a reverential awe and respect for who He is, what He has done, and what he can do. He also wants us to have hearts that are so tuned into His that we repent or turn away from our sin as soon as we realize that we have sinned against God.

King David was an imperfect man. He made some huge mistakes in his life; adultery, murder, and lying just to name a few. And yet the Bible refers to him as "A man after God's own heart." King David had a deep respect and fear of God and he was quick to repent when confronted with his sins. That is what God desired of King Jehoiakim and his officials. Because they did not respond that way God judged them and the nation of Israel and very soon they would be taken away into captivity in Babylon.

God knows that his people cannot be perfect. If they could have been perfect He wouldn't have had to send His Son as a sacrifice for their sins. He wants His people, especially those that have been called to lead to fear Him always and to repent of their sins quickly. If there are Babylonians knocking on your door, it might be time to take a hard look at your heart. Do you hold God in the reverence, awe, and respect that He deserves? Have you repented of all sin that you know about in your life? Jesus, teach us to fear You and help us to repent from anything that separates us from You.

OCTOBER 21
Read: Jeremiah 37:1 – 38:28, 1 Timothy 6:1-21, Psalm 89:38-52, Proverbs 25:28

1 TIMOTHY 6:11

But you, Timothy, belong to God; so run from all these evil things, and follow what is right and good. Pursue a godly life, along with faith, love, perseverance, and gentleness.

As Paul closes this letter to his disciple Timothy He gives him some instructions. And these instructions apply to us as well. Timothy was a young leader that Paul had trained and sent to Ephesus to deal with wrong teachings in the church that Paul had established there. Paul had spent most of the time dealing with those issues but also gave some time to giving his young pupil some tips on how to live his life in a way that brought glory to God and edified the church.

In our verse for the day Paul begins by reminding Timothy who he belongs to; God. Why is it that we need to be reminded of that? It seems that no matter how close we get to the Lord that we must be reminded that we are not our own. I thank God for reminders like we have in this verse because it is through this knowledge that we are humbled and are able to approach the throne of God.

Paul then goes on to tell Timothy about the direction that his life should be moving in. Paul instructs Timothy to run from all the evil things that he has described in this letter. This again tells us that we play a role in our relationship with God. God wants us to be holy because He is holy. One of the ways that we will become holy is to run from all the evil things in our lives.

This verse goes on to tell us that it is not enough just to run from those evil things but we must also be moving toward something else; things that are right and good. If all you do is move away from evil things without a specific direction and purpose, you are likely to find yourself moving toward another kind of evil. You must run from evil and towards things that are good and right.

Paul concludes this verse by telling Timothy to pursue a godly life. He is telling Timothy to chase after holiness. In your own life you will find that unless you are running from evil and toward godliness, your life is going to be a shell of what it could be. A godly life that is also marked by faith, love, perseverance, and gentleness does not happen by just sitting around waiting for it to happen. You must desire it and make it the goal of your life. Paul was calling Timothy to be an example to those in the church that he was leading. God is also calling you to be an example to those around you; your family, your ministry, your church, or your community. Learn what it means to live a godly life that is marked by faith, love, perseverance, and gentleness. Then pursue that life with all of your effort while also running from evil. That is a life that pleases God and draws others to Him. Jesus, teach us to live a life that pleases You.

OCTOBER 22

Read: Jeremiah 39:1 – 41:18, 2 Timothy 1:1-18, Psalm 90:1 – 91:16, Proverbs 26:1-2

JEREMIAH 39:18

Because you trusted me, I will preserve your life and keep you safe. I, the LORD, have spoken!

Jeremiah gives a word of prophecy to Ebed-melech the Ethiopian. Ebed-melech is only mentioned here in our verse for the day and in the previous chapter of Jeremiah. Jeremiah had been imprisoned in a dungeon that had waist-high mud in it. Ebed-melech went to King Zedekiah and asked the king to save Jeremiah from the dungeon. Zedekiah sent Ebed-melech to save Jeremiah.

Ebed-melech was a eunuch in King Zedekiah's court. What his role was is not mentioned in scripture. There is no mention as to why He did what he did to rescue Jeremiah. He was Ethiopian which means he wasn't a Hebrew; one of the children of God. And yet, because of his actions in chapter 38 of Jeremiah God sends Jeremiah a message to give him.

The king of Babylon is about to sack the city of Jerusalem and destroy it and kill many of its people. Those that aren't killed will be sent into exile with the exception of the very poorest people. Ebed-melech had a right to be afraid. As a part of the court, there was a good chance that he would be killed immediately. So God sends him this word of hope and encouragement.

Jeremiah was ministering to a nation of people that did not want to hear what he had to say. All God wanted them to do was to repent from their sins and turn back to him. But they wanted to go their own way, regardless what God said. Jeremiah's was a tough ministry! It must have encouraged Jeremiah to receive this message for the Ethiopian eunuch. It would have told him that someone believes; someone is trusting God. This foreigner had more faith than most of the Chosen People of God.

There may be times in life and in ministry when you feel like you are in chains in a dungeon in mud up to your waist. And you might be wondering if anything that you are doing is making a difference. Trust that God is preparing an Ethiopian eunuch to come and rescue you and it is very likely that something that you did or said influenced them to trust God enough to do it.

God told Ebed-melech that because he had trusted God that he was going to rescue him from the impending doom. He had trusted God and rescued Jeremiah and now God was going to rescue him. God's actions almost always follow our actions. To see God rescue us, we must first trust Him to do so. Do your part and then trust God to do His part. Jesus, in You we trust!

OCTOBER 23

Read: Jeremiah 42:1 – 44:23, 2 Timothy 2:1-21, Psalm 92:1 – 93:5, Proverbs 26:3-5

2 TIMOTHY 2:2

You have heard me teach many things that have been confirmed by many reliable witnesses. Teach these great truths to trustworthy people who are able to pass them on to others.

Here in Paul's last letter we see the great mandate of Christian leaders; teaching the truth. In Paul's mind this was the most important thing that he could say to his young pupil. Timothy was the pastor of the church at Ephesus. Paul did not tell him to construct a large building that glorified God. Paul did not tell Timothy to develop programs and systems to grow a large church. He simply told him to teach the truth to others.

As we lead ministries and churches, I think we sometimes lose sight of this simple mandate. This is the basic premise that created the Calvary Chapel movement of which I am a product. Pastor Chuck Smith believes that the heart of the ministry is to "Simply teach the Word simply." We too often try to complicate what God wants to be simple. Just teach the Word of God.

Within this verse we see four generations of teaching. Paul is reminding Timothy that he had taught Timothy the truth. Paul then tells Timothy to teach those truths to trustworthy men. There is then an expectation that those trustworthy men would pass on these truths to others. As leaders within families, ministries, or churches we should be in the business of teaching teachers. That means that our teaching should be purposeful. Our goal should be that those that are receiving the teaching of the truth are being equipped to teach that truth to someone else. To do that we need to spend time with those that we are teaching and looking for those that would be described as trustworthy. Please notice that it doesn't say anything about looking for people that are great teachers or speakers; just trustworthy. Another word like trustworthy is faithful. When looking for people to teach, faithfulness will always be more important than talent and ability. Look for the people that are faithful to the ministry and to the Word. That is a reflection of their heart. I believe that God loves to work with simple faithful people to do great things. Having a great spiritual resume will never replace a faithful heart toward God and His Word.

As you are teaching, look for those that are faithful and start encouraging them to teach. Provide them with any support and opportunities that you can so that they can exercise and develop their gifts. And resist the temptation to be threatened by someone that might have a greater gift than you do. In fact that is the person that you want to encourage the most. God might want to use you to prepare this person to start a new work where the Word of truth is not being taught. How many generations of teachers are there in your life, ministry or church? Jesus, help to start today to create a long lineage of people that teach the truths that were taught to us.

OCTOBER 24
Read: Jeremiah 44:24 – 47:7, 2 Timothy 2:22 – 3:17, Psalm 94:1-23, Proverbs 26:6-8

PSALM 94:9

Is the one who made your ears deaf? Is the one who formed your eyes blind?

In our reading for the day the psalmist asks some rhetorical questions of his readers to challenge the way that they are thinking about God. His comments are targeted at those that are in rebellion against God. It is as though he is asking the general question: Do you really believe that God can't see what you are doing and hear what you are saying?

That is exactly how some people believe; they believe that God can't see or hear them. It reminds me of the baby that learns to play peek-a-boo. When they cover their eyes, they think they are invisible and can't be seen. The wicked seem to think the same thing; they think that because they can't see God that He can't see them.

Sadly for them, that ignorance may cost them a lot more than they would like to pay. God is always watching and listening to us. There is never an instant when I am out of His presence. For the wicked this would be a terrifying thing for them to understand. But most of the wicked don't really care what God thinks anyway.

For the Christian this is a much more sobering thought that God sees and hears everything. I just wish that we would truly understand the depth of what it means. We too often trivialize these things about God that make Him so great in our lives. We might understand it as it relates to sin and it might keep us from certain kinds of sin but not to the level that it should.

When we sin, God is watching. When we sin, it hurts God's heart. It hurts His heart because it removes us from the kind of relationship with Him that He created us for. What we need to do is become clearer in our minds of the absolute truth that He is with us while we are sinning. It needs to be as real as if it were our mother, or spouse, or children standing there as we were committing that sin. Then it might keep us from more sins.

Another aspect of this truth is that if we were truly aware of God's presence it would also keep us from much of the fear and doubt that might fill our minds. If I could truly embrace the fact that God is seeing and hearing everything about my life I would be able to rest in the most difficult of life's circumstances and challenges. Our problem is that we can't see Jesus and so we might not always act as if He really is there with us.

It takes faith to believe God when He said that He would never leave us nor forsake us. In the stillness of our minds and hearts we must just believe that He sees and hears us; there can be no question about that. Then we need just begin to embrace the image of Him in our presence at all times. Jesus, teach us to see You at all times and in all places.

OCTOBER 25

Read: Jeremiah 48:1 – 49:22, 2 Timothy 4:1-22, Psalm 95:1 – 96:13, Proverbs 26:9-12

JEREMIAH 49:11

But I will protect the orphans who remain among you. Your widows, too, can depend on me for help.

Jeremiah is speaking out a prophecy against the nation of Edom. Because of their sins against the people of God, He is planning to destroy them as a nation. The fact that God would do something like that bothers many people. They wonder why a loving God would destroy people. What they are failing to understand is that God never destroys anyone that has not had an opportunity to turn to Him but has rejected Him. God wants all people to be His people and to rest under His loving care and protection. But those that reject Him and oppose Him fall under His judgment.

We can't fully understand why God does what he does because we are not capable of thinking like God. Instead of trying to understand we can rest in our knowledge of His character toward His people and those that He cares for. Today's verse is an example of that.

Even though God intends to destroy the nation of Edom from the face of the earth, He promises to take care of the widows and orphans of Edom. God's love, compassion, and grace towards the helpless is a source of great hope. The Bible doesn't tell us how God was going to keep this promise but we need only rest in the fact of God's faithfulness to believe that it is true.

Because we live in a world that is filled with war, violence, famine, and disease there will always be orphans and widows that need God's protection and care. It is God's desire that His protection and care are provided through His people. God blesses His people to be a blessing to others. As a nation that has been greatly blessed by God, we have an obligation to be a blessing to the orphans and widows of the world.

We can't reach them all, nor does God expect us to. We just need to do what we can. God will take care of the rest of them. We might think that we don't need to do anything, God has promised to do it, so I don't have to think about it. We need to be careful not to allow that thought to stop us from trying to do something. There is always a chance that God has chosen you to be the method that He desires to use to keep that promise to them.

God is faithful! He has promised to take care of the orphans and widows, and He will! If He intends for you to be a part of that and you do nothing, they will still be taken care of somehow but you will miss out on being used by God and you will lose the blessing that He intended to give you. You don't have to sell everything you own and give it to the poor. Be sensitive to the Spirit's leading and do what He tells you. It is usually something simple and easy. Let Him use you to do the amazing. Jesus, show us how to care for the orphans and widows.

OCTOBER 26

Read: Jeremiah 49:23 – 50:46, Titus 1:1-16, Psalm 97:1 – 98:9, Proverbs 26:13-16

PSALM 98:1

Sing a new song to the LORD, for he has done wonderful deeds. He has won a mighty victory by his power and holiness.

There is something about the word "new" that creates all sorts of emotions in people. From a marketing viewpoint "new" is a powerful tool to sell products. Everyone seems to want the newest widget on the market. From the viewpoint of our lives, the word "new" can bring the opposite emotions including fear and dread. Looked at from the viewpoint of church life, the word "new" is often viewed with suspicion or even anger.

How many times have we heard about churches being fractured because the pastor instituted something "new"? It amazes me to think that some people would rather watch a church die than to accept something new that might breathe life into it. Why is it that we will accept new in everything in our lives except in our churches?

In our verse for the day we have an example that God loves new things. The psalmist said that we should sing a new song to the Lord. We should do it because of the wonderful things that He has done. God is always doing new and wonderful things and to recognize and acknowledge that we need to sing new songs to Him. I don't believe that this is referring just to the songs that we sing to Him. I believe that it is referring to every aspect of our worship; including our churches and church services.

What might be the most deadly words that can be heard in a church or any organization are: "That is the way that we have always done it!" Look at the way that God has created nature. Look at the way that a tree grows. No two trees are exactly the same and as each tree grows it changes. Everything in nature can teach us about how God wants to operate in our lives, families, ministries, and churches. A tree is a great example for us to use to learn how to grow each of those areas in our lives.

Have you been singing a new song to the Lord because of the amazing and wonderful things that He is doing in your life? If you aren't, it might be because you have stopped looking for the new things that He is doing around you. He never stops doing those things; we just stop noticing them.

God doesn't want to stay the same in your life, family, ministry, or church. He is always looking to do something new because he is trying to stimulate growth within each of these areas. We need to look at these new things that God wants to do as opportunities to write new songs in our heart to the Lord. Look for the areas where you might be tempted to say: "That is the way that we have always done it!" and ask God if that might be an area where He might want to do something new. He might not but we need to be open to whatever He might want. Jesus, help us to see You as new and fresh every day of our lives.

OCTOBER 27

Read: Jeremiah 51:1-53, Titus 2:1-15, Psalm 99:1-9, Proverbs 26:17

JEREMIAH 51:17

Compared to him all people are foolish and have no knowledge at all! They make idols, but the idols will disgrace their makers, for they are frauds. They have no life or power in them.

Our verse for the day is found within a prophecy of the overthrow and destruction of Babylon by the Medes. In the midst of this prophecy the prophet Jeremiah breaks out in declaration of God's attributes. It is as though Jeremiah is suddenly overtaken with a sense of awe and wonder about how great God is. This is a natural thing for someone that is being used by God. When we are serving and God's Spirit is working in us or through us, we will break out in praise or adoration of God. It is almost as if we can't help ourselves, we must say something about how amazing God is or we will burst.

After seeing how great God is, Jeremiah turns back to examine mankind and declares to us what he sees in today's verse. Compared to God all men are foolish and have no knowledge. Mankind seems to take great pride in its accomplishments. We marvel at the feats of people that are greater than we are in one area of life or another. We are enthralled with the abilities of great athletes, artists, or musicians. We stand in awe of the enormous things that men have built.

This verse is proven true when we promote these things of man to a place of worship in our lives. We attribute to them some life or power that we think they might give to us, only to be disgraced because they have no life or power and all the energy that we put into worshipping them is wasted and useless.

We might think that we are immune from idol worship in modern America but we are actually guiltier of it than many of the less civilized countries of the world. We disguise our idol worship with Madison Avenue and Wall Street but we still foolishly worship things that have no life or power. We know this is true because when we are in our greatest need they have nothing to offer us.

Only God is worthy of our worship. Only Jesus can give life. Only the Holy Spirit can provide the power we need to live this life well. If we give any of the worship that should go to God to an idol we will be disgraced and we will find ourselves empty and powerless.

The more that I get to know God, the more I realize how little I actually know about Him. The more I grow in my knowledge of God, the more I realize how much greater He is than I am. As I look at the things that God has done, the things of man begin to pale in comparison. It is ultimate foolishness to worship anything that man could make rather than worshipping the God that made man. Jesus, show us those things that we have put in Your rightful place in our hearts and minds.

OCTOBER 28

Read: Jeremiah 51:54-52-34, Titus 3:1-15, Psalm 100:1-5, Proverbs 26:18-19

PSALM 100:3

Acknowledge that the LORD is God! He made us, and we are his. We are his people, the sheep of his pasture.

Within the first six words of our verse for the day is a truth that will revolutionize the walks of many Christians if they would just embrace it. This verse begins by telling us to acknowledge that the Lord is God. This means that we don't just say that the Lord is God but we believe it and accept is as truth. It also means that our behaviors prove that we acknowledge this truth. Too many people say that the Lord is God with their mouths and then deny Him with their lifestyles. That is called hypocrisy and hypocrisy is one of the things that keep many from coming to know God.

The Lord is God whether you acknowledge it or not. Just because someone doesn't acknowledge or believe in God, doesn't change His position or existence even a small amount. But it will change how their life will be lived and how God will interface with them. If you want to receive all that God wants to give you, it must be on His terms; not yours. The Lord is God and He expects you to acknowledge that.

Our verse goes on to say that He made us, therefore we are His. Because we are His creation, we belong to him. This is where many will struggle in their relationship with Jesus. We want to believe that we are self-made people. No one has ever made themselves. This is pride and arrogance even to begin to think that you had anything to do with where you are today. God gave you everything you have and arranged it so that you could be where you are.

This verse ends by saying that we are His people and one of the sheep of His pasture. This addresses our selfish natures. To acknowledge that the Lord is God requires that we acknowledge that we are not the center of the universe; God is! We are one of many that are a part of God's flock. It is not all about us; it never has been. It's all about Jesus and His plan for our lives and for this world.

When we acknowledge that the Lord Jesus is God, we open up our relationship with God to be all that it was intended to be. It gives us a right perspective about who we are and who God is. By acknowledging that the Lord is God and that we are not, we are inviting the Holy Spirit to do His work in our lives. The Lord is God and we are not! Most people would not say that they are God but their actions say that they are the god of their lives. Only by surrendering the throne of our lives to Jesus can we truly acknowledge that the Lord is God. Jesus, help us to throw all of our crowns at Your feet and to step aside from the throne of our lives.

OCTOBER 29

Read: Lamentations 1:1 – 2:22, Philemon 1-25, Psalm 101:1-8, Proverbs 26:20

PHILEMON 11

Onesimus hasn't been of much use to you in the past, but now he is very useful to both of us.

Paul writes this short epistle while he is in prison in Rome to ask Philemon to do him a favor. There is much that we could learn from these twenty-five verses but we are going to focus on just one today. Paul is writing this personal letter to his friend Philemon in Colosse. Philemon is wealthy enough to have slaves. One of his slaves is Onesimus. Onesimus had an attitude problem that resulted in him not being a very effective servant to Philemon and I am certain that this caused great frustration and friction between the two men.

Onesimus runs away from Philemon and travels to Rome where he ends up visiting Paul while he is imprisoned. It is not clear how long Onesimus is in Rome with Paul and it is not clear what transpired while he was there. At some point Paul determines that it is time for Onesimus to return to Colosse as the slave of Philemon. What does happen is that there is some sort of attitude change that takes place in the heart of Onesimus. Paul calls Philemon to view Onesimus not just as a slave but also as a beloved brother.

Paul does not condemn the act of slavery. In that age it was common and accepted; even among Christians. They were treated usually with dignity and respect as a valuable part of the household and family. Paul also does not encourage Philemon to release Onesimus from his indentured servitude but to change his viewpoint of his relationship with him. We need to see from this that just because where we are and what we are doing feels like slavery and feels onerous doesn't mean that God wants us to leave. Where you are is where God placed you; it is now all about your attitude while you are there.

During Onesimus' time with Paul his attitude changed. While we cannot know exactly what transpired during that time we can imagine that Paul spent a great amount of time teaching Onesimus about his relationship to Jesus and helped him to understand how that translates into his relationship as a slave to Philemon. We would call that discipleship; Paul discipled Onesimus.

As a result of that discipleship Paul sends Onesimus back to Philemon and tells Philemon to take him back. He also tells Philemon that because of this time that Paul has spent with him that Onesimus will be much more useful; not just as a slave but also as a brother in Christ. Part of discipleship is helping people to deal with the mistakes that they have made in their lives and helping them to restore broken relationships. As a slave Onesimus was a burden to Philemon. As a Christian brother, he would be a great blessing and support to Philemon. Paul wanted Onesimus to stay and help him but he knew that Onesimus needed to return to Philemon to make that situation right. Make sure that those that you are discipling are going back where they can to make past mistakes right. Jesus, help us to have the right attitude.

OCTOBER 30

Read: Lamentations 3:1-66, Hebrews 1:1-14, Psalm 102:1-28, Proverbs 26:21-22

LAMENTATIONS 3:25

The Lord is wonderfully good to those who wait for him and seek him.

The book of Lamentations is a record of the sorrow and grief that Jeremiah and the people of Israel were experiencing after having been exiled from the land that God had promised to their ancestors. This was a result of their rebellion and disobedience to God's command to worship Him as the only True God. Instead they turned from God to worship the gods of the people of Canaan; worthless idols that could not help them or save them.

Lamentations is an expression of the pain that they are feeling as a people over the consequences of their sins. There are many sad descriptions of what they are feeling. There are also some wonderful expressions of the character and attributes of God within this dark book. Such is the case with our verse for the day.

The prophet Jeremiah states that the Lord is "wonderfully good." That is a remarkable statement considering their circumstances. The king of Babylon has conquered the nation of Judah and taken away most of its people in exile to Babylon. God's goodness is not dependent upon our circumstances. God is always good because the very nature of God is good. Just because my circumstances are bad, it doesn't mean that God is bad. God is always good.

Jeremiah then says that God directs His goodness toward people. This goodness of God is directed to people under two conditions; those who wait for Him and those who seek him. At first glance these two conditions almost appear to be contradictory. Waiting implies inaction, while seeking implies action. Since there are no contradictions in Scripture, the problem must be in definition.

Waiting on the Lord is an active thing. It means that we trust God to complete His will in our lives and we are actively doing the things that He has instructed us to do. We are not trying to force our will upon our circumstances are striving to escape them. Waiting on the Lord means that we trust that God is in control and that He is going to act on our behalf.

Seeking the Lord happens more in our hearts than it does in our actions. It involves allowing the Holy Spirit to work within our heart and mind to conform us into the image of Jesus. The activity of seeking the Lord is to do those things that assist in this process, like prayer and Bible reading and study.

As we wait on Him and seek Him we will see the goodness of God. This verse is a proclamation of one of the attributes of the Lord. We can rest in it and trust our life to it. If we are not sensing the goodness of God, we simply must keep waiting and keep seeking. His word is absolutely true and He is faithful to keep His word. Jesus, help us to wait and teach us to seek You daily.

OCTOBER 31

Read: Lamentations 4:1 – 5:22, Hebrews 2:1-18, Psalm 103:1-22, Proverbs 26:23

HEBREWS 2:1

So we must listen very carefully to the truth we have heard, or we may drift away from it.

After a proclamation that Jesus is greater than the angels, the author of the book of Hebrews gives us a warning not to get off course. He gives us this warning because it is a lot easier than we think it is to drift. As a young man I served in the Navy in the navigation department of a nuclear submarine. We had some of the most sophisticated equipment available at the time. Part of my responsibility was to ensure that we knew where we were and that we were on course to arrive at our desired destination. On any given six-hour watch we would have to make adjustments to get back on course. We had to pay very close attention to what was going on.

The author of Hebrews is telling a similar thing. We can't just go blindly through our lives and expect to end up being where God wants us to be. We must have a plan and pay close attention to it. It has been said that if you don't know where you are going then any direction you go is the right one. That is not what our verse is telling us.

On the submarine, we cared about where we were because we didn't want to run into an underwater mountain. We had charts that told us where these mountains were but those charts were only useful if we used them. Those charts represented truth. For us to avoid the danger, we needed to know where we were in relation to the truth. Failure to do so was potentially life-threatening.

Our verse says that we must do the same thing in our spiritual lives. We must stick close to the truth or we may drift away from it. Drifting away from the truth is dangerous and has serious consequences. The problem is that most people don't realize how easy it is to drift away until they find themselves far from where they are supposed to be.

On the submarine there were many factors that caused us to drift away from our intended course; currents, equipment errors, and human errors. In our lives there are many factors that can cause us to drift off course. Satan and his demons are determined to drive us from the course that God intends for us. The world system is designed for that same purpose. Our sins and the sins of others also cause us to drift from our course.

To stay on course we must listen to and heed the truth that we find clearly spelled out in God's Word. We must regularly be checking our location to ensure that we are where we are supposed to be. We need to look for people that can help us to check our course. Staying on course with the truth is a matter of the choices we make to stay on course. Failure to make the right choices or making no choices at all is likely to result in us being in places that we never imagined going. Jesus, help us to fix our eyes on You and to use your Word to guide our path.

NOVEMBER

NOVEMBER 1

Read: Ezekiel 1:1 – 3:15, Hebrews 3:1-19, Psalm 104:1-23, Proverbs 26:24-26

EZEKIEL 2:5

And whether they listen or not—for remember, they are rebels—at least they will know they have had a prophet among them.

In our reading for today Ezekiel receives his first vision from God and his commission or call from God. Ezekiel was called by God to be a prophet to the people of Judah that had been taken into exile in Babylon. There are some interesting things about the way Ezekiel is called and his ministry. First his calling to be a prophet of God is preceded by a vision of some angelic beings and the glory of God. This sets the tone for many of Ezekiel's later prophecies.

Second, Ezekiel is given a scroll to eat that contains prophecies and funeral songs. Once he eats it he is given the specifics of his call. It is simple; tell the people what I have told you. God's instructions to Ezekiel are very simple; tell the people what I have put inside of you. But then God tells Ezekiel that the people probably aren't going to listen to him.

God gives Ezekiel virtually the same mission that He gave to Jeremiah. Ezekiel was to minister to the people of Judah that were in exile in Babylon and God told him that they were a stubborn and hard-hearted people. God is telling Ezekiel in advance that his ministry is going to be to a people that didn't want to hear what God had to say and it was very likely that they would hate him for doing it.

We also see God's purpose for doing it in our verse for the day. God wanted the people to know that a prophet of God had been among them. Ezekiel's ministry was to proclaim to the people what was going to happen to them in the future. And when those future events took place the people would think back to Ezekiel and realize that he had been telling them what God said. God's purpose was to show them their stubborn and hard-hearted ways in a hope that they would repent and turn back to Him.

God will usually pick who it is that we are to minister to. And while everyone would rather minister to those that will respond correctly, that is not always going to be the case. Sometimes we will be tasked to be an Ezekiel or Jeremiah. We might be a lone voice crying out in the wilderness of stubbornness and hard hearts. That doesn't change the fact that God called you to that wilderness and has a purpose in it. Both Ezekiel and Jeremiah had powerful ministries that lasted long after they were gone. Just because you don't see any fruit doesn't change your responsibility to be faithful to God.

God has a plan that you are given a part in. And no matter how microscopically small your part is, it is still part of God's plan to save the entire world. None of us can possibly know how our small acts of ministry might be used by God to fulfill His great plan. Jesus, help us to be faithful even while surrounded by a stubborn and hard-hearted world.

NOVEMBER 2

Read: Ezekiel 3:16 – 6:14, Hebrews 4:1-16, Psalm 104:24-35, Proverbs 26:27

HEBREWS 4:15

This High Priest of ours understands our weaknesses, for he faced all of the same temptations we do, yet he did not sin.

This is a truth about Jesus that I think we often underestimate and under-appreciate. But it is vital that we truly grasp it and make it our own. Jesus is our High Priest. That means that He intercedes on our behalf before God. Because He came as a man to this world He can relate to us as people. This works the other way also; we can relate to Him as a man. Our relationship with Jesus is not meant to be some mystical spiritual experience; it is meant to be an intimate personal relationship.

One of the things that tend to hinder people in their relationship with Christ is their weaknesses. Everyone has areas in their lives where they are not living up to God's standards. These areas are weaknesses and we view them as something that prevents us from drawing close to Jesus. What we forget is that it is these very weaknesses that Jesus came to experience and die for. Part of His reason for coming to the earth as a man was so that He could face all the same temptations that we do.

At no time could we say that Jesus doesn't understand what we are going through. The Bible says very clearly that what you are going through is not uncommon to man which means you are not the only one that is or has experienced this. All the temptations that you are faced with, Jesus was also faced with. The big difference is that Jesus at no time allowed those temptations to sway Him toward sin. It would be great if we could say the same thing, but we can't. That is why Jesus had to die on the cross. The knowledge that Jesus was tempted the same way that we are helps us to relate to Him. It is accepting what He did on the cross for our weaknesses that lead to sin that should give us hope and peace. Jesus understands you better than you could possibly imagine. He understands your weaknesses and understands what things tempt you and how they tempt you.

The reason this is important is because Jesus wants us to come to Him with these things as they are happening and talk to Him about them. We have to resist the temptation to run from Jesus every time we are experiencing temptation or struggling in our weaknesses. He wants to be there for us so that He can give us the strength that we need to resist. He knows how to resist because He has resisted all the same temptations that you are experiencing. The enemy will try to lie to you and tell you that you don't deserve to go to Jesus while you weak and being tempted. Don't buy into that lie; run to Jesus every time you sense your weakness and let Him coach you through how to deal with it. Doing that will not make you sinless but it will help you to sin less. That is why Jesus came to live as a man. Jesus, thank you for experiencing what I am experiencing so that I can come to you for the help that I need when I am feeling weak.

NOVEMBER 3

Read: Ezekiel 7:1 – 9:11, Hebrews 5:1-14, Psalm 105:1-15, Proverbs 26:28

EZEKIEL 9:11

Then the man in linen clothing, who carried the writer's case, reported back and said, "I have finished the work you gave me to do."

Ezekiel speaks about the destruction that is going to befall Jerusalem and the nation of Israel pretty soon in today's reading. God is angry because the people continue to worship idols even after He has sent prophets to warn them repeatedly. They have refused to hear what God is trying to tell them.

Ezekiel then sees a vision of six men that God sends into the city of Jerusalem, starting in the Temple, to kill everyone that is worshipping the worthless idols. One of these men is sent out ahead of the others to place a mark on the head of everyone that is saddened by all of the sin that they see. It would appear from the text that this man did not play a role in the passing of judgment but was tasked to protect those that were still loyal to God.

It is my belief that this is the role that God wants each of us to play in the world today. Too often we act like one of the five with our battle clubs out to execute God's judgment upon this wicked and sinful world. That is not our role. Our role is to precede the five men and do everything that we can to find and mark all those that will believe in Jesus.

One of the interesting things about this text is that it would appear that the man with the writing case also had a weapon. And though he carried it, it does not appear that he used it. This is inferred because he returns before the other five do. This man was armed and had the ability to execute judgment upon the wicked but that was not his task, nor his responsibility.

As we lead the families, ministries, and churches that God has entrusted to us, we need to follow this man's example. God has given us the ability and equipped us to do many things but He has not called us to do them all. We have got to be so careful to focus only on those things that God has called us to do. There may be things that God has given you incredible gifts and abilities to do that He is not asking you to do.

When this man returns to the Lord he tells Him: "I have finished the work you gave me to do." What a powerful statement! God assigns the work and we are responsible to complete it. We don't need to think up things to do for God. We just need to do the work that He assigned to us. And we need to stay at it until it is finished. Jesus, on the cross said; "It is finished!" He had completed the work assigned to Him.

Even our ability to complete the work is a gift from God. The Bible teaches that God is faithful to complete the work that He started in us. But as in all things with God, we must do our part. Our part is to do what we have been assigned and to do it until we can report back to God and say: "I have completed the work you gave me to do." Jesus, help us to stick to the task that you gave us to do for You.

NOVEMBER 4

Read: Ezekiel 10:1 – 11:25, Hebrews 6:1-20, Psalm 105:16-36, Proverbs 27:1-2

EZEKIEL 11:5

Then the Spirit of the Lord came upon me, and he told me to say, "This is what the Lord says to the people of Israel: Is that what you are saying? Yes, I know it is, for I know every thought that comes into your minds."

There is a part of us that believes that our minds are a private place that only we know what happens there. We believe that we can hide things there from God. Our verse for the day tells us something much different. There is nothing in our minds that is hidden from God's holy gaze.

In a strange way this is comforting to me. I have a desire as a man trying to be a true Christ-follower to be holy. But the truth is that I daily miss the mark of perfection that God desires for me to hit. Through Christ's blood I have forgiveness for all the sins that I commit, but God expects me to come in repentance of those sins and seek reconciliation. Knowing that I can't hide my sins from God makes it easier for me to come to Him whenever I need to.

The more intimately we are acquainted with this concept of God's absolute omniscience, the more we are willing to accept the purifying work of the Holy Spirit in our minds. Of course, this assumes that I agree with God that some of the things that come into my mind are sinful, ungodly, or impure. God is a gentleman; He will not force His purity upon us.

This is one of the reasons why a daily exposure to the written word of God is so important. It is within the pages of the Bible that we find truth. It is the truth of God revealed in Scripture that God desires to use as our guide to holiness. Without a regular feeding of God's words of life, we will mentally starve our minds of the very thing it needs to survive spiritually.

This is also why it is so important that we control what we do allow to come into our minds. The old computer saying, "Garbage in, garbage out!" applies to our minds as much as to computers. If we do not do anything to filter the things that come into our minds than we will not be able to do anything about what comes out in our lives. If you put enough garbage into your life, you can be assured garbage will come out.

It also comforts me to know that God knows not just the thoughts that come into my mind but also from where those thoughts came. The enemy is quite good at inserting thoughts into my mind. I don't understand how he does it, but I know that he does. Some of those thoughts can be very disturbing and disgusting. God does not judge me for my thoughts; it is what I do with my thoughts that determine my relationship with God. We are told to capture our thoughts and bring them under submission to the obedience of Christ. Humble your heart and mind before God and allow the Holy Spirit to help you to do that. Jesus, thank you that You know me so well and love me anyway.

NOVEMBER 5
Read: Ezekiel 12:1 – 14:11, Hebrews 7:1-17, Psalm 105:37-45, Proverbs 27:3

EZEKIEL 14:5
I will do this to capture the minds and hearts of all my people who have turned from me to worship their detestable idols.

The leaders of Israel come to Ezekiel because they want a message from God. They want to hear what God has to say about what is going on in their country. Babylonia has come and conquered them and taken many away into captivity. These leaders probably want to know what is going to happen next. There is a sense from the reading today that these leaders weren't trying to determine what God wanted but to get from God what they wanted.

God speaks to Ezekiel and has him challenge these men's hearts. They had set up idols in their hearts and God said to them that these idols would lead them into sin. God is warning them to turn their hearts and minds back to Him. These are the leaders of God's people and He is telling them that He will punish them if they do not respond to His warning. God is especially angry at the hypocrisy of these leaders. They worship their detestable idols and then come to God and ask Him about the future.

God won't share us with anyone or anything. God will not allow us to split our loyalties between two things that we worship. God wants all of us. You can't worship something else in your heart and then in your mind want to know what God thinks or is going to do. God calls that prostitution.

We are God's! We are His people and we are His bride. For us to allow anything into our hearts beside God is to commit adultery.

Nothing can take God's place in our hearts. Every day we must search our hearts to determine if we have allowed something to take God's place in our hearts and minds. This can be a person, or a thing like a car, truck, or motorcycle. It can be a position or job that fills your life as only God should. It can be money or fame. Whatever it is, God wants it to take its correct place in your life.

As leaders of families, ministries, or churches we need to take this warning seriously. God will punish those leaders that set up idols in their hearts. He will do it because it will lead them into sin. And where the leader goes; the people follow. To protect the people, God will punish the leader. The sad thing about that is that the people will suffer anyway. If God has to punish a leader, those that are following him are going to suffer too. As a leader, that may be the greatest burden that I bear; that my sin might cause someone that is following me to stumble.

The only solution is to surrender your heart and mind completely to God. Let Him capture them both. Daily ask God to reveal to you if there are any idols under construction in your heart and then do everything in your ability to destroy them before they become established. Those that are called to follow you as you follow Christ are depending upon that. Jesus, help me to open both my mind and heart to You.

NOVEMBER 6
Read: Ezekiel 14:12 – 16:41, Hebrews 7:18-28, Psalm 106:1-12, Proverbs 27:4-6

EZEKIEL 15:2

Son of man, how does a grapevine compare to a tree? Is a vine's wood as useful as the wood of a tree?

In this short chapter the prophet Ezekiel gives a message to the people of the nation of Israel. This is a tragic and terrifying message. In essence, the Lord is proclaiming their soon destruction. The Lord tells them that He is going to be tenacious and thorough about making the land desolate.

The reason for this harsh attitude of God is because the people of God have been unfaithful to their God. The Lord had made many promises to the nation of Israel about His care and protection of them. The only condition that God put on them is that they would stay away from the false gods and idols of the land and worship Him alone.

What struck me about today's verse was the comparison that God makes between the wood of a vine and a tree in relation to his people. The Lord makes the connection between usefulness and faithfulness. The Lord goes on to say that the people of Jerusalem have become useless because of their unfaithfulness.

We were all created for a purpose that God established before the foundation of the earth. As our Creator, God has the right to determine what our purpose is in this universe. We all have the general purpose of being created to worship and glorify God. Then God also has assigned us more specific purposes for accomplishing His will on this earth and for the furthering of His kingdom.

The people of Jerusalem had wandered from their general purpose; to worship God and glorify Him as the Only True God. Because they had done that, they were described as useless. They were so useless that they weren't even very good for burning. But they were to be burned just as rubbish is piled up and burned; not for a purpose but just to be disposed of.

It is difficult for me to imagine being useless to God. He created me, He knows everything about me, He takes care of me, and He loves me with an unfathomable love. The idea that I could become useless to Him is difficult to comprehend. This verse, and many others like it, makes it very clear that God expects us to be what we were created to be; God-worshippers. If we are not, then we are wasting our lives and will accomplish nothing useful in the eyes of God.

On the other hand, if I do worship God and live to glorify Him, then my life is useful to Him. I may not see just how useful it is but I can rest in the knowledge that God only asks me to be faithful so that I can be useful. God is looking for men and women that will be faithful to Him so that He can show Himself to be strong on their behalf. Jesus, help us to be faithful to You and Your plan for our lives.

NOVEMBER 7

Read: Ezekiel 16:42 – 17:24, Hebrews 8:1-13, Psalm 106:13-31, Proverbs 27:7-9

PSALM 106:20

They traded their glorious God for a statue of a grass-eating ox!

This undated anonymous psalm is referring to the Exodus and the incident that occurred when Moses went to the mountain and received the commandments on the stone tablets from God. Moses was up on the mountain for forty days. Moses had left his brother Aaron in charge while he was gone. All the people could see on the mountain was the glory of the Lord that appeared as a consuming fire.

When Moses didn't come back right away the people went to Aaron and told him that they were ready to leave and that they needed a god so that it would lead them. It is not surprising that the god that they fashioned for themselves was one of the gods of the Egyptians. Our verse for today describes how ridiculous this action was. They had the glorious presence of the Lord right in front of them and they decide they want a grass eating animal instead. And not even an animal but the image of an animal. How foolish!

But before you are too quick to judge them you need to know that we do the same thing on a regular basis. Far too often, we take our eyes off of the glorious presence of the Lord and fix our eyes on some lesser thing and allow that thing to fascinate us to distraction. It can be a person that we know or see in the media. It can be a thing like a car or a motorcycle or a house or some other toy. It can be a feeling produced by some activity or alcohol or drug. Whatever that thing is that we allow to entice us is far inferior to the glory of God.

The people came to Aaron because the glory of God was not enough from them. Aaron failed to focus them back on the glory of God and keep them from this great sin that they committed. In fact, Aaron helped them to commit this sin.

As leaders of God's families, ministries, and churches it is our responsibility to first keep our eyes on the glory of God and to encourage those around us to do the same. The Israelites were tired of waiting for something to happen. Their frustration led them to start looking for another option.

It is the responsibility of those that God has put in charge to always point people to the glory of God. We can't do that if we are not looking to the glory of God ourselves. Refocus your eyes on the glory of God and don't let the desires of those around you to stray from what God told you to do.

The glory of God is enough for all of us. There is nothing that we could possibly substitute it with that would even be a shadow of the glory of God. It is the responsibility of God's servant/leaders to faithfully remind the restless among us of that truth. Jesus, help us to see Your glory as it is meant to be seen and help us to point others to it as well.

NOVEMBER 8

Read: Ezekiel 18:1 – 19:14, Hebrews 9:1-10, Psalm 106:32-48, Proverbs 27:10

HEBREWS 9:9

This is an illustration pointing to the present time. For the gifts and sacrifices that the priests offer are not able to cleanse the consciences of the people who bring them.

Here in our reading for the day, the writer to the Hebrews is describing how Jesus is a perfect or better High Priest than the ones that had been serving in the tabernacle and temple since the days of Moses. The writer explains in great detail that Jesus' sacrifice on the cross did away with the old system or covenant and replaced it with a new covenant that was perfect.

Sometimes when we read things like this as it is referring to sacrifices and the Law of Moses we can tend to overlook the application that this has for us. We live under the Law of Grace and not under the Law of Moses. This letter was written to Jewish Christ-believers that had begun to move away from grace and toward doing the things that the Law of Moses required as their way of being right with God. The writer's purpose in writing was to draw them back to Christ's work on the cross as the only work that was necessary or able to make them right in God's eyes.

As modern day Christ-believers we are not likely to try to sacrifice sheep and goats in an effort to please God. At least I hope that is the case. Instead of sacrificing animals we will try to do other things so that we are pleasing to God. We will sometimes try to work our way into God's good graces. The problem with that is there is nothing that we can do that is able to make us right in God's eyes except for what Jesus did for us. Nothing else that we do could even come close to making us right in God's eyes.

In tomorrow's reading you will see that the only way to please God is through faith. In fact we are told that without faith it is impossible to please Him. Faith is simply believing God. The way that we are made right in God's sight is by believing what He told us and accepting it as truth. Our works and sacrifices are meaningless to God if we don't believe Him.

Our service, works, and sacrifices ought to be a fruit of our faith. That means that they should happen naturally because we believe God. Because I believe God, I serve God. Because I believe God I do works for God. Because I believe God I am willing to sacrifice of myself for God. None of these things in and of themselves will get me any closer to God. However, because I have faith, because I believe God, it pleases Him when I do them. Check yourself regularly to make sure that you are doing what you are doing because you think you have to or because you believe God and know that doing these things pleases Him. Jesus, help us to do everything out of a deep and abiding love for You and faith in You.

NOVEMBER 9

Read: Ezekiel 20:1-49, Hebrews 9:11-28, Psalm 107:1-43, Proverbs 27:11

EZEKIEL 20:39

As for you, O people of Israel, this is what the Sovereign LORD says: If you insist, go right ahead and worship your idols, but then don't turn around and bring gifts to me. Such desecration of my holy name must stop!

One of the things that God continually chastised the nation of Israel about was their worshipping of idols. Of all the sins that God spoke to them about, this was the one that He was the most upset about. Time and time again, God commanded them to worship Him alone. There are many occasions that God was close to destroying them completely because of their unfaithfulness to Him.

God is the only true and living God. All the idols that the Israelites were worshipping were lifeless and unable to do anything for them. These images of wood and stone were utterly useless and God said that by worshipping these things that the people also became useless.

Before we judge the Israelites too severely, we need to understand that we are often just like them. It is amazing how quickly we can allow something to take God's place in our lives. Worship is hard-wired into our DNA. We will worship someone or something. The question is not if we will worship, but what we will worship. God made it very clear on numerous occasions that their only choice was Him; their True and Living God.

In our verse for today, God tells the Israelites to choose. He wants them to choose between worshipping their worthless idols and Him. God is perfect and holy. When we come to Him it must be with the attitude that He is the absolute ruler of the universe and that He alone is worthy of our worship. By worshipping idols that can do nothing and then coming to God, the Israelites were either trying to elevate their worthless idols to the level of God or worse, bringing God down to the level of the worthless idols.

God will not be mocked and He will not allow us to share His place in our lives with anything or anyone else. He will give you the choice. And in today's reading it was said several times that by choosing God, you were choosing life. It was also very clear that by choosing to worship the worthless idols that they were choosing death; both physically and spiritually.

We need to search our hearts and try to determine if we have allowed someone or something to be set up as an idol in our lives. What is it that we care more about than God? What is it that we will sacrifice our life to besides God? What is it that we will sacrifice our time with God for? If there is anything or anyone in your life that you would not give up for God, then you may be at risk of choosing it or them over God. It is unlikely that God is going to ask us to give up those things that are precious to us but He doesn't want them to be more precious than our relationship with Him. Jesus, help us to sweep all the worthless idols from our lives so that our hearts can be pure before you.

NOVEMBER 10

Read: Ezekiel 21:1 – 22:31, Hebrews 10:1-17, Psalm 108:1-13, Proverbs 27:12

EZEKIEL 22:30

I looked for someone who might rebuild the wall of righteousness that guards the land. I searched for someone to stand in the gap in the wall so I wouldn't have to destroy the land, but I found no one.

God is about to unleash His fury upon the nation of Israel for their unfaithfulness to Him. In our text for today, Ezekiel also speaks for God about their adulteress behaviors with the pagan nations around them. By the end of our reading for today, King Nebuchadnezzar comes and lays siege to Jerusalem and conquers it.

God is looking for someone! God is looking for someone with eyes to see the spiritual condition around them. Righteousness is a wall that protects us from the enemies that surround us and from God's judgment of sin. God is looking for someone that can see this wall has a gap in it. God doesn't want them to just see it, He wants them to stand in the gaps of that wall and do something about it.

If you had a fortified city and there was a gap in the wall, it meant that your enemy could come into your city and defeat you. Righteousness is the wall that defends your life, family, ministry, church, or organization. If there is a gap in that wall, the enemy WILL attack you there. To defend a city with a gap in its wall you would send your best warriors to defend that section of the wall. In the spiritual battle we do this through prayer. If there is a gap in the wall of righteousness in your life, family, or ministry then start praying. The battle is often won or lost in prayer or lack of prayer. While prayer will stave off the attacks that will come, the longer that the gap remains in the wall the greater the likelihood that the enemy is going to break through and defeat you. The wall of righteousness must be repaired. That is accomplished through the Word of God and a closer walk with Jesus.

In Ezekiel's time God was looking for someone that would stand in the gap and repair the wall of righteousness for Jerusalem and the nation of Israel. God was looking for one person that would lead Israel back to Him and to His righteousness. He found no one. He is still looking for people that will lead their families, ministries, and churches back to Him. We live in a world that is set upon leading us to destruction. God wants men and women to stand in the gap and pray for their organizations and countries so that they might defend them from the enemies that are set on destroying them. One person might be all that God is looking for to prevent His Righteous Anger from being poured out.

You could be that one person that God is looking for to stand in the gap and protect those around you. You might be the one person that God is looking to help to rebuild the wall of righteous in some person's life or in some organization or even in your country. Will you stand in the gap? Jesus, help us to stand and to rebuild.

NOVEMBER 11

Read: Ezekiel 23:1-49, Hebrews 10:18-39, Psalm 109:1-31, Proverbs 27:13

EZEKIEL 23:35

And because you have forgotten me and turned your back on me, says the Sovereign Lord, you must bear the consequences of all your lewdness and prostitution.

In this chapter Ezekiel uses a graphic and powerful word picture to describe the way God feels about the way the cities of Samaria and Jerusalem have acted toward God. Samaria is the capital of the ten tribes of Israel that broke away from Judah after King Solomon died. Jerusalem is the capital of the two tribes of Judah and Benjamin. Ezekiel describes these two cities as sisters that have become prostitutes, selling their love to anyone that came along.

What caught my attention in this verse was the reference to the consequences that they were going to experience. It is strange to me how often I am confronted by people that are surprised that they must experience the consequences of their sins. It is often because they fail to see the connection between their sins and the consequences that naturally follow.

Some people also wrongly believe that forgiveness takes away the consequences of sin. The Bible nowhere teaches that principle. Forgiveness does take away the penalty of sin but it doesn't necessarily take away the consequences. God, in His sovereignty, can take away the consequences of our sins. In my experience and what I see in Scripture is that God often uses our consequences to teach us about sin. Some people respond better to the lessons taught through consequences than they ever will through God's love and grace.

In today's verse Ezekiel tells both Samaria and Jerusalem that they are going to experience all the consequences for all of their sins. The reason they were going to experience the full measure of their consequences is because they had forgotten their God and turned away from Him. We are all going to sin. As true Christ-followers that thought should repulse us and cause our hearts to hurt. As disciples of Jesus we should be growing in holiness as we allow the Holy Spirit to conform us into the image of Jesus. However, we are still sinners saved by grace and there is still a chance that we are going to sin. How we respond when we become aware of our sin makes all the difference in the world.

Repentance and humility are keys to a life that is pleasing to God. When we become aware of our sin God desires that we would humble our heart before Him and turn away from our sin and turn back to Him more fully. This is how true forgiveness is experienced from our sins. God may or may not dismiss the consequences of those sins, but I am certain that He will pour out His amazing grace upon you within those consequences. Jesus, help us to turn to You quickly.

NOVEMBER 12
Read: Ezekiel 24:1 – 26:21, Hebrews 11:1-16, Psalm 110:1-7, Proverbs 27:14

HEBREWS 11:6

So, you see, it is impossible to please God without faith. Anyone who wants to come to him must believe that there is a God and that he rewards those who sincerely seek him.

In today's reading we have a section of scripture that is often referred to as the Hall of Faith. In chapter eleven of Hebrews the writer names many of Israel's great men and women of faith. Most of the names are very familiar but some of them are a little more obscure. Some of them we are a little surprised to see in the list while others seem automatic. It makes me wonder if we won't have the same kind of responses when we get to heaven and see who God thought was a person of faith versus the ones that we thought were.

Today's verse is rich and is one of my personal favorites. In speaking of faith we are told that without faith it is impossible to please God. Faith in its simplest terms is believing God and what He says. One of the reasons why I like this verse is because it tells me very plainly that it is possible to please God. We are told that the doorway to pleasing God is faith. It is as we exercise our faith that we become a person that pleases God.

This verse also tells us that part of faith is coming to God. God is not some far off being that looks down upon us with disdain and frustration. This verse implies that there is an aspect of faith which includes our coming to God and that this pleases Him. God wants us to come to Him with everything that is going on in our lives. He cares so much about us that the things that affect us are important to Him.

The verse also goes on to say that if we are going to come to Him that we need to believe that He is there. It is a pretty foolish thing to do to go to God in prayer if you don't believe He is there and listening. Faith is believing that He is there and that He hears every last one of your prayers.

Not only do we need to believe that He is there and that He hears all of our prayers, we also need to believe that He can and will do something about our prayers. It is also foolish to pray to God if you don't believe that He can do something about what you are praying about. It shows a lack of faith and ignorance as to the awesome ability of Almighty God.

God rewards those that sincerely or diligently seek Him. It is not possible to fully describe and define what that reward might be, but one thing I do know for sure is that it is something that will please me. Believe God and believe that He is there when you go to Him and believe that He can do something about the issues of your life and then you can expect to be pleasing to Him and you can expect a reward from Him. Jesus, give us the ability to believe.

NOVEMBER 13

Read: Ezekiel 27:1 – 28:26, Hebrews 11:17-31, Psalm 111:1-10, Proverbs 27:15-16

You regard yourself as wiser than Daniel and think no secret is hidden from you.

Today's reading is mostly about the city of Tyre. It was one of the most influential cities of the time. They possessed great wealth and power. And as is usually the case, their great success led them to become proud. And God's word is quite clear about how he feels about pride. Tyre was not only prideful about their great accomplishments but also about their great wisdom. They believed they knew more than anyone else in the world. This kind of belief can lead to great arrogance and other very harmful attitudes. Once you start believing that you are wise, you begin viewing others in relation to your wisdom and you begin to put others down.

God resists the proud and He confounds the wise. Tyre was completely and utterly destroyed by King Nebuchadnezzar. All of their success, wealth, and wisdom got them nowhere. With everything they had, they were missing the one thing that would have saved them; a relationship with God.

The times that we live in today are not that much different than they were in the days of Ezekiel. There are still people, organizations, and countries that are experiencing great wealth and success. There are people that believe that they are wiser than anyone around them. There are people and organizations that believe their wealth and wisdom will protect them. There are countries that believe that they are invincible. Without God, these people, organizations, and countries will experience the same fate as Tyre. While there may not be a King Nebuchadnezzar marching on their gates, God is preparing someone or something to humble and confound them.

Churches and ministries are not immune from this disease. Some believe that because they represent God, that they can behave the same way that Tyre was with arrogance and pride. God will not hesitate to humble a church or ministry leader that behaves in this manner. We cannot even begin to believe that because we are in the church that we are immune to this kind of correction.

God is looking for strong leaders that are humble and meek. He wants His leaders to be people that know that without God they would have nothing and that compared to God they know nothing. Only this type of attitude and behavior can assure God's protection and provision. The moment we look to ourselves for anything that we do or have is the moment that God stops being able to work fully in our lives, ministries, and churches. God doesn't need us but He wants to use us to reach out to whole world to reveal Jesus to the lost. Staying humble and meek opens the door to our heart for Him to do that. Jesus, teach us to know nothing except You and to need nothing but You.

NOVEMBER 14

Read: Ezekiel 29:1 – 30:26, Hebrews 11:32 – 12:13, Psalm 112:1-10, Proverbs 27:17

PSALM 112:7

They do not fear bad news; they confidently trust the LORD to care for them.

In this psalm we see a group of people that should have no fear of bad news; those people that fear the Lord. This psalm is a great testimony to the benefits of fearing the Lord. When we get to that place of reverential awe of God, these are the rewards that await us.

One of the interesting things is that you can't get to that place of reverential awe if you have your eyes on the reward. Your eyes must be focused on the Lord. The way that you know that you have attained the description of one having the fear of the Lord is when you see these things in your life.

Bad news seems to be a part of our everyday lives. We can't turn on the news on television or read the paper without being bombarded with bad news. It seems that for something to make it into the public media that it has to be really bad. It seems to be a game to see who can find the worst "bad news."

One of those characteristics is that you don't fear bad news. Fear is removed from our lives as we fill our lives with trust in something or someone greater than ourselves. The greater that someone is the greater our trust is and the less we fear. When we fear the Lord, we recognize His greatness and begin to trust Him. As we grow in our knowledge of God and His infinite power, we learn to trust Him more.

There comes a time when we realize that God is in complete control of everything. All of us have heard that but we don't all believe it. It is that lack of belief that prevents us from truly trusting God and vanquishing fear in our lives. We can get to a place where our trust in the Lord is so great that bad news has no power over us. We can do this because we know that God knew about that bad news before you did and He already has a plan to make good come out of it.

If you go through life dreading the next phone call or the next conversation with your boss it is a sign that you do not fear the Lord. Because you do not understand who God is and what He is doing all around you, you do not trust Him to take care of all the bad things that could happen to you. This lack of trust will cause you to have fear.

Get to know God more fully through prayer and through His living Word. Spend time in fellowship with other believers and learn from them who God is and how He works in the universe. Then believe what you learn. Faith or believing God is the key to having that reverential awe of God that leads to trusting Him. Trusting God doesn't make the bad news any less bad, it just means that we don't have to be afraid because we know that God has a plan to deal with it. Jesus, teach us to fear You and nothing else.

NOVEMBER 15
Read: Ezekiel 31:1 – 32:32, Hebrews 12:4-29, Psalm 113:1 – 114:8, Proverbs 27:18-20

EZEKIEL 32:17

On March 17, during the twelfth year, another message came to me from the Lord.

Ezekiel is given another message that describes what is going to happen to Egypt and other godless nations. The Lord instructs Ezekiel to weep for these nations because they are going to be sent to the world below. It grieves the Lord's heart that anyone would refuse to choose His love and grace and instead choose to be separated from Him forever.

In today's verse Ezekiel is given "another" message. It occurred to me as I was reading that there is a reason why the Lord gave Ezekiel "another" message; it was because he was faithful with the first message. In fact, Ezekiel had received many messages from the Lord because he had been faithful to speak forth the messages that the Lord was giving to him.

God wants to speak to all of us and I believe that He desires to give messages to us that are intended for other people. I don't necessarily mean that He will use us like He did Ezekiel but I can say for certain that there are people all around you that the Lord wants to get a message to and there is a good chance that He wants to use you to do it. All around you are people that need to hear from God that do not want to or know how to listen for His voice.

It is an amazing and somewhat frightening thing to think that the God of the universe might want to use me to get a message to one of His creations. God doesn't need us; He could get these messages to people without us but He chooses people like you and me to speak on His behalf to the people around us that are heading down the wrong path. He wants them to know that it grieves His heart that they are going the way that they are. His goal in giving you a message for others is that they would turn around and follow a path that leads to fellowship with Christ and life.

What an amazing privilege it is to be used by God to help people come to know Jesus and experience eternal life. And the radical thing about that is that He can and desires to use anyone. No one is beyond the range of God to use as one of His special messengers. God can use absolutely anyone to give someone a message of God's love, or hope, or peace, or joy, or encouragement. It doesn't require training or special education; it only requires the presence of the Holy Spirit in your life.

Ezekiel was given many messages and some of them are spectacular. Because Ezekiel was faithful to give the messages he was given, he was given "another" one. I like that! I would like to receive another message from the Lord and so I will be faithful to share the one He has already given me. How about you? Jesus, help us to share with others.

NOVEMBER 16

Read: Ezekiel 33:1 – 34:31, Hebrews 13:1-25, Psalm 115:1-18, Proverbs 27:21-22

Continue to love each other with true Christian love.

The writer to the Hebrews opens this last chapter of his epistle with what looks like a very simplistic statement; love each other. I would like to challenge you to take a closer look at this verse and examine your heart. Are you continuing to love others with true Christian love? This is a question that we ought to be able to answer yes to; especially as we approach Christmas, a celebration of God's greatest gift of love, Jesus.

The epistle to the Hebrews was written to Jewish Christians. Its intent was to draw these Christ-believers back from following the Law of Moses and to draw them to the Grace of God through Christ Jesus. So as the writer tells us to love each other, he is telling us to love other Christians. We would think that we shouldn't even have to think about this, let alone have to write it in a letter and discuss it. The Holy Spirit knows our hearts so well; He knows that we will not do this unless we are reminded to.

Who are these other Christians that we are to continue to love? The obvious ones are the ones that you are close to; the ones in your family, or ministry, or church. It is also the ones that you are not close to; the ones outside your family, the ones in other ministries, and the ones in other churches. We are also called to love Christians of other nationalities, cultures, and denominations. We are also called to love Christians that worship God in ways that we don't agree with or understand.

We're not just to love them but love them with Christian love. Since the word "Christian" means Christ-like, we are to love them the same way that Christ loved them and loves them. That means that we need to understand how Christ has shown His love for us and show that same kind of love toward other Christ-believers. Here is the radical thing about that; as you learn how much Christ has loved you and loves you now and you begin to reflect that love into the lives of others, you will learn even more how much Christ loves you. The more you love others, the more you will appreciate and feel the love that Christ has for you. Try it; you will see that you can't out-love God. The more that you love others, the greater your capacity to feel love and to give love will be.

Our verse challenges us to love with "true Christian love." That means that we shouldn't be faking it; we should love people with true love. There is a place for doing acts of love while God is causing love to grow in your heart but even that would be considered a true Christian love if your heart is set on loving them the way that Christ did. You can't make it happen in your own heart, the Holy Spirit has to grow it there. False love is motivated by what it can get out of the relationship; true love is motivated by what it can give to the relationship. Examine your heart to see if you love others as Christ loves them. Jesus, fill our hearts with Your love so that we can give it to others.

NOVEMBER 17
Read: Ezekiel 35:1 – 36:38, James 1:1-18, Psalm 116:1-19, Proverbs 27:23-27

JAMES 1:5

If you need wisdom—if you want to know what God wants you to do—ask him, and he will gladly tell you. He will not resent your asking.

James, the half-brother of our Lord Jesus, wrote one of the strongest books in the Bible. It is one of the most studied books in the Bible because of its real-life application. There is hardly a paragraph that does not give us something that we can use to make our lives more Christ-like. Here in the opening verses of his epistle, James exhorts us to ask God for wisdom.

Wisdom is different than knowledge. Wisdom is knowing what to do with the knowledge that you have. Identifying a black cat-sized animal as a skunk is knowledge. Staying away from the skunk because it can spray you with a foul-smelling substance is wisdom. James gives us a further definition of what wisdom is in the verse for the day. It is not just knowing what to do with the knowledge that you have but what it is that God wants you to do with the knowledge that you have.

True wisdom is doing what God wants you to do; even when this contradicts what the world calls wisdom. The Bible teaches that the wisdom of the world is foolishness to God. Why would we want to go to the world for wisdom when God would call that wisdom foolish? And yet, that is what we do so often. We will go to secular sources of wisdom when we have a source that never fails and is absolutely perfect.

Our verse tells us to ask God for the wisdom we need. There are several things that we need to take from this verse. First, wisdom is knowing what to do with the knowledge that you have. If wisdom is knowing what God wants us to do then our knowledge of what God wants needs to be growing. This means that you need to be reading and studying your Bible. As you read and study you are increasing the knowledge that God has to work with to give you wisdom. Second, to ask God means that you need to have an active prayer life. God will usually work in your prayer life to give you the wisdom that you need. He will also work in others which means that you need to be around people that are seeking God's wisdom also.

Finally, you need to believe that God wants to give you the wisdom that you need. He will gladly give you what you need. What we often will struggle with is when God delays in giving us what we think that we need. If you don't have it right now, either you don't really need it right now or God is waiting for you to get the knowledge you need or He is waiting for you to ask. Jesus, help us to come to You often and with the right heart.

NOVEMBER 18

Read: Ezekiel 37:1 – 38:23, James 1:19 – 2:17, Psalm 117:1-2, Proverbs 28:1

EZEKIEL 37:12

Now give them this message from the Sovereign LORD: O my people, I will open your graves of exile and cause you to rise again. Then I will bring you back to the land of Israel.

God gives a message of encouragement to Ezekiel to give to the people of Israel. God had kept His threat to punish the children of Israel for turning away from Him. God had told them that if they turned to worship other gods other than the One and True God that He would drive them from the good land that He had given them. They did exactly what God told them not to do. And so God did exactly what He said He was going to do.

God used the king of Babylon to punish the children of Israel. This was after He had warned them on numerous occasions that He was going to do it. He even told them that He was going to use King Nebuchadnezzar to drive them out of the land that He had told them that they could have forever. Some might look at this situation and say that God was going back on His word. He had told the children of Israel that the Promise Land would be theirs forever. So why was He kicking them out of the land? His promise of an eternal homeland was a conditional promise; there was a part that the children of Israel played in keeping the land forever. That condition was that God was to be their only God. Because of their unfaithfulness, God was forced to keep His threat to them because of His faithfulness.

Even in the midst of punishing the nation of Israel for its unfaithfulness, God makes another promise to the His chosen people. He promises to bring them back to the land that He had promised them to keep forever. All they have to do to see this promise fulfilled is the same thing that they needed to do in the first place; worship only God. To see God bring them back from exile, all they had to do was repent from their sin of idolatry and turn back to God.

God is so faithful and full of grace and mercy. No matter how far we wander from Him, He is waiting for us to return to Him so that He can fulfill all the promises that He made to us. No matter what we might have done in our lives, He stands ready to forgive the repentant heart and bring any and all of us back from whatever exile we forced Him to send us to. God's grace and mercy are endless and difficult to comprehend. We don't need to understand; we just need to accept it and do it.

If you have wandered away from the intimate fellowship with God that He desires to have with you; just repent and turn back to Him and He will bring you back from wherever He exiled you to and into the incredible life that He desires you to have. Don't wait and don't fight. The sooner that you give in to God, the sooner you will be experiencing the life that Jesus can to give you. It all begins with repentance. Humble yourself before God and ask Him to forgive you and then watch Him begin to work in your life. Jesus, help us to ache when we are absent from your presence.

Eat the flesh of mighty men and drink the blood of princes as though they were rams, lambs, goats, and fat young bulls of Bashan.

In this prophecy a great enemy of Israel will come from the north. This enemy, Gog, is believed by many to be some form of the Russian Empire. God will convince them to attack Israel and in the process of the attack God will utterly wipe out their entire army. Most believe this to be a future event. Its purpose is to declare the power of God to an unbelieving world. God will supernaturally protect the nation of Israel from an overwhelming attack.

In today's verse God has called the birds and wild animals to come to a sacrificial feast. This great enemy of Israel and God will suffer such a great defeat that it will take months to bury all the dead. God will send birds and animals in great numbers to eat the flesh of all the fallen enemies of God. This will be a horrific scene that hopefully will take place after the Rapture of God's church.

Some might read a verse like this and wonder what it says to us today. The obvious thing is that God can and will protect His people from their enemies. It also tells us that no enemy is so overwhelming that God can't utterly defeat them. It also tells us that the mighty men and princes of this world are not as great and mighty as we might see them to be.

In this verse they are compared to sacrificial animals. In the sacrificial system of Israel the animals were sacrificed to God. Usually only a small portion was burned in the fire. The rest was eaten by the priests or by the people making the sacrifice. In this sacrificial feast mentioned here the animals are the ones doing the eating. It is backwards of what is normal.

We should not be too concerned about what the rest of the world thinks or is doing. We need to stay focused on what the Lord would direct us to do. This is especially true if we are called to lead in families, ministries, or churches. Let God take care of the world. Let God deal with the mighty men and princes that might be lining up and preparing to attack you. You focus on the things that God has set before you.

Just remember when you feel overwhelmed by the pressures of the world that Jesus has overcome the world. Remember this account today; that God can supernaturally act on your behalf and rescue you in a way that shocks the whole world. Trust Him and Him alone to be your strength. Hold fast to His truth. Walk daily in His ways and let His Holy Spirit direct your path. Jesus, help us to look for Your hand upon all things around us.

NOVEMBER 20

Read: Ezekiel 40:28 – 41:26, James 4:1-17, Psalm 118:19-29, Proverbs 28:3-5

JAMES 4:7

So humble yourselves before God. Resist the Devil, and he will flee from you.

Our verse for today is one that many people are very familiar with. We have all heard this one quoted or quoted it ourselves. Usually it is only the second half that we quote. It is my belief that is why so many people are not able to resist the Devil; they omit the first part. In many people's minds they picture the Devil in a red suit with horns and a pitchfork. That is what they are resisting and usually failing.

The context that this verse is contained in is our relationship to the world. James is telling us that if we are friends of this world, then we are enemies of God. If our goal in life is to enjoy this world and the things of this world than we are not friends of God and we cannot please God. God wants us to stand up to the attacks of the enemy; but we have to decide not to live in the enemy's camp first. It is staggering the number of people that come to us for help that will not leave the camp of the enemy when they are told that is the reason why they are in trouble.

We need to love God more than we love the world. Our verse tells us to humble ourselves before God. That means that we acknowledge to God that He is God and that He is in charge. It means that we will let Him direct our plans and the path that we take in life. It means that we will choose to accept whatever His word tells us; even when it means doing something that we don't want to do.

To be able to resist the Devil, you must first humble yourself before God. It is through humbling yourself before God that you are given the power through the Holy Spirit to resist the Devil. We don't have the strength to do it on our own. The Devil manipulating our own sinful desires is much stronger than we will ever be. By humbling yourself before God you are calling in the power of the Almighty God to assist you to resist.

This is especially true if you are called by God to lead a family, ministry, or church. As a leader you are a more visible target to the enemy. The Devil knows that if he can take out a leader through his own sinful desires that he can impact a much larger group of people. As the leader you are out in front and that can be a very vulnerable place to be. You need to have your armor on and need to have your shield up. You do that by humbling yourself before God.

There is not a man or a woman that can stand up and resist the Devil. On the other hand, the Devil cannot stand up to even the weakest man or woman that has humbled themselves before God. We only become strong enough to resist the Devil once we have learned that without God we cannot resist him at all. Jesus, help us to be humble.

NOVEMBER 21

Read: Ezekiel 42:1 – 43:27, James 5:1-20, Psalm 119:1-16, Proverbs 28:6-7

PSALM 119:5

Oh, that my actions would consistently reflect your principles!

For you trivia buffs, Psalm 119 is the longest chapter in the Bible. Psalm 117 is the shortest chapter and it is said that Psalm 118 is the center chapter in the Bible. Psalm 119 is one of my favorite of the Psalms. Within this psalm is a focus on the word of God like virtually no other text in the Bible. From verse 1 to verse 176, God's laws, commands, and statutes are praised and we are exhorted to keep them and to love them.

Another reason why I am fond of this psalm is that it is written as much like a prayer as it is a song. This anonymous psalmist loves God by loving His words and throughout this psalm we see examples of how he does that.

There is nothing particularly special about verse 5 that we are looking at today except that it was the first verse in the chapter that grabbed me and caught my attention. There are many other verses that could just have easily been used for today's devotional.

In our text for today the psalmist makes a request of God that his actions would be consistent with the principles of God's Word. What a great request! He loves God's word and he is asking God to help him show that to the whole world by controlling his actions. The psalmist wants his actions to reflect the word of God. What a perfect image! When we look in the mirror what we see is a reflection of us and the world around us. The psalmist wants the word of God to the thing that is reflected off of him. When people look at him, what they see are the commands of God being lived out.

Not only does he want his life to be a reflection of the statutes of God, he wants it to be a consistent reflection. The psalmist wants the reflection of his life to be the same every time someone looks at him. No matter where he is, he wants his reflection to be the same and to be a reflection of the perfect commands of God.

It should not be a surprise to anyone that this is what God wants from all of us. He wants our lives to be a consistent reflection of the perfect word of the Living God. God wants each of us to be a mirror that reflects Jesus Christ to everyone that looks at us. God also wants that to be a description of our families, ministries, and churches. It should be no surprise to anyone that God wants people to see Jesus when they look at our families, ministries, and churches.

And the only way that we are going to do that is to develop this same love for the word of God that the psalmist had. God's commands, statutes, and laws have got to take a central place in our lives. We must develop a hunger and thirst that can only be satisfied by the word of God. Our desire and prayer should be that God would help us to hide His word in our hearts and that He would help us to reflect His perfect law in our actions. Jesus, help us to make every action be a perfect reflection of your perfection.

Read: Ezekiel 44:1 – 45:12, 1 Peter 1:1-12, Psalm 119:17-32, Proverbs 28:8-10

You have not kept the laws I gave you concerning these sacred rituals, for you have hired foreigners to take charge of my sanctuary.

God is having Ezekiel remind the nation of Israel about the way that He told them that He wanted to be worshipped. God had given the Israelites very clear and extensive instructions on how He wanted temple worship to take place. Over time the Israelites started to treat these instructions nonchalantly. These rituals became so common that the Israelites started to bring in foreigners to do the work for them. What a powerful warning is found in this for all of us.

God had given them clear directions on how to perform the various rituals that He commanded them to keep. God didn't change His mind later. To God these rituals were as important as the first day that He gave them to the Israelites. What changed were the hearts of the people. The longer that they did these rituals the less meaningful they became; they became commonplace and mundane. At the same time the people that were responsible for conducting these rituals began to think of themselves as important. The more important they thought themselves to be, the more mundane became the rituals that they were performing.

As modern evangelical Christians we do not have the same types of rituals that the Israelites did. They had very specific ways of worshipping God. We are given much more freedom in the manner that we come to worship God. We do have some rituals like communion and baptism but most things that we do are not dictated explicitly by God. I believe that puts us at even greater risk of falling into the same trap that the Israelites did. Because we don't have clear, distinct direction from God on how we should worship Him that we are at greater risk of making our worship mundane and common.

God deserves our very best and He deserves that we treat every aspect of our worship of Him with reverence and awe. Every aspect of our lives which we do as an act of worship toward God (which should be every part of your life) should be approached as something holy. How you dress when you go to church or to your Bible study should show your reverence and awe of God. That doesn't mean you need to wear some special kind of clothes but you should ask yourself if God would be pleased with what you are wearing. When you tithe it is an act of worship; do it with joy and gladness. Prayerfully ask God to direct you in all those kinds of things.

Treat the things of God as holy because they are. God is not happy when we treat His things as common and mundane. If God has called you to serve Him in any way (which He has) then you should treat that as a holy privilege and thank Him for it by serving faithfully and diligently. God's blessings are often a product of our obedience. Don't get tired of doing those good things that He gave you do to. Jesus, teach us to serve.

NOVEMBER 23

Read: Ezekiel 45:13 – 46:24, 1 Peter 1:13 – 2:10, Psalm 119:33-48, Proverbs 28:11

1 PETER 2:5

And now God is building you, as living stones, into his spiritual temple. What's more, you are God's holy priests, who offer the spiritual sacrifices that please him because of Jesus Christ.

Peter is writing this letter to the Jewish believers that were scattered from Jerusalem because of persecution. While it was written specifically to them it was meant to be read by all believers. Peter in our verse for the day tells us that we are a work in progress; we are being built up into a temple by God and for God.

This is an amazing image that Peter paints for us. God is using us as living stones to build Himself a spiritual temple. Only God could do something like that. When something is living it typically grows and changes. That is absolutely true of people; they are always in a state of some form of growth or change. When man builds something, he uses materials that are static; they don't change or grow. He does that because he knows that living materials are going to make the building very unstable over time.

The unlimited power of God can take the ever-changing stones of our lives and combine them into something that is absolutely fantastic; His

Church. Only God could hold together the living stones that so often want to separate and build temples for themselves. The Church is a miracle and we should stand in awe of what God has done. We should also do everything that we can to cooperate with God and stop fighting with each other.

Not only are we living stones but Peter goes on to tell us that we are God's holy priests. Before you assume that is talking to the pastors and ministers and other ministry leaders and not you remember that Peter is writing an open letter to all believers. The context of this letter and this section of scripture do not limit this statement at all. It is an all-inclusive statement. The "you" in that statement literally means you.

As leaders of families, ministries, or churches we have a responsibility to teach those that we minister to what it means to be a priest. We need to help them to discover just what it means that they are to give spiritual sacrifices that please the Lord. One of the ways that we teach them that is by modeling it for them. If they can't see it in us, we shouldn't expect them to do it.

We need only study the life of Jesus and what He taught to begin to know just what those spiritual sacrifices are. It is the way that He interacted with and ministered to the people. It is the way that He taught about the Kingdom of God. It was the way that He lived His life for others rather than for Himself. Imitate the life of Christ and then encourage others to do the same. Jesus, open our hearts to see You more clearly so that we might reveal You to others.

NOVEMBER 24

Read: Ezekiel 47:1 – 48:35, 1 Peter 2:11 – 3:7, Psalm 119:49-64, Proverbs 28:12-13

EZEKIEL 48:11

This area is set aside for the ordained priests, the descendants of Zadok who obeyed me and did not go astray when the people of Israel and the rest of the Levites did.

As the Lord is describing to Ezekiel how the land should be divided out to the tribes He tells Ezekiel to give a special piece of land to the descendants of Zadok. These descendants have the distinction of having been faithful to God even when all of their fellow countrymen had turned to idolatry. Because of their faithfulness they were given the distinct privilege of ministering before God in the temple. No one else was allowed to do it.

These descendants of Zadok were no better or more holy than the other Israelites. What made them different was their faithfulness to God. What makes this especially important is the fact that they did this while the rest of the nation practiced idolatry all around them.

We live in a world where idolatry is increasingly prevalent. In the US it is not the kind that the Israelites were practicing but it is idolatry none the less. Instead of worshipping stone and wood idols, we are worshipping idols of money, position, possessions, or power. We may not sacrifice animals to these idols but we sacrifice our relationships and lives to them.

God calls us to turn away from all of those idols and worship only Him. That can be incredibly difficult because everyone around us is likely worshipping those idols. To go against the flow of everyone around you takes great courage and an unflinching faith that God is in control. God's desire is that we would be faithful to His call on our lives regardless of what the rest of the world is doing.

What Zadok and his descendants experienced from their faithfulness was a special place in the kingdom of God. One of the things that struck me in this text was that Ezekiel is talking to the descendants of Zadok. We leave a spiritual legacy behind for all of those that follow after us. When we are faithful to God's call and instructions, our descendants, both physical and spiritual will reap rewards and blessings. Of course, they also need to be faithful otherwise they risk losing the blessings and breaking the chain of reward.

Whatever the world does around you, just be faithful to God and He will look down upon you and smile. You may receive a reward in this lifetime and you may not but your descendants will likely reap a harvest of blessings and rewards from your faithfulness. The only way to do that is to keep your eyes on Jesus. Don't spend too much of your time looking at what everyone else is doing; you concentrate on what God is calling you to do. Jesus, help us to be faithful.

NOVEMBER 25

Read: Daniel 1:1 – 2:23, 1 Peter 3:8 – 4:6, Psalm 119:65-80, Proverbs 28:14

DANIEL 1:8

But Daniel made up his mind not to defile himself by eating the food and wine given to them by the king. He asked the chief official for permission to eat other things instead.

King Nebuchadnezzar came with his army and besieged Jerusalem and conquered it. In addition to the precious items from the Temple of God he also brought back many prisoners of the people of Israel. Nebuchadnezzar ordered that the "strong, healthy, good looking" young men of the captives be brought to his palace. They were to undergo a three-year training process to determine if some of them would be fit to become advisors in his royal court.

Daniel was one of the four young men named that were selected to be a part of this process. The king assigned to them the best of the food and wine that was served to him as their ration. Daniel made up his mind not to eat that food and wine because he felt that it would defile him. He then asked for permission to eat something else.

Daniel was a Jew and had been raised under the strict dietary rules of the Law of Moses. God gave to Moses to give to the nation of Israel very strict instructions as to the things they could and could not eat. These dietary laws were meant to cause the Jews to be a separated people. They were meant to be different from the world around them. The dietary laws were just one of the ways that God wanted to use to cause the Hebrews to be a people that stood out from the rest of the world.

Daniel could have easily justified in his own mind that he was a prisoner exiled from his homeland. He could have easily convinced himself that he really didn't have a choice. Daniel is showing great faith in God and resolve of character to make a choice like this. This is even more remarkable when we remember that Daniel was a teenager at this time.

In many respects we are just like Daniel. This world that we live in is not our home. As Christians we are citizens of heaven. We are just passing through this world as we wait for our graduation to heaven. The world is also trying to "train" us to be like it is. And just like Daniel, we are daily being offered things that will defile us.

We are called to be a separated people. Unlike the Jews we do not have the Law as a guideline. Instead we look upon the New Testament as our guide and we depend upon the Holy Spirit to teach us about holiness and separation from the things of the world. It all begins with a single choice, much like the one that Daniel made in our verse for the day. We must choose not to be defiled by the world around us. Even if we never fully attain it our goal must be absolute holiness and righteousness. If that is our goal then we will never even approach it. Choose not to be defiled by the world around you. Jesus, help us to choose daily to be undefiled.

NOVEMBER 26

Read: Daniel 2:24 – 3:30, 1 Peter 4:7 – 5:14, Psalm 119:81-96, Psalm 28:15-16

1 PETER 5:12
I have written this short letter to you with the help of Silas, whom I consider a faithful brother. My purpose in writing is to encourage you and assure you that the grace of God is with you no matter what happens.

As Peter closes his letter he gives his purpose in writing it. This letter was written to Christian Jews that had been scattered all over Asia. Peter's purpose was to encourage them and to remind them that the grace of God is always present in their lives. Peter was a fisherman by trade but here we see that Jesus has transformed him into a shepherd.

Peter was the main guy in the church in Jerusalem. The persecution in Jerusalem became so great that the church was scattered all over Asia. Peter is concerned about his scattered flock and so he writes this letter. Most of us probably can't imagine what it would be like to be driven from our homes and have everything taken from us because of our belief and trust in Jesus. We can't imagine how hard that might be or how vulnerable it might make us to the schemes of the enemy.

What we can imagine is life in the 21st century and all of its trials and temptations. Peter's letter applies to us in the 21st century just as it did to the 1st century church. While we are seldom going to face the persecution that they faced, we do face a seemingly endless stream of trials and temptations. Be encouraged, it will only last for a little while; the rest of your life. Our lives no matter how long they might be are only a moment compared to eternity. The thought of spending all of eternity in the presence of Jesus Christ in heaven ought to encourage and strengthen us.

Thankfully, our hope is not just in eternity. God has determined that He will also pour out His grace upon us in this life as well. No matter what trial or temptation comes your way, God's grace is right there with you to hold you through it. No matter how bad things seem to get around you, the grace of God does not fade or fail. Trust in God's grace, His unmerited favor upon your life, always but especially during the dark times of your life.

As leaders of God's families, ministries, and churches you are called to shepherd the flock that God has entrusted to you. Part of your responsibility to them is to encourage them and to remind them of the ever-present grace of God. Too many shepherds try to beat their sheep into doing what they think is right. God loves them and so should you. Show them the love of God in gentleness and meekness. Always point them back to the grace of God as their source of hope and assurance. It is there that they will become encouraged and grow stronger. Jesus, help us to live with our arm outstretched to You, pointing You out to others.

NOVEMBER 27
Read: Daniel 4:1-37, 2 Peter 1:1-21, Psalm 119:97-112, Proverbs 28:17-18

DANIEL 4:30
As he looked out across the city, he said, "Just look at this great city of Babylon! I, by my own mighty power, have built this beautiful city as my royal residence and as an expression of my royal splendor."

Babylon is said to have one of the most spectacular cities ever constructed. It was a wondrous thing to behold. King Nebuchadnezzar was very successful at his campaigns of conquest and was a prolific builder. Daniel chapter four is fascinating because much of it appears to be written from the perspective of King Nebuchadnezzar, a pagan king; it is as though he is narrating this chapter.

Early in the chapter God had warned him in a dream that something pretty dramatic was going to happen. Daniel interpreted the dream and told Nebuchadnezzar that his kingdom was going to be torn away from him and he would be driven mad and driven from the kingdom that he had built to live like an animal for seven years. This vision was fulfilled twelve months later and was triggered by Nebuchadnezzar's statement in our verse for the day.

The king looked out over the incredible city that he had built and then allowed his pride to express itself. God had determined to make an example of Nebuchadnezzar to the rest of the world. God used this seven year event to prove to the whole world that He is in complete control over everything including the pagan kings and kingdoms of the world.

As Christians, especially Christian leaders, we cannot exclude ourselves from the lesson that God is teaching here. Nebuchadnezzar's pride and arrogance was the trigger to this event. As leaders of families, ministries, or churches we can find ourselves also standing on the roof of some impressive structure or inside some amazing organization or in a place where our efforts are being recognized. What we do at that moment will determine how the rest of our life may play out.

God put Nebuchadnezzar on a seven year time-out. God will not hesitate to do that to any of the rest of us either. If we begin to look around at the things that God is doing and begin to believe in our hearts that we are responsible for it happening we can be assured that God is preparing a grassy field for us to hang out in until we figure out who is really in charge.

We can avoid that ever happening by just humbling our hearts before God. Few sins anger God like the sin of pride. The Bible is rich with warnings and exhortations against pride. It is also filled with promises for those that practice the opposite of pride, humility. Humble your heart before the Creator of the universe before He does it for you. Jesus, help us to recognize that everything in our lives is as a direct result of You working their on our behalf.

NOVEMBER 28

Read: Daniel 5:1-31, 2 Peter 2:1-22, Psalm 119:113-128, Proverbs 28:19-20

DANIEL 5:17

Daniel answered the king, "Keep your gifts or give them to someone else, but I will tell you what the writing means."

King Belshazzer of the Babylonians decided to throw a big party and during that party he had the holy vessels, gold and silver cups, from the temple in Jerusalem brought out so that his nobles could drink from them. Right in the middle of the party a hand appears and writes something on the wall. The king gets pretty freaked out about this and so he calls in all of his wisest men to determine what it means. He promised to these men great rewards if they would just tell him what the words meant. None of them could. The queen mother tells the king that there is a man that probably can interpret the writing on the wall.

Daniel is brought before the king and the king tells him that if he will interpret the writing that he will reward him including a promotion to the third highest ruler in the land. In our verse for the day Daniel tells the king that he can keep his gifts. It is very possible that Daniel knew what was about to transpire that very night and that the rewards would be meaningless once Belshazzer was killed and Darius became king.

But there is another principle that we as Christians should take careful heed of. Daniel had a gift from God to interpret things like the hand writing on the wall of Belshazzer's banquet hall. Daniel knew that it was not appropriate to "sell" that gift. Belshazzer offered to pay Daniel to use the gift that God had given Daniel freely. God has also given each of us gifts that He expects us to use for His glory and to proclaim His name just as Daniel did.

Daniel responded and told the king that the rewards were not necessary and that he was going to do what the king asked anyway. We should be just as willing to share the gifts of God with others as Daniel was. Because of his obedience to the king and to God all of the king's nobles and his guests saw the power of God at work. Daniel was willing to serve God even if there wasn't a reward.

The story continues that Belshazzer did in fact reward Daniel with all that he said that he would. Belshazzer was killed that very night and his kingdom was conquered by the Medes and the Persians so it is difficult to know how long Daniel got to keep his reward. In Daniels heart he had already determined to serve God regardless if there was a reward or not. Could you say the same thing about your service to the Lord? If there was absolutely no reward of any kind, would you continue to serve? If no one ever said thank you, would you continue to do what you are doing now? If no one appreciates you or if they take advantage of you, will you still serve? Daniel did! Jesus did! You should! Jesus, help us to look upon You as our reward.

NOVEMBER 29

Read: Daniel 6:1-28, 2 Peter 3:1-18, Psalm 119:129-152, Proverbs 28:21-22

DANIEL 6:4

Then the other administrators and princes began searching for some fault in the way Daniel was handling his affairs, but they couldn't find anything to criticize. He was faithful and honest and always responsible.

King Darius plans to reorganize his kingdom. It is quite large and so he divides it into 120 provinces and assigns a prince over each of them. He then assigns three men to oversee the 120 princes. These three men would report directly to King Darius. It was a good system to control a large territory without getting too bogged down with dealing with individual provinces. Daniel was one of the three men overseeing the princes. He quickly proved himself to be the most capable of all and so the king planned to put Daniel in charge of the whole kingdom.

All the other guys didn't like the idea that Daniel was going to be in charge of everything and so they started to watch him very carefully to find some kind of fault or flaw in his character. They could find nothing to criticize about Daniel or the way that he handled his affairs. The way that these evil guys described Daniel is the way that I want unbelievers to view me; faithful and honest and always responsible.

Daniel is working in an environment that is about as difficult as you can possibly find and still maintain his integrity. He is working closely with a pagan king. He is very likely being exposed to all of the evil and wickedness that went on around the royal chambers of the king. He is also dealing with all of the politics and intrigue that goes on in a position like his. The temptations to compromise his faith and integrity must have been tremendous and yet his accusers can find nothing with which to charge Daniel. Instead they must fabricate a scenario that will trap Daniel.

If people look into your life and examine your character, would they describe it like these men described Daniel? Is your character such that people have to contrive and scheme to accuse you? Your circumstances are probably far less tempting than Daniel's were. God would call you to a Daniel level of faith. Trust God to the point that you can work in any environment while maintaining your integrity and character.

God blessed Daniel in very real and practical ways as a result of his faith and integrity. God wants to bless you as well. Stand up for the truth and refuse to compromise your integrity. It might result in some discomfort and trials as the world fights against what you are doing but you can rest assured that if you are being obedient to God that He will protect and provide for you. King Darius knew of Daniel's integrity and was sad when he discovered that he had passed a law that would cause Daniel harm. Not only did God protect Daniel but He also dealt very harshly with his enemies. Trust God; let Him be your defender and strong tower. You just do what is right! Jesus, teach us to be like You.

NOVEMBER 30
Read: Daniel 7:1-28, 1 John 1:1-10, Psalm 119:153-176, Proverbs 28:23-24

1 JOHN 1:3

We are telling you about what we ourselves have actually seen and heard, so that you may have fellowship with us. And our fellowship is with the Father and with his Son, Jesus Christ.

The apostle John begins his first epistle with a great illustration of true evangelism. Evangelism and evangelists have gotten a bit of a bad name and have been stereotyped by our society and media as men standing behind a pulpit or on a street corner telling people that they are going to hell if they don't change their ways. Evangelism is telling people about Jesus and how they can have a personal relationship with Him and spend all of eternity with Him.

One of the ways that we do that is by helping people to understand that there is a judgment coming but that is certainly not the only way and often it is the wrong way with some people. It is the love of God and the grace of God that lead most people to repentance. The best example to share with people is the example of your life.

God has shown His grace and mercy in your life. People can look at your life and see that the power of God is real. By telling people what you have actually seen and heard, they can then relate to you. By sharing these things with other people, they are able to fellowship with you. It is as we share the things of God that God draws people into the family of God. God doesn't need us to do this, but He has chosen to use this method to reveal Himself to the world.

There is no greater tool for evangelism than a life that has been changed by the power of God. If you are a child of God, than your life has changed because of your relationship with Jesus. Share that with others so that they also can fellowship with you. And because they are fellowshipping with you as you fellowship the Father and His Son, Jesus, they also are fellowshipping with God.

Too often we look at evangelism as something that is done by some guy in a suit and tie. Jesus told all of us to go out into the world and tell people about what He has done for them. You don't have to preach to do that; you just need to be a child of God that has been changed by the power of the Holy Spirit working in your life. It has been said that we should always preach the gospel and if necessary we should use words. That means that our life is a living gospel. Nothing will reach a lost a dying world like a person that has fully surrendered their life to God and is daily in fellowship with Him and His Son, Jesus. Don't worry about what to say, your only responsibility is to live a life that is pleasing to God; He will guide when it is time to speak and He will give you the words to say. Jesus, help us to be lamp posts to guide others to You.

DECEMBER

DECEMBER 1

Read: Daniel 8:1-27, 1 John 2:1-17, Psalm 120:1-7, Proverbs 28:25-26

PSALM 120:6

I am tired of living here among people who hate peace.

Have you ever felt like the psalmist in today's reading? He feels that he is completely surrounded by enemies and they never cease to attack him. There is no peace on any side because everyone around him hates peace. The result is that he is tired of living there. I am certain that many can relate to our reading for today. You might live in a neighborhood where there is great strife and friction. You might work in a place where there is no sign of peace and it is difficult even to show up for work without being attacked. Or you might be living with someone that has no desire for peace and continually makes life miserable and difficult.

Our natural response is to think just like the psalmist did and say to ourselves and to others; I am tired of living here like this. And then we do something about it; we leave that place and go somewhere else where we think that we will find peace. We will move to a new neighborhood, or get a new job, or leave our spouse and marry another in an effort to find peace.

What we often find when we do that is that there is no peace in this new place either. The new neighborhood, job, or spouse brings no more peace than we had before. In fact, it might even be worse than it was before. Some people spend their entire lives running from one place and thing to another looking for peace.

There is only one place that peace can be found and that is in Christ Jesus. Nothing else in our lives can bring peace; not a new neighborhood, or a new job, or a new spouse, or anything else. Throughout the New Testament, especially the epistles we see the concept of being "in Christ." That means that our life is found in and defined by Jesus. The deeper we are in Christ the more peace that we experience in our lives.

What we need to understand to experience peace is not that we need conflicts and strife to go away but that our life needs to be more completely consumed by Jesus. We live in a world that "hates peace." It is determined to destroy anything that is good and of God. There is no place that we can go and nothing that we can do that is going to change the way the world is. But we can experience peace in the midst of this hateful world and we can also be an oasis of peace for everyone around us.

People desire the peace of God that surpasses understanding but they have no idea where to find it. They will go anywhere and do anything to find it. We need to find it in Jesus and then let other people see it in us. Once they see the peace of God in our lives they will want it also and they will be drawn to us and we can direct them to the only source of true peace; Jesus Christ. We can't run away from those that "hate peace" but we can experience peace in our hearts in Christ. Jesus, teach us to rest in Your peace.

DECEMBER 2

Read: Daniel 9:1 – 11:1, 1 John 2:18 – 3:6, Psalm 121:1-8, Proverbs 28:27-28

DANIEL 10:12

Then he said, "Don't be afraid, Daniel. Since the first day you began to pray for understanding and to humble yourself before your God, your request has been heard in heaven. I have come in answer to your prayer."

Daniel had received a vision that troubled him greatly. He began to pray and ask God to give understanding of what the vision meant. It took three weeks for the answer to come to Daniel and it came in a spectacular way; an angel delivered it to him. Daniel is overwhelmed by this appearance and needs to be strengthened by him.

There are some tremendous truths to be found in this verse and text. Daniel was told that God had heard his prayer from the first moment that he had begun to pray. When God doesn't answer our prayers right away I believe that we sometimes think that we need to keep praying our prayers because we think that God didn't hear us the first time. Or we might think that God didn't understand what we were praying for. God doesn't need us to repeat ourselves, He doesn't need us to speak louder, He doesn't need us to maintain a certain posture while praying; God hears our prayers.

We are taught in scripture to keep coming to God with our prayers. That is not so that we will change God's might or so that He will hear us but so that we will be changed and we will hear His voice. Persistence in prayer is not a lack of faith but proof of it and also the conduit to hearing from God.

One of the keys to getting a response from God to your prayers is also found in this verse; Daniel humbled himself before God. Daniel didn't understand the vision that he had received from God. He admitted that to God and asked God to give him understanding. Few things will set your prayer life on fire like humility. It is our pride and selfishness that often hinders our prayers from being answered.

It takes humility to admit that you don't know something or that you need help. It takes faith to believe that God is able to bring understanding and is able to give us what we are looking for. It takes both humility and faith to see our prayers being answered. In Daniel's case we see it also takes patience. Daniel waited three weeks to receive the answer to his prayers. The answer to his prayers was being blocked by one of Satan's princes. For Daniel to receive his answer God had to send reinforcements to assist this angel.

If you have been waiting a long time for your prayers to be answered, be encouraged by this verse. Be persistent; keep praying. Do what you can to make sure that you are praying according to God's will by comparing your request to God's Word. Then, check your heart and make certain that you have humbled yourself before God and that you believe that God hears you and will answer your prayer. Jesus, help us to wait.

DECEMBER 3

Read: Daniel 11:2-35, 1 John 3:7-24, Psalm 122:1-9, Proverbs 29:1

DANIEL 11:32

He will flatter those who have violated the covenant and win them over to his side. But the people who know their God will be strong and resist him.

Many of Daniel's prophecies are similar to this one, they will have dual fulfillment. This is one of those cases. In today's reading we see an event described that was fulfilled about two hundred years later by Antiochus Epiphanes. Then Jesus referred to the same prophecy as a future event, pointing to an event that is expected to take place during the Tribulation Period.

Today's reading speaks of a man that will through subtlety and diplomacy take power and will deceive many to follow him. He is the same person as the "little horn" from Daniel 8. He will even convince some to forsake their covenant relationship with God to join his side. It is very likely that this is referring to Jews during the Tribulation period. Some of them will be deceived into turning away from God to follow the Antichrist. There are many that believe that the False Prophet of Revelation is one of these deceived Jews.

In our verse for the day we are told that some will not be deceived. These are the ones that "know their God." There is a powerful lesson in this for all of us. We live in a culture and society that puts little importance on the truth or God. Much of the influences in our lives are meant to deceive us and draw us away from knowing our God. Nothing in this world could be more important than knowing God intimately and as completely as is humanly possible. While we can never know God in His infinite fullness, we can know Him as He has revealed Himself in His Word and in His Son Jesus. To stand up against the onslaught of daily influences to turn from God we must daily seek to know Him more fully.

The key to resisting the enemy and standing strong in the face of ceaseless attacks; we need to know our God. It is not necessary to develop a battle plan of defense, simply get to know the Lord and trust Him to be your strong fortress. We don't need to launch a strategic attack against our enemy. We need to rest in the strength of our Almighty God and allow Him to fight the battles of this life.

As we get to know our God better and better, we may also find ourselves recruited to get into some part of the battle as one of His soldiers. Until He recruits you, you focus on getting to know Him. Eventually everyone will be called, but we need to know Him intimately enough to recognize His voice when He calls. Too many people try to stand on their own strength and abilities. They take getting to know God as seriously as they do studying a menu before ordering a meal. They get to know just enough to place an order and then forget the rest. They are the ones that will be deceived and will turn away at the first invitation by our cunning enemy. Jesus, teach us everything there is to know about You.

DECEMBER 4

Read: Daniel 11:36 – 12:13, 1 John 4:1-21, Psalm 123:1-4, Proverbs 29:2-4

1 JOHN 4:8

But anyone who does not love does not know God—for God is love.

The apostle John is best known as "the disciple whom Jesus loved" or as one of the "Sons of Thunder" or as the writer of the incredible book Revelation. We sometimes overlook these three letters that John wrote. To do that is to miss some rich and incredible material that can have a profound impact on our lives. In our reading for today, we have a dissertation about love and God and our relationship with God. John describes God in a very simple way; God is love. While this is simple to say, it can take a lifetime to understand. Because to truly understand what it means that God is love requires that we understand what love is. We may think that we know what love is but to truly understand love we must understand it the way that God views it. Only by understanding how God views love can we begin to understand God. As we begin to understand God, we then are able to have the right kind of relationship with Him.

We know that God loves us; the Bible tells us so. John 3:16 is one of those statements that tells us that God loves the whole world. What does it truly mean that God gave His Son so that we could be saved? We know it but we don't truly understand it. The Bible tells us that we will not have complete knowledge until we are with Jesus but we are also exhorted to know God.

As we mature we even understand how God demonstrates His love for us when He chastens us and disciplines us for our sins. Even though it is not fun and we would rather it didn't happen, we know that it is a sign of His love for us. What we need to get a firm grip on in our faith is that God is love. That means that absolutely everything that He does is motivated by His divine attribute of love. And because God has complete control over all the circumstances and situations of our life, that His love is being manifested in all areas of our lives.

The area that this is the most difficult to see is within our trials and tribulations. It is when our lives are falling apart and are in shambles that we have the hardest time seeing the incredible, never-ending, never-failing love that God has for us. When "bad" things are happening to us for seemingly no reason, it is difficult to see and feel that God loves us. The Bible teaches that there is nothing that can ever separate us from the love of God in Christ Jesus.

As leaders of families, ministries, or churches we have a responsibility to know the love of God intimately. We need to study it and grow in our knowledge of it every day. We need to find ourselves resting in the center of God's love in every circumstance of our lives; including all the tough times. We also, at the same time, need to be teaching others to do the same thing. Jesus, teach us of Your love.

DECEMBER 5

Read: Hosea 1:1 – 3:5, 1 John 5:1-21, Psalm 124:1-8, Proverbs 29:5-8

HOSEA 3:1

Then the LORD said to me, "Go and get your wife again. Bring her back to you and love her, even though she loves adultery. For the LORD still loves Israel even though the people have turned to other gods, offering them choice gifts."

The prophet Hosea was sent to give the nation of Israel a message from God that was intended to shame them into returning to the Lord. They had turned away from Him and were worshipping worthless idols and God painted a picture of that in the book of Hosea as prostitution. As far as God is concerned anyone that turns away from the Lord is acting as a prostitute, selling their affection to someone that they are not married to.

God created us to be His; no one else's. We are His special possession; whether we want to be or not. When we reject His love by rejecting His Son we are playing the harlot and committing adultery against God. A person with a hard heart doesn't really care about that but those with a heart that is sensitive to God will be offended by that thought. That is good; it shows that there is hope for our restoration to a right relationship with our Lord.

Playing the prostitute doesn't always mean that we have turned totally away from the Lord. It can also mean that we have just split our affection between God and something else. Only God can be the Lord of our lives; He must have the premier position in our lives. There are many things in my life that are important to me; my wife, my children, my church, my friends, my home, and many other things. All of these things take a distant second to God in my life. If any of those are elevated to a place equal or higher than God than I am committing spiritual adultery against God.

The cool thing about God is that no matter how unfaithful we are, He is always faithful. No matter how long or in what ways I might wander from the Lord, He is always faithful to take me back and to cleanse me of my adultery through repentance and forgiveness.

The book of Hosea is targeted at the entire nation of Israel but it calls out the leaders of the nations as the cause of the prostitution in Israel. As leaders of our families, ministries, and churches we must never forget that our sins will affect the lives of those we have been called to lead. If we sin, then there is a high probability that they are going to sin as well. Where we lead, they will follow. If we lead them into sin like idolatry, we must realize that we will give an accounting for that before the Lord.

In a message that I heard recently it was said that the most important thing that a pastor needed to have for his church was his own personal holiness. To lead others toward holiness, we must first be holy. In our verse for the day we are reminded that God is faithful and loves even when we have been unfaithful. Jesus, give the ability to stay close to you.

DECEMBER 6

Read: Hosea 4:1 – 5:15, 2 John 1-13, Psalm 125:1-5, Proverbs 29:9-11

HOSEA 4:6

My people are being destroyed because they do not know me. It is all your fault, you priests, for you yourselves refuse to know me. Now I refuse to recognize you as my priests. Since you have forgotten the laws of your God, I will forget to bless your children.

The prophecies of Hosea are given in a time when the nation of Israel has almost entirely turned away from the Lord. Within this book is some very difficult imagery that is meant to shock and upset the people. God desires that they will be shocked back into a right relationship with Him.

The nation of Israel had been chosen to be the unique object of God's love and grace. No other nation experienced as intimate a relationship with God as did the Israelites. No other nation was promised God's protection and blessing like the Jews were. All God expected in return was that they worship Him alone. Time and again, they rejected God's desires and worshipped false gods. The result of turning away from God was that they did not know God. This lack of knowledge was destroying them. Not knowing God has a severe impact upon every aspect of our lives. It is not just a physical destruction, but in all aspects of our lives. An ignorance of God will destroy us emotionally, relational, professionally, and of course, spiritually.

In our verse the prophet Hosea proclaims for God that the priests were to blame for this. They had the responsibility to teach people about God. Their problem was that they really didn't know God themselves. And it wasn't because they couldn't know God; it was because they refused to. The priests had access to everything that they needed to know God better than anyone else. The one thing they lacked was a fear of the Lord. It didn't bother them that God would be upset if they didn't try to know their One True God.

The consequence of this attitude on the part of the priests was that God was going to refuse to accept them as His priests. As Christians we are a part of the priesthood of Christ. That means that all of us are called to help others get to know Christ. If you are involved in any kind of leadership in your life, family, or ministry than this responsibility is magnified. We will all stand before God some day and give an account of how well we fulfilled this calling to make Christ known to others. The text reminds us that we must know Him ourselves first.

God takes this seriously. So seriously that it comes with a severe consequence. He tells the priests that because they have forgotten His laws He will forget to bless their children. As a parent of three children, I want my children to be blessed. One of the ways that I can make sure that they are is to come to know God intimately and then teach others to know Him, including my children. Jesus, teach us to know You.

DECEMBER 7

Read: Hosea 6:1 – 9:17, 3 John 1-15, Psalm 126:1-6, Proverbs 29:12-14

HOSEA 9:8

The prophet is a watchman for my God over Israel, yet traps are laid in front of him wherever he goes. He faces hostility even in the house of God.

In the Old Testament, the office of prophet was a very important thing. This person had the mighty role of speaking to the people the things that God wanted them to know. You didn't ask for the job and you couldn't be trained to do it. God selected the people that He wanted to be prophets. When God spoke to them, they were expected to tell the intended recipient exactly what God said. There are also many accounts of people going to the prophets and asking them to inquire of the Lord for something that was going on in their lives.

The office of prophet no longer exists in the church. However, the spiritual gift of prophecy does. God still speaks to individuals and requires them to share His message with others. God is still using people to be watchmen over His people. The difference now is it is not just Israel but for all that would believe. God has chosen certain people to be His representatives to watch over and guard His people.

In the church today that is anyone that has assumed a role within a ministry or church, especially a leadership role. Within a ministry or church, your responsibility is not to do a certain job but to minister to the body as the Lord would direct. This will be accomplished through a series of tasks and activities but the objective is to do ministry, not just do the tasks and activities. Part of that ministry is to be a watchman over the flock of God. And as you are doing that ministry He is going to speak to you about things that he wants you to share with those that you come into contact with. And when He does we must be sure to share those things.

We must be very careful with this responsibility. Often we can think we are hearing from God when we are actually hearing from our flesh. We know we are hearing from God, when what we are saying lines up with the word of God. Also, what we say should draw people to God and should be edifying in nature. We must know that what we are saying is the truth. The problem is that many people don't want to hear the truth. They would much rather live their lives the way that they want to, not the way that God wants them to. And to protect themselves from the truth they will attack those that tell the truth. We might like to believe that within the church this doesn't happen but it does all too frequently.

Don't be surprised when someone within your ministry or church is hostile when faced with what God wants to say. It happened in the Old Testament to the prophets and it happened to Jesus. Why should you be any different? Jesus, help us to share the truth in love and to love those that are hostile toward your truth.

DECEMBER 8
Read: Hosea 10:1 – 14:9, Jude 1-25, Psalm 127:1-5, Proverbs 29:15-17

I say this because some godless people have wormed their way in among you, saying that God's forgiveness allows us to live immoral lives. The fate of such people was determined long ago, for they have turned against our only Master and Lord, Jesus Christ.

Jude was the son of Joseph and Mary and brother to James and half-brother to Jesus, our Lord. It is interesting to me that he doesn't claim that title in the opening of his letter. Instead he refers to himself as the slave of Jesus. He is named last in Matthew which would imply that he was the youngest son of Joseph and Mary. As such he might very well felt like a slave. As you read through this brief letter you can clearly see he was referring to his place in regards to the Risen Lord Jesus and not to his earthly role in the family.

Jude writes this letter as a warning against the false teachers that are creeping into the church. These teachers were telling the people that because of God's gracious forgiveness that it was OK for them to live in immorality. They were saying that people could continue to sin and that God's forgiveness would cover them. Jude is very harsh with these false teachers and basically says that their fate has already been sealed.

The church today is not immune from this same very thing. Much of what we see the world running to is a theology that allows them to continue to feed their sinful desires while having something that resembles a relationship with God. The people that are running to this theology are more concerned about being happy than they are about being right with God. Sadly, they are being misled by the very people that ought to be leading them to a right relationship with God.

The problem is that these teachers are coming right out and telling the people that this is what is going on. They are teaching a partial truth that causes the people to feel good about themselves. Because we are sinful creatures we are drawn to this type of theology. What Jude is trying to do is to teach people to stay away from this type of teacher. He is doing that because this theology is empty and leads to death of the soul. The only way that we can feel good about ourselves is when we have seen our sins through the eyes of God and turned from them to follow Jesus.

As leaders of families, ministries, and churches God calls us to teach "the whole truth, nothing but the truth, so help me God." Anything less or anything else and we are leading our people astray and we should expect a very severe judgment from the owner of the flock; God. Staying away from sin and denying our sinful desires is the true path to happiness. Give God glory by teaching His truth in such a way that people are led to repentance and joy. Jesus, help us to know only You; the Truth.

DECEMBER 9

Read: Joel 1:1 – 3:21, Revelation 1:1-20, Psalm 128:1-6, Proverbs 29:18

PSALM 128:4

That is the LORD'S reward for those who fear him.

There are some that would suggest that there are no rewards to living the godly life; it is just the way that we are supposed to live. Well, today's reading and verse seem to contradict that kind of thinking. God does expect us to live a life that is pleasing to Him and we should be doing it out of a deep abiding love for Him. Even our love for God comes from God and is preceded by His love for us.

There are rewards for living the life that God wants us to. This includes God's protection, provision, grace, and mercy. But there are also more tangible things that He desires to reward us with. In our text it refers to a wife and children. Our families are a reward that God gives to us. Elsewhere in scripture we are told about the blessings of our table and our home and the work that we do. Each of these can be the reward that God gives to His children. He also gives us the desires of our hearts; whatever that might be.

The factor that determines whether or not we get these rewards is our fear of the Lord. These rewards are reserved for those that fear Him. Elsewhere in the Bible we are told that the fear of the Lord is the beginning of wisdom. By this and many other scriptures we can discern that this fear that is being called out is not the idea of being terrified. The fear of the Lord has been defined as the reverential awe of God.

God is all-powerful and all-knowing; there is nothing beyond the ability of God. God is perfect and holy. The fear of the Lord comes upon a person as they begin to get to know God and compare Him to themselves and realize how much greater He is than they are; when you realize how much bigger God is than you are and how much wiser He is. The fear of the Lord also includes an understanding that He is in complete control and has the power to destroy or to save.

As our fear of the Lord grows our capacity to receive from the Lord grows. God desires to bless His children with every blessing that He has prepared for them. But it depends upon a right relationship with Him to receive those blessings and rewards. That right relationship begins when we recognize who God is and who we are compared to Him. It depends upon our hearts being humbled before a great and mighty God and our sins confessed openly before Him.

The Christian life will never be perfect and free from trials and tribulations. We live in a fallen world that seeks to destroy the things of God. But that doesn't mean that this life can't be filled with the good things that God has made for our enjoyment. As we learn to fear the Lord, we also learn to recognize the rewards and blessings that He has poured out into our lives so that we can enjoy this life as we wait for the next one. Jesus, thank you for the many things that You have given us just because we are Yours.

DECEMBER 10

Read: Amos 1:1 – 3:15, Revelation 2:1-17, Psalm 129:1-8, Proverbs 29:19-20

AMOS 3:3

Can two people walk together without agreeing on the direction?

Amos is called by God out of the sheepfolds to be a prophet to tell the people of Israel and the people that have oppressed Israel that God is preparing to judge them. The role of the prophets was to communicate the heart and mind of God to the people. Often we see this role being fulfilled just as it is with Amos; as a warning about upcoming judgment. God's desire is that the people will repent, turn from their wicked ways and turn back to Him just as Nineveh did with the warnings of Jonah.

Here in the midst of Amos' prophecies we see this interesting paragraph. In our text is the first of a series of rhetorical questions. These are questions that are not meant to be answered but to communicate a fact in such a way that no one can disagree. God is telling the people through Amos those things that are going to come to pass by the hand of God. It is a fact just as all the other questions relate to the reader facts that they can't argue with.

In our text for today we have a verse that is very applicable to life and ministry. In essence we are being told that for two people to go in the same direction together they must agree on the direction that they are going. This very simple concept is such a critical part of life and ministry that if we ignore it, we will be assured of strife and division. Within a ministry or a church, we must all be going in the same direction. To do that we must all agree to be going in that direction.

The question then is who decides what direction we are going? The leader does through the leading of the Holy Spirit. Whoever has been appointed by God as the leader of that ministry or church is the one whom God will hold responsible for determining the direction. It is then up to the rest of us to agree to go in that same direction.

If we determine that we do not agree with the direction that the leader has chosen, then we have a choice to make. We either submit to the leader and his direction, in other words choose to agree, or we choose to walk a different way. The thing that some people struggle with in ministry is the idea that sometimes it is not possible to walk together.

Paul and Barnabus reached a point in their ministry where they did not agree on the direction that they were walking and determined that they could no longer walk together. And through that dividing of the ministry God grew the missionary ministry of both of them. It is a very natural process for things to grow and divide. It doesn't have to be painful and traumatic. Just because we don't agree doesn't mean that either one of us is wrong. It might mean that God is trying to multiply the ministry. Jesus, teach us to divide and grow your ministries and churches without division.

DECEMBER 11

Read: Amos 4:1 – 6:14, Revelation 2:18 – 3:6, Psalm 130:1-8, Proverbs 29:21-22

REVELATION 3:1

Write this letter to the angel of the church in Sardis. This is the message from the one who has the sevenfold Spirit of God and the seven stars: "I know all the things you do, and that you have a reputation for being alive—but you are dead."

In our reading today, Jesus is talking to the angels of the seven churches. These angels are usually referred to as the leaders or pastors of those churches. The interpretations of these letters to the churches are as varied as the letters themselves. Some say these letters refer to the different church ages that have come and gone. Some say that they are literal letters to churches that existed at the time that John wrote this book. Some say that they refer to churches today. As with most things of God, all of them could be right or all of them could be wrong and anything in between. God's word is living and active. Every page has something for us every day.

This letter is written to the church of Sardis says that they had a good reputation in the world around it. It had all the right programs going on. It had good preaching and an impressive building. Lots of people were showing up at the services and all the best looking people were coming. But Jesus said that their appearance of life was a costume; they were actually dead. What Jesus is referring to is not their physical life but their spiritual life. They were all dressed up and made up to look alive but they weren't.

The church of Sardis was not growing spiritually. They were going through the motions of the spiritual things but they were not operating in the Spirit. They were doing church but they weren't being the church. The church exists to help people become like Jesus Christ. That means that all the people should be growing in their relationship with God on a daily basis. When growth stops, it doesn't take long for life to stop.

As we lead our families, ministries, or churches we must always be looking at those that God has entrusted to us and looking for spiritual growth. As the leaders we don't have to make people grow; we need to provide places and ways for them to grow. The angel of the church of Sardis wasn't doing that and because he wasn't Jesus counted it against him. He didn't count it against the people but against the leader. Our role is to help them to grow and if we are shepherding our people correctly they will grow.

Look around you; are the people around you growing in their relationship with the Lord? Are you growing in your relationship with the Lord? If there isn't growth; then get back to those things that you know provide growth. If you don't, then ask someone that is growing and follow their example. Jesus, teach us to be the church.

DECEMBER 12

Read: Amos 7:1 – 9:15, Revelation 3:7-22, Psalm 131:1-3, Proverbs 29:23

AMOS 8:11

"The time is surely coming," says the Sovereign LORD, "when I will send a famine on the land—not a famine of bread or water but of hearing the words of the LORD.

Amos had the difficult task of prophesying judgment upon the nations of Israel and Judah. They had turned away from God and had rejected all of the warnings of the prophets that God had sent before Amos. In today's verse we see that God is about to create a famine that will fall upon the land of Israel and Judah. This is not the usual famine that wipes out all the crops so that there is no food to eat. This famine is a withdrawal of the ability to hear the words of the Lord.

This is virtually impossible for the modern day Christian to conceive. The words of the Lord are very easy to hear with television, radio, and the internet; not to mention churches on nearly every corner. We have no lacking of the words of the Lord filling our ears. But even with all of that, there is something of a famine in our land for the words of the Lord as well. It is not that the words of the Lord are not here but that people are not hearing them.

People can hear or watch some of the best preachers in the world twenty-four hours a day and seven days a week. But if the words that they are speaking are not having an effect which results in a change in that person's life than they are not hearing those words and they are in a spiritual famine. Usually this famine is self-inflicted and is a result of a lack of faith; they simply don't believe enough to allow the Holy Spirit to make changes in their lives. Too many people now view the teachings that they are exposed to as entertainment.

God desires that we would tune our ears in to His voice. To do that we need to humble ourselves and ask Him to speak to us. We shouldn't listen to preachers to be entertained but we should be earnestly seeking a word from the Lord that will help us to make the changes that are necessary in our lives to be more like Christ. Jesus said that we need to feed upon every word that proceeds from God. We need to develop a hunger for the Word of God and to do that we need to deny ourselves some of the things that we use to fill ourselves.

If we don't seek the words of the Lord we might find ourselves in a spiritual famine. We can take steps that ensure that we are getting a steady diet of God's word. As we continue feeding upon His word we become more attuned to His voice as He is speaking to us. As we hear His words, we need to obey them and allow the Holy Spirit to make those changes that God wants to make. As we allow each of those changes we are better prepared to hear God's voice. Jesus, help us to hunger for a regular diet of Your word.

DECEMBER 13

Read: Obadiah 1-21, Revelation 4:1-11, Psalm 132:1-18, Proverbs 29:24-25

PSALM 132:12

If your descendants obey the terms of my covenant and follow the decrees that I teach them, then your royal line will never end."

This anonymous and undated psalm refers to the promise that God made to King David when he became king. God promised that there would always be a descendant of David on the throne of the nation of Israel. Like many of God's promises, this was a conditional promise. That means that God placed a condition in the promise that related to David's participation in the agreement.

For that promise to be fulfilled, David and his descendants would have to abide by the terms of the agreement and do their part. It was a very simple agreement. God told them to obey his covenant and follow His decrees. If they did then God would make sure that there was always a descendant of David on the throne of Israel.

In an agreement like this there is usually a consequence aspect that may or not be written into the agreement but it is always there. In this agreement it is implied that if David's descendants do not obey God and follow His decrees that the royal line of King David will end.

God's promises never fail! Unfortunately, people do! We know from history that David's descendants did not live up to their end of the agreement and the royal line of David did end. We also know that this is a prophetic promise and that Jesus was the ultimate fulfillment of this promise and that His royal line will never end.

As we begin and lead ministries and churches, God would make a similar promise to us. If we will obey Him and follow His decrees, He will make sure that what we are doing will live on to future generations. Everyone wants to be a part of something bigger than they are and they want to know that what they are doing is important and that it will last. This is called leaving a legacy. Everyone wants to leave a legacy.

In our verse for today, God tells us how to do that. It's very simple! All you have to do is to obey the terms of the covenant we have with God. These are found in the Bible. And then you have to follow the decrees that

He, the Holy Spirit will teach you. Obey God and respond to the leading
of the Holy Spirit and you will leave a legacy that will never end. If we don't
obey God and follow the Holy Spirit, then we are very likely to experience
the consequence aspect of the agreement; our leadership will end and God
will put someone else in our place that will obey and follow Him. It is my
desire that the things that God does through me live well past my mortal
life; should the Lord tarry. Jesus, teach us to obey and help us to follow.

DECEMBER 14
Read: Jonah 1:1 – 4:1, Revelation 5:1-14, Psalm 133:1-3, Proverbs 29:26-27

PSALM 133:1

How wonderful it is, how pleasant, when brothers live together in harmony!

This short little psalm carries a great spiritual truth that if embraced by
more people would change the face of the earth. We live in a world
where discord and disunity are rampant. Even within seemingly unified
groups these is disharmony. Sadly this is just another of the many imperfections of man manifesting itself within the world. The further we get
from God, the less harmony and peace there is in the world.

It is indeed wonderful; it is indeed pleasant when there is harmony
within a marriage, family, group, church, or nation. When we hear a group
of people singing, it is very pleasant to hear them singing in harmony. The
problem is that when you get two or more people together they seldom are
singing the same song. When a group of people are singing and they are
not in harmony, it is an unpleasant experience.

To experience harmony everyone has to agree with what is being done.
They have to agree as to the direction that they are going; they have to be
in agreement as to the goal they are trying to achieve. More than that, they
need to agree to the way that they are going to get there. When one or
more members decide that they want to go in a different direction than the
rest of the group, there is disharmony. It is as though one singer decides
to sing a different song than the rest of the group is singing. It is very
distracting and creates disharmony.

Creating harmony within a group, whether it be a marriage, family, ministry, or church is possible. To do it everyone needs to agree with where the group is going. Where most groups don't achieve harmony is the understanding that agreement comes only as a result of the members sacrificing their positions to the harmony of the group. To achieve harmony we must submit our desires and visions to the direction that the group is going. In a musical group all members agree to play the songs in a specified order and in a specific style; that brings harmony and it is wonderful and pleasant.

As we submit our wills to the God-directed needs of our marriages, families, ministries, and churches we will experience harmony and it will be sweet. Everyone wants to have harmony in every area of their lives, but most people aren't willing to sacrifice anything to get it. It is our own selfish desires that prevent us from achieving harmony in our lives.

All of our relationships can be and should be moving toward harmony. Obviously, we can only do our part but we must be doing our part. God will bless your relationships as you work toward creating harmony. Surrender your will to God and let Him direct you toward achieving harmony in all areas of your life and then you will see how wonderful and pleasant life can be. Jesus, teach us to let go of what we want.

DECEMBER 15

Read: Micah 1:1 – 4:13, Revelation 6:1-17, Psalm 134:1-3, Proverbs 30:1-4

MICAH 3:11

You rulers govern for the bribes you can get; you priests teach God's laws only for a price; you prophets won't prophesy unless you are paid. Yet all of you claim you are depending on the LORD. "No harm can come to us," you say, "for the LORD is here among us."

In Micah's prophecy he speaks out against those that are in leadership positions and attacks the motivations of their hearts. The people that were in the government were taking bribes from people to do their jobs. The priests were making the people pay so that they would teach the laws to the people and the prophets were withholding the words of God unless they were given money. And then at the same time they were saying that they were trusting God. And worse yet, they didn't think it was wrong!

All that God gives us is a gift. The gifts that He gives us, he gives freely out of the abundance of His love for us. Much of what God gives us He gives to us so that we will give it to others. How can we ask someone to pay us for something that God gave us for free? Micah was attacking the greed and faithlessness of the people of his time.

All of us can fall into the same trap that the people of Micah's time did. It can be very tempting to think that your gifts, abilities, and influence are valuable to someone. You can even justify that this is how God is going to provide for you. But what price can we really put on the gifts of God?

This is why I have a great level of respect for anyone that serves God without receiving compensation. We often refer to them as volunteers. These people serve God because it is their right and responsibility. They serve God because they receive a reward greater than anything that any man could ever give; treasures in heaven. As a full-time, paid pastor it humbles me to know that there are people all around me that work a full-time job and then come to serve God without compensation out of their love for God and for His church. In my heart I know that they are likely to receive a greater reward in heaven than I will.

In my life I have seen God bless me materially because of my service to Him and His church. My struggle is just like that of Micah's contemporaries; resisting the temptation of expecting to be paid for serving God and His people. We are to trust God to meet our every need and to share the gifts that He gives to us freely with others. My own experience and the experience of many that I know is that when I give freely and joyfully of the blessings that God has given me; that I am seldom in need of anything. It has been said; "You can't out-give God." This applies to everything in your life; your time, talents, and treasures. Give it away and watch God work. Jesus, help us to hold the gifts that you give us with open hands.

REVELATION 7:9

After this I saw a vast crowd, too great to count, from every nation and tribe and people and language, standing in front of the throne and before the Lamb. They were clothed in white and held palm branches in their hands.

The Apostle John sees during his vision a vast multitude; so great that they could not be counted. Elsewhere in our reading we saw that there was an army of 200 million. It causes me to wonder at just how large this vast multitude might be. There are about 7 billion people on the planet right now. During the seven years of the Tribulation period a vast number of them are going to be martyred for their faith in Jesus Christ.

That is a staggering thing to think about. It is estimated that more people will come to know Jesus as their Savior during the Tribulation period than all of the time that preceded it. That should give us great joy. If you are like me and believe that the Rapture is going to take place before the seven years of the Tribulation, it is good to know that there is some hope for those that are still fighting God and resisting His call to salvation.

This joy should be joined with an equal measure of fear. Revelation indicates that a very large percentage of the people of the earth are killed during the various judgments that God sends upon the wicked of the earth. Billions of people are likely to die during that terrible time. If they harden their heart then, they are lost forever.

Our only responsibility is to witness to them. We need to share with them the love of God and the future that awaits them if they refuse to accept His free gift. Then it is between them and the Holy Spirit to work out the timing of their conversion. It should be our prayer that they would make that decision before we all leave. But God, who is full of grace and mercy, will give them one more chance to choose eternity with Him in heaven or eternity separated from Him.

It is my belief that there will be widespread conversions immediately following the Rapture. Those conversions will be the direct result of people like you and me sharing the gospel and witnessing the power of God in our lives to those around us. Hundreds of millions of people will come to know Jesus during that time. How many of them will have the fingerprints of your life in their salvation testimony.

Jesus said that we should let our light shine. Our lives can be a beacon of light that can even reach into the darkness of the Tribulation period. Just share the truth of Jesus with them today. You may be blessed by seeing them with Jesus in the air during the Rapture or they may remember the things that you told them in words and showed them in your life and then be one of this vast crowd that John saw in his vision. Jesus, help us to let Your light to shine brightly from our lives.

DECEMBER 17

Read: Nahum 1:1 – 3:19, Revelation 8:1-13, Psalm 136:1-26, Proverbs 30:7-9

PSALM 136:1

Give thanks to the LORD, for he is good! His faithful love endures forever.

Too often we tend to forget what God has done for us and to thank Him. Each of us could write a psalm like this one describing the many things that God has done for us. And yet we frequently find ourselves wrapped up in some fear or worry about something that God is so much bigger than. We are reminded in today's reading to give thanks to the Lord.

Here in our verse for today the reason we are given to give thanks to the Lord is because He is good. In our church it is not uncommon to hear someone say: "God is good!" The typical response is: "All the time!" God is good all of the time. It doesn't matter what our circumstances are whether good or bad, happy or sad; God is still good all of the time. And because He is good all of the time; He is worthy of our thanks and our praise.

It is easy to thank God when things are going your way. It is easy to be thankful when the sun is shining and the birds are singing. It is easy to sing God's praises when the car is running fine and all the bills are paid. But God isn't any less good when the diagnosis from the doctor is cancer. He is no less worthy of praise when your spouse has left. God is still God even if you lose your job. God is God and God is good! All the time! He is entitled to our thankfulness all the time. He is worthy of our praise all the time. He deserves our worship all the time.

Twenty-six times in this psalm we see the phrase "His faithful love endures forever." It is God's love that is the reason we should be thankful. God doesn't do what He does because He feels some sense of responsibility toward us. He doesn't take care of us out of some sense of duty and obligation. God does what he does for us because of His love for us. That love is a faithful love. We can depend upon it. We don't have to wonder if God loves us or not. His faithful love is something that we can be absolutely sure will be there no matter what we do.

God's love will endure forever. No matter what happens in this world, we can rest in the fact that God's love will never change. There is nothing that can happen that can change the height, depth, width, or length of God's love for us. This whole world will fade away but God's love for each one of us will not fade even a small amount. God's love for us each individually will not change even if we change. God can't love you more than He does right now and He won't ever love you less than He does right now.

That is something to be thankful for. No matter what this life brings, God's love will be the one constant thing in your life. Cling to it when the waves of your circumstances are crashing all around you and be thankful for it all the time. Jesus, thank you.

DECEMBER 18

Read: Habakkuk 1:1 – 3:19, Revelation 9:1-21, Psalm 137:1-9, Proverbs 30:10

HABAKKUK 1:11

They sweep past like the wind and are gone. But they are deeply guilty, for their own strength is their god.

The prophecy of Habakkuk has to do primarily with God using the nation of Babylon to punish the nation of Israel because they turned away for the True and Living God to worship worthless idols. The Israelites were living just like the pagan nations all around them and this made

God angry. And so God used the pagan nation of Babylon to punish His people.

The nation of Babylon was a strong and vicious nation. The Bible likens them to wild animals in the way that they terrorized the peoples that they conquered. They showed no mercy and they showed no pity. And for a time they were unstoppable. One of the reasons that they were so powerful was that God wanted to use them to get His people to turn back to Him. In our text for today, God proclaims that the nation of Babylon is deeply guilty. Their guilt comes not from the way that they were treating others but because of their hearts. The Babylonians were worshipping their strength. This world that we live in today is not that different than it was 2,600 years ago, people still are worshipping their strength.

National pride can easily turn into the worship of strength. Personal or corporate success can lead to a type of worship of strength. The people that we tend to admire and sometimes idolize are those that exhibit some strength that we do not have. We have got to be so careful not to put people up on pedestals, they don't belong there; only God does. Their strength, power, ability, or success came from God. He is the only one worthy of our worship.

In our ministries and churches, we must be careful about this as well. We pray that God will make our ministries strong and successful and it is His will that our ministries and churches grow and become strong and successful. Our challenge is that once it does, we will begin to look at the strengths as the reason why the church or ministry is strong. What a dangerous trap we can fall into. The very thing that we pray for and God desires to do can be a snare that causes us to stumble.

The success of your family, ministry, or church will not be measured by how big, strong, or powerful it is. It will be measured by how well you keep Christ at the core. If Christ ever moves out of the center of your family, ministry, or church and something else is what people see at the center than you should be warned that God may be preparing a Babylon to come and get your attention. Jesus, help us to see any strength, success, power, or influence as another reason to worship You and You alone.

DECEMBER 19

Read: Zephaniah 1:1 – 3:20, Revelation 10:1-11, Psalm 138:1-8, Proverbs 30:11-14

ZEPHANIAH 3:9

On that day I will purify the lips of the people, so that everyone will be able to worship the Lord together.

The prophet Zephaniah is given a vision of what lies ahead for the nation of Israel. In that vision God describes His disappointment regarding the way that His chosen people are behaving toward each other. God's desire is that His people would be a special people; a holy people. The word "holy" means "set apart." Too often we interpret this to mean that we are to be perfect. For us a better word might be "different." God's people should be different from the rest of the world. That is what God is upset about with His people; they are just like the rest of the world.

It is not difficult to imagine that He has the same complaint about His people today. It is often difficult to tell the difference between the people of the church and the people of the world. The behaviors and attitudes of those in the church reflect those of the world. That should not be so!

Zephaniah is describing a future day when God will purify the lips of all the people so that they can worship the Lord together. It occurred to me as I was reading this that if God will cause this to happen today, that it would please Him if His church was attempting to accomplish it before He comes. God wants all of His people to worship Him together. God wants united worship within the Church. I am not suggesting that all the different denominations and church organizations should be disbanded. The One-World church is not scheduled until after we are raptured. I am suggested that we stop fighting over territory and semantics and worship God together.

We should be working toward building relationships with other groups of like mind to find ways to worship God together. We all have our own styles and doctrines but the God we worship is One. There is enough common ground between us to provide opportunity to fellowship and worship. Obviously, there are some groups that we should avoid because they are apostate or heretical, but for those we should band together.

Even as I write that I know that it is very difficult. People are suspicious of other groups and will defend their territory tenaciously. Personally, I believe that is a lack of trust in God's plan and ability to build His church. My only concern is that we pursue God's will in all things of the church and leave the actual building of it to Him.

Some day we will all worship the Lord together. The Lord will need to purify our lips first but it is going to happen. I would rather that He do that now in my life so that I can enjoy the fruits of that worship today. Let's stop quibbling over spiritual pedigrees and meaningless details and worship our Lord. Jesus, purify my lips.

DECEMBER 20
Read: Haggai 1:1 – 2:23, Revelation 11:1-19, Psalm 139:1-24, Proverbs 30:15-16

REVELATION 11:5
If anyone tries to harm them, fire flashes from the mouths of the prophets and consumes their enemies. This is how anyone who tries to harm them must die.

In today's reading we learn about the two witnesses that are sent to Jerusalem to warn people about God's impending judgment of the world. For three and a half years they will speak out against the Anti-Christ and his followers and warn people to turn back to God. God will protect these two witnesses supernaturally by allowing them to protect themselves against any attack that will come against them. There are no such attacks mentioned in scripture but it is not hard to imagine that they will happen. At that time the world will be in chaos and under the control of the Anti-Christ and the One-World religion.

Earlier in Revelation we read that there will be 144,000 Jews that are marked by God and they also are protected supernaturally from harm. It doesn't say exactly how that is done but the imagination can create some interesting scenarios. As I reflected on that I was reminded that God is fully capable of protecting anyone He chooses from anything that He chooses, anytime He chooses. That is powerful stuff as we go through this life. While life on earth is nothing like it will be during the time of the Tribulation period, God is no less able to protect us today as He will then.

Fortunately for most of the people reading this we will not actually have to concern ourselves with God's protection because we will be in His presence then and for the rest of eternity. Depending on how long the Lord tarries we will still be living in a world that is at least somewhat hostile to God and to His people. We will have lots of opportunities to trust in the protection of God.

The account of God's protection of His chosen people in Revelation is a graphic example of His ability to overcome anything this world or our enemy can throw against us. There is nothing that God can't overcome to protect those He has chosen to protect. We need to also keep in mind that hundreds of millions of people will be killed during this same time because they believe in God and have accepted His Son Jesus. Just because God might choose not to protect us from something is not an indication that He loves us any less or that we are not chosen by Him. It just means that His plan for the universe includes you experiencing a different form of protection than you might wish.

God's protection is not just about keeping us from harm but could also include things like keeping us from some sins and temptations. God's protection may come in the form of the Holy Spirit dispensing to us His gifts in abundance. We just need to trust that as long as we hold on the Lord; His protection is ever-present with us. Jesus, thank you that You are a strong tower that we can run to.

DECEMBER 21

Read: Zechariah 1:1-21, Revelation 12:1-17, Psalm 140:1-13, Proverbs 30:17

ZECHARIAH 1:3

Therefore, say to the people, "This is what the Lord Almighty says: Return to me, and I will return to you, says the Lord Almighty."

The book of Zechariah was written after the exile. The people had begun to return and the second Temple had been started but not finished. Zechariah's prophecies are filled with fascinating imagery that points to a future time when the Messiah will restore the glory of the city of Jerusalem.

The book was written to encourage and exhort the people of God to hold fast to their faith.

The book opens with a clear exhortation to return to God. As we read an exhortation such as this we need to keep in mind that it wouldn't have been written if they hadn't turned away from God. Turning away from the Lord and returning to Him are a common theme throughout much of the Old Testament. If anyone struggles with believing in the base sinfulness of man he just needs to read the Old Testament and keep track of the number of times it is recorded that God's people turned away from Him after He supernaturally rescued them from their enemies.

In our verse for the day we see the system that God uses to restore His people. He expects them to return to Him. It is then that God will return to them. It is this idea that God will return to them. God's word clearly teaches that God will never leave nor forsake His people. So the idea of God returning to His people must mean something other than a physical return. It relates to His activity in the lives of His people.

God will never leave us nor forsake us. But if we rebel and turn away from Him He will withdraw His hand of blessing, provision, and protection from us. All that we have is from God and all that we will receive will come from God. Every circumstance that has come into our lives has been directed by the Lord. Without God's hand of protection and provision the things that come into our lives will be seen as curses rather than blessings. But God's purpose remains true; he desires that we would return to Him. He will use whatever method He must to see that happen. He will even allow terrible things to happen if that is what it is going to take to get you to return to Him.

God doesn't want to see that happen. He would much rather that we would always want to be His people and would seek Him with our every breath. God wants to pour out blessings in our lives that are so great that we have to share them with others. He wants to provide for our every need. He wants to protect us from every enemy. But if we insist on having our own way and not following His way, we leave Him with no choice but to withdraw from us. God's love for us is so great that if we will humble ourselves and return, He will never reject us. If you find yourself feeling distant from God, simply return to Him and you and expect Him to return to you. Jesus, help us to run to You.

DECEMBER 22

Read: Zechariah 2:1 – 3:10, Revelation 12:18 – 13:18, Psalm 141:1-10, Proverbs 30:18-20

ZECHARIAH 3:2

And the Lord said to Satan, "I, the Lord, reject your accusations, Satan. Yes, the Lord, who has chosen Jerusalem, rebukes you. This man is like a burning stick that has been snatched from a fire."

Zechariah is given a vision of things going on in the spiritual world. In this vision he sees Jeshua, the high priest, standing before the angel of the Lord. Right beside Jeshua is Satan accusing him of many things. This is a familiar scene. The Bible teaches us that Satan is the accuser of the brethren. That means that he is constantly bringing charges against God's people to God.

We also know that Satan is a liar and the father of lies. What is not clear based on Scripture is whether or not he lies in the presences of God. We do know that it is impossible to lie to God; He knows everything, all the time. It would seem to me that God wouldn't permit him to lie in His presence.

What this means is that when Satan accuses us, it is about things that are true. Satan accuses us before God of sins that we have committed. I believe that is what is going on here. That is evidenced later by the fact that his clothes are filthy. The angel of the Lord instructs others standing around to remove the filthy clothes and replace them with clean ones. This is a picture of God's grace specifically in the area of forgiveness. God's forgiveness cleanses us of the filth of our sins.

Jeshua is the high priest and represents the priestly order. Just because Jeshua was the high priest doesn't make him automatically righteous and holy. He was just as much a sinner as anyone else. And just like everyone else Jeshua needed God's grace.

The Lord says to Satan, "I reject your accusations." It doesn't say that they are not true but that He rejects them. This is one of those incredible truths about our relationship with the Lord. He knows that we are sinners and he knows that we sin. He also has Satan standing there in His presence accusing us at every opportunity. But rather than being disappointed or upset, he rejects those accusations.

For us as Christians this is because of the finished work of Jesus Christ on the cross. Jesus paid the price for every sin and wrong thing that we have ever done or will do once for all time. I would think that it must be very frustrating to Satan that his accusations are regularly rejected by Jesus. But for us it means that we never need to concern ourselves about whether or not Jesus will accept us. That doesn't give us a license to sin. God hates our sins and wants us to repent or turn away from them. But having done that, our relationship to God is open and free. Satan is a powerful enemy and a tenacious accuser of Christians but his accusations are rejected by the Lover and Savior of our souls. Jesus, thank You for knowing us and loving us anyway.

DECEMBER 23

Read: Zechariah 4:1 – 5:11, Revelation 14:1-20, Psalm 142:1-7, Proverbs 30:21-23

ZECHARIAH 4:10

Do not despise these small beginnings, for the Lord rejoices to see the work begin, to see the plumb line in Zerubbael's hand. For these seven lamps represent the eyes of the Lord that search all around the world.

As we begin this work that the Lord has set before us we need to meditate on this verse. The prophet Zechariah gives this message from the Lord to Zerubbabel as he is rebuilding the temple in Jerusalem. The work is going slowly and so God sends a word to Zerubbabel and the people to encourage them.

God's eyes go throughout the whole earth and when He sees His people working on the projects that He has set before them, it pleases Him. This verse asks us the question, if God is pleased how can we be displeased? God hasn't asked us to build Him a huge temple, He has asked us to build this church.

As we look at the work that is going on we should respond as God does. In the NLT this verse says that God rejoices to see the work happening. That should be our exact response, to rejoice at what the Lord is doing in our midst, so matter how small.

The old people of Zerubbabel's time wept as they saw the temple being built because it was so much less than what they thought it should be. Let us not suffer from that same sin of thinking we know better than God.

The parable of the mustard seed reminds us that small things in the kingdom of God can grow to be great. And 1 Corinthians reminds us that God uses the humble things and the despised things and the small things to do His work.

Let us rejoice in the things that God has done! Let us celebrate as each stone is laid in this house of worship that we are building for Him! Let us faithfully and diligently keep at the work until it is completed to glory and pleasure of God.

DECEMBER 24

Read: Zechariah 6:1 – 7:14, Revelation 15:1-8, Psalm 143:1-12, Proverbs 30:24-28

REVELATION 15:2

I saw before me what seemed to be a crystal sea mixed with fire. And on it stood all the people who had been victorious over the beast and his statue and the number representing his name. They were all holding harps that God had given them.

The Revelation of the Apostle John is one of the most fascinating books in the Bible. It is filled with incredible imagery and terrible prophecies. Bible teachers will often over-emphasize the importance of this book or avoid it all together. This book starts with a promise telling us that we will receive a blessing for reading it and sharing it with others. And while it is an amazing book, it must be counted as equal with all the other books of the Bible, Old Testament and New Testament, as the complete and total Word of God. No one book can be placed higher than any other and no books can be avoided; all must be read and studied so that we can know as much about God as is humanly possible.

In our verse for the day John sees in his vision a group of people. It seems that all of these people had harps. This is likely where the image that everyone in heaven has a harp comes from. That is probably not true. These people were special and God chose them for a very special task in heaven; to play those harps and sing praises to Him that sits on the throne.

What makes these people special is that they have been victorious over the beast and his statue. These people have believed God and trusted in the salvation of Jesus Christ while the rest of the world has believed the lies and miracles of the Anti-Christ. They have not accepted the beast's mark nor bowed in worship to his statue. The penalty for failing to take the mark or worship the beast is death; which most commentators believe will be by beheading.

God says these people that have been martyred are victorious over the beast. What we need to see from this is that their victory is not a military one but a personal one. Their victory is not that they beat the Anti-Christ in some battle but in that they persevered in their faith until death. Their victory over the beast is that they ran their race all the way to the end without denying God and worshipping the beast.

For those of us that are Christ-believers we will be watching this event take place from the comfort and security of heaven. We are also called to run our race with endurance. During the Tribulation the Anti-Christ will reveal himself. Until then his boss, the Devil is still at work in the world trying to get people to deny God and worship him instead. We are called to persevere until the end of our lives so that we can also stand before God as being victorious over our enemy. Whether we get a harp or not is not important. It would be better to spend all of eternity in heaven with nothing than to spend even one moment in hell with all the riches of the world. Jesus, give us the strength to persevere.

DECEMBER 25
Read: Zechariah 8:1-23, Revelation 16:1-21, Psalm 144:1-15, Proverbs 30:29-30

REVELATION 16:15
Take note: I will come as unexpectedly as a thief! Blessed are all who are watching for me, who keep their robes ready so they will not need to walk naked and ashamed.

As you read through chapter sixteen of Revelation and hear of the terrible judgments being poured out on the wicked of the world during the Tribulation, suddenly this statement appears. It appears within this chapter just as its speaker will appear to the world. Jesus interrupts this account of the seven vial judgments to remind us that we are to be watching for His imminent return.

It occurred to me as I was reading this on Christmas morning that there are some days that we are not expecting Jesus to return. Our attention is focused on some other event or activity. There may even be days when we don't want Him to return. We might be saying in our heart, "Lord, please wait until next week."

It is one thing if our desire is to see a loved one or friend accept Christ before He returns, it is quite another to be asking God to wait until you have opened your Christmas presents or taken a trip or attending some event or achieved some status. Our desire for His immediate return should be greater than anything of this world. Our love for Christ should be so great that we long for it even over our wedding day or the birth of a child.

Nothing should even come close to our desire for His quick return. Even as we work to begin a new work for Him, we should desire to joyfully lay that work at His feet unfinished because He returned before we finished it. As servants, our task is to do the work. As the Lord, Jesus determines if we will be allowed to complete it.

This verse speaks specifically about our being ready. The Lord desires that we would be always ready for Him to return. We are not to let the things of the world distract us from what God wants to do. The Lord is warning us against being involved in some sin when He returns because we will experience shame if we are.

As we do this work for the Lord, we must keep our eyes on Him, watching for His quick, sudden return. We must keep our hands clean, especially as we are called to be touching His bride, the church. And we must keep our hearts pure and undefiled from the sin of this world.

Come quickly Lord!

DECEMBER 26

Read: Zechariah 9:1-17, Revelation 17:1-18, Psalm 145:1-21, Proverbs 30:32

ZECHARIAH 9:12

Come back to the place of safety, all you prisoners, for there is yet hope! I promise this very day that I will repay you two mercies for each of your woes!

Today's reading is an incredible section of scripture. It is rich in prophecy about the first and second coming of Christ. In the midst of today's reading is this promise that we find in the verse that we are looking at today. We should all make a habit of looking for and noting the promises that God makes in scripture. Some of those promises were made specifically for the nation of Israel and they don't apply beyond them but a great many of them apply to anyone that will believe in and trust God.

Our verse for today is one such promise. It is intended for everyone and is intended to be believed and lived by anyone that desires it. The promise is a precious gift that we need to treasure but it also needs to be shared. Just like almost every other gift that God gives us, He wants us to share it with others.

Zechariah is speaking to people that understand what it means to be in captivity. Many of the people that would have heard this message first hand had experienced captivity in Babylon. And while they were not physically in prison they knew that they were not free. They had been exiled to Babylon by King Nebuchadnezzar.

This is a promise of hope! God has promised to the prisoners that every woe that they have experienced will be repaid with two mercies. What a beautiful thing that is! That means that God sees each and every struggle or trial that goes on in my life. Not only does He see them but He also keeps a record of them. And that record is kept so that God can counter them with twice as many mercies. That means that for each of these tough times that God has allowed into our lives that He is going to also bless us twice as much in areas that we don't deserve.

We live in a world that has very creative ways of taking people into captivity. There are people all around us that are prisoners. They are prisoners to some kind of sin or idolatry. Many of these are sins of the flesh but more people are prisoners of sins of the mind than of the flesh. Many of them do not even know that they are prisoners. What they do know is that their lives are not what they are supposed to be. They need a place of safety and hope. And that is where we come in. We may have already experienced the truth of this promise and now God wants us to share it with others. As leaders of families, ministries, or churches it is our responsibility to get this truth out to those that need it so desperately. They need to know that there is hope and they need someone to tell them how to get it. Jesus, help us to be the ones that share this promise of safety and hope with others.

DECEMBER 27

Read: Zechariah 10:1 – 11:17, Revelation 18:1-24, Psalm 146:1-10, Proverbs 30:33

PSALM 146:3

Don't put your confidence in powerful people; there is no help for you there.

As we look around the world and see the great and influential people there is a temptation to put our trust and confidence in them. It is our desire to have a person in our lives that we can put our confidence in; it brings us peace and comfort. Our verse for the day warns us against that very thing.

That desire to find someone to place our trust and confidence in was placed in us by God. He put it there so that we would not depend upon ourselves and so that we would turn to Him to meet that need in our lives. Our human nature tends to try to find a person to meet that need because God is spirit and we cannot see Him. We look for a person that we can reach out and touch.

Our verse tells us that there is a problem with that idea; that powerful person cannot help us like we think they can. No matter how powerful that person is they cannot provide you with the things that you need. The reason they can't is, they are not God and only God can give you what you truly need. Another reason why we shouldn't put our confidence in powerful people is because we don't know if God will allow them to continue to be powerful. All of us have seen very powerful people brought low by a scandal or by death. Only God is constant and dependable enough to be where we place our confidence and trust.

As leaders of families, ministries, or churches we also must protect against this tendency of people to place their confidence in us. None of us may describe ourselves as powerful but you probably have some amount of influence on someone which makes you powerful in their eyes. We must teach them not to put their confidence in us. We need to always be directing them to God and His provision for their lives.

We must never forget that we are a tool that God is using to lead and guide them. We have no idea how long God is going to allow us to do that. God's plan might include you or them leaving and going somewhere else. If they have not learned to depend upon God, they will wander around looking for someone or something that they can put their confidence in. You owe it to them to teach them to put their confidence in the Lord and in Him alone. That way, no matter where they go they will always have the Lord to depend upon. This will also protect them from those that might want to take advantage of them or harm them. As much as I desire never to fail, I know that there will come a time when I let down those that put their trust in me. If I do not teach them to put their trust in God first, it might cause them great harm; it might even cause them to fall away from the Lord. That is too great of a burden for me to bear. Instead, I will teach them to put their confidence in God because He will never let them down. Jesus, teach us to see You as the only powerful person in the world.

DECEMBER 28

Read: Zechariah 12:1 – 13:9, Revelation 19:1-21, Psalm 147:1-20, Proverbs 31:1-7

REVELATION 19:7

Let us be glad and rejoice and honor him. For the time has come for the wedding feast of the Lamb, and his bride has prepared herself.

Few things in life are more beautiful than a bride as she walks down the aisle of her wedding. Everything that can be done to make this bride glorious in appearance has been done. Great effort, not just by the bride but by her family and friends has been expended for this day. The gown was selected and has been given great care.

Everyone that has trusted in the Lord has been invited to a feast, the marriage feast of the Lamb. And at this feast all will celebrate the marriage of the Lamb to His bride. The Lamb is Jesus and His bride is the church. The church is everyone that has accepted Christ's gift of salvation. As a man, I have a little challenge picturing myself as the bride but as a part of the church that is exactly what I am.

Revelation 19:7 says that this bride has made herself ready. Christ's bride will do this the same way that a woman would. The church must do everything it can to be as beautiful as it possibly can. When speaking of a woman on her wedding day this would be her physical appearance. But with the Bride of Christ, it refers to holiness. God looks on the inside, not the outward appearance.

God is not impressed by large, ornate buildings. He is not impressed by giant sanctuaries filled with people. God is impressed when people gather together to meet His Son, Jesus. God is impressed when people are being changed on the inside. God is impressed when people are working out their salvation.

As we exercise ourselves toward godliness, we become more beautiful to God. The sins of our lives are like dirt, filth, and stains on a wedding dress. God wants us to be cleansed of the stain of our sins by the washing of the blood of Jesus.

As ministers of God, meaning you are in some sort of ministry for God, this is even more critical. As you minister, you are called to place your hands on the Bride of Christ, the church. The sin of your life can stain the beautiful gown of the Bride. We have all seen or heard of a church leader that had a moral failure, and it was a stain on the whole church.

Each of us must do everything in God's ability to be cleansed of all sin and unrighteousness so that we will do nothing that leaves a stain on the Bride of Christ. It is our responsibility to prepare ourselves for the wedding feast and also to help to prepare the bride. Lord, help us to keep our hands clean as we touch your bride.

DECEMBER 29

Read: Zechariah 14:1-21, Revelation 20:1-15, Psalm 148:1-14, Proverbs 31:8-9

REVELATION 20:12

I saw the dead, both great and small, standing before God's throne. And the books were opened, including the Book of Life. And the dead were judged according to the things written in the books, according to what they had done.

There will come a day when everything that we have done will be judged by God. Every deed will be examined and tested by God. For what purpose would God do this? This "white throne judgment" is for believers as they stand before God in heaven. God does nothing without a reason and a purpose.

If God is going to judge our deeds there must be a reward for good judgments and a penalty for bad judgments. Many would say that once you are in heaven everyone is equal and there is no difference between how people experience heaven. I believe scripture says something different. Scripture speaks of rewards in heaven and it is our deeds here on earth that will determine what those rewards are. And for those deeds that judged as bad, there will be a loss of reward.

And if that is true, it is important for us to focus our attention on deeds that will result in rewards. But we need to be careful not to do those deeds for the rewards. God's judgment of our deeds will be based on whether we did what He wanted us to do, when He wanted us to do it, how He wanted us to do it, and for the reason that He wanted to do it. It is all about being completely surrendered and submitted to the leading of God through the Holy Spirit.

Why do you want to do this thing for God? Is your motivation right? Do you hope to get something out of it? The Bible teaches us to examine ourselves so that God doesn't have to. Is your heart right? Is your motivation pure? Or is there too much of self in your selfless acts?

Our rewards for doing a work for God will come as a result of God looking at our deeds and seeing the right intention, motivation, and expectation. Our desire should be to please God. Our hope should be that everything that we do pleases Him. Our wish should be that our deeds are judged as good.

My greatest desire is to stand before God and hear Him say; "Well done, good and faithful servant."

Read: Malachi 1:1 – 2:17, Revelation 21:1-27, Psalm 149:1-9, Proverbs 31:10-24

MALACHI 2:10

Are we not all children of the same Father? Are we not all created by the same God? Then why are we faithless to each other, violating the covenant of our ancestors?

Malachi challenges the people of the nation of Israel in regards to the way that they are treating one another and God. In our verse for the day Malachi asks three questions that each of us should answer in our hearts. The greatest commandment tells us that we are to love God and to love others. Today's verse asks us if that is what we are doing.

First we are asked about our relationship to one another. We are all children of the same Father; that makes us brothers and sisters. That is not usually how we treat people that are not in our immediate family; instead we treat them like strangers. If we would start looking at everyone that we come in contact with as a brother or sister, we might behave differently toward them. We would be less likely to sin against them.

Then we are reminded that the same God created all of us. This speaks of a common design; we are all created with a common purpose. God created us to love Him and to love others. We were all created with that same purpose. This also should have an impact on how we view and treat people. People were created for God not for themselves; we need to be a vessel that God can use to model and teach people how to be the people of God.

Knowing these things then begs the question as it does in our verse; "Why are we faithless to each other?" We cannot treat people with disdain and contempt and expect that God would be pleased with us. We need to be treating people faithfully because of our relationship to them as brothers and sister in Christ and because of our common purpose in the world.

One of the big problems with the world is ignorance of this fact and the result is that most people do what they can to please themselves even if it means being faithless to others. Most people don't care what happens to most other people. There is a real lack of love that can be easily seen in the way that most people treat those around them.

Our ability to love God is manifested or revealed by the way that we love other people. They are directly linked and cannot be separated. If you can't love other people then you really can't love God the way that you are supposed to. Love is the key to our relationship with God. We show our love to God by showing our love to others. As we do acts of love to our brothers and sisters we are actually loving God. Each time we do something as an act of love we are fulfilling the purpose that God created us for and that is pleasing to God. Each day we should look for ways to show God that we love Him by showing His love to someone else through acts of faithful love. Jesus, teach us to love.

DECEMBER 31

Read: Malachi 3:1 – 4:6, Revelation 22:1-21, Psalm 150:1-6, Proverbs 31:25-31

PROVERBS 31:30

Charm is deceptive, and beauty does not last; but a woman who fears the LORD will be greatly praised.

The Proverbs 31 woman is a person of great beauty and character. Women throughout the centuries have looked at this text and seen it as an impossible inventory of the things that they need to do so that they can be considered a godly wife. That is not what this text is saying at all; it is rather a picture of how this husband views his wife. Within each verse of this text we find examples of godliness within this wife but more importantly we see how this woman brings her complete self into the relationship with her husband.

No woman may be able to do and be all the things that this woman was, but every woman can give all of herself to her marriage and her family. If more men and women studied what it was that God would like us to learn from this text there would be fewer women struggling to find their place in life and in their family. God has not, in this text, given us a template of what He thinks a godly woman looks like; He is celebrating the amazing things that women can do in their lives, marriages, and families.

In our verse for the day we see the most important characteristic a godly woman has. It has nothing to do with the things that she does or how she looks. It has everything to do with the relationship she has with

God. It is the fear of the Lord that will determine whether or not she is a godly woman. Her charm may influence people greatly but it is not the real her. And no matter how beautiful a woman is, her beauty will only last for so long; time and gravity march relentlessly on. But a woman that fears the Lord will experience success in her life and will be praised by her husband, children, and everyone else around her.

Charm by itself is not enough because there is always someone more charming than we are. Beauty is not lasting and it can become an idol that entraps us. There is nothing wrong with charm or beauty but they are nothing compared to the fear of the Lord. A woman can be completely devoid of charm and as homely as a stone and be an amazing woman of God. In fact a woman with charm and/or beauty is often distracted by those things and cannot become the woman that she could be.

This culture is far too consumed with charm and beauty and puts very little emphasis on character. God looks at the heart and cares more about character than He does on physical appearances or personality traits. Most women (and men) would be much better served by working on their character than they would on their appearance or social standing. If we would just develop a healthy fear of the Lord, God would work out within us the other characteristics that please Him and will allow us to become the people that He desires us to be. Jesus, teach us what true beauty and charm look like.

PASTOR RICK LANCASTER

FAVORITE SCRIPTURE: JOHN 15:13
"Greater love has no one than this, than to lay down one's life for his friends.

My testimony is that of the power of a praying wife. Kelly and I were married in 1981. Kelly has been a Christian since she was a young child. I had gone to Sunday school, but have no recollection of meeting Jesus there. My life before Christ can best be described as one based on self-confidence and self-reliance. I seemed to succeed at everything I tried. I did well in the military and well in my job. This left me with the attitude that I didn't need God. Kelly prayed for me and witnessed to me for 16 years. A major job change put me into a place where I had a great amount of time to think and reflect. It seemed important to me to find out what it was that Kelly believed in. I was traveling a lot and, thanks to the Gideons, I started finding some answers in the Bibles in hotel rooms. There came a point that I realized that my attitude toward God was based on my ignorance of who He is and what Jesus has done for me.

In October 2004, God called my family and me out of Revival Christian Fellowship to plant a church in the French Valley area of Murrieta, California. With us came a small group of faithful friends that have grown to be more like part of our family.

In starting Calvary Chapel French Valley, God impressed upon me the desire to help the people of our community to build strong healthy families. I am looking forward to serving the Lord by serving the families of this area for as long as the Lord wills or as long as He tarries.

Rick Lancaster is founder and Senior Pastor of Calvary Chapel French Valley in Murrieta, California. Rick has studied and taught through the Bible for more than sixteen years and has published a wide range of articles and devotional materials aimed at drawing Christians into a deeper faith with Jesus.

He and his wife Kelly live in Southern California and have three adult children.

For more from or to connect with Rick, visit www.radicalword.com/social.

* 9 7 8 1 6 0 0 3 9 1 2 4 8 *